Becoming
Divine

Becoming
Divine

An Introduction to Deification in Western Culture

M. David Litwa

CASCADE *Books* · Eugene, Oregon

BECOMING DIVINE
An Introduction to Deification in Western Culture

Copyright © 2013 M. David Litwa. All rights reserved. Except for brief quotations in critical publications or reviews, no part of this book may be reproduced in any manner without prior written permission from the publisher. Write: Permissions, Wipf and Stock Publishers, 199 W. 8th Ave., Suite 3, Eugene, OR 97401.

Cascade Books
An Imprint of Wipf and Stock Publishers
199 W. 8th Ave., Suite 3
Eugene, OR 97401

www.wipfandstock.com

ISBN 13: 978-1-62564-155-7

Cataloguing-in-Publication data:

Litwa, M. David.

    Becoming divine : an introduction to deification in western culture /
M. David Litwa.

    xvi + 274 pp. ; 23 cm. Includes bibliographical references and indices.

    ISBN 13: 978-1-62564-155-7

    1. Apotheosis. 2. Deification (Christianity). I. Title.

BT767.8 L489 2013

Manufactured in the U.S.A.

For Lucy
τύτθον ἐμόν

Contents

Preface | ix

Abbreviations | xi

Introduction: Enter Deification | 1

1 Merging with the Sun: The Deification of Amenhotep III | 9

2 The New Dionysus: Divine Assimilation in Greco-Roman Ruler Cult | 26

3 "You Have Been Born a God": Deification in the Orphic Gold Tablets | 42

4 "We are Being Transformed": Paul and the Gospel of Deification | 58

5 "Immortalized in This Very Hour": Deification in the "Mithras Liturgy" | 69

6 "I Have Been Born in Mind!": Deification in the Hermetic Literature | 86

7 "I Have Become Identical with the Divine": Plotinus on Deification | 102

8 "The Flash of One Tremulous Glance": Augustine and Deification | 117

9 "I Am the Truth": The Deification of Husayn ibn Mansur al-Hallaj | 134

10 "God's Being is My Life": Meister Eckhart's Birth in God | 144

11 "Uncreated by Grace": Deification in Gregory Palamas | 155

12 "By Faith a Human Becomes God": Martin Luther on Deification | 172

13 "Then Shall They be Gods . . .": The Mormon Restoration of Deification | 190

14 "Rather be a God Oneself!" Nietzsche and the Joy of Earthly Godhood | 205

15 The Posthuman God | 222

Conclusion | 231

Bibliography | 241

Subject Index | 261

Ancient Document Index | 265

Preface

DEIFICATION IS ONE OF the most terrifying and exhilarating ideas imagined by humankind. I still remember the response of an old friend (at the time a fellow seminarian), Ben Wiles, who read a first draft of this book with a mixture of stunned aporia and enraged disbelief. He generously peppered the text with a series of red question marks and exclamation points, frequently asking—whenever he would run across the language of becoming god—"what does this *mean*???" Ben was a pastor and concerned with (Christian) orthodoxy; but his response was no less fiery than the atheist for whom deification is an impossible, farcical dream, nothing but atavistic wish fulfillment. Humanists—whether theists or not—appear no more sympathetic. For them, becoming divine seems an entirely misguided goal for moderns who should embrace their human lot and do everything possible to enrich its native potential. The goal of becoming "fully human" has become so popular that modern Christian writers proclaim that this is what deification actually means. Apparently this is an attempt to translate an ancient and admittedly bizarre idea, making it palatable to the aspirations of our own culture. In my view it is a bit of an over-translation—and one that tends to drain the discourse of deification of its power and mystery.

I was introduced to the topic of deification when I heard a lecture on Gregory Palamas in the fall of 2003. It has taken me nearly a decade to trace the discourse of deification from Egypt all the way to my own context in modern America. The project—both for me and for others—is hardly complete. Many more chapters in the history of deification can be written—and will be written, I trust, by a new generation of scholars and theologians who recognize the importance of this topic for our times.

With some trepidation, I have entitled my introductory chapter "Enter Deification." Although the vocabulary of deification has been with us for some time, we stand on the brink of a new discourse. For the first time, deification is being used as a scholarly category in religious and biblical studies for understanding humanity and the human vision of salvation. This new scholarly category includes Christian forms of deification, but is not restricted by the norms of Christian theology. In light of this new discourse—already flourishing—a general introduction to the topic of deification, in all its diversity, is long overdue. So I present the fruits of my research.

Throughout what follows I speak as a historian, but hardly a dispassionate one. From the very first time I heard of it until the present day, I have remained strangely fascinated by the idea of deification and its modern import. If through this book I have done anything to spark interest in the topic of deification and further its research, I rest content.

I append three brief notes on technical matters before my acknowledgements. First, for Greek and Latin texts my practice has been to offer a fresh translation. When this is not the case, it is indicated in the notes. Second, all Gods who are attributed supreme status and universal power (for example, Zeus, Yahweh, Helios Mithras) are referred to with a capital "G." Lesser gods and demigods are signified by a small "g." When the "Gods" are referred to in the plural—implicating both high Gods and minor deities—I also capitalize the "G." Third, I avoid the convention of distinguishing Christians as God's "sons" from Jesus as God's "Son" by a capital "S." The convention adheres to a Christian orthodoxy that in some cases is anachronistic, and in other cases obscures the assumed parity between Christ and believers. In other cases, however, the Christian author clearly exalts Christ over God's human children making the capitalization of "Son" appropriate. These spelling conventions obviously involve a judgment call on my part—a judgment for which I take full responsibility.

Here I gratefully acknowledge Blaire French for committing herself a second time to proofing an entire book. Her labors will not be forgotten. Karl Shuve read an earlier version of the chapter on Augustine, and I appreciate his comments. Ben, you have my thanks as well—in addition to all my teachers and friends who over the years have tolerated my fascination with this topic, and kept up the conversation.

This book is dedicated to Lucy, my most beautiful baby daughter whom I will love always.

MDL
Charlottesville, Virginia
June, 2013

Abbreviations

Note: Abbreviations of biblical books follow the *The SBL Handbook of Style*, edited by Patrick H. Alexander et al. Peabody, MA: Hendrickson, 1999, 73–74. Other abbreviations are as follows.

1 Apol.	Justin Martyr's *First Apology*
Acad.	Augustine's *Against the Academicians*
Ad Thalass.	Maximus the Confessor's *To Thalassius*
Adul. am.	Plutarch's *How to Distinguish a Flatterer from a Friend*
Aen.	Virgil's *Aeneid*
Aet.	Philo's *On the Eternity of the World*
Alc.	Euripides' *Alcestis*
Alex.	Plutarch's *Life of Alexander*
Amb.	Maximus the Confessor's *Ambigua*
An.	Aristotle's *On the Soul*
ANET	*Ancient Near Eastern Texts*, ed. Pritchard
ANRW	*Aufstieg und Niedergang der Römischen Welt*, ed. Haase
Ant.	Plutarch's *Life of Antony*
Anab.	Arrian's *Anabasis of Alexander*
Arian.	Augustine's *Againt the Arian Sermon*
Asc. Isa.	*The Ascension of Isaiah*
Ascl.	The *Asclepius* or *Perfect Discourse*
Autol.	Theophilus of Antioch's *Ad Autolycum*

AWA	*Archiv zur Weimarer Ausgabe*, eds. Hammer and Biersack
Bibl.	Pseudo-Apollodorus' *Library*
Bibl. hist.	Diodorus of Sicily's *Library of History*
C. Jul. op. imp.	Augustine's *Against Julian, an Unfinished Book*
Cal.	Lucian's *Slander*
Cap.	Gregory Palamas' *One Hundred and Fifty Chapters*
CCSL	Corpus Christianorum: Series Latina
Cels.	Origen's *Contra Celsum*
Cf.	Compare
CH	Corpus Hermeticum
Ch.	Chapter
Chron.	Eusebius' *Chronicle*
Civ.	Augustine's *City of God*
Cleom.	Plutarch's *Life of Cleomenes*
Comm. Jo.	Origen's *Commentary on John*
Conf.	Augustine's *Confessions*
Cons. ev.	Augustine's *Harmony of the Gospels*
Crat.	Plato's *Cratylus*
CSEL	Corpus Scriptorum Ecclesiasticorum Latinorum
DC	*Doctrine and Covenants*
Dec.	Philo's *On the Decalogue*
Deipn.	Athenaeus' *Learned Banqueters*
Dem. ev.	Eusebius' *Demonstration of the Gospel*
Descr.	Pausanias' *Description of Greece*
Dial.	Justin's *Dialogue with Trypho*
Dial. mort.	Lucian's *Dialogues of the Dead*
Div. Aug.	Suetonius' *Divus Augustus*
Div. Inst.	Lactantius' *Divine Institutes*

DK	*Die Fragmente der Vorsokratiker*, eds. Diels and Kranz
Doct. Chr.	Augustine's *On Christian Teaching*
Duab.	Augustine's *Two Souls*
DW	*Deutschen Werke* of Meister Eckhart, eds. Quint and Steer
Enarrat. Ps.	Augustine's *Expositions of the Psalms*
Enchir.	Augustine's *Enchiridion*
Ep.	Epistle
Esp.	Especially
Esu carn.	Plutarch's *On the Eating of Flesh*
Exp. Gal.	Augustine's *Exposition of Galatians*
FGH	*Die Fragmente der griechischen Historiker*, ed. Jacoby
Frag.	Fragment
Gen. litt.	Augustine's *Literal Commentary on Genesis*
Gen. Man.	Augustine's *On Genesis Against the Manicheans*
Geog.	Strabo's *Geography*
Georg.	Virgil's *Georgics*
Gig.	Philo's *On Giants*
Gorg.	Plato's *Gorgias*
Haer.	Irenaeus' *Against Heresies*
Hom.	Homily
IG	*Inscriptiones Graecae*, ed. Kirchner
Il.	Homer's *Iliad*
Inc.	Athanasius' *On the Incarnation*
Inwood	*The Poem of Empedocles*, ed. Inwood
JET	*Journal of Evolution and Technology*
JRS	*Journal of Roman Studies*
KJV	King James Version
LÄ	*Lexikon der Ägyptologie*, eds. Helck and Otto

LCL	Loeb Classical Library
Leg.	Athenagoras' *Legatio*
LSJ	*A Greek-English Lexicon*, eds. Liddell and Scott.
LW	*Lateinische Werke* of Meister Eckhart, ed. Weiss, et al.
LXX	Septuagint
Met.	Apuleius' *Metamorphoses*
Mor.	Plutarch's *Moralia*
MT	Masoretic Text
Nat.	Pliny the Elder's *Natural History*
Nat. bon.	Augustine's *The Nature of the Good*
Nat. grat.	Augustine's *Nature and Grace*
Nem.	Pindar's *Nemean Odes*
NHC	Nag Hammadi Codices
n.p.	No pages
NRSV	New Revised Standard Version
Od.	Homer's *Odyssey*
OF	*Orphicorum Fragmenta*, ed. Bernabé
OGIS	*Orientis Graeci Inscriptiones Selectae*, ed. Dittenberger
Ol.	Pindar's *Olympian Odes*
Op.	Hesiod's *Works and Days*
Opif.	Philo's *On the Creation of the World*
Or.	Orations
Ord.	Augustine's *On Order*
Par.	Parallels
PGM	*Papyri Graecae Magicae*
PL	*Patrologia Latina*
Praep. ev.	Eusebius' *Preparation for the Gospel*
Princ.	Origen's *On First Principles*

Protrep.	Clement of Alexandria's *Protrepticus*
Prov.	Philo's *On Providence*
QE	Philo's *Questions on Exodus*
QG	Philo's *Questions on Genesis*
Quaest. rom.	Plutarch's *Roman Questions*
Quant. an.	Augustine's *On the Quantity of the Soul*
Resp.	Plato's *Republic*
RGRW	Religions in the Greco-Roman World
Rom. Hist.	Cassius Dio's *Roman History*
SEG	*Supplementum Epigraphicum Graecum*, ed., Hondius et al.
Sera	Plutarch's *On the Delay of Divine Justice*
Serm.	Sermon
SJT	*Scottish Journal of Theology*
Spec.	Philo's *Special Laws*
Symp.	Plato's *Symposium*
Tr.	Gregory Palamas' *The Triads*
Tract. Ev. Jo.	Augustine's *Tractates on the Gospel of John*
Trans.	Translator
Trin.	Augustine's *On The Trinity*
Ran.	Aristophanes' *Frogs*
Res gest. divi Aug.	Velleius Paterculus' *Exploits of the Divine Augustus*
Strom.	Clement of Alexandria's *Stromateis*
Tim.	Plato's *Timaeus*
VC	*Vigiliae Christianae*
Ver. rel.	Augustine's *On True Religion*
Vit. philosoph.	Diogenes Laertius' *Lives of Philosophers*
Vit. Plot.	Porphyry's *Life of Plotinus*
Vulg.	Vulgate

WA   *Werke Martin Luthers, Weimarer Ausgabe*

WUNT   Wissenschaftliche Untersuchungen zum Neuen Testament

Enter Deification

The impulse toward truth, and especially truth concerning
the Gods, is a desire for divinity.

—PLUTARCH, *MORALIA* 351E

SOME HAVE CALLED IT the essence of sin, others the depth of salvation.
Regardless of one's evaluation of it, however, deification has been a part
of human aspiration throughout Western history. From the ancient pharaohs
to modern transhumanists, people have envisioned their own divinity. These
visionaries include not only history's greatest megalomaniacs, but also mystics, sages, apostles, prophets, magicians, bishops, philosophers, atheists, and
monks. Some aimed for independent deity, others realized their eternal union
with God. Some anticipated godhood in heaven, others walked as gods on
earth. Some accepted divinity by grace, others achieved it by their own will to
power. There is no single form of deification (indeed, deification is as manifold as the human conception of God), but the many types are united by a set
of interlocking themes: achieving immortality, wielding superhuman power,
being filled with supernatural knowledge or love—and through these means
transcending normal human (or at least "earthly") nature.

What is deification? In its etymological sense, deification means
the process of making (from the Latin *facio*) someone (or some thing)
a god (*deus*). In its broadest sense, deification is the attainment of some
sort of superhuman transcendence. In theistic cultures, the Gods have
always represented to human beings a wonderfully blissful and superior
form of life. (Indeed, Ludwig Feuerbach argued that God represents the
human ideal under infinite magnification.[1]) If humans are to experience

---

1. Feuerbach, *Essence of Christianity.*

transcendence—even ultimacy—they must in some way become like (the) God(s), and even gods themselves.

Deification comes under many names. They include "divinization," "theosis," "apotheosis," and "exaltation." The term "divinization," formed from the Latin *divinus*, means to become "divine," which in itself is an even vaguer concept than *deus* ("god"). According to Homer, the "divine" (*theios*) can even describe salt![2] "Theosis" (from *theos*, the Greek word for "god") is most often used to designate Christian forms of deification.[3] "Apotheosis," in turn, is now a common way to refer to deification in non-Christian contexts (esp. Greek and Roman ruler cult).[4] "Exaltation," finally, is a term used chiefly in Mormon thought to describe the postmortem godhood of Latter-day Saints. For the sake of clarity and simplicity, I adhere throughout this book to the term "deification," employing it as an umbrella category that includes the other terms.

In the past, deification in Western thought has been treated as a peripheral topic shelved as a subcategory of patristic soteriology or (chiefly Greco-Roman) ruler cult. In spite of this history, this book attempts to show that deification is a pervasive theme in Western spirituality. The Egyptians first explored the path to godhood for their Pharaoh. Greek philosophers like Heraclitus taught a way of thinking that melded the divine and human.[5] Plato taught the West about the ultimate (Beauty, the Good, God), how to yearn for it, and how to assimilate to it. Platonized Christianity was (and is) a religion of transcendence, teaching human beings to go *beyond* sin, the world, and the earthly self with the result that they become immortal and divine. From the first century C.E. until the present day, Christianity has been a vehicle carrying different traditions of deification in Western culture. Since the nineteenth century, forms of deification have developed in various non-Christian and post-Christian venues.

The main purpose of this book is to present a historical introduction to deification in its various forms and manifestations in Western culture. Western culture is understood in its broadest sense as including the cultures of ancient Palestine, Persia, and Egypt which had a profound influence on Greco-Roman religions including (perhaps most obviously)

2. Hom., *Il.* 9.214.

3. The term "theosis" was coined by the Christian writer Gregory of Nazianzus. The term was used by the late Christian writers Pseudo-Dionysus, Maximus the Confessor, and John Damascene (Russell, *Doctrine of Deification*, 341). It is now ubiquitous in Christian scholarship.

4. For a survey of apotheosis terminology, see ibid., 333–37; 341–42. See further Litwa, *We Are Being Transformed*, 59–60, 61–62.

5. See most recently Miller, *Becoming Divine*.

Christianity. This book assumes no prior familiarity with deification. (Those interested in a more technical discussion can follow the sources cited in the notes.) Nor is it a theological introduction that focuses only on Christian forms of deification.

Although the book aims to be representative, the visions of deification presented are not exhaustive. Deification, as the reader will come to discover, is too broad a topic to cover in one volume. The thinkers and movements discussed here were chosen because they bring together the themes and elements of deification that are variously combined in distinct systems of thought in diverse times and cultures.

The representatives selected are fifteen—spanning the period from Egypt's New Kingdom (in the fourteenth century B.C.E.) to the present day. Following roughly chronological order, this book treats deification in ancient Egypt, the Greco-Roman cult of rulers, Orphic mysteries, various Christian sources (Paul, Augustine, Meister Eckhart, Gregory Palamas, Martin Luther, Joseph Smith), the "Mithras Liturgy," the Hermetic writings, the Sufi Husayn ibn-Mansur al-Hallaj, and, Friedrich Nietzsche. A final chapter presents a version of deification in modern transhumanist thought. For none of these individual figures or movements do I claim to provide a comprehensive treatment. They are examined only with reference to their particular versions of deification.

Roadmap

The story of deification begins in chapter 1 with the Egyptian pharaohs, commonly viewed as sons of Re (the Sun God) and, at death, incarnations of the divine Osiris. I focus specifically on one pharaoh: Amenhotep III (reigned ca. 1391–53 B.C.E.). Called the "sun king," every year Amenhotep III was ritually reborn from the Sun God in the Opet Festival. After the ceremony, his divine aura dissipated. In year thirty of his reign, however, Amenhotep III celebrated his jubilee or Sed Festival and became permanently divine. In story, symbol, and in his statues, Amenhotep III was identified with Amun-Re the Sun God, the creator, and the embodiment of all divinity. This chapter tells the story of how his enduring deification occurred, and the arcane rites employed to perform it.

When Amenhotep III died, he became one with the god Osiris. In the Greek world, Osiris was identified with the god Dionysus. Dionysus was the god of theater and wine—but he was also the wild conqueror of the east. According to legend, Alexander the Great imitated Dionysus when he conquered India in the 320s B.C.E. The heirs of Alexander in the Macedonian kingdom of Egypt—the Ptolemies—escalated their assimilation to the wine god. Chapter 2 tells of the fabulous parades of Ptolemy II, the revels of Ptolemy IV, and the opulence of Ptolemy XII—a bazaar of wealth and power aimed to show these kings' Dionysian divinity. Later, the Roman triumvir Marc Antony had himself styled the "New Dionysus" during his stint with Cleopatra. In imitation of the god, Antony attacked the Parthians in the east, and later triumphed in Alexandria adorned in the garb of the god. Antony's own jocular character and opulent displays assimilated him to Dionysus' persona, power, and prerogatives, which—to the Egyptian people at least—meant more than mere play-acting.

In the ancient world, typically only kings and pharaohs claimed the divine prerogatives of immortality and ruling power. Yet in the mysteries of Dionysus—the topic of chapter 3—deification was made available to all who underwent initiation. A version of these Dionysian mysteries are partially revealed in the Orphic gold tablets—mysterious writings found all over the Mediterranean world. A central message of these tablets is postmortem deification: an immortal life of feasting and joy in the underworld. The basis of Orphic deification is the divine kinship of the initiate with the Gods. Orphic deification is experienced, interestingly, as a postmortem rebirth from the goddess Persephone and consequently an assimilation to Persephone's divine son, Dionysus.

As Orphic initiates identified with the god Dionysus, so the Apostle Paul morphed with the divine Christ. "I have been crucified with Christ," he once claimed, "I no longer live—Christ lives in me" (Gal 2:19–20). Assimilation to Christ, as chapter 4 relates, comes to fruition in two events: (1) the reception of immortality (*the* fundamental divine trait), and (2) rule over "all things" (including superhuman beings). The cosmic rule of Christians begins after death, but their transition to immortality begins in this life. They receive divine Spirit (*pneuma*) and slowly become spirit from the inside out. Those led by the Spirit become God's children. Christ was the first human declared to be son of God. But the promise of divine kinship is not for him alone. Rather, it is for all who obtain the immortality and divine power of the crucified god.

In chapter 5 we examine an ancient rite of immortalization buried in a book of magical spells. It has come to be called the "Mithras Liturgy." Whether or not this spell was ever part of the Mithraic mysteries remains moot; the spell's intent, however, is more secure: the deification of all those initiated into its "mysteries." In the spell, the magician is instructed to use magical ointment, protective charms, and bizarre formulae as means to zoom, star-like, to the fiery gates of the divine Sun. Reaching this point requires that the magician leave this world of change and birth to be wholly reborn as spirit (*pneuma*). His immortalization is admittedly temporary, but it can be experienced in the present and repeated many times. It has a glorious end: the sight of the greatest God Helios Mithras and the attainment of his wondrous revelations.

Around the time that the Mithras Liturgy was composed, the Hermetic writings began to appear in Egypt. The literature is named after Hermes—the Greek equivalent of the Egyptian god Thoth. As is discussed in chapter 6, Hermes teaches a mode of deification based on the essential divinity of the human mind. In this respect, Hermetic thought agrees with Gnostic Christian teaching: deification is a process of realizing one's own inner divine identity. Hermes teaches a Platonic path of contemplation beginning with the physical world and rising to the lights of the stars. By this path, one returns to what humanity once was. Present-day humans are a fallen version of an intelligible Human, made in the image of God and equal to God. The goal of life is to return to this "essential Human"—to strip off the body and its passions in order to become pure mind.

Both the Mithras Liturgy and the Hermetic literature were born in Egypt, a land that produced one of the greatest philosophers of ancient times: Plotinus (205–70 C.E.). To him we turn in chapter 7. Like Hermes, Plotinus taught a Platonic path of deification through identification with divine Mind. The human soul, he said, is an image of divine Intellect. Fixed between a corruptible body and intellectual Beauty, the goal of the soul is to purify itself through virtue and contemplation, preparing for a postmortem ascent to the intelligible world. As thought thinking intellect, the human soul can unite with divine Mind briefly in this life but permanently in the course of its post-mortem transformations. Despite his bold language, however, Plotinus does not envision a loss of human individuality when it unites with Intellect. Nor does he anticipate an indistinct union with ultimate divine reality—what he calls "the One."

A key moment in St. Augustine's theological development was his reading of the "books of the Platonists"—among them works of Plotinus. Originally a Manichaean Christian, Augustine of Hippo (354–430 C.E.) agreed with popular Platonic thought that the human intellect was essentially divine and could ascend back to divinity. When he converted to Catholicism, however, Augustine eventually rejected the idea that humans had an innately divine core. Their only path to divinity, he concluded, was participation in the divine qualities of Christ—the only human being who shared the essence of the Father. Deification occurs by external divine aid, not by a spark of divine grace woven into the human constitution. God's creation of humans from nothing produced a permanent separation between humans and God. As a result, humans become only the adopted—not natural—children of God. They are justified, incorporated into Christ's body, made immortal and happy—but remain human. In Augustine—who set the course for Christian orthodoxy in the West—deification becomes a metaphor for the complete salvation of human nature.

The Sufi Husayn ibn Mansur al-Hallaj (858–922 C.E.) is perhaps most famous for declaring: "*Ana' l-Haqq*"—"I am the Truth," or "I am God." This statement, as is shown in chapter 9, is a mystical deduction from the most central concept in Islamic theology—*tawhid*, or God's unity. God's unity, according to Hallaj, is so all-encompassing that it even excludes the claim of personal self-substantiality—what Hallaj called "I-ness." To claim to be a self, for Hallaj, is to claim what the devil did of old: "*I* am better than Adam!" Selfhood is an illusion that draws people—even good Muslims—away from realizing their fundamental unity with Allah. Hallaj was a witness to this unity. He declared God's oneness, which for him meant that there was nothing other than Allah. "I am the Truth" thus becomes a declaration of Allah himself, coming from the lips of a man who lost himself in God.

Chapter 10 turns to the medieval theologian Meister Eckhart (1259–1327). Like al-Hallaj, Eckhart viewed reality through the eyes of eternity. Drawing on Augustine's reflections on eternity, the Meister taught that the good human being is identical to the only-begotten son of God. If the son of God is God's eternal Word, and all things are in the Word, humans exist eternally in and as God's Word. This simultaneously scholastic and mystical deduction allowed Eckhart to overcome Augustine's distinction between adopted and natural children: in God, humans are eternal, and God's eternal offspring. As the Word is being begotten eternally, so are other human children as one and the same Word or son of God. But there is a deeper mystery: in the ground of human beings remains the imprint of eternity. Thus, in the vortex of this inward eternity, humans everlastingly give birth to the son of God just as the Father.

Marking the culmination of a long tradition in the eastern Mediterranean world, Gregory Palamas (1296–1359)—the subject of chapter 11—taught a version of deification simultaneously acknowledging humanity's union with God's energies and separation from God's essence. Unlike in Latin theology, the energies (roughly speaking, the attributes or activities) of God, Palamas insisted, *are God* so that by sharing in them the human can even become "uncreated by grace." Nevertheless God in his ultimate aspect remains enveloped in mystery and ineffability. The process of Palamite deification is not by grace alone, but must be worked out in a life of virtue, love, and contemplative prayer. The great model of prayer and deification is Christ himself transfigured on Mount Tabor. Monks who practiced Christ-like prayer, Palamas believed, participated in Christ's deifying light.

Chapter 12 shows that the Protestant reformer Martin Luther (1483–1546) continued to advance the vocabulary and uphold the notion of deification as it was handed down by the Catholic (broadly Augustinian) tradition. Luther's first contact with the idea of deification, however, appeared to come through his reading of medieval mystics like John Tauler and the author of *Theologia Germanica*. Assimilating their themes of deification through humility, love, and self-annihilation, Luther quickly wove deification into the fabric of his own theology of paradox. For Luther, the Christian is both fully deified and a sinner, married to Christ though naturally divorced from God, ruler of all things, but—without Christ—spiritually empty and even nothing at all.

We arrive at the American continent in chapter 13. Coming out of a Protestant tradition largely tone-deaf to deification, the prophet Joseph Smith (1805–44) boldly preached a theology of human godhood. Nevertheless, the founder of the Mormon church had a new storyline—a grander vision of the past that guaranteed a brighter human future. Not only were humans to become gods along with Christ, Smith preached, but even God the Father had once been a man. In a lofty vision of cosmic evolution, Smith pictured God himself evolving from humanity to deity, then calling up all his spirit children to equality with him. This lofty destiny is primarily placed in the afterlife when most humans are parceled out into three levels of heaven. Only those in the highest, or celestial, level have a chance to be deified. Of these, only those who submit to the rite of eternal marriage have the privilege of producing spiritual children in the afterlife and becoming full-fledged gods. In a singular move in the history of deification, Latter-day Saints reserve godhood not for the individual alone, but for the entire family.

The year Smith died is the year Friedrich Nietzsche (1844–1900) was born. In chapter 14 it is argued that Nietzsche's famous book *Thus Spoke Zarathustra* is a quest for godhood in a godless age. The "old grimbeard" of a God (i.e., the Judeo-Christian God) has died. Zarathustra preaches a new gospel. A new god-man is coming: the overman (*Übermensch*). Yet Zarathustra is ultimately unsatisfied with a human god who *will* come. The future alone cannot justify the shortcomings of the past. Zarathustra realizes that if god is going to make an appearance, it must occur in him—that is, in his affirmation of life, his will to power, and his acceptance of eternal return. By declaring "yes!" to past, present, and future, Zarathustra identifies with Fate and becomes a "creator"—one who not only submits to necessity but who shapes it like a god, and dances like Dionysus.

A brief final chapter discusses a contemporary model of deification currently developing in the movement called "Transhumanism." In this model, deification is achieved by evolution now directed by advanced technology.

The transhumanist vision involves (1) the implantation of bio-technology into the human body to extend human life and performance, and in some versions (2) the "uploading" of human consciousness onto a virtual world, giving the human mind limitless life and intelligence. The result of these events is the posthuman—a being who will be superior to modern-day humans as much as we are superior to apes. Although most transhumanists are secular, they admit that they are seeking after goods traditionally provided by religion and possessed only by the ancient gods: immortality and cosmic power. In a religious framework, then, it is not implausible to characterize the posthuman as a (techno-)god, the hope of a better world, and the future ruler of the cosmos.

Chapter 1

Merging with the Sun

The Deification of Amenhotep III

Hail to you, O Re, in your rising,
Amun in your beautiful setting.
You rise and you shine upon your mother's back,
Appearing in glory as king of the ennead. . . .
As to the gods, their hearts are glad
When they see you in the morning bark.
Re has a (following) breeze continuously.
As to the evening bark,
it has destroyed the one who attacked it.
You cross both your heavens in triumph!

—*HYMN TO THE RISING SUN*[1]

IN AN INSCRIPTION FROM western Thebes (modern Luxor), the god
Amun-Re hails Pharaoh Amenhotep III as "my son of my body, my
beloved Nebmaatra, my living image, my body's creation."[2] According to
ancient Egyptian lore, the god Amun-Re had visited Amenhotep's mother
Mutemwia in the form of her husband Thutmoses IV. Mutemwia was
asleep in one of the inner rooms of the palace. In a temple inscription we
read, "She [Mutemwia] awoke on account of the aroma of the god and
cried out before him. . . . He went to her straightaway, she rejoiced at
the sight of his beauty, and love for him coursed through her body. The

1. Epigraphic Survey, *The Tomb of Kheruef*, 38.
2. *ANET*, 376.

9

palace flooded with the God's aroma." Reliefs in the Luxor temple show Mutemwia delicately touching the fingertips of Amun-Re.[3] Actual intercourse is not described. We only learn that "the majesty of this God did all that he desired with her," with the result that Mutemwia declared, "Your dew fills my body!" After the transfer of divine "dew," the God Amun-Re informs Mutemwia that the name of her child is "Amenhotep, ruler of Thebes. . . . He shall exercise the beneficent kingship in this whole land, he shall rule the Two Lands [of Egypt] like Re forever."[4]

Such is the miraculous birth of Pharaoh Amenhotep III (ruled 1391–53 B.C.E.), one of the most famous and powerful Pharaohs in Egyptian history.[5] Although the deity of the Pharaohs is a commonplace in Egyptology (a standard title of the Pharaoh was "the good god"[6]), only three Pharaohs—Hatshepsut, Amenhotep III, and Ramesses II—provide an extended account of their literal birth from a god.[7] It is often alleged that Hatshepsut—a female Pharaoh—engineered her divine birth to legitimate her rule. Amenhotep III and Ramesses II, however, did not need a divine birth story to justify their authority. They—along with presumably many other Pharaohs—did not doubt their physical birth from Amun-Re. Then as now myth was reality, because myths constitute a world.[8]

Amenhotep III ruled in the period of the New Kingdom (ca. 1550–1069 B.C.E.), a time when the deification of the living ruler became prominent in Egypt. He was the ninth ruler of the Eighteenth Dynasty, son of great conquerors, and grandfather of king Tutankhamen (the famous "king Tut"). Amenhotep was a powerful and long-lived Pharaoh, but was not eccentric like his son and successor Akhenaten (sometimes considered to be the first "monotheist"). Nor was he a great general like Ramesses II, "the Great," who ruled a century after him. The divinity that Amenhotep III claimed—at least initially—was based on his kingly office, and was sealed by royal ritual. Virtually all Egyptian Pharaohs considered themselves to be sons of Re, the Sun God. Late in his reign, however, Amenhotep seems to have considered himself to be a living manifestation of the Sun God himself. We will follow him—as best we can—on his road toward this new self-understanding.

---

3. Brunner, *Die Geburt des Gottkönig*, plate 4.

4. Fletcher, *Chronicle of a Pharaoh*, 12.

5. Amenhotep can also be called by his Greek name "Amenophis."

6. "Amenhotep's titles repeatedly call him 'the good god' with an insistence never before seen in royal inscriptions" (Kozloff, *Amenhotep III*, 121).

7. For the deity of the Pharaoh, see esp. Silverman, "Egyptian Kingship," 49–94; Wilkinson, *Complete Gods*, 54–63; Frandsen, "Aspects of Kingship," 47–73.

8. See further Shaw, *Ancient Egypt*, 93–100; Pinch, *Egyptian Myth*, 70–74.

The King's *Ka*

In the twelfth scene of his birth story depicted on the walls of the Luxor temple, Amun-Re mentions the king's "*ka*." The *ka* was the divine spirit of the king, a spirit he shared with all pharaohs who came before him and all who would come after.[9] Although the king's *ka* was shaped and molded as the "twin" of the king at his birth, it was officially inherited at his coronation. For the Pharaoh, the *ka* was the divine principle in his person: the "immortal creative spirit of divine kingship."[10] It was the spirit of the creator and king of gods Amun-Re himself.

Apart from his *ka*, Amenhotep III was a normal human being, subject to all human foibles and frailties. Endowed with the divine force of *ka*, however, Amenhotep III was son of the living God and a god himself. Although one can focus on the human or the divine side of the Pharaoh, privileging one aspect misses the point. Was Pharaoh divine? Yes—insofar as he was the incarnation of the royal *ka*. The *ka* was different from the king, and yet one with him. It entered him in his coronation, and only left him at death.[11] "When the king died," writes Lanny Bell, "his body was buried with Osiris . . . and his *ka* returned to heaven. There the *ka* continued to be worshiped as a form of the Sun God, whose essence it shared and into whom it now again merged."[12]

Coronation Titulary

At his coronation, Amenhotep—like all pharaohs since the fourth dynasty—had invoked over him five royal names, each with an individualized epithet that reflected the power and future policies of the monarch. Two of the names—the "Horus name" and "Golden Horus name" served to identify the pharaoh with the god Horus, falcon-headed god of the skies. That Horus was "golden" is important since gold was "the flesh of the gods." In the modern world, one of the billboard signs for Pharaonic Egypt is the flashing gold mask of "king Tut." This mask—one of the few surviving—shows Pharaoh encased in the flesh of a deity.

The birth name of the king—Amenhotep (meaning, "Amun is at peace")—was his "son of Re name." All kings were considered to be sons of the Sun God Re. Amenhotep's specific throne name was "Nebmaatra,"

9. Kozloff, *Amenhotep III*, 85–86.

10. Bell, "Divine Temple," 140.

11. Ibid., 140–42.

12. Ibid., 144.

meaning, "Re, lord of truth." Implicitly this name identified him with the Sun God himself.

Amenhotep later came to prefer names that associated him with the Sun: "heir of Re," "chosen one of Re," "image of Re." Egypt's vassal states in western Asia spoke of Pharaoh in solar terms. Abi-Milku, for instance—who ruled the Phoenician city of Tyre during Amenhotep's final years—was one of the many Canaanite chieftains who addressed Pharaoh simply as "the Sun." In one letter he writes,

> The [Egyptian] king is the Sun who comes forth over all lands day by day according to the way of being the Sun, who gives life by his sweet breath and returns with his north wind. Who gives forth his cry like Baal and all the land is frightened by his cry.[13]

The cry of the king is that of the solar falcon "soaring high on the thermals of a cloudless day, invisible against the blinding sun, its shriek seeming to come from the orb itself."[14]

An epithet that Amenhotep III later coined specifically for himself was "Dazzling Sun Disk."[15] More than any other name, this one indicates that Amenhotep not only associated himself with the Sun, but in some sense morphed with it.

Amun-Re

To understand Amenhotep's identification with the Sun, we must understand the Sun God himself—particularly in his manifestation as Amun-Re. In Egyptian theology, the Sun God Re came under many names: "Horakhty," "Khepri," "Atum," and later "Aten." Horakhty was associated with the horizon, Khepri with the dawn, Atum with the sunset, and Aten with the visible sun disk. In Heliopolis (Greek for "Sun City"), the god Re headed the pantheon. By the time of Amenhotep III, however, Amun of Thebes had become the universal and supreme God—the king of the gods. Amun—whose name means "the Hidden One"—was the primeval creator deity. As the might of Amun grew, other deities merged into him and became manifestations of his power. To become the ultimate manifestation of power, Amun absorbed the energies and being of the divine Sun.

Amun-Re reigned from Thebes, which became the capital of the sun king Amenhotep III. By the time of Amenhotep, however, temples were

13. Quoted in Kozloff, *Amenhotep III*, 121.

14. Ibid.

15. Berman, "Overview of Amenhotep III," 2–3.

erected to Amun-Re all over Egypt. The two most significant were in the heart of ancient Thebes and—about a mile north—in the massive temple complex at Karnak.[16]

As king of the gods, Amun-Re was also the protector and Father of earthly kings. The king himself was son of Amun-Re, as well as his image. Accordingly, king and God shared a striking resemblance. In some cases, the statue of Amun can only be distinguished from that of a Pharaoh by the shape of the beard.[17]

Conqueror

Amun-Re had made Amenhotep king over both upper (the southern highlands) and lower Egypt (the Delta region). One of Amenhotep's five coronation titles—the "Two Ladies" name—emphasized his universal rule. Universal rule was declared at his accession, but it also needed to be proved militarily. Amenhotep's royal predecessors had secured an empire ranging from Sudan in the south to Syria in the north. In the fifth year of his reign, Amenhotep III invaded Nubia, the "land of gold" south of Egypt. In Egyptian culture, winning battles was important for a divine king, since the substrate of divinity was power. War and military might expressed this divine power in striking—often shocking—ways. In Amenhotep's victory stela, he is shown stepping on the face of a prostrate enemy, grabbing the hair of two others whom he lunges toward in order to cut off their heads.[18] At Philae, one of Amenhotep's monuments describes him as "stout-hearted while killing, and cutting off hands." According to Egyptian military custom, the amputated hands of enemies were displayed as gory trophies.[19]

Amenhotep's victory stela over the Nubians depicts him not only as a conqueror, but as a god: "His majesty led on to victory, which he completed in his first campaign of victory. His majesty reached them [the enemy] like the wingstroke of a falcon, like Montu [falcon god of war] in his transformations; . . . [Pharaoh] Nebmaatra [i.e., Amenhotep III] the fierce-eyed lion, whose claws seized vile Cush [i.e., Nubia], who trampled down all its chiefs in their valleys, and cast them down in their blood, one on top of the other."[20] In battle, Amenhotep III became a manifestation

---

16. Tobin, "Amun-Re," 18–21.
17. Mysliwiec, "Atum," 25.
18. For the image, see Kozloff, *Amenhotep III*, 75.
19. Ibid., 77.
20. Fletcher, *Chronicle*, 44.

of the Theban war god Montu. Pictured as a falcon, Montu-Amenhotep clawed his enemies to pieces.

In Egyptian theology, divine power was symbolized by the savage strength of animals. Every New Kingdom Pharaoh bore the epithet "Mighty bull" as his Horus name. Both bulls and lions were associated with rule. By depicting himself as animalic in his victory stela, Amenhotep III accentuated his divinity.

"I made the chiefs of wretched Cush come before you, carrying their tribute on their backs!" declared Amun-Re to Amenhotep. But it was not enough for Amenhotep to be lord of the southern lands of Cush. Amun-Re gave his son dominion over all four corners of the earth. In the same inscription, the God declares:

> Turning my face to the north I did a wonder for you, I made the countries of the ends of Asia come to you carrying all their tribute on their backs. They offer you themselves and their children, begging you to grant them the breath of life.
>
> Turning my face to the west I did a wonder for you, I let you capture Tjehenu, they can't escape! Built is this fort and named after my majesty, enclosed by a great wall that reaches up to heaven, and settled with the princes' sons of Nubian bowmen.
>
> Turning my face to the eastern sunrise I did a wonder for you, I made the lands of Punt come here to you, with all the fragrant flowers of their lands, to beg your peace and breathe the air you give.[21]

Universal dominion was technically only enjoyed by the king of the Gods himself—Amun-Re. It is this divine sovereignty that the God bestowed on his son, Amenhotep III.

The Story of the Sun

The greatest symbol of life and divinity was (and perhaps is) the sun. It is the source of all energy, warmth, light—and thus life on this planet. Unlike other places on the globe, the Egyptian sunrise and sunset was (and is) not blocked by lush forest. Nor did clouds create many dour days over the land of the Nile. The golden eye of the sun was constantly present and powerful. When Pharaohs came to depict their divinity, they spoke of it in solar terms.

Egyptians viewed the sky as the surface of a cosmic ocean above the air (cf. the "waters above the firmament" in Genesis 1:7). On this ocean,

21. Ibid., 36–37.

the Sun coasts along on his "Dayboat." During the night, in turn, the Sun God sails on his "Nightboat" along the underbelly of the cosmos called the "Duat" or netherworld. The next morning, the Sun is reborn as Egypt's creator and life-giver. The Sun's daily movement through the sky was viewed as a journey from birth to death. His rebirth at dawn was made possible by merging with Osiris in the underworld.

Although depicted as a mummified corpse, Osiris was also god of life and fertility. His life-giving power permeated the floodwaters of the annual Nile inundation, which brought renewed vitality to Egypt's fields. He caused seeds to germinate, eggs to form chicks, and fetuses to become fully fledged animals. Osiris was viewed as the corpse of the Sun. When night turned darkest—at the stroke of midnight—the Sun merged with his corpse. Light was energized by darkness, order by chaos, and life came out of death.

Opet Festival

As son of the Sun, Amenhotep III would follow the glittering path of his divine Father on earth. The symbolic solar rebirth of Amenhotep occurred at the Opet Festival. This sacred celebration was an ancient rite revived and elaborated a century before Amenhotep III by Pharaoh Hatshepsut. Opet was an annual festival held at Thebes and celebrated in the temple of Amun-Re. The festival was a time of joy. There was stick fighting, trumpet blowing, acrobatic dancing, the butchering of animals, and piles of food. Despite some fluctuations, the date of the festival coincided with the rising of the Nile in early summer. This was a time of national celebration—the sandy soil of Egypt was being replenished with mineral-rich black mud.[22] Life would continue another year. This life was the gift of the Sun in heaven, and his Pharaonic representative on earth.

"During the temple's annual *Opet*-festival," writes Bell, "the reigning monarch was identified with the royal *ka*, divine kingship was reborn, and the individual king's right to rule was reconfirmed. At the climax, Amun-Re's powers were transferred to the king, and he then came into appearance before the representatives of the populace who waited anxiously in the public areas of the temple for the first glimpse of the transfigured monarch."[23]

This "transfiguration" occurred through the most sacrosanct of rites. The main ceremony conveyed the God Amun-Re from his resting place in Karnak to the temple in Thebes (modern Luxor). According to reliefs carved on walls of the Luxor Temple, Amenhotep III initiated the Opet

22. In my reconstruction of the Opet Festival, I follow Bell, "Divine Temple," 158.
23. Ibid., 157.

festival from his residence at Karnak, a palace named after himself, *Neb-maatra-tjehen-Aten*, "Nebmaatra Is the Dazzling Sun Disk." Traveling with the king was a portable bark carrying a statue of his own *ka*. Surrounded by shaven-headed priests, bright feather plumes and fans, he proceeded on foot a short distance to the temple of Amun-Re. There the priests ceremoniously collected the statues of Amun-Re with other deities and boarded them on gold-gilded barks.[24] The prows and sterns of the barks were shaped to resemble the heads of the deities carried inside them. The actual cult images of the Gods—too sacred to be seen by impure eyes—were veiled on the prows. Four bald prophets with leopard-skin cloaks marched beside each boat. Other priests burned incense for the Gods and gave them fresh water. Like floats in a parade, the barks swayed on the shoulders of the carriers until they reached the Nile. There they were set on massive river barges studded with flags. Accompanying them were a fleet of tow boats—called "duck boats" because their prows were carved into mallard heads. On the banks, gangs of men guided the barges with ropes to protect the Gods from drowning in the Nile. Reliefs in the Luxor Temple still depict them as they haul their burdens. An inscription over their heads refers to the king: "[The] ruler of glorious appearances is in his bark like Re in heaven! All the earth is united, jubilating at seeing his excellence in his river bark like Re in the night bark."[25] The assimilation of the king to the Sun God was in the minds of the people as he rode on the river.

Spectators crowded the shores of the Nile, clapping like thunder at the sight of their king and Gods. They were kept in control by Egyptian and foreign army units who marched along the banks, carrying ornate battle axes, bows, spears, clubs, and shields. Army generals rode in state on chariots drawn by stallions. Musicians plucked lutes, shook sistrums, and beat drums. In the midst of the din, trumpeters bleated the sacred cadence of the drama. Processing along, the people prayed to Amun-Re on behalf of their king: "May you set his lifetime to be like the duration of heaven, that he might appear like the Sun disk within it!"[26]

When the king arrived at the Luxor quay, it was already lined with princes, princesses, and high officials carrying bouquets and other offerings. Behind them priests drove fattened, festooned cattle destined for sacrifice. The barks of king and Gods were lifted off the barges and marched toward a massive pylon gate exploding with painted hieroglyphs.

---

24. Kozloff, *Amenhotep III*, 86.

25. I take this translation from the official Epigraphic Survey, *The Festival Procession of Opet*, 7.

26. Ibid., 9.

People—both common and elite—lined the road to worship Amun-Re and kneel before their king.

Through the gate was the temple complex. There the priests set the barks down and heaped offerings before them.[27] In the vast, sunlit courtyard, the king stood before the ram-headed staffs of Amun-Re representing the royal and divine *ka*. From his bark, the god ritually declared to his son, "I have given to you the lifetime of Re and the years of Atum, every foreign land being beneath your soles."[28]

The king now proceeded into the temple beyond the court where the common people buzzed. The eyes of the king and his retinue needed a moment to adjust from the brightness of the day to the sudden blackness within. When the image of Amun-Re entered the sacred enclosure, it was removed from its bark, and placed inside a special shrine within the temple. Before the shrine, the king purified himself with water, burned incense, and poured a libation. Behind the king an official announced: "The protection of all life, stability, and dominion, all health, all joy, all valor, and all victory surround him like Re."[29]

In the Chamber of the Divine King, Pharaoh's coronation rites were recapitulated. One by one, elaborate diadems were placed on the king's head. One of them featured the horns of Amun-Re himself. During each separate crowning, the king knelt before Amun-Re with his back toward the statue. Reliefs show the deity placing his hands on the king's head from behind in a protective gesture. Through the laying on of hands, the God's spirit and power—the royal *ka*—was transmitted like electricity from Father to son.

In the Chamber of the Divine King, the temple appeared to end. But there was a low door to the north. At the climax of the sacred rites, the king and high-ranking priests solemnly entered through the door to go deeper into the divine realm. In the inner sanctum of Amun-Re, the priest recited sacred texts as the king presented a series of precious offerings to Amun-Re and other ancient deities of Thebes. As the king renewed the God, the God vitalized the king. Pharaoh presented to the Gods pure water—the first fresh, invigorating liquid collected from the flooded Nile. He gave bouquets of fresh flowers for rejuvenation. He burned incense, the aroma of the Gods. The sweet-smelling smoke suffused the king himself.

After the offerings, the king approached the cabinet-like shrine holding Amun-Re. He opened the doors and finally laid eyes on his divine

27. Bell, "Divine Temple," 160–61. Sometimes, Bell notes, the procession from Karnak to Luxor took the land route along a highway lined with sphinxes.

28. Epigraphic Survey, *Festival Procession of Opet*, 22.

29. Ibid., 24.

Father. Instantly Amun-Re's golden glory burst upon the king, and the pharaoh became a renascent god, with a renewed persona and additional sacred names. The king then knelt before Amun-Re—facing the God—and the deity crowned him definitively.[30]

At some point during these rituals, the king turned left and arrived in a majestically decorated hall now called the "birth room." Worshipers believed that, in this sanctuary of the Luxor temple, Amun would reunite with the mother of the reigning monarch so that she could once again give birth to the royal *ka*. In the birth room, the king fully merged with his newborn *ka* in a secret ritual.[31]

After his rebirth, the king entered a long hall oriented east-west with twelve pillars. The twelve columns may have represented the twelve hours of the Sun God's journey through the netherworld. By processing through the colonnade, the king imitated the voyage of the Sun God in his journey by night in the netherworld.[32]

Now seething with divine energy, the king finally reappeared as if from a divine womb into the sunny court. The assembled throng had been anxiously awaiting to see if the rites had proved efficacious. When the Pharaoh emerged from the shadows, he reflected the bright Sun with his robe of shining gold and silver. The people roared at the sight of the regenerated divine king, splendidly crowned and glorious in triumph.[33] By now, the humanness of the king had almost been fully submerged. The king was glittering with divinity. As the living manifestation of the Sun God, the people adored their transformed king as the source of their own life.[34] Pharaoh Amenhotep III called the Luxor temple "his palace of justification in which he is rejuvenated, the palace from which he sets out in joy at the moment of his appearance, his transformation being visible to all."[35] As the king marched out of the temple he heard proclaimed over his royal *ka* statue: "The good god, lord of the two lands, Nebmaatre, given life, stability, and dominion like Re forever!"[36]

30. Bell, "Divine Temple," 174.

31. Fletcher, *Chronicle*, 115.

32. Kozloff and Bryan, *Egypt's Dazzling Sun*, 86.

33. Bell, "Divine Temple," 176.

34. Ibid., 135.

35. Van De Mieroop, *A History of Ancient Egypt*, 196.

36. Epigraphic Survey, *Festival Procession of Opet*, 30. Cf. the mystery rite in which Lucius becomes the living image of the Sun god—and even the Sun himself (Apuleius, *Met.* 11.23–24).

The Sed Festival

Amenhotep's identification with the Sun in the Opet Festival seems to have been only temporary. The electric surge of divinity—recharged in the rite—gradually began to wane in the realm of the everyday. In the thirtieth year of his reign, however, Amenhotep's transformation into the Sun God may have become permanent. During this year, Amenhotep celebrated his first Sed Festival (or jubilee), an ancient rite renewing the powers and promoting the divinity of the king who now (given short life expectancies) must have seemed as old as a god.

Not since the Twelfth Dynasty (a millennium earlier) was there a Sed Festival envisioned on so lofty a scale. Amenhotep III ordered his chief scribe—Amenhotep son of Hapu—to scour the records of the past in order to recover and adapt traditional elements.[37] The festival began around late April. All of Egypt was involved in the celebration. The common people loved the jubilee for its promise of rich food and fanfare. Faithful officials received more permanent boons: jeweled collars, gold bracelets, gold amulets shaped like ducks and fish, and green linen bands to tie around their heads.[38] All around Thebes, there was much dancing, singing, and jubilation. It was an international affair—kings as far away as Babylonia expected an invitation.

In the tomb of Kheruef—a high official of Amenhotep III—the pharaoh is depicted during his first Sed Festival participating in the ancient rites. Once again, the ceremonies portray the king's union with the Sun God. Kheruef says that "the king appeared gloriously at the great double doors of his palace," west of Thebes.[39] Before his palace was a manmade lake Amenhotep called the "Lake of His Majesty." The king and his court sailed across the lake in barks made to look like the Dayboat and Nightboat of Re.[40] High officials, including Kheruef, "grasped the tow-ropes of the evening bark and the prow-rope of the morning bark and they towed the bark at the great palace." The lake's northeast-to-southwest orientation imitated the path of the Sun through the sky.[41]

To symbolize himself as the Sun in his second Sed Festival (ca. 1358 B.C.E.), Amenhotep wore copious amounts of gold jewelry, which glittered magnificently in the glaring Egyptian sun.[42] When he presented himself, the

---

37. Berman, "Overview," in *Amenhotep III: Perspectives on His Reign*, 17.
38. Epigraphic Survey, *Tomb of Kheruef*, 43.
39. Kozloff, *Amenhotep III*, 184.
40. Johnson, "Monuments and Monumental Art," 86–87.
41. Kozloff, *Amenhotep III*, 186.
42. Fletcher, *Chronicle*, 154.

people beheld him no longer as their king, but as an immortalized "living god imbued with the powers of the sun."[43]

Arielle Kozloff depicts the king's rebirth at the Sed Festival as a kind of "resurrection":

> [It was the] culmination of a process of deification that had begun with Amenhotep III's coronation. At that time, like all Egyptian kings, he was the representative and high priest of each god on earth (son of Re, heir of Geb, and Horus incarnate) and was treated as nearly divine. He had his own cult statue, like a god, and in his palace, he was approached with great ceremony—prostration and bowed heads—like a god in a temple. Over the decades, however, and passing through difficult times, Amenhotep III's own divinity had intensified. Substantial amounts of statuary and stelae identified him . . . not just as the deities' representative, but as the gods themselves: as Amun, Min, Montu, Horus, Thoth, even the Aten. One of his inscriptions on Karnak's Third Pylon states that the statues of himself he has placed there are actually images of Re, "divine and beautiful." Now at the time of his jubilee, Nebmaatra himself became a god in his own right.[44]

In reliefs showing his third jubilee, Amenhotep wears the *shebyu* collar—a finely coiled double necklace. Wearing this collar meant that Amenhotep III was assimilated and identified with his Father Amun-Re. Such assimilation, according to Raymond Johnson, represents "an official statement that Amenhotep III had united with the sun god while still alive." "For the last eight years of his reign," Johnson notes, "Amenhotep is represented in a timeless, youthful form, more cult image than actual man. The changes in the representation of this king proclaim his deified state as the sun god's 'living image on earth.'"[45] The fact that statues of the gods bear the faces of the rulers who made them is widely recognized among Egyptologists. Amenhotep III, it appears, was the first Pharaoh who depicted the Gods in his own image.[46] "As a living manifestation of the creator god [Amun-Re]," Johnson argues,

> Amenhotep was essentially all gods in one. As such he appears to have been worshipped in every divine form imaginable. Material

---

43. Ibid., 125.

44. Kozloff, *Amenhotep III*, 191.

45. Johnson, "Images of Amenhotep III," 37. In some of these images the wife of Amenhotep, queen Tiye, plays the role of the goddess Hathor, the "companion of the sun god who stood for all aspects of regeneration" (Hornung, *Akhenaten*, 27).

46. Kozloff, *Amenhotep III*, 121.

from Memphis indicates he was worshipped there as "Neb-maat-Re united with Ptah" in a gigantic temple.... He was worshipped as Thoth in Hermopolis in the form of immense quartzite baboons twenty feet high crowned with limestone moon disks, as the creator god Atum-Re at Heliopolis, as Osiris at Abydos, as Ptah-Sokar and Atum at his mortuary complex in Thebes. He was worshipped as Amun-Re and Re-Horakhty at Karnak, as Sobek-Re at Armant; as a falcon at Hierakonpolis; as Khnum at Elephantine; and as the sun, the moon, and lord of Nubia at Soleb.[47]

Soleb

Many of these statues and temples of Amenhotep have crumbled like dry sand. The temple of Soleb, however—near the Third Cataract in modern Sudan—preserves some faint reflection of Amenhotep's self-conception. This sandstone edifice was dedicated to two gods: Amun-Re of Karnak and Nebmaatra lord of Nubia. Nebmaatra, as we have seen, was Amenhotep's own throne name. One of the gods worshiped in Soleb was none other than Amenhotep III himself.

The statues that have survived show the king dressed in a kilt associated with deities, hooded with the traditional pharaonic headcloth (the *nemes*-headcloth). Sprouting from his head are the ram horns of Amun-Re, which serve to identify Amenhotep with the high God. On top of the statue is a lunar crescent with a sun disk.[48] The symbols indicate that the king had already come to represent (perhaps embody) Sun and Moon.[49]

Cult statues were important for expressing the king's permanent deification because they did not decay like flesh. The *ka* of the creator could permanently inhabit the stone, even if it could not always reside in the fleshly body of the king. In this way, the divine spirit of the king could inhabit multiple bodies and appear in distant locations.[50] Statues thus stabilized the king's divinity, like batteries whose divine charge would never fade. Buried under the sands, some images have remained pristine long after the corruption of the king's mortal husk.

47. Johnson, "Images of Amenhotep III," 41, cf. 37 and Johnson, "Monuments and Monumental Art," in *Amenhotep III: Perspectives on his Reign*, 87–88.

48. Kozloff and Bryan, *Egypt's Dazzling Sun*, 107–8.

49. Ibid. Cf. Fletcher, *Chronicle*, 155; Kozloff, *Amenhotep III*, 191.

50. Kozloff and Bryan, *Egypt's Dazzling Sun*, 126.

Death and Rebirth

Although his mummy was moved and reburied in ancient times, scholars are fairly sure that they have recovered the body of Amenhotep III. Judging from the remains, writes Kozloff, the king

> seems to have lost a huge amount of weight toward the end [of his life] because his skin was so loose that packets of materials had to be inserted to plump it up. His teeth and jaws were in disastrous condition, with caries and dental granuloma (a disease mass forming at the root of the tooth inside the jawbone). He may not have been able to eat, and he certainly must have been in great pain, with nothing but opium and magical spells to dull the suffering.[51]

Pharaoh Amenhotep III died about a year after his third Sed Festival.

In the second century C.E., Clement of Alexandria mocked the deification of Alexander the Great (made Pharaoh in 332 B.C.E.) because the Macedonian Pharaoh had died.[52] In Egyptian culture, however, death was not the denial of deification, but its fulfillment. The Pharaoh's final union with the Sun God was described in Pyramid Texts composed a thousand years before Amenhotep III. From these texts we know that the Sun did not sail alone in his journey through the netherworld. On his bark were a host of deities and other souls. Among them was the pharaoh's own soul (or *ba*). Just as the Sun God merged with the body of Osiris, so did the pharaoh's soul. Through this union, the pharaoh gained strength not simply to become one among many living spirits. He received power to rise *with* and *as* the Sun God himself.

Pharaoh's journey through the netherworld is depicted on the tomb walls of several Eighteenth-Dynasty pharaohs—including that of Amenhotep III. The oldest version of the story, called the *Amduat*—or "What is in the Netherworld" was originally called the "Treatise of the Hidden Chamber." The *Amduat* divides the underworld journey into twelve hours. At the first hour, the sun god is greeted by the ecstatic jubilation of solar baboons—somewhat like earthly baboons who honk and screech at the appearance of the morning sun.[53] In the second hour, the Sun God passes through the waterway of Re, a region named "Wernes." Here the blessed dead spend their afterlife in the Field of Reeds. The journey through the reeds continues into the third hour, through the waterway of Osiris. Channels of water

---

51. Kozloff, *Amenhotep III*, 228.

52. Clement of Alexandria, *Protrep.* 10.96.4.

53. Forman and Quirke, *Hieroglyphs and the Afterlife*, 118.

become zigzag paths of fire in the fourth hour. For quick travel over burning sands, the bark of the Sun transforms into a double-headed serpent vehicle. During the fifth hour, the serpent chariot winds through a narrow pass under the tomb of Osiris. In the sixth hour—at the stroke of midnight—the Sun is nearly swallowed by an abyss of watery darkness. The whole cosmos comes near to being plunged into eternal night. Yet in the deepest blackness, the Sun's light is rekindled by merging with the corpse of Osiris.

Although the entire story of the *Amduat* is concerned with the renewed life of the king after death, the "Kings of Upper and Lower Egypt" are only addressed in the sixth hour. They are shown as mummified figures with crowns standing behind the Sun's corpse. Above them are shown their symbols of power: scepters, crowns, and uraeus serpents.[54] Like Osiris, their mummified bodies remain in the caves of the underworld, but their souls rise with the Sun.

When we reach the seventh hour, the Sun God battles and defeats Apopis, also known as "Horrible of face." He is a huge serpent representing chaos. The eighth hour is the time for the newly rekindled Sun to cloth himself—along with other Gods and souls—in preparation for the new day. Twelve oarsmen appear in the ninth hour before the bark of Amun-Re. In front of them are three divine images who "cause all the trees and all the plants to be created."[55] Those who drowned in the Nile appear in the tenth hour. Although their bodies could not be recovered on earth, they are preserved in the underworld. The punishment of evildoers is shown in the eleventh hour.

At the end of the twelfth hour, the Sun God is reborn by being towed on his bark through the body of a gigantic serpent named "Life of the Gods." Traveling with the Sun God on his bark, the Pharaoh's soul is digested in reverse—moving from the tail of the serpent to the mouth. He enters as an old man and exits as a child. When the bark is spewed from the snake's mouth, it is pulled up by the god of air Shu. Suddenly the bark of the sun bursts out from between the thighs of the sky goddess—a new dawn breaks forth!

Out of the darkness, twelve Gods are heard to proclaim: "Born is he who is born, who has emerged, has emerged! . . . [T]he sky belongs to your *Ba*-soul, that it may rest in it, the earth belongs to your corpse, Lord of veneration! You have seized the horizon, that you rest in your shrine . . ."[56] This proclamation is addressed to the Sun God Re, but it equally applies to the soul united to the Sun—the pharaoh.

54. Hornung, *Knowledge for the Afterlife*, 83.

55. Ibid., 112.

56. Hornung and Abt, *Egyptian Amduat*, 364.

In the Pyramid Texts, the pharaoh is identified with the Sun (here called Atum) in his rebirth.

> He [Pharaoh] has come to you, his Father; he has come to you, O Sun . . .
>
> You shall evolve with your Father Atum, you shall go high with [your] Father [Atum], you shall rise with your Father Atum and release needs . . .
>
> You will go up and go down; you will go up with the Sun and rise up . . .
>
> You have developed, you have gone high, you have become effective, it has become cool for you inside your Father's arms, inside Atum's arms.
>
> Atum, elevate him to you, encircle him inside your arms: he is your son of your body, forever.[57]

Atum the Sun God encircles the pharaoh in his fiery arms, and the pharaoh's spirit merges with the sun. Egyptian artists represented this union when they depicted Atum as a male wearing the royal double crown of Lower and Upper Egypt.[58] Atum inhabited the form of the pharaoh, and pharaoh absorbed the essence of the Sun. In death Amenhotep III finally attained the permanent deification of his soul.

Conclusion

Across the Nile from Luxor was Amenhotep III's funerary temple. The temple gate was (and is) guarded by two seventy-foot high seated statues of the king now called the *colossi* of Memnon (after an Ethiopian king in Homer's *Iliad*). Although they are gone now, long ago when one entered the solar court of the funerary complex, one beheld a series of twenty-six foot statues of the king as Osiris standing between massive columns.[59] Already in his statuary, then, the king had anticipated his union with Osiris in the underworld.

Buried in Amenhotep III's tomb, on his massive red-granite sarcophagus we find the words of Osiris addressed to the king: "My son, Nebmaatra, my beloved heir, Amenhotep, ruler of Thebes, you have come together with the Gods, and I have given to you the necropolis of the West

---

57. Der Manuelian, *Ancient Egyptian Pyramid Texts*, 39–40.

58. Mysliwiec, "Atum," 25.

59. Fletcher, *Chronicle*, 142–43.

[the netherworld]."[60] As a manifestation of Osiris, Amenhotep would never leave his underworld crypt. As one identified with Amun-Re, however, those who dwelt along the Nile would see their king rise every morning as Egypt's dazzling Sun.

60. Ibid., 161.

Chapter 2

The New Dionysus

Divine Assimilation in Greco-Roman Ruler Cult

His face was as the heav'ns, and therein stuck
A sun and moon, which kept their course and lighted
The little O, the earth . . .
His legs bestrid the ocean; his reared arm
Crested the world. . . . For his bounty,
There was no winter in't; an autumn 'twas
That grew the more by reaping. His delights
Were dolphin-like, they showed his back above
The element they lived in. . . .
Realms and islands were
As plates dropped from his pocket . . .

—SHAKESPEARE, *ANTONY AND CLEOPATRA*

A S EARLY AS HERODOTUS in the fifth century B.C.E., the Egyptian god
Osiris was identified with the Greek god Dionysus.[1] Of all Hellenistic
deities, Dionysus had the greatest ability to bridge the gap between the human and the divine. "Humanity emerges from nature and aspires to divinity,"
observes Richard Seaford. "Dionysos, by transcending these fundamental
divisions, may *transform the identity* of an individual into animal and god."[2]

1. Herodotus, *History*, 2.144.

2. Seaford, *Dionysos*, 5.

Dionysus, like Christ, was born of a woman, but called son of the most high God. The mortal woman was Semele, princess of Thebes in central Greece. After her union with Zeus, Semele was deceived by Hera into asking her paramour on oath to reveal his true form. Zeus was forced to fulfill her request, thus killing his mistress in a shock of light and heat. Nevertheless he saved her fetus by carefully removing it and sewing it into his thigh. The god Dionysus was thus said to have been born twice.

As an infant, Dionysus (also called Bacchus) had to be hidden from his jealous stepmother, and so was spirited off to Nysa in Arabia. There, he wore women's clothes as a disguise, and "spent his time at dances and with bands of women and in every kind of luxury and amusement."[3]

Dionysus' companions were satyrs, silens, and maenads. Satyrs and silens (used more or less interchangeably) were sex-crazed, snub-nosed, wild-haired young men with horse tails and hooves. Since they were immortal, they combined aspects of humanity, animality, and deity. Maenads (sometimes called "Bacchae") were literally "crazy women" with whipped-up snaky hair and flailing arms. In Dionysiac revelry, they moved in concert like a flock of birds and could make milk, honey, and wine spew from the ground. As members of Dionysus' sacred band (or *thiasos*), they carried thyrsi (fennel sticks topped with a pine cone), ivy wreathes, and torches. Their ecstatic cry was "*Euhoe!*" and "*Iobacchus!*"

When Dionysus reached adolescence, he formed the maenads "into an army, equipped them with thyrsi, and made a campaign over all the inhabited world."[4] The focus of Dionysus' invasion was the east. Never had a drunken band of women and satyrs proved so formidable against fierce warriors. His battles won, Dionysus triumphed over his enemies in a boisterous parade with marching pans, a showcase of exotic treasures, and rumbling elephants.[5]

The war was so successful that it was later imitated by the most famous of conquers, Alexander the Great. In the foothills of the Hindu Kush, Alexander discovered ivy (sacred to Dionysus) and thought that he had found the site of Nysa. These lands, he concluded, were the old haunts and battlefields of the god. To celebrate his own military successes, the story goes, Alexander imitated Dionysus' triumphal parade. In the florid account of Plutarch, Alexander

---

3. Diodorus of Sicily, *Bibl. hist.* 3.64.5.

4. Ibid., 3.64.6; cf. 4.4.2–4. For a similar campaign attributed to Osiris, see 1.17.1.

5. The word for triumph, *thriambos*, first appears in an invocation to Dionysus (Seaford, *Dionysos*, 45). Later authors claim that the ritual of triumph originated with Dionysus (Diodorus of Sicily, *Bibl. hist.* 3.65.8; Arrian, *Anab.* 6.28.2). Scenes of Dionysus' triumph become popular on Roman sarcophagi in the second century C.E.

set out through the region of Carmania celebrating a week-long revel. Eight horses were leisurely conveying him while he feasted day and night continuously with his companions on a dais fastened upon a lofty and conspicuous scaffolding. A host of wagons followed—some with purple and embroidered canopies, others overshadowed with branches of trees ever fresh and green. They conveyed the rest of his friends and generals, who were crowned and drinking. There you would see neither shield nor helmet, nor pike—but soldiers with mugs, drinking horns, and flagons along the whole highway ladling from large kegs and mixing bowls drinking to each others' health, some as they marched forth together and went along, others as they lied down. Plentiful music of fifes, pipes, song, chanting, and the frenzied cries of women dominated the whole scene. Tricks of bacchic license accompanied the disordered and wandering troops as if the god [Dionysus] himself were present co-leading the revel.[6]

The imitation of Dionysus reached Hollywood proportions in Alexandria, Egypt sometime in the 270s B.C.E. Ptolemy II Philadelphus—son of one of Alexander's generals—put on a Grand Procession in honor of his father, Pharaoh Ptolemy I. The parade depicted various scenes from the life of Dionysus in the form of gigantic and richly decorated floats. A snippet from the description of Callixeinus (an eyewitness) gives some taste of the extravagant efforts of the Ptolemies to conform themselves to the god.[7] At one point there was rolled in a

four-wheeled cart, which contained the "Return of Dionysus from India." [It featured] an eighteen-foot statue of Dionysus reclining on an elephant. He wore a purple cloak and a golden crown of ivy and vine. He held in his hands a golden thyrsus-lance, and he wore felt slippers embroidered with gold. In front of him on the neck of the elephant there sat a young Satyr seven feet tall, wreathed with a golden crown of pine, signaling with a golden goat-horn in his right hand. The elephant had gold trappings and a golden ivy crown about its neck.

Five hundred little girls followed him, dressed in purple gowns and golden girdles. The first one hundred and twenty girls were wreathed with golden pine crowns. One hundred and twenty Satyrs followed them, some wearing silver armor, others bronze. After them marched five troops of donkeys on which rode crowned Silens and Satyrs. Some of the donkeys had frontlets

6. Plutarch, *Alex.* 67.1–6. Cf. Arrian, *Anab.* 6.28.1.

7. Athenaeus, *Deipn.* 5.196a–203b.

and harnesses of gold, others of silver. After them marched twenty-four elephant quadrigae, sixty bigae of goats, twelve of saiga antelopes, seven of oryxes, fifteen of hartebeest, eight bigae of ostriches, seven of onelaphoi, four bigae of onagers, and four quadrigae of horses.[8]

The text proceeds with lavish lists of exotic "eastern" animals (with equally exotic names) that convey cartfuls of spoils (including pretended prisoners of war) from Dionysus' Indian campaigns. The fact that Ptolemy II's statue followed the scenes from Dionysus showed how eager the king was to assimilate himself to the god.[9]

Ptolemy II's grandson Ptolemy IV Philopator had a particularly close relationship with Dionysus. He founded festivals involving sacrifices of all sorts in honor of the god including a "Wine Flask-Carrying Festival."[10] According to Plutarch, the king himself played an active role in these religious rites. In his palace he would go about gathering devotees while holding a timbrel, devoting "himself to women and Dionysiac routs and revels."[11] It was said that Philopator was tattooed with ivy leaves, the plant sacred to Dionysus.[12] According to Clement of Alexandria, Ptolemy IV also received the nickname *Neos Dionysos*—the "New (or Young) Dionysus."[13]

From inscriptions we know that "New Dionysus" was a title borne by Ptolemy XII Auletes ("Flute-Player").[14] The flute (*aulos*) was a Dionysiac instrument. Though generally seen as unfit for royal lips, it perfectly fit a Dionysian pharaoh. Lucian of Samosata tells this colorful tale, which probably refers to Auletes:

8. Trans. Rice, *Grand Procession*, 17–19, modified. See his commentary on ibid., 83–86.

9. Athenaeus, *Deipn.* 201d.

10. This report comes from Eratosthenes of Cyrene (in Athenaeus, *Deipn.* 7.276a–c), who lived in the court of Ptolemy IV.

11. Plutarch, *Cleom.* 33.2, 34.2; cf. Justin, *1 Apol.* 30.1.

12. *Etymologicum magnum* s.v. *Gallos*, 220.19–20; cf. 3 Macc 2:29. Ptolemy IV also undertook a reform of the administrative organization of Alexandria, giving to the "Berenice" tribe the name "Dionysia" and replacing the ancient names of the demes of this tribe by the new names borrowed from the Dionysiac cycle (Satyrus in Theophilus of Antioch, *Autol.* 2.7). This reform showed the spread of Dionysiac mythology in the Alexandrian milieu and the desire of the king to place his capital under the patronage of his ancestor Dionysus (Fraser, *Ptolemaic Alexandria*, 2.120, n. 48; Dunand, "Les associations dionysiaques," 87–88).

13. Clement of Alexandria, *Protrep.* 4.54.2.

14. *OGIS* 186.9–10, 191.1, 741.1; *SEG* 8.408; Porphyry *ap.* Eus *Chron.* = *FGH* 260.2 [12] and [15]. For other references on inscriptions and papyri to Ptolemy XII as *Neos Dionysos*, see Tondriau, "Rois Lagides," 137–38.

At the court of Ptolemy surnamed Dionysus, a man accused Demetrius, a Platonic philosopher, of drinking water and of being the only one who did not assume the feminine habits in the Dionysiac festivals. Now if Demetrius—called in the next morning—had not drunk wine under the eyes of all the court, or clothed himself in a robe of Tarentum [a city known for its luxury], striking cymbals and dancing, he would have perished as one displeased with the life of the king, as one who tried to refute and oppose the opulence of Ptolemy.[15]

Antony-Dionysus

At the end of the Hellenistic period, Dionysiac royal ideology was absorbed by Marc Antony, the Roman triumvir (83–30 B.C.E.).[16] Although Antony claimed to be a descendant of Heracles, his temperament was Dionysian through and through. A lover of luxury yet also a soldier, Antony officially donned the mask of Dionysus when he became autocrat of the eastern Mediterranean. Soon embroiled in the clash of propaganda, spontaneous religious enthusiasm, and the cords of his own destiny, Antony found that the mask of Dionysus had fused with his persona and could not be removed.

If drunkenness was a kind of possession by Dionysus, then Antony was clearly inhabited by the god. In his famous *Life of Antony*, Plutarch humorously observed that sober Romans

were disgusted at his [Antony's] ill-timed bouts of inebriation, his heavy expenditures, his cavorting with tramps, his snoozings during the day, his wandering about while beside himself and hung over—not to mention his nightly revels and trips to the theater, his loitering around with married women, playing the mime and making a fool of himself. It is said at any rate that when he was feasted at the nuptials of Hippias the mime—drinking through the night—that in the morning when the citizens called him into the Forum he came out still over-stuffed with food and barfed, while one of his friends held a cloak underneath [to catch the chunks].[17]

Antony's reputation as a drinker became so bad that the triumvir eventually had to "vomit up"—to use the expression of Pliny the Elder—a

15. Lucian, *Cal.* 16; cf. Strabo, *Geog.* 17 795.6 and 796; Dio Chrysostom, *Or.* 32 383, 22; Athenaeus, *Deipn.* 4 176e–f.

16. Hölbl, *History*, 291.

17. Plutarch, *Ant.* 9.5–9.

treatise called *On His Own Drunkenness*.[18] Since the text does not survive, we can only imagine some of the Dionysian humor it contained.

According to ancient traditions, Dionysus had yoked his chariots with lions while on his great eastern campaign.[19] In apparent imitation of Dionysus, Antony was the first to try lion-hitching at Rome. The deed was part of a larger program of extravagance that smacked of Dionysian triumph after Antony and Julius Caesar beat Pompey in the battle of Pharsalus (48 B.C.E.). While Caesar sailed on to secure his power in Egypt, Africa, and Spain, Antony came to Rome to celebrate. There his critics

> were grieved at the sights of the gold goblets carried around in his excursions like those in parades, his pavilions set up along the highway and in groves, the outlays of his lavish luncheons by rivers, the lions yoked beneath his chariots, along with the houses of sober men and women quartered with prostitutes and female fiddlers. They made it out to be something terrible that [Julius] Caesar himself was in the open air outside Italy, mopping up what remained of the war with immense toil and danger, while others on his account lived in luxury and outraged the citizens.[20]

Like Dionysus, Antony had the amazing ability to change his identity by putting on tragic and comic masks. Although he was always an aristocrat and became proto-emperor of the east, his favorite part to play was the slave. When kicked out of the senate by Caesar's enemies in 49 B.C.E., Antony dressed up as a slave, and hired a horse and buggy to escape to Caesar in Gaul.[21] When Caesar was killed in the senate chamber five years later, Antony immediately jumped into his handy slave suit and skulked in a corner until passions cooled down.[22] Having a night of fun at Alexandria, "slave Antony" popped his head through random doorways and windows, teasing people innocently going about their business.[23] Fulvia, an early wife of Antony, was a strait-laced type-A who liked to wear the pants in their relationship. To loosen her up, Antony put on the following play:

---

18. Pliny, *Nat.* 14.148. Scott ("Octavian's Propaganda," 133–41) provides the ancient sources and context, but his interpretations are flawed and outdated. See further Griffin, "Propertius and Antony," 17–26; Huzar, "The Literary Efforts of Mark Antony," 657; and Marasco, "Marco Antonio," 539–48, who cites Seneca the Younger, *Ep.* 83.24–25 (ibid., 541).

19. Dionysus with yoked lions is shown in vase painting as early as the sixth century B.C.E. Cf. Seneca the Younger's *Oedipus* 424–26.

20. Plutarch, *Ant.* 9.5–9; cf. Pliny the Elder, *Nat.* 8.55; Traina, *Marco Antonio*, 33.

21. Plutarch, *Ant.* 5.9

22. Ibid., 14.1.

23. Ibid., 29.2–3.

Once when large crowds departed to meet [Julius] Caesar after his victory in Spain, Antony too went out. Then when a rumor suddenly reached Italy that Caesar had perished and his enemies were at hand, Antony returned. He dressed up in slave clothes, came to his house by night, and claimed to bear a letter to Fulvia from Antony. He was brought into her hooded and covered up. His wife was beside herself with worry. Before she read the letters she asked if Antony was still alive. In silence, Antony held out the letter. When she broke the seal and started to read, he threw his arms around her and planted a kiss on her face.[24]

After Caesar's victory in the civil war, Antony bought (or simply occupied) the house of the defeated general, Pompey the Great. He made it into the quarters of a Dionysian bazaar, filled with actors, performers, and stuntmen. Once again, Plutarch provides the critical (that is, criticizing) report. Upright men, he says, "were grieved when they saw it [the house] closed for the most part to leaders and generals and ambassadors—outrageously pushed from the doors—but full of actors and miracle-mongers and hung-over flatterers, on whom most of his [Antony's] cash was expended in the most violent and offensive way."[25]

Antony's assimilation to Dionysus intensified in his eastern exploits. In 39 B.C.E., the Athenians with their wives and children met him on his arrival and greeted him as Dionysus. Antony issued coins portraying his bust wreathed in a crown with ivy leaves and blossoms. "By this means," says Dietrich Mannsperger, Antony "appears not only as the 'charge of Dionysus' . . . but as the *Neos Dionysus*, the new, young, or even second Dionysus himself."[26] A surviving Athenian inscription refers to Antony as "New Dionysus the god."[27]

According to Seneca the Elder, the drama in Athens took an unexpected turn. Athenian officials proceeded to offer Antony in marriage to their (virgin!) Goddess Athena, and to entreat him to wed her. "Antony said he would marry her, but exacted 1000 talents as dowry. At this one of the Greeks said: 'Sire, Zeus had your mother, Semele, to wife without a dowry.' This jest passed unpunished, but the betrothal cost the Athenians 1000 talents."[28] The "betrothal" sum was probably one sixth of this amount,[29]

24. Ibid., 10.7–9.

25. Ibid., 21.2–3.

26. Mannsperger, "Apollo gegen Dionysos," 385–86. For the coins, see ibid., Plate XXI.3–6.

27. *IG* II2 1043.22–23.

28. Seneca the Elder, *Suasoria* 1.6.

29. Dio Cassius, *Rom. Hist.* 48.39.2.

but still a blow to the Athenians. Socrates of Rhodes reveals more about Antony's stay in the center of Greek culture:

> He had a roughly framed hut built in a conspicuous spot above the theater [of Dionysus at Athens] and covered with green brushwood, as they do with Bacchic "caves" [gateways to the Underworld associated with Dionysus]. In it, he hung drums, fawn skins, and other Dionysiac paraphernalia of all sorts. He lay inside with his friends, beginning at dawn, and got drunk. Musicians summoned from Italy entertained him, and the whole Greek world gathered to watch. Sometimes . . . Antony moved up onto the Acropolis, and the entire city of Athens was illuminated by the lamps that hung from the ceilings [of the temple buildings]. He also gave order that from then on he was to be proclaimed as Dionysus throughout all the cities.[30]

In 41 B.C.E., Antony left Lucius Censorius in charge of Greece and crossed over into Asia Minor (modern Turkey). At the time, Antony's partner—and rival—Caesar Octavian was worn down at Rome with civil strife and rioting. Antony, however, began an extended vacation with ample peace and good cheer. Kings loitered at his doors. Royal women vied with one another in bestowing gifts—and their beauty.

According to the mythology of Dionysus, wherever the god went "he held great festive assemblages and celebrated musical contests."[31] In the same way, Antony proved to be a magnet for the bests artists and performers of Greece. Musicians and dancers accompanied him everywhere, producing a constant carnivalesque atmosphere.

As he traveled along, many cities welcomed Antony with incense and paeans—honors they knew were meant for gods. In Ephesus—the *de facto* capital of the province of Asia—Antony's divine identity was revealed: "women were led out dressed as bacchants with men and boys as satyrs and pans. The city was full of ivy Dionysian wands, little harps, pipes, and flutes. People were calling Antony 'Dionysus Giver of Joy' and 'Gentle.'"[32] Jollity and festivity surrounded Antony's advent, and the people were swept up in Dionysian transport.

The climax of this Dionysian drama occurred in Tarsus when Queen Cleopatra sailed up the Cydnus river in a barge outfitted with a golden prow, purple sails, and silver oars. "She herself," wrote Plutarch, "reclined under a parasol embroidered with gold, adorned graphically like Aphrodite, with

---

30. In Athenaeus, *Deipn.* 148b–c = *FGH* 192 F2.

31. Diodorus of Sicily, *Bibl. hist.* 3.64.7; cf. 4.4.2–4.

32. Plutarch, *Ant.* 24.1–2, 4.

young boys looking like cupids do in pictures standing on each side fan-
ning her. Likewise there were the most beautiful servant girls, having the
robes of mermaids and graces, some at the rudders, others at the rigging."
Cleopatra—like Antony—came as a deity, and made her epiphany known
by her scent. "The most wonderful aromas from heaps of incense," Plutarch
continued, "took hold of the riverbanks." As she was ferrying along, Antony
was holding court in the marketplace. When people got word of Cleopatra's
advent, they poured out of the city leaving Antony alone and blinking on
the tribunal. "There was a saying which spread among all the people, that
for the good of Asia Aphrodite had come to revel with Dionysus."[33]

We cannot ignore the fact that to some Greeks Antony was, as Plutarch
remarked, Dionysus "the Savage" and "Wild" (other cult epithets of the
god). Many people—especially rich aristocrats—resented the hike in taxes
and political corruption. Plutarch believed that the triumvir was too trust-
ing, allowing his courtiers to collude. When abuses were boldly brought to
Antony's attention, he remedied the wrongs and laughed at his own expense.

There was, however, an appropriate time for Antony to be Dionysus
Savage and Wild—in war. During Antony's rule over the east, Parthian
armies hovered like a cloud over the provinces of Syria and Armenia. As a
general, Antony was motivated to recover the Roman standards lost to the
Parthians in 53 B.C.E. Yet there were also deeper religious undercurrents
motivating Antony's invasion. As the "New Dionysus," he was likely induced
to imitate the god's invasion of the east: like the god, he would conquer and
bring back exotic spoils.

Tragically, Antony's major campaign was a disaster. He lost, according
to Plutarch, 28,000 infantry and 4,000 cavalry—mostly to disease. Although
Antony had to accept defeat, months later he captured the king of Armenia
as a consolation prize. This king had betrayed him in the previous invasion,
and so was hauled to Alexandria to be the gem in the crown of Antony's "triumph" in 34 B.C.E. During the festivities, Antony wreathed his head with
ivy and dressed in the gold-embroidered gown of Dionysus. In this garb, he
rode along Alexandria's Canopic Way, holding the thyrsus stick in his hand
and wearing high laced boots worn by tragic actors.[34]

In Alexandria, Antony and queen Cleopatra formed a certain club,
called "Those who Live Like None Other." They feasted each other daily,
and expended an enormous amount of wealth. Plutarch refers to the well-
known "luxuries, excesses, and parades of Antony" while in the Egyptian
capital. Although the historian was critical of these events, Antony took

33. Ibid., 26.1–5.
34. Velleius Paterculus, *Res gest. divi Aug.* 2.82.4.

them to be "cheerful and beneficent actions."[35] The Alexandrians—known for their love of carousal and comedy—did not seem to mind. In fact, Plutarch admits that they "enjoyed his buffoonery and joked with him. . . . They loved him and said that with the Romans he used the tragic mask, but with them the comic."[36]

Meanwhile in Rome, two of the charges leveled against Antony were that he gave himself the title of "Osiris" or "Dionysus"[37] and posed for portraits and statues as Dionysus.[38] These charges are not implausible. Like the Ptolemies, Antony desired to be known officially as the "New Dionysus"[39] and to assimilate himself to the god in art.[40]

In fact, rulers assimilating to gods was an established tradition—popular even at Rome. Antony pointed out that Octavian once held a lavish ritual banquet (a *lectisternium*) in the garb of the god Apollo. Eleven friends surrounding him impersonated the other twelve Olympian gods. "The scandal of this banquet was greater," the historian Suetonius noted, "because of death and famine in the land at the time, and on the following day there was an outcry that the gods had eaten all the grain and that Caesar was in truth Apollo—but Apollo the Tormentor (a surname under which the god was worshipped in one part of the city)."[41] The battle of Antony versus Octavian that ensued would thus be a battle of the gods.[42]

When Antony was in crisis, he had learned—like any good Roman soldier—to deal with want.[43] When war flared up with Caesar Octavian, however, Antony did not halt the opulence of Dionysus. He sailed with Cleopatra in good spirits to the island of Samos. He had already ordered every king, chief, and tetrarch of the nations and cities between northwest Greece and the north coast of the Black Sea to bring military supplies. In a similar manner, Antony ordered every famous actor, dancer, musician, and performer to come ready to entertain him.

---

35. *Adul. am.* 12 [*Mor.* 56e]; cf. Strabo, *Geog.* 17.11.

36. *Ant.* 29.4.

37. Dio Cassius, *Rom. Hist.* 50.25.2–4.

38. Ibid. 50.5.3.

39. Plutarch, *Ant.* 60.3.

40. Tondriau, "La dynastie ptolemaique," 283; Dunand, "Les associations dionysiaques," 87. See also the bust in Bianchi, *Cleopatra's Egypt*, 155, cat. 58.

41. Suetonius, *Div. Aug.* 70.2.

42. For further associations of Augustus and Apollo, see Wickkiser, "Augustus, Apollo," 267–89.

43. Plutarch, *Ant.* 17.5–6.

So when nearly the entire inhabited world was wailing aloud and letting out a groan, one single island was day after day charmed with flute playing and stringed instruments. The theaters were full and the choruses competed. Every city sacrificed, sending a steer, and kings competed with each other in their entertainments and gifts for one another.[44]

Antony even presented the entire city of Priene to the artists of Dionysus as a kind of perpetual Woodstock.[45]

Tragically, Antony—though superior to his opponent on land and by sea—prematurely retreated in the sea battle off Actium in northwest Greece. Fleeing to Libya and then to Egypt, he lost the confidence of his troops and eventually the war. After a brief dally with cynicism and misanthropy, Cleopatra drew Antony back into the palace at Alexandria. Though he knew his fate, Antony "turned the city to feasts and drinking bouts and acts of largess." Plutarch recounted that

Drinking parties, revels and festivities took possession of the city of Alexandria for successive days. Antony and Cleopatra dissolved their club of "Those Who Live Like None Other." They formed a new club not at all falling short of the old one in splendor, luxury, and expenditure. They called it the band of "Those Who Die Together"—for their companions were enrolled as those who were themselves going to die with them. They lived life this way in good spirits cycling from feast to feast.[46]

In August of 30 B.C.E., Octavian's ships occupied the harbor of Alexandria, and his army stood armed at the gates. The last evening Antony was alive, "he bid his household servants to refill the cups and feast him more zealously."[47] During the night, precisely at midnight,

when the city was in silence and dejection on account of the fear and expectation of what was to come, suddenly there was heard the melodious sounds of all kinds of instruments and the cry of a crowd singing "*Euhoe!*" with satyr-like leaps—like some Dionysian band driving forth with no little tumult. The onrush passed almost through the middle of the city, and then it turned toward the outer gate facing the enemies. At this point the din began more and more to fade away. It seemed to those who read the sign that the god [Dionysus] had abandoned Antony, the

44. Ibid., 56.6–9.
45. Ibid., 57.1.
46. Ibid., 71.3–5
47. Ibid., 75.2.

god to whom he most of all assimilated himself and associated with until the very end.[48]

The next morning, Antony's fleet betrayed him and sailed to Caesar Octavian. The defeated Dionysus returned to his quarters and ordered a slave to kill him. The slave raised the sword to strike, but suddenly plunged it into himself. Antony, musing on his example, drew the curtain on his own life.

Propaganda and Reality

Antony was an ambiguous and multi-faceted character; his soldiers were loyal to him and many people loved him. The historical sources that describe him, however, are almost universally hostile. Plutarch, whom I have used heavily in my reconstruction, was a conservative moralist and sober Platonic philosopher. For him, Antony was no hero, but a paragon of vice paired with Greece's most passionate and ill-fated king—Demetrius the Besieger. As one loyal to the traditional gods, Plutarch also did not take kindly to rulers assimilating to deities. "Is not almost any king," the historian once asked, "called Apollo if he hums a tune, Dionysus if he gets drunk, and Heracles if he wrestles?"[49]

Although the ancient sources are full of jokes and hostility toward Antony, one cannot simply brush aside his assimilation to Dionysus as imaginative propaganda. Antony's enemies did not make up the fact that he assimilated to a god—they exposed it with relish. Although scholars have proved willing to take the romance between Antony and Cleopatra with utmost seriousness, they tend to view Antony's assimilation to Dionysus as pure political calculation with no religious meaning.[50]

Accordingly, scholars fumble when it comes to explaining what it meant for Antony to be a "New Dionysus." "The real significance of such a title," F. W. Walbank comments, "is not easy to discover," but it was likely "a

---

48. Ibid., 75.4–6. Most scholars when they read this report think of the Roman custom of *evocatio*: the calling out a god from a captured city. There is no evidence, however, that Octavian performed an *evocatio* or that this ritual explains the ghostly parade.

49. Plutarch, *Adul. am.* 12 (*Mor.* 56f).

50. Huzar is a good example of this trend (*Mark Antony: A Biography*). She remarks that Antony's role-playing as Dionysus was "an amusing game" (ibid., 156), and that he did not have "any illusions of divinity. . . . He viewed divinity as a moral force of control, a skillful propaganda to organize the east" (ibid., 195). Before him, Sulla, Pompey and Caesar had been worshiped as gods in the east, "not because they were actually believed to be gods but because this was how political allegiance was invariably displayed" (ibid., 193).

political gesture."[51] Other scholars see the designation as "little more than a cult title."[52] To Duncan Fishwick, the title indicates only that the ruler "reproduces here and now the qualities and achievements of Dionysus and in so doing appears as a new, fresh edition of that god."[53] This is careful, scholarly language, but evades the central question of religious importance: Was the *appearance* of Antony as Dionysus also felt to be a *religious reality*?

To answer this question we must pay attention to the cultural context. The religious matrix of the Hellenistic world did not assume that deity was something "out there" separate from the world. In a saying attributed to the philosopher Thales, "All things are full of gods!"[54] Deity was something that humans—and nature—shared with gods on various levels. Dead men could become heroes with divine powers. While still alive, people could be swept up to heaven. The gods could inhabit the gold and marble bodies of statues, and come in the form of human beings. Deity was defined most of all by power, and those with supreme power were kings. No great gap separated ruler and god in the minds of Greeks—least of all the Egyptians. In their statues and pictures, the gods looked like rulers, and rulers were thought to be the images of gods.[55]

In this context, Antony's assimilation to Dionysus cannot be passed off *merely* as a piece of political propaganda. In the modern West, when religion is separate from politics and deity from human beings, it is hard to take seriously the divine aura surrounding a political figure. To be charitable, however, we should assume that ancient Mediterranean peoples took their religion seriously. The mask of Dionysus—whether on an actor or a ruler—was not empty. Regardless of Antony's perceived failings, he was widely believed to manifest the power and persona of Dionysus—in cheer, in luxury, and in military might. It is not unreasonable to think that many of

51. Walbank "Monarchies and Monarchic Ideas," 86.

52. Fraser, *Ptolemaic Alexandria*, 1.244 (cf. 237). In principle, Fraser concedes that the "New" in "New Dionysus" seems "to imply reincarnation of the god."

53. Fishwick, *Imperial Cult*, 29–31. Biographers of Antony are generally uninterested in the question of Antony's assimilation to Dionysus and the meaning of his title "New Dionysus." Bengtson briefly noted that Antony's assimilation to Dionysus was conscious and that the triumvir, inflated by his universal authority over the east, probably believed that he was Dionysus (*Marcus Antonius*, 296). Chamoux considered the title "New Dionysus" to be "clever flattery" (*adroite flatterie*) in accord with Greek custom and Antony's disposition (*Marc Antoine*, 235–36). For Southern, Antony's "lavish play-acting as the new Dionysos impressed but did not convince the easterners" (*Mark Antony*, 74, cf. 86). None of these authors address the religious meaning of the title or other aspects of divine assimilation.

54. Aristotle, *An.*, 411a7.

55. See further Litwa, *We Are Being Transformed*, 37–50; 62–78.

his devotees believed that Dionysus inhabited Antony in some special way. If scholars today assume that Antony's actual identification with Dionysus is not possible given the sober Roman mentality, they should recall that Antony was not the average Roman—and he was not sober.

Incarnation and Deification

To seem cautious and not expose themselves to undue criticism, scholars typically deny the possibility of a real incarnation of god in Antony. Antony was the new Dionysus, *but he was not Dionysus*. Although historically "safe," this judgment represents, I think, a failure of our religious imagination. Part of the problem is that scholars appear to assume a Christian version of incarnation wherein a divine being somehow permanently unites with the soul and body of a single human being. Consequently, one cannot separate the persons—or personalities—of the human Jesus and the Word of God. In a Hellenistic context, however, incarnation may only imply a temporary "enfleshment" of a god—a divine epiphany in a human body.[56] Dionysus was known to possess people through wine, acting, and other ecstatic behaviors. Identity was permeable for Dionysus—he could identify with various humans simultaneously and many individuals with him.

Antony proved susceptible to possession because of his Dionysian disposition—his reckless abandon, his joy in life, his zeal for honor. His impersonation of the god was not a masquerade. Cities genuinely honored him as Dionysus, and spent great sums of money to do so. When Antony died a temple for him stood half-built in the center of the larger harbor of Alexandria. Near the temple was found a statue base that a devotee of Antony had dedicated on 28 December 34 B.C.E. The inscription read: "To Antony, the Great, the Inimitable . . . God and Benefactor."[57]

From a purely political perspective, Antony remained in control of the play—choosing when he would appear as the god, to what extent, and to what ends. From a religious perspective, however, the spirit of Dionysus took control of Antony. In him the god became flesh, and directed the final acts of his life.

---

56. Note, for instance, Dionysus in Euripides' *Bacchae*, who takes the form (*morphēn*) of a mortal in exchange for that of a god (ibid., 4), and later says: "I have taken and keep the form (*eidos*) of a mortal, and I have altered my *morphēn* to that of a man" (ibid., 53–54)." See further Buxton, "Metamorphoses of Gods," 85–86.

57. Hölbl, *History*, 292.

To think of Dionysian possession as incarnation is not an inappropriate category in the Egyptian context.[58] There the Pharaoh was traditionally viewed as an incarnation of the god Horus. At death, the Pharaoh was thought to become Osiris, who (as I mentioned) was identified with Dionysus. Antony was not the Pharaoh, but the Pharaoh's patron. Nevertheless, his rule was interwoven into the pattern of Ptolemaic assimilation to Dionysus. The king manifested the power and prerogatives of the god. On statues and on coins, these powers appeared on the faces of kings decorated with Dionysian horns, headbands, and ivy crowns.

If Antony's identification with the god was functional, it was nonetheless real. There was no claim that the king fully exhausted the reality of the god—ancient Egyptians and Egyptianized Greeks were not unintelligent. When their kings died, they did not believe that their god died. Rather, the next king became a new epiphany of the god—a Horus reborn. In spite of our cultural and religious distance, then, the idea that Antony could be an "incarnation" of Dionysus-Osiris—a new appearance of the god's power and persona in human flesh—fits well with the religious imagination of his time.

Conclusion: The Closing of the Curtain

Did Dionysus abandon Antony in the end? This is a difficult question. Plutarch's response has already been given—but his is not the only answer. As Egyptians knew, a dead Antony could still be Dionysus-Osiris in the underworld. Let us admit that there was heard the night before Antony's death the sound of a Dionysian band departing Alexandria. Such an omen can be interpreted in different ways, a fact that always grants freedom to offer a new reading.

It seems to me that Dionysus did not so much leave Antony as leave *with* him. As Plutarch reports, the ghostly procession of Dionysus occurred the night before Octavian's takeover. In the morning, Alexandria would be given over to a new master, Egypt would lose its queen, the royal line would be decimated, and the land would be ruled by a distant emperor.

Yet even if Dionysiac rule in Egypt had come to a close, the assimilation of rulers to gods had not. Octavian as the new Apollo was Egypt's next Pharaoh. If kings died, the tradition of deification did not. Octavian's takeover of Egypt would begin a new period in the Mediterranean world. This new age is represented in our own timetables as marking the transition from the "Hellenistic" to the "Roman period." For the Egyptians, it was a

---

58. Nock, "Notes on Ruler Cult IV," 1.147, 151–52; Huzar, *Antony*, 149, cf. 193; Hölbl, *History*, 292.

transition from an age of ecstasy and release to one of burden and decay. In the words of the Hermetic tractate *Asclepius*,

> O Egypt, Egypt, of your reverent deeds only stories will survive, and they will be incredible to your children! Only words cut in stone will survive to tell your faithful works, and the Scythian or Indian or some such neighbor barbarian will dwell in Egypt. For divinity goes back to heaven, and all the people will die, deserted, as Egypt will be widowed and deserted by god and human.[59]

59. Trans. Copenhaver, *Hermetica*, 81.

Chapter 3

"You Have Been Born a God"
Deification in the Orphic Gold Tablets

Life. Death. Life.
Truth.

—ORPHIC BONE TABLET "A" OF OLBIA[1]

SPREAD OVER AN EXCEEDINGLY large area, inscribed between a time ranging from the fifth century B.C.E. to the second century C.E., the Orphic gold tablets testify to a strikingly persistent and widespread—if uncommon—religious discourse in the ancient Mediterranean world.[2] Central to this discourse was the promise of deification. "You have been born a god, from the human that you were!" declares a tablet found in ancient Thurii, Italy.[3] One found nearby announces: "Happy and fortunate, you will be god, from the mortal that you were!"[4] Hundreds of years later on a gold leaf found at Rome, a mysterious speaker addresses a woman: "Come, Caecilia Secundina, having become a goddess by law!"[5]

---

1. Text and translation in Graf and Johnston, *Ritual Texts*, 214.

2. Evidence for an actual Orphic community is sparse, appearing only in the ancient Milesian colony of Olbia on the Black Sea (in present-day Ukraine) (on which see Zhmud, "Orphism and Graffiti from Olbia," 159–68). The best short introduction to Orphic thought and practice is still Parker "Early Orphism," 483–510. See also Frede, "Die Orphik," 229–46.

3. For the Orphic fragments, I use the edition of Bernabé, *Orphicorum Fragmenta* (hereafter Bernabé *OF*) 487.4. A corresponding English translation of the tablets can be found in Bernabé and Jiménez San Cristóbal, *Instructions for the Netherworld*.

4. Bernabé *OF* 488.8.

5. Ibid., 491.4.

The gold tablets were all found in the graves of those who became initiates in the mysteries of Dionysus. They were often placed in their mouths or on their chests, and seemed to serve partly as memory aids for the recent dead who stumbled—bewildered—into the dank caverns and confusing crossroads of the underworld. Some of the texts of the gold leaves are terse, pronouncing only the names of the initiates, passwords, or an epistolary greeting to the king and queen of the underworld (for example: "To Pluto and Persephone, greetings!"). One long text is filled with nonsensical strings of words from which some scholars extract an esoteric hymn to Persephone.[6] In this chapter, I will focus on the tablets with longer and (for the most part) metrical texts. There are twenty-two of these published to date: seven from south Italy, one from Sicily, seven from Crete, six from Thessaly, and one from Rome. Thematically speaking, these tablets fall into three groups (with somewhat fluid boundaries): (1) those in which the speaker pronounces his or her purity before the gods of the underworld, resulting in a declaration of deification or supplication for it, (2) those tablets that provide a brief "map" of the underworld and instruct the initiate to declare his or her divine kinship before potentially hostile guards, and (3) the tablets which speak of the rebirth of the (recently deceased) initiate as a god.

The gold leaves are often called "Orphic" because they are linked with Orpheus the ancient Thracian bard. According to legend—widely credited in the ancient world—Orpheus founded the mysteries of Dionysus (or particular brands of them).[7] In the fifth and fourth centuries B.C.E., a "hubbub" of books (to use Plato's term) were fathered on Orpheus and his son Musaeus.[8] Some of these books included a poem (or poems) about the birth of the gods (called a "theogony"). Others included spells for healing diseases, purifications for expunging guilt, as well as instructions for bloodless sacrifice. The point of undergoing purification was to avoid dire punishments in Hades like lying in mud, carrying water in a sieve and (more humorously) swimming in "ever-flowing diarrhea."[9] One of the books Orpheus reputedly wrote was called *Descent to Hades*. Excerpts of the content of this book—or one like it—may also have been incised onto the gold tablets, along with ritual formulae.[10] Making Orpheus the author of such tablets would have

6. Ibid., 492.

7. Ibid., 501 (Ps.-Apollodorus, *Bibl.* 1.3.2) and 502 (Diodorus of Sicily, *Bibl. hist.* 3.65.6).

8. Plato, *Resp.* 364e (*biblōn homadon*).

9. Plato, *Phaedo* 69b–d (lying in mud); *Gorg.* 493b–c (water in sieve); Aristophanes, *Ran.* 144–46 (diarrhea).

10. Herrero de Jáuregui, "Orphic Ideas of Immortality," 300. Riedweg reconstructs the sequence of the descent ("Initiation-death-underworld," 219–56).

been apt since—according to widespread legend—he had already visited Hades and returned.[11] The great Latin poets Virgil and Ovid depict Orpheus as singing his way into Hades in order to bring back his wife Eurydice—only to lose her at the last moment.[12] Earlier traditions, however, hint that Orpheus may have been more successful.[13]

The focus of this chapter is not Orpheus, however, but the version of deification found on the gold tablets.[14] That these tablets represent Orphic teaching and ritual has of late been convincingly defended.[15] With discretion, then, we can call deification as it is depicted on the tablets "Orphic," with the caveat that it is just as appropriate to refer to it as "Dionysian" or "Bacchic." Whatever we call it, however, the form of deification represented in the gold leaves was offered to common (though probably well-off) people who yearned for an alternative to the predominant "Homeric" view of the dead as bloodless shades gibbering with minds full of oblivion.[16] The gift of Dionysus, as proclaimed by his prophet Orpheus, was a conscious life in a paradise wherein one banqueted eternally, crowned with the other heroes and demigods.

The Zagreus Myth

In some circles of scholarship, the master narrative used to explain Orphic deification is the so-called "Zagreus myth." The Zagreus myth is the final scene of an Orphic theogony variously told (as all myths are). We pick up the story with Zeus, who is reported to have swallowed the ancient first-born god (later called "Phanes")—allowing Zeus to beget the gods anew. He fathers Persephone (queen of the Underworld) from Demeter (goddess of grain) and then has relations with Persephone herself to produce the last and future king, Dionysus.[17] Displeased, Zeus' wife Hera incites the Titans—primordial, barbarous gods from an earlier epoch—who set upon the child

11. Euripides, *Alc.* 357–62; Plato, *Symp.* 179d; Isocrates, *Busiris* 7–8.

12. Virgil, *Georg.* 4.467–505 ; Ovid, *Metamorphoses* 10.1–77.

13. Klodt, "Der Orpheus-Mythos," 57–58. Cf. Graf, "Orpheus," 80–106, esp. 81–82. For Orpheus and his netherworldly function in art, see the "Iconographical Notes" in Bernabé and Jiménez san Cristóbal, *Instructions*, 273–326.

14. On Orpheus himself, see the testimonies in Bernabé *OF* 864–1095. Important introductions include Warden, *Orpheus*; Charles Segal, *Orpheus*, 165–84.

15. Bernabé and Jiménez San Cristóbal, "Are the 'Orphic' Gold Leaves Orphic?" 68–101.

16. Homer, *Od.* 11.36–50, 24.1–18.

17. Bernabé *OF* 280–83; 296–300.

Dionysus, tear him to bits, and consume him raw.[18] In rage at this impiety, Zeus launches his thunderbolt, instantly blasting the Titans to smoke.[19] Out of their sooty vapor (*aithalē*) was born the human race. Human nature is thus marked not only by the rebellion and barbarity of the Titan gods, but also by their horrible guilt for their ancient deicide. Yet mixed together with the murky vapor—like glittering sparks—were the remnants of the divine Dionysus. These remnants, then, come to constitute human nature like flecks of gold in mud. It is these embedded pieces of godhead that make human nature divine. It is the purpose of Orphic ritual to inform—or rather remind—the initiate of her true nature, and provide her the means and power to return to the purely divine, Dionysiac state.[20]

Although the story of the Titans tearing apart Dionysus is old (fourth, possibly fifth century B.C.E.), the age of the final element—in which humans are made from bits of Dionysus—has long been disputed. We find this last element of the story only in the sixth century C.E. Neoplatonic commentator Olympiodorus. Although some scholars imply that Olympiodorus teaches a divine soul (as one would expect from a Platonist), Olympiodorus makes clear that it is human *bodies* that are Dionysiac, not their inner selves. He speaks of our "Dionysiac" bodies in an argument against suicide (in short: we should not kill the body because it is part of Dionysus).[21] This new element of the story carries all the earmarks of Olympiodorus' idiosyncratic interpretation to support his own philosophical position.[22] These sorts of additions to myth are common and acceptable when no canonical version

18. Ibid., 301–17.

19. Ibid., 318–31.

20. Guthrie, *Orpheus and Greek Religion*, 84, 120. "The beginnings of [Orphic] salvation," Guthrie writes, "lie within every one of us, since they are identical with the germ of divinity which it is our nature as human beings to possess." The Orphic life, he soon adds, "aims at the exaltation and purification of our Dionysiac nature in order that we may in the end shake off the last trammels of our earthly selves and become actually, what we are now potentially, gods instead of mortals" (ibid., 156 cf. 129).

21. For the argument of Olympiodorus and its context, see Gertz, *Death and Immortality*, 27–50.

22. Luc Brisson argues that the Dionysiac body is Olympiodorus' "'mystical' interpretation of an alchemic operation reconciled to an episode of the Orphic theogony." Originally the punishment of the Titans was not connected with the origin of the human race ("Le corps 'dionysiaque,'" 494–95). Edmonds argues that "the anthropogonic part of the myth of Zagreus does not appear to be linked with the murder of Dionysos and the punishment of the Titans in any evidence before the Neoplatonists, and that the doctrine of original sin derived from it is, in fact, an invention of modern scholars" ("Tearing Apart," 42). Bernabé opposes both views, asserting that Olympiodorus passes on ancient tradition ("Autour le myth orphique," 25–39). Edmonds offers a counter-response in "A Curious Concoction," 511–32.

of a story exists. Due to its thin and late attestation, however, it cannot safely be used as evidence for Orphic belief from the fifth century B.C.E. to the second century C.E. (the period of the gold leaves). It is better to base our interpretation of Orphic deification on the tablets themselves.

Divine Kinship

The tablets show that deification is largely based on one's divine lineage. In the tablet from the ancient city of Hipponion (around 400 B.C.E.), the initiate is instructed to say: "I am the child of Earth and starry Heaven (*Gēs pais eimi kai Ouranou asteroentos*)."[23] A majority of the gold leaves contain a version of this phrase.[24] In most cases, it is spoken (or the initiate is instructed to speak it) before the inquisitive guards of the netherworld. When the guards learn of the divine kinship of the initiates, they allow them to drink from the lake of Memory, and shuttle them along to the netherworld's king and queen.

The phrase "child of Earth and starry Heaven" is reminiscent of the line from Hesiod's *Theogony* that the gods "were born from Earth (*Gēs*) and starry Heaven (*Ouranou asteroentos*)."[25] It was common knowledge that Gaia and Uranus (i.e., Earth and Heaven) were the parents of the most commonly worshiped deities (the Olympians). Orphic initiates thus proclaimed themselves as part of the same family as the gods.[26]

But the immediate offspring of Earth and Heaven, according to the *Orphic Hymns* (second–third century C.E.?), were the Titans.[27] Do the tablets thus refer specifically to their Titanic origins?[28] The fact that the Titans are not mentioned elsewhere in the tablets inspires suspicion. In one Orphic theogony, the Titans are only sons of *Earth*, born to take vengeance on "starry Heaven."[29] This detail highlights the fact that the Titans—even though gods of a sort (ruling before the Olympian gods)—are almost universally

23. Bernabé *OF* 474.10.

24. Ibid., 474–84a (a total of twelve tablets).

25. Hesiod, *Theogony* 106.

26. Cf. Hesiod, *Op.* 108: "As the gods and mortals had a single origin." Thus also Pindar: "One is the race of humans, one of gods / Since we both breathe through a single mother (Earth) (*Nem.* 6.1–3). Porphyry attributes to Euripides the line: "Earth and Heaven, common parents of all" (*De abstinentia* 3.25).

27. *Orphic Hymns* 37.1–2 (Athanassakis). In these *Hymns*, the Titans are referred to as "the ancestors of our fathers" (*hēmeterōn progonoi paterōn*). Morand notes that, though the *Orphic Hymns* do not make direct reference to the murder of Dionysus by the Titans, it is probably presupposed (*Études*, 216).

28. Bernabé and Jiménez San Cristóbal, *Instructions*, 41–42.

29. Bernabé *OF* 83 = Athenagoras, *Leg.* 18.6.

associated with evil and rebellion in Greek literature.[30] Most disturbingly, they are the murderers of Dionysus—the chief Orphic god. Announcing one's Titanic nature to the guards—or Persephone herself (Dionysus' mother)—would thus be an off-putting and counterproductive way to announce one's divine lineage.[31] The Titans are the roots of human guilt, not godhood.

How then do we interpret, "I am a son of Earth and starry Heaven?" It is tempting to identify one's earthly legacy with the body and one's heavenly heritage with the soul. In making this distinction, however, one may already be adopting later Platonic reinterpretations of Orphic thought. In Hesiodic and Orphic theology, Earth is just as divine as Heaven.[32] The "son of Earth and starry Heaven" is thus divine by virtue of both parents. But if being a child of Earth and Heaven signifies one's dual (earthly and celestial) states, the emphasis falls on the celestial. Several tablets make this clear by immediately adding a clause: "but my race is heavenly (*ouranion*)."[33] The heavenly heritage of the initiates indicates their relation to the celestial [Olympian] gods. The Titans, by contrast, were thought to be buried in Tartarus.[34]

In a tablet from Pharsalus in Thessaly (350–30 B.C.E.), the heavenly origin of the initiate is expressed by a new name: "My name is Asterius."[35] "Asterius" is a mystical name of initiates derived from *astēr*, the Greek word for star. Thus the name means "Starry" and amounts to another way of saying "my race is heavenly." Whether "Starry" as a name indicates that one's destiny is to dwell in heaven with the other Olympians is less certain. As ancient poets knew, the underworld has its own heaven and stars.[36] For Orphics, it seems, Hades—or a region of it—was the place of paradise, and the final destination of the deified.[37]

---

30. See esp. Plutarch, *Esu carn.* 996b–c; Plato, *Leges* 701b–c. Other sources in Bremmer, "Greek Fallen Angels," 73–74.

31. Zuntz, *Persephone*, 312; Graf and Johnston, *Ritual Texts*, 115.

32. Significantly, the *Orphic Hymns* contain both a hymn to Earth (Hymn 26) and Heaven (Hymn 4).

33. Bernabé *OF* 476.7; 484.4; cf. 489.3; 490.3.

34. *Orphic Hymns* 37.2–3 (Athanassakis).

35. Bernabé *OF* 477.9.

36. Pindar writes: "For them [underworld beings] the strength of the sun (*menos aeliou*) shines below while it is night here" (frag. 129.1–2 [Maehler]). According to Virgil, "[T]hey [in the Blissful Groves of the underworld] know their own sun, and stars of their own (*solemque suum, sua sidera norunt*)" (*Aen.* 6.641). Cf. Apuleius, *Met.* 11.23.

37. Note that the deified enjoy rites "*under the earth*" (*hypo gēn*) (Bernabé *OF* 485.7).

Rebirth

In a tablet from Thurii, the initiate is greeted by underworld beings as if already a god: "Hail (*chaire*), after having had an experience such as you never had before!"[38] The experience, as we find out, is rebirth into godhead. "You have been born a god! A kid (*eriphos*), you fell into milk!"[39] The odd statement about a young goat (*eriphos*) plunging into milk seems to refer to a rebirth in which the initiate returns to infancy, and sucks the milk of his new divine mother, Persephone. That the initiate is depicted as a "kid" may involve an identification with Dionysus, who was known by the epithet "kid" (*eriphos*).[40] Pseudo-Apollodorus, moreover, tells the tale of Zeus changing Dionysus into a young goat (*eriphon*) to protect him from a maddened stepfather.[41]

In two tablets from Pelinna, however, it is not only a kid that leaps into milk, but a bull and a ram.[42] Dionysus was, to be sure, depicted as a bull,[43] but the ram remains elusive.[44] The Greek scholar Yannis Tzifopoulos offers an explanation: the initiates of Dionysus "become identical with him, i.e., they become *bacchoi*, just as the god in his earthly manifestations becomes a bull, a ram, or a kid. . . . These animals were selected because their movements (which were perhaps consciously imitated by Dionysos' followers) came close to the movements of the ecstatic ritual dance, through which communion with god and the god's epiphany were effected."[45] His interpretation has yet to be weighed by scholars. But if the idea of identification with

---

38. Ibid., 487.3; cf. 487.5. Sourvinou-Inwood argues that greeting the dead with *chaire* before the fourth century B.C.E. was an "acclamation of deification" in which the deceased was recognized as a hero (*"Reading" Greek Death*, 196).

39. Bernabé *OF* 487.4. Cf. 488.9–10.

40. This epithet is known from the (admittedly) late lexicons of Hesychius (under the words "*Eriphios*" and "*Eiraphiotes*") and Stephanus of Byzantium (under the word "*akrōreia*"). Identification with Dionysus was popular for rulers (see above, ch. 2). For common people identifying with Dionysus, see Henrichs "Changing Dionysiac Identities," 157–58; Kingsley, *Ancient Philosophy*, 269 (with earlier sources); Cole, "Voices from beyond the Grave," 286–88, 290; Taylor, *Moral Mirror*, 90–99.

41. Ps.-Apollodorus, *Bibl.* 3.4.3.

42. Bernabé, *OF* 485.3–5; 486.3–4.

43. Plutarch, *Quaest. rom.* 36 (*Mor.* 299a–b). Translation and discussion in Furley and Bremer, *Greek Hymns*, 1.369–72; 2.373–77.

44. Graf points out that there is "no ram Dionysus" ("Dionysian and Orphic Eschatology," 245).

45. Tzifopoulos, *Paradise Earned*, 203–4.

Dionysus remains controversial, the notion that the milky plunge signifies rebirth and deification is not.[46]

Rebirth imagery is also present in another tablet from Thurii (quoted in part above):

> I plunged beneath the lap [or sunk beneath the womb (*kolpos*)[47]] of my lady, the subterranean queen [i.e., Persephone] . . .
>
> "Happy and fortunate, you will be a god, from the mortal you were!"
>
> A kid, I fell into milk.[48]

Based on this description, the initiate appears to enter into the goddess' womb in order to be born again as a deity. A terracotta figure of Persephone from Kamarina in Sicily interestingly shows a winged figure (an initiate?) in the womb of the goddess Persephone.[49] In this light, falling into milk would imply that the newly born initiate is able to drink from the full breasts of the goddess.[50] Plunging into the lap of Persephone apparently leads to a second birth from the divine mother. The fact that in Orphic theology, Persephone is depicted as the mother of Dionysus suggests once again that the initiate is being identified with the god. It is worth noting that a third century B.C.E. papyrus which describes a Dionysiac ritual and prayer (the Gûrob Papyrus) mysteriously refers to the "tokens . . . god through bosom (*symbola . . . theos dia kolpou*)."[51] Dionysus is also called *hypokolpie* ("one beneath the lap") in an Orphic Hymn, although the reading is disputed.[52]

Rebirth as a god is reminiscent of the experience of perhaps the most famous deified man of the ancient world, Heracles. Although his stepmother

---

46. Janda revives an interpretation of Albrecht Dieterich that leaping into milk implies traveling to the milky way. In support of this interpretation, he notes that kid, bull, and ram are all names of constellations (*Elysion*, 328–30). Graf points out that "to be in milk" (*einai en galaxi*) can indicate "any new beginning" ("Dionysian and Orphic Eschatology," 246). For rushing into milk as indicative of ritual assimilation to Dionysus, see Faraone, "Rushing into Milk," 310–30.

47. For *kolpos* as "womb," see *LSJ* under the term *kolpos* I c.

48. Bernabé *OF* 488.7–10.

49. Hadzisteliou-Price, "To the Groves" 51–55. Figure on Plate 29.1 (cf. also figures on Plate 30.1, 3, 6). The figure of Persephone holds, as Zuntz points out, a phiale (a saucer used in sacrifice) and a cista (a box typically concealing secret objects revealed in a mystery ritual) (*Persephone*, 175–76). Hadzisteliou-Price points out that souls in the ancient world were depicted as winged ("To the Groves," 53–54).

50. Bernabé and Jiménez San Cristóbal, *Instructions*, 130–31.

51. Bernabé *OF* 578. English translation in Graf and Johnston, *Ritual Texts*, 218. See Graf's comments on *ibid*. 151.

52. *Orphic Hymns* 52.11 (Athanassakis).

Hera was his constant opponent during his life, when the hero died and rose to heaven, she formally adopted him. Diodorus of Sicily (first century B.C.E.) describes the ritual that they underwent: "Hera got onto the bed and, placing Heracles next to her body, dropped him down to the ground through her clothing, thus imitating genuine birth."[53] As a result of this ceremony, Heracles was made a fully fledged god and given a place among the Olympians. A fragment of Hesiod's *Catalogue of Women* says that Heracles "died (*thane*) and then went to the grievous house of Hades, but now he is a god (*theos esti*), released from all evils."[54]

Lightning

In three of the Thurii tablets, we hear that the initiate is overcome by "the star-flinger with lightning [evidently Zeus]."[55] The references to lightning could be literal (the initiates were electrocuted in a storm). But the lightning could just as easily be metaphorical. In this view, Zeus' thunderbolt is the instrument by which one passes from a mortal state to a divine one.[56] For ancient Greeks, death by lightning was a commonly recognized means of attaining heroic status.[57] "For no one who has been struck by a thunderbolt is without honor," observes a second-century dream interpreter, "wherefore he is revered even as a god."[58]

According to ancient myth, the funeral pyre of Heracles was struck by lightning, allowing him to ascend to his father Zeus.[59] Semele, mother of Dionysus, came to live on Olympus after being struck by a thunderbolt.[60] Asclepius, doctor and demigod, shared a similar fate.[61] In each case, lightning purified the hero from his or her mortal parts and brought about deification.

53. Diodorus of Sicily, *Bibl. hist.* 4.39.2.

54. Hesiod frag. 25.25–28 (Merkelbach and West). Cf. Homer, *Od.* 11.602–4.

55. The line is variously inscribed on the tablets, most clearly on the tablet printed as Bernabé *OF* 488. Here we read *assteroblēta* (nominative) *keraunōi* (dative). This reading should probably be taken as original for all three tablets found in the Timpone Piccolo at Thurii (Bernabé *OF* 488–90). See the comments of Zuntz, *Persephone*, 314–15.

56. Bernabé and Jiménez San Cristóbal, *Instructions*, 113–14.

57. Kingsley, *Ancient Philosophy*, 258.

58. Artemidorus, *Oneirocritica* 2.9.76–77.

59. Diodorus of Sicily, *Bibl. hist.* 4.38.4–5. According to Ps.-Apollodorus, a cloud stood under the burning Heracles, and sent him up to heaven with a peal of thunder (*meta brontēs*) (*Bibl.* 2.7.7).

60. Pindar, *Ol.* 2.27; Achilles Tatius, *Leucippe and Clitophon* 2.37.4; Philostratus, *Imagines* 1.14; Nonnus, *Dionysiaca* 8.409; 9.206.

61. Hesiod frag. 109; Lucian, *Dial. mort.* 13; Minucius Felix, *Octavian* 23.7

But Zeus, as some commentators point out, also doles out lightning to punish crime. The Titans, for instance, were blasted by lightning when they murdered Dionysus. Could it be that the lightning mentioned in the tablets at Thurii indicates some kind of penalty? According to Martin West, the statement in the Thurii tablets, "fate overcame me, and the star-flinger with lightning," refers to the soul sent *into* the world by Zeus' thunderbolt, not out of it.[62] He compares this thunder to that which accompanies the souls' dispatch to new incarnations in Plato's *Republic* (621b): "But around midnight there was a clap of thunder and an earthquake, and they [the souls] were suddenly carried away . . . this way and that, up to their births, like shooting stars." If the thunderbolt does bring about birth in this world it can stand as form of punishment, since bodily life, according to Orphic thought, amounts to imprisonment.[63]

Heroization

As the examples of Heracles (son of Zeus) and Asclepius (son of Apollo) show, it was typically the great heroes of the past who could boast of their close kinship to the gods and go on to experience a blessed afterlife.[64] According to widespread tradition, the hero Achilles died in Troy by Paris' arrow (in later sources, the dart was said to hit his heel). In the eighth-century B.C.E. epic *Aethiopis*, Achilles' mother Thetis resurrects (literally "seizes") her son fresh from the funeral pyre and brings him to "White Island" to enjoy eternal life.[65] In a similar tradition, Thetis brings Achilles to the Isles of the Blessed after asking this favor from Zeus, king of the gods.[66] Another hero, Menelaus, was only Zeus' son-in-law, but for this reason still earned a

---

62. West, *Orphic Poems*, 23.

63. Plat, *Crat.* 400c. In fact, lightning as (1) castigation and (2) deification are not mutually exclusive. In mythology, Asclepius is first struck by lightning as a punishment, but later deified (Hesiod frag. 125; Euripides, *Alc.* 1–4; Ambrose, *De Virginibus* 3.176.7). Semele, according to some accounts, was first killed by Zeus' lightning-like appearance. She was only deified when Dionysus stormed Hades to bring her up—not just to earth—but to the stars (Ps.-Apollodorus, *Bibl.* 3.5.3; Diodorus of Sicily, *Bibl. hist.* 4.25.4; 5.52.2; Pausanias, *Descr.* 2.31.2; 2.37.5; Plutarch, *Sera* 27 [*Mor.* 566a]).

64. See esp. Homer, *Il.* 21.187; 14.113; 20.241 and Herrero de Jáuregui, "Dialogues of Immortality," 271–90.

65. The *Aethiopis* is lost, but is summarized in Proclus' *Chrestomathy* (text and translation in West, *Greek Epic Fragments*, frag. 113). Cf. Euripides, *Andromache*, 1260–62. Also in the *Aethiopis*, Memnon, son of Dawn, is granted immortality after being killed by Achilles. See on Memnon Rohde, *Psyche*, 64–66.

66. Pindar, *Ol.* 2.79–80; cf. Plato, *Symp.* 179d–180b.

place in the paradise of Elysium.[67] In fact, all the men of the heroic age, according to Hesiod, live after death with carefree hearts on the Blessed Isles.[68] By claiming their divine kinship, then, Orphic initiates implicitly likened themselves to the ancient heroes who enjoyed better afterlives. According to widespread Greek belief, by contrast, the age of heroes was long over, and now (in a degraded, iron age) actual deification no longer occurred.[69] Orphic initiators rejected these limitations, and promised that the glory of the age of heroes could be relived in Hades.

Indeed, Orphic deification can be categorized as a form of heroization. By definition, a hero is a type of lesser god, often called a "demigod" (*hēmitheos*) in Greek literature. He (or she) is immortal, chthonic (that is, living underground), and possesses some kind of superhuman power. In the Orphic tablet from Petelia (mid-fourth century B.C.E.), the initiate is told that "You will reign with the other heroes."[70] In a tablet from Entella in Sicily, the initiate is referred to simply as a "hero."[71] In the so-called "great tablet" from Thurii, we also find the mysterious phrase: "Hero. Light to the intelligence."[72] Pindar, a fifth-century B.C.E. Theban poet, refers to souls that, after their final reincarnation, "Until the end of times are called 'sacred heroes' (*hērōes hagnoi*) by human beings."[73] The term "heroization," however, is not meant to exclude the broader category of deification. Becoming a hero makes one a god, but one of subordinate status—that is, a demigod.[74]

Empedocles the Fallen Daimon

One rightly asks how Dionysian initiates with their divine pedigree became human in the first place. The Sicilian philosopher and physician

67. Homer, *Od.* 4.563.

68. Hesiod, *Op.* 170–71.

69. Pausanias, *Descr.* 8.2.4–5.

70. Bernabé *OF* 476.11. In Homer's *Il.* 4.61, Hera speaks to Zeus in similar language: "And you rule with all the other immortals" (*su de pasi met' athanatoisin anasseis*). Cf. 14.94; 23.471.

71. Bernabé *OF* 475.2.

72. Ibid., 492.8.

73. Pindar, frag. 133 (Maehler) from Plato, *Meno* 81b–c.

74. Cf. Bernabé, "Imago Inferorum Orphica" 123–24. *Pace* Bernabé, the gold leaves do not offer "an ambiguous testimony" regarding the status of the deceased initiate (ibid., 123). Initiates are deified. If deification is rare in the Greco-Roman world, the gold tablets indicate that it is not as rare as some scholars suppose.

Empedocles (494–34 B.C.E.) may hold the answer.[75] Empedocles believed that he was a daimon (a divine being) exiled from the gods. Although at one time he lived with the other gods in bliss, for some "sinful murder"[76] the self destined to become Empedocles was hurled into sea, air, and land, where (by his own testimony) Empedocles lived the life of a boy, a girl, a fish, a bird, and even a bush.[77] His blistering cycle of incarnations and reincarnations was riddled with pain, and all the cosmic elements (by his own report) "abhorred" him. Empedocles himself confesses (perhaps recalling his first incarnation), "I wept and shrieked when I saw this unaccustomed land!"[78] But his long journey through different bodies was meant to purify him. In his incarnation as a Sicilian doctor and philosopher, Empedocles felt that he had reached the final stage of his journey. He was so near to his divine state that he could proleptically—and publically—declare to his fellow citizens: "I am for you an immortal god (*theos ambrotos*), no longer mortal!"[79] When he died Empedocles evidently expected to break free from the cycle of transmigration. His experience is rightly compared to that of the initiate who declares on a gold tablet: "I flew away from the circle of painful, heavy grief!"[80]

The myths surrounding Empedocles' death represent the reality of his postmortem deification. Perhaps the best known account is that Empedocles jumped into the crater of Mt. Etna—an immense, active volcano in Sicily—which soon spewed back one of the philosopher's bronze boots, licked by fire. According to Peter Kingsley, Empedocles' leap into Etna "represents, mythologically, a descent into the underworld," which served as a "prelude to a celestial ascent."[81] In his fiery death, says Kingsley, Empedocles was imitating Heracles, who was burned alive on Mount Oeta, and enjoyed festivities with the gods after his apotheosis.[82] Based on a fragment of his own

---

75. For Empedocles and Orphic tradition, see Kingsley, *Ancient Philosophy*, 259–69; 308–9; 312

76. DK 31 B 115 = Inwood 11.

77. DK 31 B 117 = Inwood 111.

78. DK 31 B 118 = Inwood 115.

79. DK 31 B 112 = Inwood 1. In formulating his theory of metempsychosis, Empedocles may have been thinking of the god Apollo, who according to myth was exiled from the Gods for killing the Cyclopes. Apollo became a shepherd, and was forced to build the walls of Troy. Significantly, Pythagoras was reported to be an incarnation of Hyperborean Apollo.

80. Bernabé *OF* 488.5.

81. Kingsley, *Ancient Philosophy*, 250–51.

82. Ibid., 255. Cf. Homer, *Od.* 11.602–3; Horace, *Ars poetica* 464–66.

works, it seems that Empedocles likewise expected to share hearth and table "with the other immortals," being free from human pain and weariness.[83]

Like Empedocles, the Bacchic initiates who employed the gold tablets were formally deified only after their deaths. They viewed human life as a time when one pays the penalty for their sins.[84] The body is a "safe" or "prison" meant to protect the soul "until one's debts (*ta opheilomena*) are paid."[85] Bodily existence is a kind of purification. Genuine life begins after death, when one springs from the body and returns to one's divine state in an underworld paradise.

Netherworldly Life

We do not know much about the paradisiacal life lived by the initiates. In two Thurii tablets, the place is called the "seats of the pure" (*hedras . . . euageōn*).[86] There is mention of "sacred meadows and groves of Persephone."[87] The deified initiate is not alone, but part of a band of "other famous initiates and Bacchics."[88] Plato speaks of a "symposium [or drinking party] of the holy ones."[89] In the same passage, he condemns Orphic missionaries for preaching a gospel of "eternal drunkenness (*methēn aiōnion*)."[90] In the tablets from Pelinna we do find the promise: "You have wine as a happy honor," but no reference to intoxication.[91] The image of the symposium is meant to suggest a primeval period when humans (to quote Hesiod) "were mixed together with gods. For then the feasts were common, and common were the seats for immortal gods and humans who are mortal."[92]

83. DK 31 B 147 = Inwood 137.

84. Bernabé OF 489.4; 490.4; cf. 493.2.

85. Plato, *Crat.* 400c. In this passage, Plato does not explicitly attribute the famous play on words *sōma sēma* ("the body [is] a tomb") to the Orphics, but only to "some people" (*tines*). See further Dodds, *Greeks and the Irrational*, 169–70. Elsewhere Plato attributes the body-as-tomb doctrine to "the sages (*tōn sophōn*) . . . perhaps some Italian or Sicilian man [Pythagoras or Empedocles?]"—again, not to Orphics specifically (*Gorg.* 493a). In *Phaedo* 62b, Plato says that the idea that the body is a prison is an account (*logos*) told in "secret language" (*en aporrhētois*). In the *Axiochus* (attributed to Plato) this doctrine (body = prison) appears as standard Platonic teaching (365e).

86. Bernabé OF 489.7; 490.7.

87. Ibid., 487.6.

88. Bernabé OF 474.15–16; cf. *mystōn thiasous* ("bands of initiates") in 495a.

89. Plato, *Resp.* 363c.

90. Ibid., 363d.

91. Bernabé OF 485.6.

92. Hesiod, *Eoiae*, frag. 1.5–7 (Merkelbach-West). In context, Hesiod is speaking of the heroic women of old. Cf. Edmonds, *Myths of the Underworld*, 84.

Ethics

Plato criticizes popular Orphic missionaries of his day for preaching postmortem liberation by ritual alone.[93] This (strangely Protestant) criticism should be taken with a grain of salt. The Orphic tablets place strong emphasis on being pure. On several leaves, the initiate is instructed to say to Persephone: "I come pure (*katharos*) from among pure!"[94] Although the confession undoubtedly refers to ritual purity, one should not hastily infer that it excludes morality. An Athenian orator in the fourth century B.C.E. quoted a well-known Orphic saying, that Justice (*Dikē*) is enthroned alongside Zeus, and watches over the deeds of humans.[95] According to Aristophanes, Orpheus taught people to abstain from murder (*phonōn*).[96] He means, naturally, that Orphics did not practice blood sacrifice; but *phonos* is a broader term that applies to all kinds of killing (humans and animals). Plato reports the view of (likely Orphic) "priests and priestesses": "They say that the human soul is immortal; at times it comes to an end, which they call dying; at times it is reborn, but it is never destroyed, and one must therefore live one's life as piously (*hosiōtata*) as possible."[97] According to Clement of Alexandria, it was Orphic teaching that "if we live throughout holily and righteously (*hosiōs kai dikaiōs*), we are happy here, and shall be happier after our departure there, not possessing happiness for a time, but enabled to rest in eternity."[98] In the stories of Musaeus (son of Orpheus), it is "the just" (*tois dikaiois*) who are led to Hades, seated on couches, crowned with wreathes, and provided with drink.[99]

For many Orphic specialists, moreover, ritual performance alone was not enough to achieve salvation. What is also needed, as the author of the Derveni papyrus (fourth century B.C.E.) stresses, is knowledge.[100] For him, it is not enough simply to go through the right rituals or hear the right cosmogony. One must understand what the myths and symbols mean. The need to understand what one is doing—to know underworld geography as well as the passwords needed to access salvation—is distinctive among

---

93. Plato, *Resp.* 364b–c; cf. 364e–5a; 366a–b.

94. Bernabé *OF* 488.1; 489.1; 490.1; 491.1.

95. Ibid., 33 = Ps.-Demosthenes, *Or.* 25.11. Cf. Bernabé *OF* 34.

96. Aristophanes, *Ran.* 1032–33. Aristophanes places this point in the mouth of the tragedian Aeschylus, who speaks with utmost seriousness.

97. Plato, *Meno.* 81b.

98. Clement of Alexandria, *Strom.* 5.14.122.2.

99. Plato, *Resp.* 363c

100. Bernabé *OF* 470, esp. Col. XX. Translation and commentary in Kouremenos, et al., *Derveni Papyrus*, 136; 238–42.

Greek mysteries that typically emphasize experience (*pathein*) rather than learning (*mathein*).[101]

The Work of Memory

Based on these observations, one could argue that deification in Orphic thought is primarily based on human works—what two tablets call "the work of memory."[102] But Memory (*Mnemosyne*) is also a goddess, daughter of Earth and Heaven, and thus sister of the initiates.[103] The work of Memory thus also refers to her work, or rather the work that she performs for those in her divine family. Significantly, the tablet found at Rome replaces the "work (*ergon*) of Memory" with the "gift (*dōron*) of Memory," and immediately announces the deification of the initiate: "You have become a goddess by law!"[104] The "law" (*nomos*) would seem to refer to a ritual regulation or the decree of fate. But law (*Nomos*) is also a god addressed in an Orphic hymn who serves as cosmic and moral regulator, who is "present in the most upright thoughts . . . dwelling peacefully with all lawful human beings (*tois nomimois*)."[105] In short, there is indication that for Orphic initiates paradise—although indeed "earned" by moral and ritual purity—was still rooted in divine favor.

One's divine lineage is a kind of natural grace inherent in all human nature. To activate the potential of this nature, however, a savior god is necessary. This savior is none other than the son of the goddess of the underworld himself. In a tablet from Pelinna, the initiates are instructed to say to Persephone: "Bacchius [i.e., Dionysus] himself has liberated you!"[106]

Conclusion

Orphism, if not a popular movement, was an important and widespread discourse spanning a period from the Classical Age to Late Antiquity. One could argue that the discourse also represents a religious mentality, a mentality that cannot be fully explained by portraying Orphic thought as a "deviant path"

101. Aristotle, frag. 15 (Rose). I am thus skeptical of viewing "the golden leaf" as a "'ticket to Heaven'" (*pace* Bremmer, "Death and Immortality," 121).

102. Bernabé *OF* 474.1; 476.12.

103. Bernabé and Jiménez san Cristóbal, *Instructions*, 15–16.

104. Bernabé *OF* 491.3–4.

105. *Orphic Hymns* 64.9–11 (Athanassakis).

106. Bernabé *OF* 485.2.

diverging from the mainstream religion of Greek cities.[107] It was a mentality that was part and parcel of the Greek world and Greek culture in its many phases and motley variety. The basis of this mentality is the recognition of the infinite value of the individual self, its great potential, and its worthiness to be (eternally) preserved. The temporal maintenance of family, city, and empire through the cycle of birth and rituals of bloody sacrifice did not sufficiently quench the thirst of some people's spiritual longing. The loss of the individual at death, and the sinking of the human mind into the mire of oblivion was perceived to be too much a contradiction of human significance. The Homeric immortality of *kleos*, or fame, was understood as too fleeting and limited to too few in a past that was too far away. What was needed was life after the cruel blow of death—life in all its vivid color and concreteness. Fascinatingly, those who shared this "Orphic" mentality believed that death is not that which separates human beings from the gods; it is what joins them to the table of the gods, and makes them demigods and gods themselves.

107. Detienne, "Le chemins de la déviance," 49–80; Detienne, *Dionysos Slain*, 70–72, 94. Plato notes that Orphic ritual practitioners persuaded whole cities (*poleis*) to undergo their purifications (*Resp.* 364e).

Chapter 4

"We are Being Transformed"
Paul and the Gospel of Deification

> "Immortality" conceded to every Peter and Paul has so far been
> the greatest, the most malignant, attempt to assassinate *noble*
> humanity.
>
> —FRIEDRICH NIETZSCHE, *ANTICHRIST* §43

As Orphic initiates identified with the god Dionysus, so the Apostle Paul morphed with the divine Christ. "I have been crucified with Christ," he once claimed, "I no longer live—Christ lives in me" (Gal 2:19–20). In a letter to the Corinthians, he writes, "the one who cleaves to the Lord [Christ] is one spirit with him" (1 Cor 6:17). The hope of union with Christ is not individual. Paul speaks of his converts as sharing a single body with their divine Lord (1 Cor 3:6; 6:3; 12:1).

This union of Christ and believers is well demonstrated by Paul's striking use of "co-" compounds. His converts are said to be "co-heirs" (*sugklēronomoi*) with Christ (Rom 8:17; cf. Eph 3.6) if they "co-suffer" with him (*sumpaschomen*) (Rom 8:17; cf. 2 Cor 1:5; Col 1:24). Paul calls himself "co-crucified" (*sunestaurōmai*) with Christ (Gal 2:19; cf. Rom 6:6). He apparently expects a similar destiny for his followers, insofar as they are "co-grown" (*sumphutoi*) into the likeness of Christ's death (Rom 6:5; cf. 6:8; 2 Cor 4:10; Phil 3:10; Col 2:20), and "co-buried" with Christ (*sunetaphēmen*) (Rom 6:4; Col 2:12). Subsequently they "co-live" (*suzēsomen*) with Christ (Rom 6:8; 2 Tim 2:11) by being "co-glorified" with him (*sundoxasthōmen*) (Rom 8:17; cf. 2 Thess 2:14).[1] Perhaps the strongest statement of union be-

---

1. According to Deutero-Pauline literature, Christians are "co-raised" (*sunegeirō*)

58

tween Christ and Christian is in 2 Cor 3:18, where believers become the "same image" (*tēn autēn eikona*) of (or as) Christ—who is soon identified as the image of God (4:4).

This union with Christ assumes a kind of kinship. Pauline Christians become children of God (Rom 8:14; 9:26; Gal 3:26; 4:6) just as Christ was declared "son of God" (Rom 1:4). Christ and Christians are thus siblings (*adelphoi*) (Rom 8:29), images of the same divine Father (cf. Gen 5:1–3). This kinship language seems to express a kind of relatedness rightly called "genetic," that is, having to do with the *genos*—the race or class into which two entities belong. Christ and believers as kin belong to the same class of beings, namely divine "sons of God." Christians as divine children of the Father are pictured as subordinate to Christ their elder brother. The fact, however, that believers are pictured as Christ's siblings, made in the same image, and heirs of the same world, indicates a relative parity between Christian and Christ.

Immortality and Deification

The key trait of deity in the ancient world is immortality.[2] The creation story of Genesis shows that humans, though made in (or as) the image of God (Gen 1:26–27), were kept from eternal life (Gen 3). Paul's gospel taught that humans could attain immortality through assimilation to the divine Christ (1 Cor 15:35–53). The Pauline mode of assimilation is corporeal. That is, believers assimilate to the glorious *body* of Christ. In this way they receive an immortal nature made up of a fine, ethereal stuff called *pneuma*.

According to Paul, Christ has a "body of glory" (*sōma tēs doxēs*) (Phil 3:21)—or, as it can be translated, a "body constituted by glory." This is the body that Christ gained in his resurrection, when he was raised by the "glory" of the Father (Rom 6:4). Accordingly in 1 Corinthians, Christ is called the "Lord of glory" (2:8). When believers "behold the glory of the Lord" (2 Cor 3:18), they behold Christ himself, who is the image of God (2 Cor 4:4; cf. 4:6; Col 1:15).

Yet if Christ has a *body* of glory, why does Paul call him a "life-making spirit" (*pneuma zōopoioun*) (1 Cor 15:45; cf. 2 Cor 3:17)? The word translated "spirit" here is again the Greek word *pneuma*. Scholars and exegetes are more and more coming to the conclusion that pneuma did not mean

---

with Christ (Eph 2:6; Col 2:12; 3:1), and are "co-enlivened" (*suzōopoieō*) with him (Col 2:13; Eph 2:5). Subsequently, they "co-reign" with Christ (*sumbasileuō*) (2 Tim 2:12), sitting "co-enthroned" with him in the heavenly realms (*sugkathizō*) (Eph 2:6).

2. Litwa, *We Are Being Transformed*, 44–45.

a Platonic, immaterial "spirit." It is more suitably translated by "breath" or "wind." Among ancient philosophers and medical professionals, it was thought of as a corporeal substance, though not a solid, earthly substance like earth and water.[3] It was much more like air. Air, however, was thought to be naturally cold and misty, whereas pneuma was hot, fiery, fine, and extremely subtle. Many Stoics described pneuma as a fine mixture of air and fire, and identified it with the substance of aether, or the fiery air thought to exist in the upper reaches of the universe.

That Christ's pneuma is also his body is indicated by the fact that those conformed to Christ (v. 49) are said to inherit a "pneumatic *body*" (*sōma pneumatikon*) (1 Cor 15:44). Christians become like Christ by conforming to Christ's pneuma (vv. 48–49). Elsewhere Paul speaks of assimilation to Christ's body of glory (Phil 3:21). Pneuma and glory thus appear to be parallel expressions—both describe the "stuff" of a resurrection body.

In 1 Corinthians 15:39–53, Paul discusses the nature of the resurrection body in answer to the question "With what sort of body do they [i.e., those resurrected] come?" (v. 35). He responds:

> Not all flesh is alike, but there is one flesh for human beings, another for animals, another for birds, and another for fish. There are both heavenly bodies and earthly bodies, but the glory of the heavenly is one thing, and that of the earthly is another. There is one glory of the sun, and another glory of the moon, and another glory of the stars; indeed, star differs from star in glory.
>
> So it is with the resurrection of the dead. What is sown is perishable, what is raised is imperishable. It is sown in dishonor, it is raised in glory. It is sown in weakness, it is raised in power. It is sown a psychic body, it is raised a pneumatic body. If there is a psychic body, there is also a pneumatic body. Thus it is written, "The first man, Adam, became a living soul (*psychē*)"; the last Adam [Christ] became a life-giving pneuma. . . . The first man was from the earth, a man of dust; the second man is from heaven. As was the one of dust, so are those who are of the dust; and as is the one of heaven, so are those who are of heaven Just as we have borne the image of the one of dust, we will also bear the image of the celestial one [i.e., Christ].
>
> What I am saying, brothers and sisters, is this: flesh and blood cannot inherit the kingdom of God, nor does the perishable

---

3. Cf. Origen: "It is a custom of holy scripture, when it wishes to point to something of an opposite nature to this dense and solid body, to call it 'pneuma'" (*Princ.* 1.1.2; cf. his preface §8).

inherit the imperishable. Listen, I will tell you a mystery! We will not all die, but we will all be changed, in a moment, in the twinkling of an eye, at the last trumpet. For the trumpet will sound, and the dead will be raised imperishable, and we will be changed. (1 Cor 15:39–52, NRSV, modified)

Paul characterizes the pneumatic body by incorruptibility, glory, and power (1 Cor 15:42–43)—all divine qualities. It is also conformed to Christ's body, consisting of "life-making" pneuma (v. 45) associated with "heaven" (v. 47). The nature of the pneumatic body is thus celestial (v. 48); it is not, Paul adds, made up of "flesh and blood"—the constituents of present bodily life (v. 50).

This latter remark is striking. Most ancient peoples admitted that bodily life on earth is constituted by flesh—by which is meant not only skin, but bones, arteries, muscle, nerves, and all the various tissues and organs that make life possible on this planet. Flesh is the stuff of terrestrial life. "Mortals," to quote Homer, are "those who have blood in their veins."[4] To exist in a body without flesh and blood is not to be human in the way the ancients normally conceived of it. It is to be celestial, and not terrestrial; it is to exist in a corporeality existing *above* the conditions of earthly life, without disease or decomposition. It is to be "bloodless" (*anaimones*)—a Homeric epithet of the gods.[5]

When Paul talked about the bodies of earthly beings, he used the term "flesh" (*sarx*). When he turned to heavenly bodies, he used the term "glory" (*doxa*, vv. 40–41). Although glory may simply mean "brightness" or "illumination," there is strong indication that in the latter half of 1 Corinthians 15, glory is meant to contrast directly with flesh (v. 39). If flesh is the substance of earthly bodies, then glory is the brilliance of pneumatic bodies. In short, a pneumatic body is a glory body. Pneuma, like the aether in ancient cosmology, shines like the stars. Since Christ is pneuma (1 Cor 15:45), he has a body of glory (Phil 3:21). In short, to receive a pneumatic body is to gain a body of glory like the divine Christ.

These glory bodies can, to be sure, be on heaven or earth (1 Cor 15:40), but their chief location is heaven where the glory-bodies—sun, moon, stars—shine according to their purity or "weight of glory" (15:41; cf. 2 Cor 4:17). The Danish scholar Troels Engberg-Pedersen comments: "A 'psychic' body belongs *on earth* as exemplified by the 'earthly bodies' mentioned in [1 Cor] 15:39; a 'pneumatic' one belongs *in heaven* as exemplified by the

---

4. Clay, *Wrath of Athena*, 144.

5. Homer, *Il.* 5.342.

'heavenly bodies' mentioned in 15:41. Or to be even more precise: a 'pneumatic body' *is* a heavenly body like the sun, moon and stars."[6]

In other words, there is an implicit contrast between heavenly and earthly bodies underlying 1 Cor 15:39–49, and Paul associates the future pneumatic body of believers with the heavenly bodies. The mention of the heavenly nature of Christ's body in 1 Cor 15:47 recalls the contrast between earthly and heavenly bodies in 15:40.[7] Paul seems, then, to be alluding to the fact that the pneumatic bodies of Christ and believers show the same brilliance (*doxa*) as the heavenly bodies. In a word, they are "glorified." In a later letter, Paul promises believers a "glorification" (*doxazō*) of their bodies in conformity to the resurrected body of Christ (Rom 8:29–30).[8] This passage from Romans is structurally similar to 1 Cor 15:49: "Just as we have borne the image of the one of dust (Adam), we will also bear the image of the celestial one (Christ)." In Paul's letter to the Romans, to be conformed to Christ's image means to be glorified; in 1 Corinthians, to bear Christ's image is to become celestial (like the pneumatic Christ). Paul's language of "glorification" is thus a way of talking about becoming pneuma and living a life among the stars.[9] Engberg-Pedersen goes even so far as to say that resurrected Christian become stars who "*will live on* in the upper regions of the cosmos."[10] He bases his comments partially on Paul's statement that his converts "shine like stars in the world" (Phil 2:14–15). Although in this passage, believers are still on earth, Paul declares that their true city is in heaven—the realm of the stars (3:20). Engberg-Pedersen observes:

> Apparently, by acting here and now in conformity with Christ's resurrection into heaven, which has already taken place, and with a view to their own future salvation (cf. 2:12–13), the Philippians already proleptically appear *like* having the form that they will eventually have *in fact* when they have left this crooked and perverse generation behind. . . . If the pneuma is already present now among the Philippians—as what is elsewhere called

6. Engberg-Pedersen, *Cosmology and Self*, 28.

7. Ibid., 30.

8. On Pauline glorification, see Sprinkle, "Afterlife in Romans," 201–34.

9. Why does Paul not speak directly of glorification in 1 Cor 15? Although glorification and the "glory body" was a concept intelligible to a Jewish audience (or those familiar with the Jewish heritage), it would seem to be less intelligible to a Greek one. Paul's "pneumatic body" may then be an attempt to redescribe the concept of "glory" in terms intelligible to Greek physics. The closest physical concept to corporeal "glory" was the Stoic pneuma: an ethereal, fiery, fine, subtle substance, not subject to decay. Since it existed in the heavens, pneuma was envisioned as a bright or luminous body. Such was the substance of the Stoic soul, and—as it turns out—also the substance of the stars.

10. Engberg-Pedersen, *Cosmology and Self*, 12, emphasis his.

a "down payment"—when they shine *like* stars, then we are very close to the idea we found in 1 Corinthians 15 to the effect that the pneuma will eventually turn those who are resurrected *into* "stars in the world." Then they will no longer shine *like* stars: they will *be* stars.[11]

Deification and Assimilation

That Paul's version of celestial immortality is also a form of deification is indicated by the fact that glorification involves assimilation to the "super body" of a divine being (Christ). Alan Segal's interpretation of Philippians 3:21 ("He [Christ] will transform the body of our humiliation that it may be conformed to his body of glory") is elegantly simple: "The body of the believer eventually is to be transformed into the body of Christ."[12] It seems, at any rate, safe to conclude that in Phil 3:21, Paul proposes that Christians will share in the "glory body," or brilliant corporeality of a divine being. The analogous passage in 2 Cor 3:18 ("We all, beholding the glory of the Lord as in a mirror, are being metamorphosed into the same image from glory to glory") indicates just how closely believers are conformed to the glory of the Christ: they are to become the *same* image, that is the *identical (corporeal) form* as their divine Lord. Insofar as Christians participate in Christ's pneumatic corporeality, they participate in Christ's divine identity. The result is the human attainment of the clearest of all divine attributes: immortality (1 Cor 15:50–52).

Paul's language of meeting the Lord "in the air" (*eis aera*) (1 Thess 4:17), of having a heavenly city (or citizenship) (Phil 3:20), and of bearing the image of the "Celestial Being" (*ho epouranios*) (1 Cor 15:48–49) indicates that he envisioned an ascent to heaven or celestial sojourn after death (or when Christ comes to earth) (cf. 2 Cor 12:1–4). When believers make this ascent, their pneumatic element will wholly envelop and replace their mortal flesh. Like Christ, they will be sons of God and gods themselves.

11. Ibid., 42–43, emphasis his. Cf. 103, where he remarks that the "souls [of the Philippian Christians] will live on as stars in heaven until the conflagration." Alan Segal also talks of the believer being "subsumed into the body of a heavenly savior" and becoming "a kind of star or celestial immortal" ("Paul and the Beginning," 104).

12. Segal, "Paul and the Beginning," 113.

Cosmic Rule

What will believers do when they soar to the heavenly realms? According to Paul's gospel, they will stand before Christ and receive incorruptible crowns (1 Thess 2:19; 1 Cor 9:25; cf. 2 Tim 4:8). Each will be revealed as sons of God (Rom 8:18), co-heirs with the divine Christ (8:17). As divine children and equal heirs, they will be given a share in Christ's divine sovereignty. It is Christ who has the right to sit at the judgment seat (2 Cor 5:10). But Christ gives this power to "the holy ones" (i.e., Pauline Christians) to judge the world and angels (1 Cor 6:2–3). Though the subjection of all things (including demonic powers) is given only to the Messiah, those "in Christ" rule with him in eternal life (Rom 5:17; cf. 2 Tim 2:12). Christ's victory is their victory. Christ's divine sovereignty is their sovereignty. By assimilation to the divine Christ, the faithful take on Christ's divine function: universal rule.

We must flesh these points out. Along with Christ, Paul makes his converts heirs of the world. When arguing against factionalism in Corinth, Paul told his converts that "all things (*panta*) are yours" (1 Cor 3:21). This does not appear to be rhetorical hyperbole divorced from reality. In Paul's apocalyptic mindset, "all things" includes real superhuman entities: the powers of death and life, all present and future things, even the world itself (*kosmos*) (1 Cor 3:22).[13] To have possession of these cosmic realities (cf. Rom 8:38)— and the cosmos itself—is at the very least to have some degree of power over them. But to have power over death is the prerogative of the divine Messiah who will defeat death when the "end" comes (1 Cor 15:25–27). Christ is the one who truly owns "all things." He is the "heir of all (*pantōn*)"—to borrow a phrase from Hebrews (1:2).

Paul's transfer of cosmic ownership to his converts appears to be an implication of their being "in Christ." They are "coheirs" with Christ (Rom 8:17) to whom the whole world submits as the Lord of all (Phil 2:10–11). As participants in Christ, then, believers gain a share in the world. Therefore they should not be worried about mere human things (1 Cor 3:21). Paul implies that they are called to be something more than mere human beings (3:4).[14]

---

13. *Kosmos* is variously understood in this verse. Weiss understood it as "the unlimited fullness of all living beings, human and angel (cf. 4:9)" (*Der erste Korintherbrief*, 89). Robertson and Plummer opted for "the physical universe" (*Critical and Exegetical Commentary*, 73). More recent commentators who want to limit "the world" to something smaller have trouble explaining why death, life, as well as all present and future things are included in it.

14. "For when one says, 'I belong to Paul,' and another, 'I belong to Apollos,' are you not merely human (*ouk anthrōpoi este*)?" Origen comments on this notion: "the pneumatic is greater than 'human,' who is characterized either by soul or by body or by both,

That having "all things" entails a narrative of future rule seems to be implied also in 1 Corinthians 4:8. Here Paul chides the Corinthians: "Already you have all you want! Already you have become rich! Quite apart from us you have become kings!" That Paul was not merely mocking his converts but affirming his own doctrine appears from his next remark (which does not seem altogether wry): "Indeed, I wish that you had become kings, so that we might be kings with you!" Reigning as cosmic kings was evidently not the private fantasy of the Corinthians, or the doctrine of Paul's enemies. It is, it appears, what Paul had told them of their final destiny. As owners of all things and heirs with Christ, they will rule as kings with Christ (*basileusousin*) (Rom 5:17; cf. 2 Tim 2:12),[15] and come into possession of all there is (*ta panta*) (Rom 8:32).[16]

Ownership of "everything" is a form of sovereignty—a universal sovereignty to which only Christ has claim. To him God makes "all things" (*panta*) subject (1 Cor 15:27; Phil 3:21). Strictly speaking, sovereignty over "all things" is the sovereignty that only the Creator—or the one through whom all things were made (1 Cor 8:6)—can lay claim to. This is the sovereignty that makes up the divine identity of Christ, the Messiah, who is made Lord and heir of the world. Paul, it appears, envisions believers as sharing this universal sovereignty through their assimilation to Christ, the divine son (Rom 8:29).

If believers in Christ will own the cosmos and rule over it as co-heirs with Christ, they also will have the authority to judge it. In 1 Corinthians 6:2, Paul asks his readers, "Do you not know that the saints [i.e., believers] will judge the cosmos (*ton kosmon*)?" Included in the cosmos are both humans and angels (1 Cor 4:9). Naturally, then, Paul asks: "Do you not know that we are to judge angels?" (6:2–3). Paul's "Do you not know . . . ?" indicates that the future world dominance of believers was a well-known teaching (and evidently his own). The *kosmos* may refer to those judged on Judgment day. More broadly, however, it could designate the creation in general. If this is correct, then the "judging" may not be viewed as a one-time event, but as

---

and not by the pneuma which is more divine than these. By very strong participation in the pneuma the pneumatic gains this name" (*Comm. Jo.* 2.21.138, my trans.).

15. The problem of the Corinthians is not that they speed up the time of their rule (*pace* Hay, *Glory at the Right Hand*, 62) but that they rule without Paul (*chōris hēmōn*) (in an emphatic position, 1 Cor 4:8).

16. "All things" here probably refers to creation as a whole, the most common meaning in Paul (Rom 11:36; 1 Cor 8:6; 11:12; 15:27–28; Phil 3:21). In the words of Dunn, "what seems to be envisaged is a sharing in Christ's lordship . . . over 'the all'" (*Romans 1–8*, 502).

a continuous action. In this sense, judging would imply authority over the angels, and likely governance over them.[17]

Important to note is exactly who believers will judge. They will judge "angels," beings—whether good or evil—that are normally held to be superior to humanity. Human superiority over angels is only natural for those who have been made into "the same image" as Christ, the image of God (2 Cor 3:18; 4:4). Properly speaking, however, only Christ has power over the angelic or superhuman world (1 Cor 15:24; Phil 2:10–11). His power to judge is what gives him the honor of the Father (cf. John 5:22–23). Humanity granted the power to judge angels is evidently humanity sharing in Christ's divine prerogatives and honor.

In 1 Corinthians 15, Christ's role as the divine Messiah is "to destroy every Rule and Authority and Power" (v. 24). James Tabor asserts that "this cosmic conquering role belongs not only to Jesus as son of God, but to the 'many' sons to come as well. The very notion," he says, "of 'inheriting the kingdom of God' has to do with participating in a role of cosmic rule and judgment (1 Cor 15:50). Jesus only heads a group of transformed, immortal, glorified sons of God who have been given power over 'all things' to bring about God's final purposes in history."[18]

The logic of Tabor's reading is supported by Romans 16:20, where Paul promises Christians that Satan will soon be crushed beneath their feet. It is this opponent who is (if conflated with Death) the "last" enemy (1 Cor 15:26). He is, at any rate, generally considered to be the greatest and most powerful adversary of God. Satan is, in Paul's language, the "god of this world" (2 Cor 4:4). This is the enemy that Christians are said to stomp on. He will be their "footstool." Properly speaking, only the divine Messiah uses his enemies as a footstool (Ps 110:1; 1 Cor 15:27). By stomping on Satan, Christians inherit Christ's own sovereignty.

The sovereignty that Christians gain in Christ is greater than the sovereignty Adam had over beasts and birds in Genesis 1:26 and 28. It is a sovereignty of the Image of God, who is a divine being, Christ (2 Cor 4:4). It is a universal sovereignty insofar as it includes ownership of all things and the judgment of the cosmos.

---

17. A good case for the "ruling" sense of the verb "judge" (*krinō*) can be made from LXX usage, where this is often the meaning of the term (e.g., Judg 4:4; 10:2–3; Ps 66:5 [MT 67:5]; Hos 13:9–10; cf. Luke 22:30). Cf. also Judg 3:10, 30; 12:7–9, 11, 13–14; 15:20; 16:31. It also seems to be the sense in Ruth 1:1, 1 Sam 4:18; 2 Chr 26:21; Pss 2:10; 9:9; 71:2, 4; 95:10, 13; 97:9; 134:14; Prov 29:14; Mic 4:3; Isa 19:20; 51:22; Wis 1:1; 3:8; 12:13–14, 18; Tob 3:2; 1 Macc 9:73; Pss Sol 17:29; *Odes* 3:10; Sir 4:15; 45:26. This sense of *krinō* does not seem to appear at all in the Pentateuch, although see Deut 32:36.

18. Tabor "Paul's Notion," 94.

Sharing the Divine Identity

In more than one essay, Richard Bauckham has argued that the "one who functions as God shares the divine identity with God,"[19] and "it is the cosmic scope of Christ's sovereignty which places it in that unique [divine] category."[20] Although Bauckham speaks of Christ, his logic works just as well for Christians. The universal sovereignty Paul envisions for his converts could only be a divine sovereignty. It could only stem from God as a part of his identity which he shares with the divine Christ, and which Christ then shares with his siblings and co-heirs. Christ's rule is a cosmic, and thus a divine rule. It is this divine rule that he shares with believers. Christ as the prototype for believers is not just a human being. He is a *divine* prototype, one with God himself.

God made Christ an heir of the world (1 Cor 15:27). He will own it and rule over it. According to Paul's gospel, believers are made "heirs of God and co-heirs with Christ" (Rom 8:17).[21] As co-heirs, they will have an equal share of Christ's divine ownership of the world and dominion over it. Christ has first priority to it as the elder brother, but he willingly shares it with all those called his "siblings" and "sons of God" (Gal 3:26; Rom 8:17, 19, 29). They fulfill, or help Christ fulfill, a divine function.

Similarly, the authority to judge the world (both human and superhuman) is a widely recognized divine function.[22] According to Paul, it is God who judges the world (Rom 3:6; cf. Ps 96:13), along with the divine Christ (2 Cor 5:10). If, according to Bauckham, "[t]he one who functions as God shares the divine identity with God,"[23] the implications for deification are evident. For God (through Christ) to give humans ownership of "everything" (*ta panta*) and judgment over the "world" (*ton kosmon*) is to give them a share of his divine sovereignty which constitutes his divine identity.

It is thus primarily three factors, all closely intertwined, that suggest a form of deification in Paul, namely: (1) ruling over "all things" (including

19. Bauckham, *Jesus and the God of Israel*, 138.

20. Ibid., 176. Cf. 180: "Thus, it is because the Son exercises the uniquely divine sovereignty that he will and should be honoured just as the Father is."

21. "The term 'heirs of God,'" notes Cranfield, "is not to be explained as meaning simply 'heirs of Abraham,' who are to receive in due course the blessings which God promised to him and his seed." Christians will share "not just in various blessings God is able to bestow but in that which is peculiarly His own, the perfect and imperishable glory of His own life" (*Romans*, 927).

22. According to Hoskins, "In Jewish thought the judge of angels is also a position that is held solely by God" ("Biblical and Extrabiblical Parallels," 292). As evidence, he cites *1 En* 9–10; 90:20–27.

23. Bauckham, *Jesus and the God of Israel*, 138.

superhuman beings), together with (2) the expectation of existing in a superhuman, immortal, and incorruptible body. Both of these factors are viewed as functions of (3) assimilation to Christ, a divine being.

Conclusion

Paul's gospel was a gospel of immortality and deification. In the ancient world, typically only kings and pharaohs claimed divine prerogatives. Only they were immortal, and boasted of world rule. The Apostle Paul preached a gospel wherein those privileges were granted to all—including (and perhaps especially) commoners, slaves, women, and children. The only conditions were belief in Christ and moral rectitude.

One might accuse Paul of preaching a gospel of compensation since he projected divine life and rule into the future. Antony the triumvir could be a god while alive, whereas Paul's vision of deification required death or the second coming of Christ (whichever came first). On the other hand, Paul's version of deification avoids the dangers of self-promotion in the ruler cult. For the Apostle, one is deified not by heroic victories and acts of benefaction, but by following the divine Christ who lived and died to benefit human beings.

Pauline deification means assimilation—and ultimately identification—with the divine Christ. It is thus appropriate to call it Christification, or "Christosis," provided that one does not jettison Christ's divinity.[24] For Paul, Christ was the first human being to become "son of God" by his resurrection from the dead (Rom 1:4). Like the God(s) of Plato, Christ is a moral God able to lead his devotees into a virtuous life. All who follow him—in this life and the next—will share the same divine destiny and inheritance: an incorruptible body and power to defeat the Angel of Death.

> For this perishable body must put on imperishability, and this mortal body must put on immortality. When this perishable body puts on imperishability, and this mortal body puts on immortality, then the saying that is written will be fulfilled:
> "Death has been swallowed up in victory!"
> "Where, O death, is your victory?
> Where, O death, is your sting?" (1 Cor 15:53–56)

24. Blackwell, *Pauline Soteriology*, 264–67.

Chapter 5

"Immortalized in This Very Hour"

Deification in the "Mithras Liturgy"

Mithras, God of the Midnight, here where the great bull lies,
　　Look on thy children in darkness. Oh take our sacrifice!
Many roads Thou has fashioned: all of them lead to the Light,
　　Mithras, also a soldier, teach us to die aright!

　　　—RUDYARD KIPLING, "SONG TO MITHRAS"

IT IS A BLACK, moonless night. A magician stands with a female initiate (whom he calls his "daughter") and smears a mysterious ointment around her eyes. The ointment is a mixture of rose oil and beetle flesh (the original "beetle juice"?). The beetle is the "sun scarab"—said to have twelve sun rays—representing the ancient Egyptian solar deity Khepri.[1] The essence of the scarab is thus a sort of "sun substance," the very ingredient needed to obtain an oracle from the divine Sun.

　　Some days prior to the rite, the magician had placed the scarab in a deep turquoise cup on the new moon, together with seeds of lotus pulp and honey. He rubbed the seeds and honey together until they formed a little cake. The scarab, seeing the cake, ate it and perished. The magician then plopped the beetle into a glass vessel filled with the finest rose oil (an expensive perfume) and set the vessel on a circle of "holy sand." Over it the magician repeated a formula for seven days at the time of high noon (when the Sun is most powerful): "I consecrate you [O scarab], so that for me your

---

1. Khepri was thought to represent the morning (i.e., rising) sun (Hornung, *Conceptions of God*, 117, with plate IV; Assmann, "Chepre," 1.934–40; Jacq, *Egyptian Magic*, 141–42).

substance might become of use for so and so [the magician names himself] alone." Then he spoke the magic words which consisted of vowel sounds: "IE IA Ē EĒ OU EIA." Immediately, he revealed his identity (consisting of a magical name): "For I am PHŌR PHOR A PHŌS PHOTIZAAS." The final words PHŌS PHOTIZAAS sound like the Greek words for "light, giving light." The magician, as it seems, identified himself as a sort of light being, worthy to approach the King of Light himself, the Sun.[2]

The consecrated scarab ointment "immortalizes" the eyes, allowing them to see the immortal Sun shining above this world.[3] The ointment is a necessary preparation for a rite called the "Immortalization" (*apothanatismos*).[4] At the beginning of the rite, the magician prays to Providence and Soul that his "daughter," his "only child" receive immortality (*athanasian*).[5] The magician soon prays for himself that he be transferred to immortal birth (*athanatoi genesei*).[6] In the midst of the ritual, he declares that he has been reborn (*metagennēthentos*) and—"out of so many myriads"—immortalized (*apathanatistheis*).[7] His immortalization is also his deification.[8]

2. For the recipe of the ointment, see *PGM* IV.750–71. The *kentritis* ointment with its accompanying ritual is designed for preparing a fellow initiate (*PGM* IV.772–92). According to Edmonds, the magician who performs the rite attempts to avoid the malign influence of the Moon ("At the Seizure," 223–40). He infers that Mithras' instructions to perform the rite on a "full moon" (*PGM* IV.792–98) are "clearly added later" ("At the Seizure," 236, n. 49). See further Edmonds, "Faces of the Moon," 275–95.

3. *PGM* IV.516–17.

4. *PGM* IV.741, 747, 771.

5. *PGM* IV.475–78. On this text, I follow the emendations of Betz, "Mithras Liturgy," 94.

6. *PGM* IV.501.

7. *PGM* IV.647–48.

8. Guthrie, *Greeks and their Gods*, 115, 239. Morton Smith, "Transformation by Burial," 109; Tabor, *Things Unutterable*, 94; Betz, *Antike und Christentum*, 171. Temporary immortalization still amounts to a form of deification (*pace* Johnston, "Rising to the Occasion," 179). Although Diodorus of Sicily shows that "to be immortalized" can simply mean "to live on in memory" (*Bibl. hist.* 1.2.5.1; 4.7.4.18), "to immortalize" (*apathanatizō*) also clearly means "to deify." The same Diodorus says that the Getae immortalize Zalmoxis (*Bibl. hist.* 1.94.2; cf. 2.20.2). Strabo makes the meaning clear when he says that Zalmoxis was proclaimed a god (*theos*) (*Geog.* 7.3.5; cf. Lucian, *Deor. conc.* 9; *Scyth.* 1). Aristonicus (a first-century C.E. Greek grammarian from Alexandria) calls the deified Heracles the "immortalized" (*apēthanatismenon*) Heracles (*De signis Odysseae* on *Od.* 11.601). Philo's use of *apathanatizein* indicates the flexibility of the term, but it includes (I contend) the concept of deification. The human being is immortalized by philosophy (*Opif.* 77); the richness of the mind, brought up to and assimilated to God, is for this reason immortalized (*Post.* 123); souls are immortalized by virtue (*Conf.* 149; cf. *Det.* 111; *QG* 1.51); reason immortalizes the human being (*Spec* 4.14; cf. *Virt.* 15); people are immortalized by hearing the music of the stars (*Somn.* 1.36); Moses is immortalized in his bodiless ascent to heaven after death (*Mos.* 2.288).

Papyri Graecae Magicae

This "Rite of Immortalization" (as I will call it) is recorded in a magical handbook called the "Great Magical Papyrus of Paris."[9] It is a thirty-six-page book of spells written in Coptic and Greek. The book was reportedly found as part of a large cache of papyri from a Theban tomb sometime before the year 1828. Along with other papyri, it was auctioned off by adventurous collectors to European libraries and museums. In 1857, the book was bought by the Bibliothèque Nationale in Paris, and catalogued as "Supplément grec. #574." It was published in 1885 by the Vienna papyrologist Carl Wessely. Karl Preisendanz gave it its scholarly name *Papyri Graecae Magicae* (or *PGM*) IV in his famous edition of the Greek magical papyri (1928).[10] Although *PGM* IV was written in the early fourth century C.E., it "has more the character of a text composed two hundred years earlier."[11] Preisendanz's predecessor, the great Albrecht Dieterich, believed that our Rite of Immortalization originated between 100 and 150 C.E.[12] The historical author of the text is unknown (magicians preferred to remain anonymous), but may have been a learned Egyptian priest. According to the text of the Rite, however, the author is a son of the Sun God himself.[13]

It was Dieterich who called the Rite of Immortalization "the Mithras Liturgy," in large part because the God who gave the rite to the magician (through an "archangel") is called "the great God Helios Mithras."[14] When this God wondrously reveals himself at the end of the Rite, he indeed appears with the traits of the God Mithras. Mithras, called "the Unconquered Sun," was the center of a widespread mystery cult that flourished in the Greco-Roman world (including Egypt) from the second to the fourth centuries C.E.[15] Dieterich thought that he could extract from the Rite of Immortalization a Mithraic "liturgy" (what he called "an entirety of practices

---

Justin Martyr uses *apathanatizein* both for the deification of Roman emperors (1 *Apol.* 21.3) and of Christians (21.6).

9. *PGM* IV.475–820. Greek text in Preisendanz and Henrichs, *Papyri*, 1.89–101. English translation in Betz, *Greek Magical Papyri*, 48–54.

10. Brashear, "Greek Magical Papyri," 3402–3, 3407, 3410–11.

11. Ibid., 3419.

12. Dieterich, *Mithrasliturgie*, 46.

13. *PGM* IV.548. Perhaps this son of the Sun is the "archangel" referred to in IV.483. The initiate who uses the spell is also meant to declare his divine sonship (IV.535–36). Due to the use of magical names, however, it is unclear whose son he is.

14. *PGM* IV.482.

15. For an introduction to Mithras, see Clauss, *Roman Cult of Mithras*. Clauss briefly treats the Mithras Liturgy on 105–6. The astrological significance of the cult is brought out by Ulansey, *Origins*.

and prayers").[16] The Rite, he believed, was later adapted by Egyptian magicians who aimed to receive an oracle from Mithras. These same magicians, appending the recipes for the ointment and instructions for making protective amulets, made slight editorial changes throughout the Rite itself.[17]

Dieterich was correct that the text underwent several stages of production. (Evidence for this is the fact that the "daughter" addressed in the introduction abruptly drops out. In her place, we find a male magician addressed throughout as an initiate practicing "mysteries."[18]) It is now recognized, however, that a division between the Rite of Immortalization and its magical adaptation has little basis in the text itself.[19] It remains unknown whether deification in the "Mithras Liturgy" is actually Mithraic (note that the boundaries between religions in this period are fluid).[20] In its current state at least, the Rite of Immortalization is an integral part of a magical spell found in a larger handbook of spells and thus should be considered through and through a magical rite itself.

The Meaning of Magic

Magic has been variously defined and exhaustively discussed in recent times.[21] As opposed to "religion," which is commonly portrayed as public, collective, civic, and characterized by understandable prayers of supplication, magic is often depicted as secret, individual, anti-social, and typified by manipulative prayers filled with gobbledygook. But "magic" and "religion" are in fact ideal types, and the differences between them are frequently blurred. Moreover, in certain cultures (especially ancient Egypt) magic is

16. Dieterich, *Mithrasliturgie*, 93 (*ein Ganzes von Handlungen und Gebeten*).

17. Note esp. *PGM* IV.478–82, and Dieterich's comments in *Mithrasliturgie*, 83–84.

18. *PGM* IV.476. See further Betz, *Hellenismus und Urchristentum*, 209–29.

19. Betz, "Mithras Liturgy," 6.

20. Scholars today have pointed out additional Mithraic elements in support of Dieterich's thesis. See Beck, "Mithraism since Franz Cumont," 2051; Alan Segal "Heavenly Ascent," 1382; Betz, "Mithras Liturgy," 32–38.

21. Aune defines magic as *"that form of religious deviance whereby individual or social goals are sought by means alternate to those normally sanctioned by the dominant religious institution"* ("Magic in Early Christianity," 1515, emphasis his). For Assmann, "magic is to be defined as *religion applied to the domestic sphere*" ("Magic and Theology," 3, emphasis his). Alan Segal refused to define magic since its meaning is culturally determined ("Hellenistic Magic," 350). Jonathan Z. Smith encourages the use of "other generic terms (e.g., healing, divining, execrative) to replace the label "magical" ("Trading Places," 16). For a defense of the term "magic," see Hoffmann, "Fiat Magia," 179–96. The best introduction to ancient magic is Graf, *Magic*, supplemented by Dickie, *Magic and Magicians*.

considered to be a gift of the gods, a respected part of the official religion, and vital for maintaining the welfare of society and the state.[22]

Many magic spells are known for being supremely practical and indeed quotidian. They aim to entice a lover, bind an enemy, expel a demon, or otherwise obtain some service from a god or demigod. Some magic spells, however, aim at higher ends. The Christian rhetor Lactantius complained of those "who aim at heaven itself with their magic spells!"[23] In a fascinating story, the author of Acts accuses a certain Simon of Samaria of practicing magic (8:9–11). His fellow Samaritans called him "the Great Power of God"[24]—a divine title (cf. 1 Cor 1:24) that influenced later legends.[25] In the mid-second century, the Christian philosopher Justin reports that Simon "accomplished powerful acts of magic. . . . He was considered a god (*theos*) and was honored by you [Roman emperors] as a god with a statue. . . . Nearly all Samaritans and a few among other nations as well worship him, confessing him to be the Primal God (*prōton theon*)."[26] A quarter century later, the Platonist critic of Christianity Celsus spoke of Palestinian prophets in his day who proclaimed: "I am God, or a son of God, or a divine Spirit—and I have come!" "They then go on," Celsus sardonically relates, "to add incomprehensible, incoherent, and utterly obscure utterances," which give "an opportunity for any halfwit or sorcerer to appropriate the words however he wants."[27]

The deifying potential of magic is confirmed in several spells of the *Greek Magical Papyri*. One spell relates how to become attached to Helios (the Sun God). With the Sun at mid-heaven, the practitioner lies down on his roof naked and wrapped like a mummy.[28] He recites a series of "I am he" formulas, identifying himself as a companion of the Sun.[29] A sea falcon (symbolizing Horus, a manifestation of the Sun) appears, strikes the magician with

22. For magic as divine gift, note Graf, *Magic*, 92–96.

23. Lactantius, *Div. Inst.* 5.9.17.

24. Acts 8:10. Other manuscripts read: "The power of God that is called (*kaloumenē*) great." *Kaloumenē* may be "Luke's" editorial addition designed to cast doubt on Simon's status.

25. For Simon's "deification," see esp. Lüdemann, *Untersuchungen* (Simon as great God). For Simon as representative of the Great God, see Heintz, *Simon "Le Magicien,"* 118–22; Theissen, "Simon Magus," 418–19; Zangenberg, "Δύναμις τοῦ θεοῦ," 530–34.

26. Justin, *1 Apol.* 26. Cf. Apollonius of Tyana, who by virtue of his miracles is thought to be a god (Philostratus, *Vit. Apoll.* 8.5.1; 8.7.1).

27. Origen, *Cels.* 7.9; cf. 1.9, 68. On the significance of magical words (*voces magicae*), see Betz, *Antike und Christentum*, 162–64.

28. *PGM* IV.170–79.

29. *PGM* IV.179–208. For the magician's identification with various deities in *PGM*, see Betz, *Antike und Christentum*, 180–81.

his wings. This is the sign that the sorcerer has been permanently united to the Sun's "holy form."[30] As a result, he becomes "lord of a godlike nature."[31] According to another spell, the so-called "spell of Pnouthis," the magician "will be [worshiped] as a god" since he has obtained a god as an assistant and friend.[32] When the magician dies, the divine assistant will keep the "aerial spirit" of the sorcerer in heaven, free from the terrors of the underworld.[33]

The Rite of Immortalization

The Rite of Immortalization narrates an ascent to heaven while the magician remains alive. To ascend into the celestial world where all things are immortal demands that the sorcerer be immortalized as well.[34] He begins with a prayer to the four elements: pneuma, fire, water, and "earthy substance." The magician is made up of all four elements. All are considered to be divine, but only one element will enable the ascent: pneuma.[35] Pneuma, as we saw in Paul, designates a fine fiery breath, or "spirit." Although ancient authors were able to make a distinction between human and divine pneuma, the Rite of Immortalization does not do so explicitly. The writer of the spell nonetheless distinguishes certain kinds of pneuma. He instructs the participant to inhale pneuma specifically "from the sun rays."[36] By sucking in sun-spirit—as much as he can—he takes in the divine, and incorporates it into himself. Psychologically, the act of inhaling quickly and with full force may have induced a trance state (or at least lightheadedness). At any rate, we are told that the magician feels himself growing lighter and (in his mind's eye) sees his pneumatic self floating upward.

Having ascended, the initiate encounters an eerie silence. The sounds of all humans and earthly beings cease. He has entered the immortal realm, and sees a "divine arrangement" (*theian thesin*)—which seems to refer to his

---

30. *PGM* IV.215–16.

31. *PGM* IV.219–20.

32. *PGM* I.190–91.

33. *PGM* I.178–80.

34. Cf. Philo, *QE* 2.40; *1 En.* 71; *Asc. Isa.* 11.22–33. Alexander pithily observes: "descent from heaven involved 'incarnation,' ascent from earth 'deification'" ("From Son of Adam to Second God," 103). See further Morton Smith, *Clement of Alexandria*, 236–43; Janowitz, *Magic*, 80–85.

35. Note that water is "immortal" in *PGM* IV.506. Empedocles identified the four elements with the gods Zeus, Hera, Hades, and Nestis (DK 31 B 6 = Inwood 12). See further Kingsley, *Ancient Philosophy*, 13–68.

36. *PGM* IV.537–38. See further Edmonds, "Did the Mithraists Inhale?" 13–22.

horoscope.[37] He immediately observes the "visible gods" or the planets.[38] They zoom through the sun disk, past a vast cosmic pipe through which the east and west winds blow.

All of the sudden the sorcerer observes the planetary gods glowering at him as if he were an intruder; terrifyingly, they start to rush at him. To deflect them, the author of the spell instructs the magician to put his right index finger into his mouth and proclaim: "Silence! Silence! Silence![39] [This is the] token of the living incorruptible God: (Guard me, Silence!): NECH-THEIR THANMELOU." The initiate whistles long and make a popping sound (repeatedly pronouncing the letter "p" with his lips), proclaiming more magical words.

Interestingly, the magician addresses Silence as a goddess. The "token" he mentions is apparently the magical name (untranslatable) and the magical words that follow. The finger-in-mouth pose is that of the god Harpocrates (or Horus the child). Again, Horus symbolized the victorious Sun. In his infant manifestation Greeks and Romans identified him with the god of silence.[40] By assimilating himself to (and possibly even identifying himself with) Harpocrates, the initiate gains right of access to the solar realm. In accordance with his new identity, the planetary gods start smiling at him and cease their attacks.[41]

But the sorcerer's troubles are not yet over. Out of the blue comes a roar of thunder, driving him out of his wits. Again he is instructed to pray the same prayer to Silence, this time addressing the planets: "I am for you a star [i.e., a planet], wandering with you, shining up from the abyss, the XY, the XERTHEUTH!"[42] Again the sorcerer assumes a magical name—apparently one known to the planets. The claim to be a star reminds us of the Orphic declaration: "My name is Starry."[43] But is the sorcerer's claim "I am for you a star!" just play acting?[44] We must keep in mind that in his pneumatic state, the magician would have a fiery, brilliant appearance.[45] Physically, he could

---

37. *PGM* IV.541–45, with comment of Merkelbach, *Abrasax* 3.237.

38. Plato, *Tim.* 40d. Six times Philo calls the stars "(sensible) gods" (*Opif.* 27; *Spec.* 1.19; *Aet.* 46, 112; *QG* 1.42, 4.157). Further references in Betz, "Mithras Liturgy," 142, n. 307.

39. *PGM* IV.559–60.

40. Meeks, "Harpokrates," 2.1003–11. See further Budde, "Harpare-pa-chered," 15–110.

41. *PGM* IV.566–68.

42. *PGM* IV.573–75.

43. Bernabé *OF* 477.9.

44. See further Betz, *Antike und Christentum*, 175–77.

45. Cf. Jesus' promise in Matt 13:43: "Then the just [at the end of time] will shine

appear as a star—a "visible god." The fact that he is a star *"for you (hymin)"* is reminiscent of Empedocles: "I am for you *(hymin)* an immortal god!" In both cases, the divinity claimed is relative to the audience addressed.

In his star form, the magician sees the sun disk slowly extending itself. Immediately an explosion of five-pronged stars fills the entire atmosphere. For a third time the magician calls upon Silence for aid. Finally the sun disk opens and he beholds a gigantic circle and, within it, fiery gates locked fast. He closes his eyes and prays the following prayer to the Sun:

> Hear me! Hear me! I am so and so [the magician names himself]
> O Lord, you who have bound with pneuma the fiery bars of the four roots!
> You of the fiery pole, PENTITEROUNI!
> Creator of light! (others say: "Encloser"), SEMESILAM!
> You of the fiery breath, PSURINPHEU!
> You of the fiery heart IAŌ!
> You of the spiritual light, ŌAI!
> You of the joyous fire, ELOURE
> You of the beautiful light, AZAÏ
> Aiōn AKBA![46]

The prayer continues with many other epithets, twenty-one in all (seven times three—a significant number).[47] The names prove fascinating. The initiate calls the Sun "Lord" (*kyrios*), a name Christians applied to the divine Christ (ubiquitous in Paul). The epithet "Creator of light" hearkens back to the God of Genesis who says to the darkness: "Let there be light!" (Gen 1:3). There immediately follows a Semitic epithet (SEMESILAM), which apparently means "Eternal Sun" (perhaps an old Phoenician or Syrian deity).[48] The Sun God is then addressed directly as IAŌ, the Greek word for "Yahweh," or the Jewish God. (IAO is immediately taken as a palindrome—ŌAI—apparently for added effect). Subsequently, the God is addressed as ELOURE—a possible spelling of the Greek word for "cat" (*ailoure*—pronounced the same way).[49] Apparently we are dealing with a cat-headed Yahweh, identified with the Sun God.[50] Finally the God is called Aiōn, a Greek word meaning

---

forth like the sun." Further parallels in Gundel, *Sterne und Sternbilder*, 104–26; cf. 301–46.

46. *PGM* IV.588–94.

47. *PGM* IV.588–602. Betz calls this section an "aretalogy" ("*Mithras Liturgy*," 156).

48. Bohak, *Ancient Jewish Magic*, 197.

49. For the mythological and magical significance of the cat in Ancient Egypt, see Jacq, *Egyptian Magic*, 139–40.

50. For Helios in Jewish magic, see Bohak, *Ancient Jewish Magic*, 251–53.

"Eternity," here an attribute of the Sun, and seemingly identified with him.[51] This bizarre combination of symbols and divine names is called "theocrasy" (literally, "the blending of gods"). To the magician, however, the combination of divine names rightly emphasizes the manifold powers and various manifestations of the same (Sun) God.[52]

The prayer ends with an impressive concatenation of vowel sounds; sounds that were probably understood to represent the language of the Gods.[53] The magician is instructed to repeat this prayer seven times for each of the "immortal gods of the cosmos."[54] These seven gods are apparently the seven planets, who need to be appeased before the magician ascends to a higher level.

Before the transition, however, the magician is disturbed and shaken by another barrage of thunder booming all around him. He prays to Silence a fourth time. Finally he opens his eyes and—lo and behold—the fiery doors of heaven stand open![55] The sorcerer beholds "the world of the gods"—a reference to the circle of the fixed stars above the planets.[56] To withstand the sight, the magician inhales more solar pneuma and prays, "Enter, Lord!"—pronouncing magical names. Suddenly rays of light whirl round to meet him. He stares into them with his immortal, sun-like eyes. Suddenly—swimming in the light—he perceives the silhouette of the Sun God (Helios) coming towards him.

Helios appears young, beautiful, with a fiery crown set on fiery hair, in a white tunic draped with a red cloak. The magician pronounces the appropriate "fiery" address: "Greetings Lord! You of great power and might, king, greatest of the Gods, Helios, Lord of earth and heaven, God of Gods!"[57] Again, some of the locutions here remind us of the God Yahweh in the Hebrew Bible, who is also called "Lord," "Lord of heaven and earth" and "God of gods."[58] The initiate confesses that he is a human being, with a

---

51. Aiōn is earlier spoken of as "master of the fiery diadems" (*PGM IV*.520–21). See further Clauss, *Roman Cult*, 162–65; Festugière *Révélation*, 4.176–99; Lewy, *Chaldean Oracles*, 99–105.

52. See further Betz, *Antike und Christentum*, 160–61; Fauth, *Helios Megistos*, 8–33.

53. *PGM IV*.610–16. Compare the phenomenon of glossolalia (the "tongues . . . of the angels," 1 Cor 13:1), and the divine pneuma's "groans" uttered by believers (Rom 8:26).

54. *PGM IV*.617–20.

55. Cf. the open door of heaven in Rev 4:1.

56. *PGM IV*.625.

57. *PGM IV*.639–41.

58. "Lord" (*kyrios*) is ubiquitous in the LXX as a translation for Yahweh. "Lord of heaven and earth": Gen 24:3; Tob 7:17 (Text Family BA); 10:14 (Sinaiticus); Matt 11:25; Luke 10:21; Acts 17:24. "God of gods": Ps 49:1 (LXX); Dan 2:47.

human mother, born from a mortal womb. Nevertheless he declares that—through the power of the Sun God—he has been reborn and immortalized (*apathanatistheis*). The immortalization is recognized as something special (he is one "out of myriads"), present ("in this very hour") and according to God's good pleasure (*dokēsin*). Interestingly, Helios turns out to be only a mediator necessary to introduce the initiate to "the greatest God." This is the God who fathered Helios. This is the God who will give the oracle. This is the God Helios Mithras.

Helios (the son) zooms to the axis on which the whole universe revolves. He is pictured on the top level of the universe, strolling on the firmament of the fixed stars. His father Mithras is beyond even these stars. To have him appear, the initiate needs a favorable arrangement of these stars (a new horoscope, fit for an immortalized being). He is instructed to stare (apparently at Helios) and make a mooing sound long and hard—straining his sides until complete loss of breath. He kisses his protective amulets and declares: "Protect me PROSUMHRI!"

The magical invocation serves as an open sesame: a door in heaven creaks open and the seven stars of the Great Bear constellation march out. Symbolically, they appear as replicas of the Egyptian goddess Hathor—young women with the faces of asps.[59] The initiate undertakes a formal greeting of each star. As if on cue, the seven stars of the Little Bear constellation also emerge. They wear linen aprons and have the faces of black bulls. The initiate offers each of them an even more elaborate greeting. In response, both sets of stars interlock in a favorable arrangement. The right horoscope has been achieved.

What follows is the final scene of the Rite—the sight of the most sacred mystery. Bolts of lightning streak downwards; lights sparkle out of nowhere; the initiate feels his body shake on earth—but in fact it is the whole earth that trembles! Out of the great Beyond, a gigantic God descends, his face like the sun. This God, Helios Mithras, appears almost exactly like Helios—a pictorial reminder of the oneness of Father and son.[60] He is young, with golden hair in a white tunic, wearing a golden crown and Persian-style trousers. In his right arm, he wields the gold shoulder of a bull. This shoulder represents the stars of the Great Bear constellation (depicted in the last scene). The

---

59. Hathor was "also a sky goddess, regarded as the Eye of the Sun God, Re; and as the personification of the sky itself" (Watterson, *Gods of Ancient Egypt*, 113). "The Seven Hathors were a group of goddesses, all of whom were forms of Hathor, who had the power to foretell the fate of a new-born child and to bestow gifts upon it. The Seven Hathors were thus analogous to the Greek *moirai* (Fates)" (ibid., 120).

60. Cf. John 10:30 ("I and the Father are one"). For Mithras as the hypercosmic Sun, see Ulansey, "Mithras," 257–64.

Egyptians called the Great Bear "the bull's shoulder," and Mithras wields it as the steering wheel of the whole universe.[61]

The appearance of Mithras is strikingly like the divine Christ depicted in the book of Revelation (Rev 1). Both have a gleaming face, fiery eyes, and hold seven stars in their right hands.[62] John, the seer of Revelation, falls as though dead before the divine Christ (Rev 1:17). The initiate in the Rite of Immortalization, by contrast, bellows like a bull, straining his abdomen, making his sense whirr. He kisses his protective amulets, stares at the God, and prays this sublime prayer:

> MOKRIMO PHERIMOPHERERI!
> My life! (of so and so) [the initiate names himself]
> Abide!
> Dwell in my soul!
> Never leave me, for I bid you: ENTHO PHENEN THROPIŌTH
> . . .
> Greetings, Lord, master of water!
> Greetings, dominator of earth!
> Greetings ruler of pneuma! [more magical names follow] . . .
> Speak an oracle, Lord, about such and such a matter [the magician fills in the blank].
> Lord, having been reborn (*palingenomenos*), I come out of the state of generation (*apogignomai*)!
> Increasing in power, and having been increased, I come to an end [as a mortal being] (*teleutō*).
> Coming out of animalic birth (*apo geneseōs zōogonou genomenos*), I, having been released, advance toward a state beyond birth (*eis apogenesian*),
> as you have brought into being,
> as you have legislated,
> as you have made this mystery;
> I am PHEOURA MIOURI!

The entreaty to "abide" (*mene su*) is reminiscent of Jesus' injunction in the Gospel of John: "Abide in me (*meinate en emoi*) and I in you" (15:4). As Jesus is the "life" (*zōē*) of the Christian (John 14:6), so Mithras is the "life" (*zōē*) of his devotee. Mithras is the master of creation (summed up by the elements). He is also the source of revelation.

---

61. *PGM* IV.700; cf. Manilius, *Astron.* 1.275–93. See further Beck, "Ponza Zodiac: II," 125–27; Ulansey, *Mithraic Mysteries*, 104–7; Edmonds, "Did the Mithraists Inhale?" 11–12; Edmonds, "Seizure of the Moon" 237.

62. Gleaming face: *PGM* IV.696–97; Rev 1:16. Fiery eyes: *PGM* IV.703; Rev 1:14. Seven stars: *PGM* IV.699–700; Rev 1:16.

In order to receive this revelation, the initiate must give his "qualifications" as it were. Having soared to the realm of the fixed stars—far above the world of change and entropy—the initiate has been reborn (*palingenomenos*) into a new condition, having left the state of becoming (*apogignomai*). Hans Dieter Betz takes the word *apogignomai* as a "death formula" comparable to Paul's declaration in Romans 14:7–9 ("we die to the Lord . . . we are the Lord's").[63] But in the context of an immortalization rite, *apogignomai* ought to mean "I come out of the state of generation (i.e., the realm of birth and death)."[64] The parallel verb *teleutō* means not "I am dying" (Betz)—an odd thing to say if the initiate is now immortalized—but "I come to an end [as a mortal being]."[65] This interpretation is confirmed by the next line, where the initiate comes out of animalic birth (literally "out of the birth of animalic reproduction," *apo geneseōs zōogonou*). The secret name of the initiate is reminiscent of the hidden name given to the Christian in Revelation 2:17 (written on a mysterious white stone).

Finally, Mithras pronounces his oracle. He offers it, we learn, in verse (as many Greek oracles were given). Not being able to bring pen and papyrus to heaven, the initiate is given an inexhaustible and infallible memory to retain the oracle—even if it turns out to be ten thousand lines![66] Back on earth, the oracle emerges from the mouth of the magician while he is in a state of prophetic ecstasy.[67] Divine revelation is spoken by human lips. The magic has worked marvelously! The narrative of the Immortalization breaks off.

Divinization or Divination?

It has long bothered commentators that the Rite of Immortalization presents such an odd juxtaposition of the awesome and the pedestrian. The magician becomes a god! But for what purpose? To receive an oracle "on whatever topic" he wants.[68] The Rite is called "Immortalization"—but in fact the main

---

63. Betz, "*Mithras Liturgy*," 192. He cites other interpretations on ibid., 191–92, n. 601.

64. Apogenesis must signify something similar to the "immortal birth" (*athanatos genesis*) mentioned in *PGM* IV.501; cf. 533. In Porphyry, "to go into apogenesis" means "to be raised again to life" (*anabiōskomenoi*) (*Antr. nymph.* 23). For the sun's role in apogenesis, cf. ibid., 29–31; Plutarch, *Fac.* 943a–945d; Plutarch, *Soc.* 591b; Julian, *Or.* 5.17; 12.14–32. See further Beck, "Place of the Lion," 48; Edmonds, "Did the Mithraists Inhale?" 14.

65. Cf. Betz, *Antike und Christentum*, 182.

66. *PGM* IV.727–32.

67. *PGM* IV.725–26.

68. *PGM* IV.718.

purpose appears to be *divination* not *divinization*.[69] Immortalization seems secondary. It is required to go to heaven (where only immortal things abide), but is not the goal in and of itself. It would be convenient to editorially extract an "original" Rite of Immortalization from the "magical" divination rite, but the two fit together seamlessly.[70] We might observe that the magician (having gone to such an effort to ascend!) would not ask the God to report on something trivial.[71] Other spells of divination, however, make one suspicious. In another encounter with Helios, the supreme God is called upon to "fetch lovers, send dreams, ask for dreams . . . attain goals, win victories, in short—everything."[72]

Temporary Eternal Life?

Another striking feature of the Immortalization Rite is that it is wholly temporary. Although a narrative of descent is not recounted, we can assume that at the end of the revelation, the magician's pneuma reenters his body allowing him to resume normal human life. The temporary nature of deification is underscored by the fact that it can be performed three times a year.[73] Interestingly, the magician who writes the spell (possibly a later editor) appends a later revelation of Mithras, who allows the immortalization to be performed once a month![74] But can the reception of eternal life be temporary? Here again we are reminded that deification comes in many different forms. We might suspect, however, that these temporary immortalizations anticipate a final deification of the magician after death.[75]

---

69. On magic and divination (equated since the first century C.E.), see Graf, "Magic and Divination," 283–98; Johnston and Struck, *Mantikê*; Johnston, *Ancient Greek Divination*, 144–82.

70. Calling the deification "religious" and the request for an oracle "magical" seems artificial (rightly, Segal, "Hellenistic Magic," 372).

71. Reitzenstein asserted that the object of the divine will for the magician is nothing other than deification (*Vergottung*) (*Die hellenistischen Mysterienreligionen*, 170).

72. *PGM* XIII.339–40, trans. Morton Smith, modified. Cf. lines 777–78 of our spell: "Ask the God for whatever you want and he will give it to you." This statement has parallels in the Christian Gospels (Matt 7:7–8; 21:22, par.).

73. *PGM* IV.747–48.

74. *PGM* IV.797.

75. Compare the "spell of Pnouthis" cited above (*PGM* I.190–91). According to Dieterich, the Rite of Immortalization "is the sacramental image of the soul's heavenly ascent, the obtaining of immortality which the believer in Mithras hoped to obtain with the actual end of his bodily life" (*Mithrasliturgie*, 83). See further Bousset, "Himmelsreise," 136; Tabor, *Things Unutterable*, 95; Betz, *Antike und Christentum*, 175–86.

Divine-Human Difference

Scholars often repeat that for non-Christians in the ancient Mediterranean world (sometimes called "pagans"), the boundary between the human and the divine was fluid.[76] The Rite of Immortalization, interestingly, does not support this idea. The deified magician—far from confusing the human and the divine—repeatedly states their difference. Three times he confesses his mortal condition—twice in rather vivid terms:

> . . . born mortal from a mortal womb.[77]

> . . . born from a mortal womb of so and so and from spermatic fluid.[78]

As a human being, he acknowledges that he cannot ascend to heaven on his own, and certainly not in his fleshly state.[79] Four times, moreover, the magician repeats a "formula" of Necessity:

> . . . after the present and immense need pressing down upon me![80]

> . . . after the present, bitter, and inexorable necessity pressing me down![81]

> . . . after the inexorable and pressing necessity![82]

> . . . on account of the pressing and bitter and inexorable necessity![83]

As a human being, the sorcerer knows that he is subject to his particular fate determined by the arrangement of stars at his birth. Only by ascending to the one who controls the stars—entering a state that is beyond birth itself—can he escape his fate. This freedom from fate is the fruit of the magician's deification.

76. Clauss, *Mithras*, 9–10. Cf. Johnson, *Among the Gentiles*, 36. The view is ubiquitous.

77. *PGM* IV.517–21; 529–32.

78. *PGM* IV.645–49.

79. *PGM* IV.529–32. This is the third time he confesses his mortality.

80. *PGM* IV.503–4.

81. *PGM* IV.525–26.

82. *PGM* IV.534–35.

83. *PGM* IV.605–6.

In the Body or Out of the Body?

An interesting question is whether the magician ascends in the body or out of it. He prays, notably, to be reborn "in mind" (*noēmati*). In addition, he is able to see himself ascend in his mind's eye. We should not conclude, however, that the ascent is purely imaginary. The initiate ascends to heaven by inhaling pneuma.[84] Pneuma—although a divine substance—is also a physical element. It is solar breath that becomes part of the "self" of the initiate. The initiate ascends by pneuma, because he *becomes* pneuma. In the Rite itself, we note that only the pneuma of the magician seeks to "run up and soar upward" past the gates of the Sun.[85] When he is in heaven, pneuma is the sole carrier of the magician's self. The Apostle Paul believed that divine pneuma could enter the self, but only when Christ returned could one fully become a "pneumatic body" (1 Cor 15:45) and rise to the stars. In the Rite of Immortalization, the magician achieved a fully pneumatic and star-like state in this present life.

Nature or Grace?

As a mortal being, the magician acknowledges that he cannot ascend to the stars. His repeated prayers to an assortment of gods and goddesses show that he is fully dependent on the divine for his ascent. The fact that he uses magical ointment and protective amulets only further reinforces his obedience to Mithras—for it is Mithras who revealed the recipes for the ointment, as well as how to construct the charms. The *practice* of deification does not annul the grace of the God who bestows it.

Importantly, the human nature of the magician is not totally opposed to divine grace. Above I noted that the four elements that constitute the human are also considered to be divine. The element of pneuma—which makes up the true self of the magician—is clearly divine, as it is the efflorescence of the Sun God. It must be breathed in (that is, come from outside)—although it is quickly integrated into the self. In sum, the magician must *pray* to be transferred to immortal birth (expressing his dependence on Helios Mithras), but this birth (as he confesses) is "consistent (*echomenōs*) with my underlying nature."[86]

84. Cf. *Chaldean Oracles* frag. 123 (Majercik).

85. *PGM* IV.586–87.

86. *PGM* IV.501–2. The manuscript reads *echomenos*, commonly emended to the adverb *echomenōs* (which I understand to mean "as is consistent with"). For other translation options, see Betz, "*Mithras Liturgy*," 113.

Ethics

Importantly, no ethical requirements are listed for the Rite of Immortalization. What is needed is (ritual) purity. The initiate is "in states of holiness made holy by holy rites" (*hagiois hagiastheis hagiasmasin*).[87] In the instructions appended to the Rite, we learn that for a week both the magician and his (optional) fellow initiate must keep themselves pure before their experience of immortalization. Specifically, they must abstain from meat and the bath (or bathhouse). In addition, the magician must test his co-initiate to see whether he (or as the introduction has it: she) is worthy and of stable character. He is required to judge her just as he would wish to be judged if he were undergoing the Rite. If his apprentice is refractory and does not follow instructions, for her the rite will be of no effect.[88] None of these stipulations (from our modern point of view) are strictly speaking ethical. The moralization of deification, as we shall see, only becomes thematic in philosophical and Christian circles.

Conclusion

For Albrecht Dieterich, "The heavenly ascent of the soul was the highest sacrament which the Mithraic initiate could participate in."[89] "The highest purpose of all religious thought," he believed, was "the exaltation of the soul to God,"[90] and it is "union with God" that, in the Rite of Immortalization, is "the purpose of the whole action."[91] Dieterich himself was uncomfortable with the idea that so lofty a religious goal could be attained by what he called "hocus pocus"—but this is exactly what the Rite of Immortalization teaches.[92] The indecipherable words, the protective amulets, the bizarre array of gods, the scarab ointment—even the whistling and popping sounds—all have a role to play in the magician's deification. But if the ancients pursued immortalization by magical means, the mystery of deification loses none of its power. Just as it was for Paul, deification is given as a gift by a supreme divinity, results from the reception of divine pneuma, and is accomplished through assimilation to God's son. Differences between the two forms of deification are obvious (Helios is not Christ), but the structural similarities

87. *PGM* IV.522.
88. *PGM* IV.739–43.
89. *Mithrasliturgie*, 91–92.
90. Ibid., 94.
91. Ibid., 179.
92. Ibid., 92.

are striking all the same. Deification, historically speaking, is the pursuit of both priest and sorcerer, both magician and apostle. In a particularly powerful way, the "Mithras Liturgy" creates a space where the vast arcs representing magic and religion converge.

Chapter 6

"I Have Been Born in Mind!"

Deification in the Hermetic Literature

Who in his own skill confiding
Shall with rule and line
Mark the border-land dividing
Human and divine?
Trismegistus! Three times greatest!
How thy name sublime
Has descended to this latest
Progeny of time!

—HENRY WORDSWORTH LONGFELLOW

I N COMPANY WITH HIS master Hermes, says the *Perfect Discourse,* Asclepius enters the inner shrine. Hermes bids Asclepius to take with him one other initiate: the beloved Tat. Only a few are invited into the shrine, for only a few have spiritually prepared for the revelation of holy mysteries. It would be impious to make public a teaching filled with "so great a majesty of divinity."[1] With one other initiate, then, Asclepius and Hermes silently enter the inner shrine.

It is the shrine, the reader discovers, of the holiest temple: the inner sanctum of the human mind. The mind, Hermes says, has the ability and vocation to meditate on the cosmos: land, sea, sky, and stars. These meditations lead like stepping stones to loftier levels of reality, deeper and deeper into the self. With Hermes as a guide, Asclepius and Tat reach the

1. *Ascl.* 1.

86

inner depths of their own self-consciousness. Their minds meditate on their minds. In themselves, they realize that they can transcend all the boundaries of the universe. They perceive themselves to have infinite ability. In their minds, Asclepius and Tat conclude, they are the same reality as the greatest and most divine power. Through intellect, they discover that the essence of God and humanity is one.

Asclepius and Tat are the most frequently mentioned disciples in the Hermetic literature. What group did they belong to or represent? Where did this group meet, and what did they do in their meetings? Theories have come and gone. Jean-André Festugière found "no trace in the Hermetic literature of ceremonies belonging to supposed believers in Hermes, nothing that resembles sacraments. . . . There is no clergy, no appearance of hierarchical organization, no degrees of initiation. . . . On the contrary . . . Hermeticism forthrightly expresses its loathing for material acts of worship."[2] In contrast, Gilles Quispel wrote that "It is now completely certain that there existed before and after the beginning of the Christian era in Alexandria [Egypt], a secret society, akin to a Masonic lodge. The members of the group called themselves 'brethren,' were initiated through a baptism of the Spirit, celebrated a sacred meal and read the Hermetic writings as edifying treatises for their spiritual progress."[3] More recently, Jean-Pierre Mahé asserts that the prayers in the Hermetic corpus "provide evidence that there were communities placed under the patronage of Hermes in which . . . prayer, characterized as . . . 'sacrifice of speech,' . . . could have the place of a true sacrament."[4] Today most scholars seem persuaded that references to "holy food,"[5] a holy embrace,[6] and formal prayers[7] suggest some sort of community and ritual life.[8]

2. Festugière *Révélation*, 1.81–84.

3. Quispel, "Preface," 10.

4. Mahé quoted in Copenhaver, *Hermetica*, 123. See further van den Broek, "Religious Practices," 77–96.

5. *NHC* VI.66.6.

6. *NHC* VI.6, 57.26–27; VI.7, 65.4.

7. E.g., *The Prayer of Thanksgiving* in *NHC* VI.7.

8. Most recently Van den Kerchove concludes that the "way of Hermes" is "a sequence of concrete ritual practices, some regular, some occasional, some temporary, others developing as a consequence of the disciple's formation. Some are a simple gesture, like a kiss. Others combine words and gestures like the rite of absorption or certain prayers. Almost all are based on a performative word, that of the teacher" (*Le voie d'Hermès*, 374–75). On the question of communities, she writes, "Collective prayers like the *Prayer of Thanksgiving*, common meals, the use of the term 'brother' in *CH* I 32 or in *NH* VI 52–54, suggest the existence of such groups" (ibid., 375). See further Giversen, "Hermetic Communities?" 49–54.

The Hermetic writings are called "Hermetic" because they are attributed to the god Hermes. Who was Hermes? In 1460, when a collection of Greek Hermetic treatises were put into the hands of the Italian scholar Marsilio Ficino, he identified Hermes with the hoary figure of Thoth. Thoth, the ancient Egyptian god-scribe, was believed by Ficino to have once been a man. He was older than Plato (427–347 B.C.E.), and a contemporary (possibly even teacher) of Moses the lawgiver who putatively lived in the thirteenth century B.C.E. Thoth-Hermes was called the "Thrice Great" ("Trismegistus"), according to Ficino, because "he was the greatest philosopher and the greatest priest and the greatest king," who stood first in the holy line of ancient theologians.[9]

If all this were true, the Hermetic writings would be dated to sometime in the 1200s B.C.E., or earlier. As it turns out, the great Calvinist scholar Isaac Casaubon in the seventeenth century demonstrated that the writings we have were most likely written sometime between 100 and 300 C.E. Though this fact sinks the (sensational) Renaissance theory of authorship, it opens up a fascinating new set of questions.

The author(s) of the literature, believed to be centered on the western banks of the Nile delta, are unknown. We do know, however, that they were prolific. Hermes the Thrice Great was renowned in Roman Egypt for his wisdom. Thus if Egyptian magician-priests desired to be widely read, they could attribute their works to Hermes. Even as early as 275 B.C.E., the Egyptian scholar Manetho wrote that Hermes already had credited to him 36,555 books![10] What remains of Hermetic literature is only a fragment of what it once was. The writings examined in this chapter are a fragment of this fragment. They include seventeen treatises written in Greek (called the *Corpus Hermeticum*), and the *Perfect Discourse* or *Asclepius* (originally written in Greek, but preserved in Latin and partially in Coptic).[11] This group of texts is often called "philosophic"—though it is acknowledged that Hermetic philosophy is indistinguishable from its theology.[12]

Although these texts seem to contradict each other at several points, the tensions can partly be explained in terms of the differences of intended audience that individual treatises presume.[13] My aim in this chapter is to

9. Copenhaver, *Hermetica*, xlviii.

10. Ibid., xvi.

11. For a discussion of other Hermetic texts, see ibid., xxxii–xliv. Below I will also make brief use of *The Discourse on the Eighth and Ninth* as well as the *Prayer of Thanksgiving* both preserved in Coptic in the Nag Hammadi Library (VI, 6–7).

12. The magic and alchemical branch of Hermetic literature—the so-called "technical Hermetica"—is not to be viewed as a lower form of literature or thought. See further Kingsley, "An Introduction," 17–40.

13. Fowden, *Egyptian Hermes*, 93, 103.

introduce the elements of what I take to be a basically coherent Hermetic theology of deification. For simplicity and convenience, I will refer to the Hermetic teachings under the (pseudonymous) name of its most prominent exponent, Hermes himself.

Although Hermes will not open a window onto a pre-Mosaic theology, he offers an important glimpse into a religious worldview that hoary Thoth could never have introduced: a Greco-Egyptian worldview existing at the same time that Christianity emerged and developed in Egypt. At the time, the Egyptian city of Alexandria was bursting with religious and philosophical pluralism—well represented in the Hermetic writings. Indeed, the Hermetic worldview incorporates and synthesizes a number of Platonic, Stoic, Jewish, and Egyptian ideas about God and human beings.[14] Consequently the Hermetic literature provides a diverse approach to God and deification.[15]

The Hermetic God

"It is God, O Asclepius, God led you to us so that you would take part in a divine discussion."[16] Who is the Hermetic God? Hermes calls him the "Unbegotten,"[17] the "Beginning,"[18] the "Lord of eternity,"[19] the "Lord of all"[20] who "transcends the height of the highest heaven, extending everywhere";[21] the Singular One similar to no one, who is "in himself and by himself . . . completely full and perfect."[22] He is "not muddied [by matter], limited by boundaries," nor is he subject to change. He is the unalterable, incorporeal, supreme Good.[23] He is not accessible to the senses, and he "lies beyond limitation, comprehension, and calculation."[24] The Hermetic God is mind, but

14. For the Egyptian roots of the Hermetica, note Mahé, *Hermès*, 2.449–56; Fowden, *Egyptian Hermes*, and Kingsley, "Poimandres," 44–76.

15. For the relation of Gnostic and Hermetic literature, see Layton, *Gnostic Scriptures*, 449; van den Broek, "Gnosticism and Hermetism," 1–20; Salaman points out that "The inclusion of four Hermetic works in a collection of Gnostic devotional literature [the Nag Hammadi Library] is an indication that Hermetic literature was considered an integral part of Gnostic study or devotion" (*Asclepius*, 27).

16. *Ascl.* 1.

17. CH 5.1.

18. CH 3.1.

19. *Ascl.*, 10.

20. *Ascl.*, 20.

21. *Ascl.*, 27.

22. *Ascl.*, 30.

23. CH 13.6.

24. *Ascl.*, 31.

beyond mind; spirit, but beyond spirit; light, but beyond light.[25] To speak most truly of this God, where and when and whence and how and what he is—is known to no one.[26]

Nevertheless the Hermetic God loves to reveal himself as Light and Life.[27] According to Hermes, God is "totally revealed and luminous."[28] His most appropriate names are "Supreme Goodness" and "Father." He is the Father because he begets all things and rules over all.[29] He is Supreme Good because he gives to all and receives nothing in return.[30] In his infinity, he is the source of all things and is all things.[31] "He has therefore all names," says Hermes, "because all names come from one Father, and that is why he himself has no name."[32] Thus the Divine Being, according to Hermes, is fully transcendent and fully present to everything. Or, in a maxim well known to medieval theologians, the Hermetic God "is an infinite sphere whose center is everywhere, and whose circumference is nowhere."

Since God is both totally distinct from and yet one with the world, one can hardly say that he hoards his divinity in a heavenly vault. Rather, like the sun, he lets his divine richness gush from him like an ever-flowing stream. In the Hermetic worldview, it is as if this mighty stream flows down over a giant staircase to form a graded hierarchy of divinity. This process of flowing out, or emanation, is the Hermetic way of explaining the begotten or "gener-ate" aspects of divine reality—aspects that subsist on a lower level than the high Deity. We find the graded hierarchy of divinity first emphasized in the visionary text *Poimandres*.[33]

According to this treatise, the first two emanations of God the Father are the Word (*Logos*) and the Cosmos (called *caelum*, or "Heaven" in the *Asclepius*). These two divinities, "born" from God the Father, fill the uppermost slots in the graded hierarchy of divinity. The Word is the intelligible aspect of God. The Cosmos, according to the *Asclepius*, is the "sensible god" (that is, the god who can be perceived).[34] In the *Poimandres*,

25. CH 2.14.

26. *Ascl.*, 29.

27. *Ascl.*, 29.

28. Literally "naked and appearing," CH 13.6.

29. CH 2.17.

30. CH 2.16.

31. CH 4.10.

32. CH 5.10.

33. *Poimandres* forms the first tractate of the *Corpus Hermeticum*. For the meaning of Poimandres as "the knowledge (or mind) of Re," see Kingsley, "Poimandres," 41–76.

34. For the sensible God distinguished from the "supreme" God, see *Ascl.* 16.

the Cosmos—fused with the Word—is depicted as the great Craftsman god who shapes and creates the material world.[35] Cosmos is made of air and fire, whereas the Word seems to be an entirely intellectual god. The Cosmos and the Word are the first two perfect images and "out-flowings" of God. From these flowed out all other levels of divinity: the sun, intelligible gods, *daimones*,[36] and the visible gods (i.e., astral bodies)—all variously discussed in the Hermetic literature.[37] Nevertheless the most important of these divine emanations, according to the *Poimandres*, was a being far superior to these lower gods, an entity called the Human Being.

Creation

The Father wished that there be another being beside him to enjoy the extraordinary beauty of the sensible god (the Cosmos). So he created the Human. It is right to capitalize the "h" in "human" because the first Human was the divine archetype, or perfect model of humanity. He (or s/he—since the archetypal Human was both male and female) emerged directly from the Father's essence, and was hence equal to God himself.[38] Since there is no matter in God, and the Human proceeded directly from God, the Human was at first wholly spiritual or intellectual and not bodily.

The Father fell in love with the Human as one falling in love with one's own self. Lovingly, the Father gave to the Human Being the power to complete the work of the physical world that Cosmos and the Word began. The Human set about this task which became for him his greatest danger.

Fall

As the story is told in *Poimandres*, the Human Being fatefully peeked beneath the clouds of the material creation. When he saw his image reflected in the water and earth below, he willed to inhabit this lower world. Instantly—since the Human was divine—his will was actualized. The Human Being assumed a human body, and was interwoven with nature. Creation was complete.

35. CH 1.10–11, cf. 4.1.

36. *Daimones*, whence we derive the English "demons," are not to be thought of as evil beings or fallen angels. In this time period, they are intermediate divinities, bodiless but subject to human-like passions.

37. *Ascl.* 19, 22–24, 37–38; CH 3.2–3.

38. CH 1.12.

In this account of creation, the first Human was not initially created from clay and then invested with the divine breath (or spirit) of life to become a living being (as in Gen 2:7). Rather, the archetypal Human was first directly given birth by God as an entirely spiritual (or intelligible) reality who fell into the flesh. When the Human whirled into the world, and other humans were produced from him, the human mind was intermixed with matter and corrupted. This mixing was so severe that a large number of people—in fact most—were drained of mind altogether. Nevertheless a minority of humans preserved intellect, even if it was hidden under a fog of forgetfulness.

Redemption

This small number of mind-endowed human beings, according to the Thrice Great, have a twofold nature.[39] One nature is bodily and mortal, the other is intellectual and immortal. The first nature is the material body. The material body is a corruptible substance foreign to intellect. Intellect is original and essential to humanity, and it cannot die.

Immortality, as a basic divine attribute, is an indicator of humanity's fundamental divinity.[40] Hermes stresses this point in the strongest possible terms. "Whatever lives," he says, "owes its immortality to mind, and most of all do humans, who are both most receptive of God and most coessential (*sunousiastikos*) with him."[41] The elect's recognition of their co-essentiality with God is the content of saving knowledge (*gnosis*) and the essential human task while existing on earth.

To sum up: true humanity and God, according to Hermes, are in essence one. Therefore, knowledge of God and knowledge of self are not only mutually related, but identical. The Delphic command to "know thyself" and the biblical command to "know the Lord" (Jer 31:34) end up being the same injunction. On what basis? On the basis of mind. Hermes says:

> Intellect, O Tat, is of God's very essence (*ousias*)—if there is such a thing as the essence of God, and whatever it is, he alone accurately knows it. The [human] mind, then, is not separated off from God's essentiality (*ousiotētos*), but is united to it, as light to the sun.[42]

39. For the language of dual natures, see *Ascl.*, 22.
40. Litwa, *We are Being Transformed*, 44–45. Cf. Bell, *Greek Mythology*, 51–52.
41. CH 12.19.
42. CH 12.1. Hermes goes on to teach that "in humans this mind is God; among humans, therefore, some are gods and their humanity is near to divinity."

Humans who possess intellect are not strictly speaking identical to God. They are like rays, while God is the sun. Nevertheless there is a genetic continuity between human and divine reality based on mind. Hermes calls humanity an "awesome wonder! (*magnam miraculum*), a living thing to be worshiped and honored" because humans, through their power of intellect, can change their nature into divine reality.[43] The specific power that humans use to transport themselves into divinity in the *Poimandres* is called "recognition": "let the one who has mind recognize that he is immortal!"[44] According to Hermes, it is a divine revelation that "he who has understood himself advances toward God."[45]

The logic, as the figure of Poimandres explains, is as follows: God is life and light, and humans are from life and light. To recognize this divine derivation is to recognize oneself and to reenter life.[46] Recognition is redemption. Those endowed with mind merely need to be aroused from their "drunkenness." Then they need to be baptized (literally, "dunked" or "submerged") into the name of Intellect.

> Baptize yourself into the mixing bowl [of mind] if your heart has the strength, if it believes, you will rise up again to the one who sent the mixing bowl below, if it recognizes the purpose for its existence.[47]

This baptism does not remove original sin, but grants knowledge of one's original divinity. No priest is needed for this rite—only the human self, which realizes its divine origin and end. Those who are able to make this realization ensure their future ascent to God. These initiates do not have to recite a creed; instead they must realize why they have come into existence. Unless people renounce and even despise their material husk (the false self) they will not be able to fulfill the human task: the realization of their natural union with God.[48]

---

43. *Ascl.*, 6.

44. CH 1.18.

45. CH 1.21.

46. Ibid.

47. CH 4.4.

48. CH 4.6. Hermes, by the standards of other contemporary philosophies, is unusually approving of bodily pleasures, and in particular sexual union (see *Ascl.* 21 and CH 2, where Hermes demands that every man have at least one child to avoid hellfire).

Hermetic Deification

In Hermetic thought, the major distinction between the human and the divine Mind is that the divine Mind is vastly purer. Yet human beings, by shedding impure thoughts, can become God. They can, through a process of spiritual ascension, strip off the body and its passions to become entirely Mind.

The way to be saved, Plato said of old, is to take flight from this world and be assimilated to God.[49] Hermes carries on this tradition. The surest method to attain this assimilation is the death of the material encasing. The *Poimandres* teaches that the holy and good soul makes its ascent to God after the body dies.[50] Nevertheless the ascent can partially begin in this life through contemplation.[51] In the *Asclepius*, Hermes defines death as "the extinction of bodily consciousness."[52] Contemplation is a kind of death insofar as it is the process whereby the Hermetic initiate abandons the bodily senses together with the false way of thinking guided by earthly perception.

Hermetic contemplation begins with a vision of the cosmos. Its initial stage might be likened to science, which is founded on repeated and studied empirical observation. In a dialogue with his mind, Hermes asks, "Is God unseen?" His mind replies, "Hush! Who is more manifest than he? For this reason alone has he made all things—that through them all you may see him."[53] God is invisible, incorporeal, and beyond the reach of the mind, but his ordering power and divine majesty are clearly visible through the things that have been made.[54] The God visible in creation is the Craftsman God. In the *Poimandres*, the Father gave birth by his Word to another Mind, the Craftsman Mind, who is a God of fire and wind. This God, united with the Word, designed and organized the physical world.[55]

The organization of the physical world is important. In ancient cosmology, there was a basic division between reality that was above the moon and reality that was below it. Although sublunar reality is constantly in flux, superlunary bodies move in perfect order.[56] This order presumes an intelligence. The intelligence that people are able to observe in the cosmos is, according to Hermes, God the Craftsman Mind. "If you wish to contemplate

---

49. Plato, *Theaetetus* 176b.
50. CH 1.24–25; see also 10.16, 18.
51. CH 1.4. The human can "ascend" while not leaving the earth (CH 10.25).
52. *Ascl.* 27.
53. CH 11.22; cf. 12.20.
54. CH 5.4; cf. Rom 1:20.
55. CH 1.9–11.
56. For the world as constantly changing, see *Ascl.* 30.

him," Hermes proposes, "behold the arrangement of the cosmos and the fine order of this array, and behold how all that is visible is so by necessity, how all that has happened and now happens is through providence. Observe matter, most full of life, this god of such magnitude, being moved with all that is good and beautiful."[57]

"Observe matter!" Hermes says, and there you will see God. Specifically, he tells his disciples to study the sciences of geometry, music, and astronomy for what they can reveal about the Craftsman's design. Both geometry and music, Hermes avows, bestow knowledge of the order of all things, which is "whatsoever God's reason has decreed."[58] Even more does astronomy manifest the majesty of God. "If you would see God," Hermes declares, "think of the sun, think of the moon's course, think of the order of the stars!"[59]

Nevertheless, the object of these sciences is never the physical phenomena themselves. It is rather the everlasting power and divinity of Intellect intuited by the human mind. Hermes expects his disciples to observe material reality with their physical eyes—but only to awaken spiritual vision. Physical phenomena, in this view, are stepping stones toward the sight of more ultimate reality, reality that culminates in a vision of the whole universe—an ecstatic flight through the cosmos. Hermes declares:

> Would that you could grow wings and fly up into the air, lifted between earth and heaven to see the solid earth, the fluid sea, the streaming rivers, the pliant air, the piercing fire, the coursing stars, and heaven speeding on its axis about the same points. Oh, this is a most happy sight to see, my child, to have a vision of all these in a single instant, to see the motionless set in motion and the invisible made visible through the things that it makes! This is the order of the cosmos, and this is the beauty of the order.[60]

But there is no ultimate satisfaction even with the coursing stars of the upper world. The Hermetic spirit searches for a Being higher than this universe.

> Do you see how many bodies we must pass through, my child, how many troops of daimones, [cosmic] connections and stellar circuits in order to hasten toward the One and Only? For the

57. CH 12.21.
58. *Ascl.* 13.
59. CH 5.3.
60. CH 5.5.

Supreme Good is untraversable, infinite, and unending. . . . So
let us . . . travel with all speed.[61]

At its heart, the Hermetic vision calls for an assimilation to a God who
is superior to fire and wind. This upward journey requires eyes that penetrate deeper than physical eyes, and knowledge that transcends scientific
knowledge. It requires the eyes of intellect, a spiritual seeing that Hermes
calls *noēsis*.[62]

Noēsis has a twofold meaning in the Hermetic literature. In its initial
phase, it means something akin to "understanding." Understanding,
according to Hermes, begins with imagination. Great artists and writers
use imagination to take in the images of their environment, transform it in
the smelting chamber of their minds, and then pour out worlds of fantasy,
which can become great literature or works of art. For Hermes, the imagination is not the stuff of fantasy. It holds the ideas of a superior world—
forms that really and eternally exist in the Mind of God. "You must think of
God in this way," he says, "as having everything—the cosmos, himself, the
universe—like thoughts within himself."[63] God has within his intellect the
entire universe in an intelligible form. All reality exists in a truer form in
God's mind as eternal Ideas. Since the Ideas are immaterial, there is no actual
space between them in the divine Intellect.[64] Thus the Hermetic contempla-
tor, thinking the transcendent Ideas of India, ocean, and sky in Intellect, can
be at all three places at once. "Imagine (*noēson*)," Hermes urges, "from your
own inherent powers":

order your soul to travel to India, and it will be there quicker
than your command. Bid it to cross over to the ocean and again
it is there at once—not as having passed from place to place but
simply as being there. Order it to fly up to heaven and it will
not lack wings, nor will anything impede it, neither the fire of
the sun, nor the ether, nor the whirlwind, nor the bodies of the
other stars—but cutting through them all it will soar up to the
last body. And if you wish to break through the universe itself
and to contemplate what is beyond (if there is anything beyond
the cosmos)—it is within your power.[65]

61. CH 4.8–9.
62. CH 5.2; 7.2; 10.5. Hermes calls the eyes of the intellect the "eyes of the heart"
(CH 4.11; 7.1; cf. 7.1).
63. CH 11.20.
64. CH 12.8; cf. *Ascl.* 34.
65. CH 11.19.

Imagination, in this view, leads to ecstasy. Ecstasy literally means "standing outside" of oneself. For Hermes, it means transcending the limits of one's bodily (space-bound) nature. "It is impossible, my son," urges Hermes, "for the soul who has beheld the beauty of the Supreme Good to become a god while in the body."[66] But if the body can be transcended, a deifying union with God's Intellect can become reality.

As Intellect, God's Ideas make up the very substance of God. To think these Ideas is thus in some way to be God already. Thinking is being, being is thinking. As the stuff of the divine Mind, the Ideas are cosmic, unchanging, and one. Therefore, for Hermes to comprehend these Ideas—and indeed, the entire intelligible world—is for him to become cosmic, unchanging, and one. His goal is to become all mind, and therefore equal to God: "If you do not make yourself equal to God, you cannot understand God. Like is understood by like. Make yourself grow to immeasurable immensity!"[67]

According to Hermes, the human mind, as coessential with God's mind, not only transcends space. It can also transcend time. Thus he commands in tractate 11: "Leap out from every body—transcend all time. Become eternity and thus you will understand (*noēseis*) God!"[68] Just as everything in Intellect is one, so it is always the same. Thus there need be no measure of change, or time. God's Mind is eternal. In Mind, Hermes himself is eternal. He thinks, and therefore is God.

Hermes' equality with divine Intellect seems unlimited. He readily bids his disciples to ascribe to themselves a host of divine attributes: unbounded power, everlasting life, limitless knowledge, even omnipresence:

> Suppose nothing to be impossible for yourself. Consider yourself immortal and able to understand everything, all art, all learning, the temper of every living thing. Become higher than all heights and lower than all depths. Sense as one within yourself the entire creation: fire, water, the dry, and the wet. Conceive yourself to be in all places at the same time: in earth, in the sea, in heaven; be not yet born, be within the womb, be young, old, dead, beyond death. And when you have understood all these at once—times, places, things, qualities, quantities—then you can understand (*noēsai*) God.[69]

This kind of ecstatic, deifying understanding is not foreign to Hermes' own experience. He testifies at one point: "Whenever I see within myself the

66. CH 10.6–7.
67. CH 11.19.
68. Ibid.
69. Ibid.

simple vision brought to birth out of God's mercy, I have passed through myself into a body that can never die. And now I am not what I was before; but I am born in Mind."[70]

In *The Discourse of the Eighth and Ninth* (another Hermetic document), Hermes enters into the highest spheres of the cosmos and sees a light along with "indescribable depths." Although still on earth, he feels himself become Mind, and he sees himself as Mind.[71] The universe rejoices, and is filled with the life of an intellectualized Hermes. Hermes becomes lord and "master of the universe."[72] He becomes providence, "aeon of the aeons, great divine spirit, and "by a spirit he gives rain upon everyone."[73] The vision is itself deifying as is made clear in the prayer of thanksgiving added after the *Discourse*: "We rejoice because You [God] have shown us Yourself. We rejoice because while we were in [the] body, You deified (*apotheiōsas*) us through knowledge of you" (64.16–19).[74]

In Tractate 13 of the *Hermetic Corpus*, Hermes declares that he feels himself become simple and one like God. "Yes," he says,

> my former form, even of my own [composite] constitution is of no concern. Color, touch, or size I no longer have; I am a stranger to them. Now you see me with your eyes, my child, but by gazing with bodily sight you do not understand what I am.[75]

Just as Intellect is not beheld with physical eyes, so Hermes is not beheld with human vision. He is intelligible, just like the intelligible God. In his inner nature Hermes was always of a piece with the intelligible. He does not need to make himself God. He has always been God, and has merely to realize it. The dynamics of such a holy realization is still, however, a true mode of deification. As Poimandres says in the tractate that bears his name: "This is the good for those who have attained gnosis: to become God (*theōthēnai*)."[76]

If the attainment of gnosis is deification, then deification can be begun in this life. In *The Prayer of Thanksgiving*, Hermes rejoices because, "while we were in (the) body, you [God] have deified us through knowledge of

---

70. CH 13.3.

71. *NHC* VI,6, 57.28–59.17.

72. *NHC* VI,6, 59.18–19.

73. *NHC* VI,6, 58.32–59.9.

74. See further Mahé, "A Reading," 79–86.

75. CH 13.3.

76. CH 1.26; cf. 10.6.

you."[77] Since divine mind is Hermes' true being, he is not limited by the strictures of material bodies—even when his own body breaks down. Hermes' mortality is thus not an objection to his divinity because Hermes is *not his body*. Therefore, what humans normally call death is, for Hermes, an ascent into a truer, more divine life. When his body and passions are finally sloughed off, his self can truly be what it is without obstruction. At this time, Hermes will experience the ultimate transformative and deifying ascent. "Stripped of the effects of the cosmic framework," Poimandres says, "the human enters the region of the eighth sphere [outside our cosmos]; he has his own proper power, and along with the blessed he hymns the Father. Those present there rejoice together in his presence, and, having become like his companions, he also hears certain powers that exist beyond the eighth sphere and hymn God with sweet voice. They rise up to the Father in order and surrender themselves to the powers, and, having become powers, they enter into God."[78]

Qualifications

I have spoken of God as Mind (*Nous*) and Hermes as one with divine Mind. Nonetheless, mind is not the deepest aspect of God. God is also the source or cause of Mind.[79] Therefore Hermes' union with divine Intellect is not his ultimate goal. He yearns "to make the eyes of [his] mind fly up and gaze at the beauty of that Supreme Good, incorruptible and incomprehensible."[80] For Hermes, there remains a God beyond Mind, beyond intelligibility, beyond essence, beyond definition, and beyond name.[81]

This God, unlike Intellect, is not able to be thought. Hermes affirms in one treatise that the essence of the mind is God, but he is quick to express hesitation about whether God, in his deepest aspect, has an essence.[82] God as the Supreme Good is totally transcendent and thus beyond essence. Thus one must be careful about calling the deified Hermes coessential with

---

77. NHC VI.7, 64.18–19. The Coptic has "you made us gods [or divine: *akaan nnoute*]." Papyrus *Mimaut* (followed here) preserves the Greek term for deification (*apetheōsas*) (PGM 3.599–601). The Latin loosely translates the phrase: "because while sown in bodies you considered it worthy (*fueris . . . dignatus*) to consecrate us to (or in) eternity (*aeternitati . . . consecrare*)." For the texts, see Parrott, ed., *Nag Hammadi Codices*, 382.

78. CH 1.26, trans. Copenhaver, modified

79. CH 2.14.

80. CH 10.5.

81. For the Hermetic God as "greater than any name" see CH 5.1, 10, *Ascl.* 20, cf. 31.

82. CH 12.1; cf. 2.5, 6.4.

God. As mind, Hermes can embody God's ultimate power, knowledge, omnipresence, simplicity, and even eternity. Yet he will never be the maker of eternity,[83] unbegotten,[84] or supremely Good, as the ultimate God is. God alone, Hermes underlines, is the Supreme Good.[85]

> All the immortal gods are honored with the name of "God."
> However, God is good, not by honorary title, but by his nature.
> For the nature of God is one: Supreme Goodness.[86]

All other beings, mortal or divine, are separable from Goodness—even Intellect. The ultimate God, according to Hermes, is not Mind, but the source of Mind, the source of all reality,[87] and of all divinity.[88]

Conclusion: Grace

If Hermes becomes one with divine Mind, it is not because he has climbed to heaven by his own resources. Hermes' birth in and as Mind is, as we have seen, "brought to birth out of God's mercy."[89] Deification in Hermetic literature is cooperative: Hermes ascends to God, but the actual vision "is experienced as a gift from the other side."[90] In *The Discourse of the Eighth and Ninth*, Hermes and his son Tat undergo strict mental and spiritual preparation to attain to the vision of God. Ultimately, however, God must come to meet those who would be one with him. Thus before the vision Hermes cries out in ecstasy: "The power which is light [i.e., the intelligible God] is coming to us!"[91]

Hermes does not end his discourse by trumpeting his identity with God. Although Hermes has been deified, he acknowledges a higher God: "For it is right before God that we keep silent about what is hidden."[92] To be sure, at one point Hermes says that by empirical knowledge and gnosis, humans are better than gods (*efsatp annoute*).[93] But the gods he mentions

83. CH 11.2.
84. CH 8.2, 2.4.
85. CH 2.14.
86. CH 2.16; cf. 11.5.
87. CH 10.1; cf. 9.1.
88. CH 9.1.
89. CH 13.3.
90. Van den Broek, "Religious Practices," 95.
91. *NHC* VI, 57.29–30, cited by van den Broek, "Religious Practices," 95.
92. *NHC* VI 59.13–14.
93. *NHC* VI,8 67.23—68.15.

here are stars and aerial *daimones*.[94] Moreover, the reason why humans become superior to these mediate divinities is because—although these gods are mortal—humans are both immortal *and* mortal. Thus ironically it is their mortality that makes humans superior.

With the high God matters are different. Hermes frequently calls Asclepius and Tat to thank the high God and recognize his eternal superiority. Choosing the incorporeal and divine, Hermes says, not only "makes the human into a god," it also "shows reverence toward God."[95] This is the humble attitude of Hermes the Thrice Great. As the paradigmatic deified human being, Hermes is not prideful, but pious. At the end of the *Poimandres*—after his vision of post-mortem deification—he bursts forth in song to the highest God:

> Holy are you, stronger than all power
> Holy are you, transcending preeminence
> Holy are you, who surpass praises.
> Accept my reason's pure offerings, from soul and heart stretched
> up to you, O unutterable, unspeakable, whose name nothing
> but the silence can express. Give ear to me who pray that I may
> never fail of gnosis, which is our common being's nature . . .

Hermes' spiritual wonder ends in the quiet of perfect stillness. God, he concludes, is he "of whom no words can tell, no tongue can speak, whom silence only can declare." "When you have nothing to say about it," says the Thrice Great, "then you will see it; for its *gnosis* is sacred silence."[96]

94. Mahé, "La voie d'immortalité," 353.
95. CH 4.7.
96. CH 10.5; cf. 1.30, 31; 10.5, 9.

Chapter 7

"I Have Become Identical
with the Divine"

Plotinus on Deification

After his deliverance from the body the god says that he came
to "the company of heaven," and that there affection rules
and desire and joy and love kindled by God, and the sons of
God hold their stations, who are judges of the souls. . . . These
are their companions, Plato, Pythagoras, and all who "set the
dance of immortal love."

—PORPHYRY, *LIFE OF PLOTINUS*, 23.29–37

THE PHILOSOPHER PLOTINUS (205–70 C.E.) famously wrote that "Our
concern . . . is not to be out of sin, but to be god (*theon einai*)" (*Enn.*
1.2.6.2).[1] His last words according to his disciple Eustochius were: "Try to
bring back the god in you (*ton en humin theon*) to the divine in the All (*to
en tōi panti theon*)."[2] One might say that the entire philosophy of Plotinus
is the path of realizing one's own divinity as part of a greater journey of the
cosmos toward God.

As one "who seemed ashamed to be in the body," Plotinus was hesitant
to tell the story of his race, nation, and family.[3] He refused even to reveal
the date of his birthday, lest anyone should celebrate it with a sacrifice or

1. The *Enneads* are a set of fifty-four treatises written by Plotinus and edited by his
student Porphyry. Translations are taken from the LCL edition of A. H. Armstrong.

2. *Vit. Plot.* 2.26–27.

3. Ibid., 1.

feast.[4] What we do know are fragments of a life: he was born in Lycopo-
lis in Upper Egypt, and studied philosophy in Alexandria for eleven years
under the great Platonist Ammonius Saccas. After briefly joining Gordian
III's campaign against the Parthians, he came west to Rome and set up his
school of philosophy.

In Rome, Plotinus was to become one of the greatest philosophers of
the ancient world. This short chapter cannot cover his philosophy in any
depth. The aim is to unravel his understanding of deification. To do this, I
will reconstruct a narrative—pulling from a variety of his treatises—of what
one might call Plotinus' story of God and the soul. The two basic questions I
seek to answer in telling this narrative are basic to any vision of deification,
namely, "what is God?" and "what is human?"

What is God?

"Upon the king of all do all things turn; he is the end of all things and the
cause of all good. Things of the second order turn upon the second principle,
and those of the third order upon the third."[5] Adapting this enigmatic text
from Plato's *Second Letter*, Plotinus envisions three fundamental levels of
divinity: the One, Intellect, and Soul (*Enn.* 5.1.10.1–4).[6] The One (*to Hen*),
or Good, is the source of all divinity—but beyond divinity (6.9.6.12–14) as
well as beyond speech, thought, awareness, and even being (5.3.14.19–20).[7]
Intellect (*Nous*)—analogous to the Christian Logos—emerges from the One
as Thought (subject) thinking Itself (object), always in union with itself.
Intellect, or Being, is the fullness of the Platonic world of Forms, where the
models of things on earth abide in an unimaginable intensity of light "boiling with life" (6.7.12.23).[8] Soul (*Psychē*) is the third grade of divinity whose
nature is to turn toward and imitate Intellect. The World Soul is the mind
of our universe, effortlessly making and directing the material world, while
itself completely focused on Intellect.[9] The stars in heaven are visible gods
made up of a pure form of Soul (5.8.3). A vast number of individual disembodied souls float about the universe as daimones (who are, in Platonic
theology, fundamentally good beings). For the completion of the universe,

4. Ibid., 2.
5. Plato, *Epistles* II.312e.
6. Cf. *Enn.* 2.9.1.12–16.
7. See further Meijer, *Plotinus on the Good*, 3–64; Gerson, *Plotinus*, 15–41;
Bussanich, "Plotinus' Metaphysics," 38–65.
8. On Intellect, see further Gerson, *Plotinus*, 42–58.
9. See further ibid., 58–64.

many individual souls are incarnated in earthly bodies: humans, animals, and plants. As one descends from humans to plants, however, the purity of soul degrades as it is more and more mixed with matter and becomes less and less conscious of itself and God. For earthly beings, embodied life is a only a brief interval in the eternal life of souls who constantly go in and out of bodies (4.3.12.1–25).

For Plotinus, there is a basic difference between the divinity of Intellect (or intelligible divinity) and the divinity of Soul (or psychic divinity). Intelligible divinity is the divinity of Intellect and the Forms; it is divinity "out of this world" (or extracosmic). Psychic divinity, on the other hand, is divinity that belongs to this world. It pervades the universe through the World Soul and inhabits beings from stars to starfish. Since soul is divine, all beings enlivened by soul can be called divine as well. Thus Plotinus says that the world is made up mostly of gods (*to pleiston tou kosmou theoi*) (3.2.8.5).[10] When he affirms that the human mind is a god of sorts, he means that the human possesses the "soul grade" of divinity. When a human soul reaches its fullest potential, however, it can perfectly reflect and participate in the higher divinity of Intellect. The key element of Plotinian deification is in fact the transition from the soul level to the intelligible level of divinity. For Plotinus, to be "one with God" is to be one with Intellect.

According to our philosopher, contracting all divinity into a single divine being does not increase the glory of God. What displays the greatness and power of divinity is its ability to infinitely expand and radiate to the farthest reaches of the universe. The expanse of divinity ends only at matter, which Plotinus thinks of as non-being. Thus in Plotinus' thought, deification is the return of radiated divinity to its divine epicenter. The immutable, all-powerful God (or Intellect) retains his supremacy, unjealous of the souls below who advance toward him. "Abiding who he is, he makes many gods (*pollous poiēi* [*theous*]), all depending upon himself and existing through him and from him. This universe exists through him and looks to him, the whole of it and each and every one of the gods in it" (2.9.9.38–40).

What is the Human?

For Plotinus, the source of life in all embodied beings is soul. The soul, regardless of what organism it enlivens, is inherently immortal. It has "life of itself (*ex heautou zōē*), which cannot perish" (4.7.11.2). As an immortal reality, the soul is also divine, or part of the divine world. Humans are made

---

10. Cf. Thales, who taught that the world was alive and full of daimones (Diogenes Laertius, *Vit. philosoph.* 1.27).

up of bodies linked with souls, but the link is not direct. Body is united with a "trace" or "illumination" of soul resulting in an entity that Plotinus calls "the composite" (*to sunamphoteron*) (1.1.5.9, 17) or "the living being" (*to zōon*) (1.1.5.1). The composite is the "we" or the center of our everyday consciousness. The soul in itself, however, remains apart as a higher element in the human constitution. According to Plato's dialogue *Alcibiades I*—which often served as an introduction to Platonism in the ancient world—the true self is the soul (130c). Plotinus affirms this teaching even more thoroughly. There is a part of ourselves—the soul or mind—completely unaffected by the confusion of this world and the turbulence within.[11] The body and bodily passions are not part of human nature in itself. It is the mind (*nous*) that is the true human within (1.1.7.18–19; 1.1.10.7–8).[12] The human mind makes us who we are and gives us the opportunity to be higher than we now are.

Plotinus believes that there is even a part of our mind that remains "undescended" as an autonomous component of Intellect (2.9.2.7–19). In this way, the summit of our soul always abides in the intelligible world (4.8.8.1–6). As we are typically unaware of our subconscious mind (so Freud), we are also usually unaware of our "superconscious" mind (so Plotinus). Our unawareness, however, does not lessen the fact that in eternity humans exist in union with God (Intellect). Paradoxically, this union is both undifferentiated (since Intellect as a substance is one), and allows humans to be distinct (since thoughts in Intellect can be distinguished). The experience of the upper divine Mind is open to all, but known only to a few who are practiced in contemplation.[13]

According to Plato's *Timaeus*, the Maker of the world (or Demiurge) formed the souls of human beings from the same reality as the World Soul, but at a second and third grade of purity.[14] Though lesser than the World Soul, Plotinus wrote, the human soul is still her "sister" (*Enn.* 4.3.6.13–14; 2.9.18.16), part of a common family (*genos koinon*) (4.3.2.1–3).[15] Consequently, the human soul is "something divine" (*theion*) (5.1.10.11–13; 1.6.6.31). Since soul is divine reality (at two removes from the One) Plotinus can sometimes call the soul a "god" (5.1.2.41–47; cf. 1.2.2.25). Nevertheless, he makes plain that the human soul is a god of the lowest rank (*theos ousa ho husteros*) (4.8.5.25–27). The low standing is due to the fact that, although

11. See further Dillon, "An Ethic," 326.

12. Cf. Plato, *Resp.* 590a9; 588c7.

13. See further Wald, *Self-Intellection*, 157–59. Narbonne traces the undescended intellect to Gnostic teaching (*Plotinus in Dialogue*, 55–77).

14. Plato, *Tim.* 41d; cf. Plotinus, *Enn.* 4.3.6.27–34.

15. See further Helleman-Elgersma, *Soul-Sisters*, 57–88.

the highest aspect of the human soul is on the level of the intelligible, it is on its lowest rung" and has "a common boundary with the perceptible" (4.8.7.6–8).[16] Stuck between gods and animals, the human soul can be viewed as sinful, earthly, and even evil. Yet if we examine the soul itself apart from its relation to body, Plotinus says, humans "deviate very little from the beings [i.e., gods and daimones] above" (4.7.10.20–21). Plotinus thus applies the old line from Empedocles to every human being: "Greetings! I am for you an immortal god!"[17] One's godhood is fully realized when one has ascended fully to the intelligible level of divinity and is "concentrated totally on becoming like to it" (4.7.10.40).

The Image of God

As in Christian theories of deification, the Plotinian human is an image of God. For Plotinus, the primary image of God is in fact a higher divine entity: the World Soul (cf. 2 Cor 4:4; Col 1:15). Nevertheless, he occasionally calls humans the image of God, and specifically God as Intellect. The human soul, Plotinus says, is an image of Intellect (eikōn tis esti nou) (Enn. 5.1.3.8). When the soul engages in thinking it becomes deiform (theoeidē)—since God is Mind (5.3.8.47–49). The goal of the image is to conform to the archetype (6.9.11.45). One does so not simply by living immortally (all souls are immortal), but by exercising and identifying with one's mind. For Plotinus, to become the form of Intellect (nooeidē) is to become the form of God (theoeidē).

The History and Destiny of the Soul

The human soul, though it is divine (theion) and comes from above (ek tōn topōn tōn anō), enters into the body and "comes to this world by a spontaneous inclination" (4.8.5.25–27). In its embodied state, the human soul indwells the middle place between the souls of cosmic gods (e.g., stars, daimones) and beasts (3.2.8.9–12). The human soul is not a stable, immutable entity. "[T]he soul is many things, and all things, both the things above and the things below down to the limits of all life" (3.4.3.21–23). The soul can rise up or down on the scale of being, modulating itself to fit the existence of an animal or a god. Plotinus, in other words, accepts a system of karma wherein souls who do evil or good are reincarnated in respectively lower or higher forms of life. Accordingly—along with deification—Plotinus presents

16. Cf. Enn. 4.1.1; 4.8.7.6; 4.7.10.
17. DK 31 B 112.4

the possibilities of both theriofication (becoming an animal) and phutification (becoming a plant). If one refuses to cultivate one's mind and becomes absorbed in sense-perceptible objects, one will become an animal in the next life. "[I]f their sense perceptions have been accompanied by passionate temper," Plotinus states, "they become wild animals . . . those whose sense-perceptions went with desires of the flesh and the delight of the desiring part of the soul become lustful and gluttonous animals.[18] But if they did not even live by sense along with their desires but coupled them with dullness of perception, they even turn into plants" (3.4.2.18–23). Those, however, who concentrate their minds on God, identifying with their intellect, eventually break the cycle of re-enfleshment and rise to the level of the Forms.

Nevertheless, the disincarnate soul does not immediately become a god on the level of Intellect. The transition to the higher levels of deity is more gradual. It is likely that in the next life a virtuous person will transition into a daimonic state (3.4.3.18–21). A daimon is a god of sorts, since it belongs on the same order as a god (6.7.6.28–32). Nevertheless a daimon is not wholly removed from the world of matter (consequently, it is not wholly pure) (3.4.6.31–32). In Plato's *Symposium*, the female sage Diotima teaches that a daimon is a mediating being between gods and humans—more divine than a human, but less than a full-fledged god (202d–203a). In Plotinus' language, a daimon "is an imitation of a god (*mimēma theou*), dependent on God" (6.7.6.28–32).

In the *Timaeus*, Plato calls the upper soul of human beings (or mind) a daimon (*daimona*) dwelling on top of the body.[19] Plotinus interprets this saying to mean that everyone has a guardian daimon as a higher, noetic "second self." "If one is able to follow the daimon which is above him," he observes, "one comes to be oneself above, living as the daimon, and giving the pre-eminence to that better part of oneself to which one is being led; and after that daimon one rises to another, until one reaches the heights" (3.4.3.18–21). Even on earth, the noble person (*ho spoudaios*) is "himself a daimon (*daimōn autos*) or on the level of a daimon (*kata daimona*), and his guardian daimon is a god (*theos*)" (3.4.6.3–4).

In his *Life of Plotinus*, Porphyry tells the story of Plotinus going to an Egyptian priest in order to call up Plotinus' guardian daimon. After the secret ritual, what appears—to the surprise of everyone present—was no mere daimon, but a god (*theon*).[20] Plotinus was one of those saints who

---

18. Cf. Plato, *Phaedo* 81e–82b; *Resp.* 10.620; *Tim.* 91–92.

19. Plato, *Tim.* 90a.

20. Porphyry, *Vit. Plot.* 10.15–25.

after death may have risen immediately to the level of a god.[21] In a normal scenario, however, a human who transitions into a daimonic state after the death of the body continues to have an "element of involuntary impulse" (1.2.6.4). When this impulse is eventually removed, "one will be simply a god (*theos monon*), and one of those gods who follow the First [i.e., Intellect]. For this one is the God who came from There [from the intelligible world], and one's own real nature, if one becomes what one was when one came, is There" (1.2.6.7–9).

Purification by Virtue

For Plotinus, godhood is attained by moral and physical purification, which he conceives of as the removal of everything alien to us. He uses the image of a sculptor who continually chisels off pieces of marble in order to reveal the lovely face of a cult statue within (1.6.9.9–12). Plotinus' favored metaphor for purification, however, is undressing. First one strips off the vices caused by the soul's association with body, then the soul strips off the body itself. The two stages are nicely summarized in Plotinus' tractate *On Beauty* (1.6). First the soul separates "from the lusts which it has through the body with which it consorted too much, and freed from its other affections, purged of what it gets from being embodied, when it abides alone has put away all the ugliness which came from the other [material] nature" (1.6.5.54–59). Then "the soul when it is purified becomes form and formative power, altogether bodiless and intellectual and entirely belonging to the divine (*holē tou theiou*)" (1.6.6.14–15).

In embodied life, virtue is the means of purification and deification. One can think of virtues as the moral qualities that disengage or detach a person from bodily life. The body is not evil per se, but ties down our thoughts, and involves people in distressing and disturbing passions (jealousy, madness, rage, etc.). Human bodies are needy, naturally somewhat greedy, and amazingly vulnerable. They demand food at regular intervals, which (in the ancient world at least) took hard work to produce and process for consumption. The majority of the population in the time of Plotinus spent their lives as farmers or slaves who had no opportunity for education or the life of the mind. The rich, on the other hand, had abundant food, and moralists like Seneca the Younger often fulminated against the tendency to overindulge on dainties. The social disparity between rich and poor sometimes led to jealousy and anger in the latter, self-satisfaction and snobbery in the former. Among the poor, malnutrition was one of the main causes of

21. Ibid., 22.13–63.

disease and death. Thus, when grain shipments to Rome were obstructed, the plebs surged with fear. All these vices—fear, social injustice, gluttony, and lack of wisdom—are all rooted in our bodily state.

Virtues are qualities of the soul that limit or eliminate these passions. As a man involved in the city life of Rome and not divorced from politics, Plotinus advocates civic (or political) virtues. He sometimes summarizes these under the headings of the four cardinal virtues: justice, moderation, courage, and prudence. Civic justice orders the self and society, moderation harmonizes passion and reason, courage "has to do with the emotions," and prudence "has to do with discursive reason" (1.2.1.17–21).[22]

Nevertheless, Plotinus believes that the civic virtues are only the first step toward living up to one's full potential. They make us good humans; but we are to be assimilated not to good people, but to gods (1.2.7.27–28). Accordingly, Plotinus posits the need for a superior set of virtues he calls "intelligible." Each of the four cardinal virtues, for instance, have a higher, intelligible form. Intelligible justice is activity towards Intellect, self-control is inward turning to Intellect, courage is freedom from passions, prudence is true wisdom or knowledge of Intellect (1.2.6.24–28).[23] These virtues lead one away from active life in the world and ultimately away from attachment to one's body. Instead, they aim at the contemplative life—to ever deeper and more intense levels of consciousness.[24] One does not have to attain these intellectual virtues from without. They are already within the self like "splendid statues all rusted with time" (4.7.10.46–47). One merely has to scrape off the layers of passion and vice (emotional attachments to the body) in order to expose the virtues that lie within.

Every human will eventually die and leave this bodily life behind. For most people, when they breathe their last the task of purification lies incomplete or hardly begun. The disembodied soul carries with it the passions it nurtured while still in the body. These passions are like weights that hold the soul down close to earth. The soul with the ability to ascend is the soul of the sage, unburdened by passion. This soul has grown wings, as it were, with which it can fly past the upper reaches of the cosmos.

For purified souls, therefore, exit from the body leads to a second, postmortem stage of deification: the ascent to the Intelligible realm. When the soul is released from the body it mounts up to "the fair and divine which no one masters" (2.3.9.25–26). It reaches the upper realm of the universe, and enters the world of Mind.

---

22. Cf. Plato, *Resp.* 4.428b–444a.

23. Cf. *Enn.* 1.6.6.6–13 and Plato, *Phaedo* 69b–c.

24. On levels of virtue, see Dillon, "Grades," 92–105.

In a book called the *Epinomis*, an imitator of Plato envisions the soul as becoming one from many parts (992b). For Plotinus, the human soul is assimilated to the unity of Mind as it enters the divine Mind (*Enn.* 3.8.8.1–9). In our current state, humans are not Intellect, but the *activity* (*energeia*) of the Intellect (1.4.9.29). One's goal is not merely to *have* intellect, but to *be* Intellect (1.4.4.15).

The realm of Intellect is the realm where all things, though of different form, are of the same reality: pure consciousness. When one attains to this realm, one is wholly Mind, and thus one with divinity. As Plotinus says, "the whole of Intellect is all together and not separated or divided, and all souls are together in the eternal world, not in spatial separation" (4.2.1.5–7). When one enters the intelligible world, one becomes one with it (3.8.11.33). The logic of union is inescapable. If all is knowledge, the distance between knowing subject and known object disintegrates. "[I]n Intellect both [subject and object] are one, not in close relation . . . but in essence, because 'thinking and being are the same'" (3.8.8.6–8).[25] For Plotinus, one *is* what one *thinks*, and by thinking the thoughts of God, one becomes those thoughts. But the thoughts of the God who is Mind *are* God. Thus, by thinking God's thoughts one's own divine reality is actualized.

Perhaps the finest exposition of the transformation into divine Mind appears in Plotinus' tractate *On Difficulties about the Soul II* (4.4):

> [W]hen it [the soul] is purely and simply in the intelligible world it has itself too the characteristic of unchangeability. For it is really all the things it is: since when it is in that region, it must come to unity with Intellect (*henōsin . . . tōi nōi*), by the fact that it has turned to it, for when it is turned, it has nothing between, but comes to Intellect and accords itself to it, and by that accord is united to it (*henōtai*) without being destroyed (*ouk apollumenē*), but both of them are one and also two (*hen estin amphō kai duo*). When therefore it is in this state it could not change but would be unalterably disposed to intelligence while at the same time having a concurrent awareness of itself (*sunaisthēsin hautēs*), as having become one and the same thing with its intelligible object (*hōs hen hama tōi noētōi tauton genomenē*). (4.4.2.26–33)

Modern Christians sometimes think of "pagan" (including Plotinian) deification as a form of absorption into God, whereas Christian deification always keeps the divine and human identities distinct. Although Plotinus

---

25. The statement about the identity of thinking and being comes from Parmenides (DK 28 B 3).

envisions a realistic form of union with Mind, the nuances of his teaching show that the integrity of the individual soul is not forsaken. He is clear that when the soul is united with Intellect, it is not destroyed (*ouk apollumenē*), but retains its own reality in a paradoxical fashion: "both of them are one and also two." The deified (or noeticized) soul, moreover, also retains an awareness of itself, even as it is aware of its identity with Intellect. According to Henry Blumenthal, "everything that exists in Intellect remains discrete, *qua* both subject and object, notwithstanding the identity of knower and known which is characteristic of this level of cognition." Thus "by raising ourselves to the level of Intellect we are in no sense losing our identity."[26]

It is widely acknowledged today that Plotinus even ultimized human individuality by his notion that the *forms* of individuals exist within the divine Mind.[27] Thus, in God there is always a Socrates, a Plato, and a Plotinus with all their idiosyncrasies. In this view, who they are *as individuals* will never—and can never—perish.

Union with Intellect

For Plotinus, union with divine Intellect can partially occur in this life. The one who knows oneself according to Intellect has already become Intellect (5.3.4.10–11). "One has certainly become Intellect," he says, "when one lets all the rest which belongs to one go and looks at this [Intellect] with this [intellect] and oneself in oneself: that is, it is as Intellect that one sees oneself" (5.3.4.29–32). The philosopher once testified:

> Often I have woken up out of the body to myself and have entered into myself, going out from all other things. I have seen a beauty wonderfully great and felt assurance that then most of all I belonged to the better part, that I have actually lived the best life and come to identity with the divine (*tōi theiōi eis tauton gegenēmenos*); and set firm in it I have come to that supreme actuality, setting myself above all else in the realm of Intellect. Then, after that rest in the divine, when I have come down from Intellect to discursive reasoning, I am puzzled how I ever came down, and how my soul has come to be in the body, when it is what it has shown itself to be by itself, even when it is in the body. (4.8.1.1–11)

26. Blumenthal, "On Soul and Intellect," 106. Corrigan notes that in Intellect "individual identity is enhanced precisely because the individual also manifests the whole" (*Reading Plotinus*, 36).

27. See esp. *Enn.* 5.7.1–3; cf. 5.9.12; 2.4.4.1–5.

Here and in other passages Plotinus describes union with Intellect as a sort of vision. Plato spoke about a vision of the Good (*Resp.* 506d–509a) or of Beauty (*Symp.* 211b–212a). For Plotinus, the true Beauty and reflection of the Good is Intellect. He testifies:

> Anyone who has seen it knows what I mean when I say that it is beautiful. It is desired as good, and the desire for it is directed to good, and the attainment of it is for those who go up to the higher world and are converted and strip off what we put on in our descent; (just as for those who go up to the celebrations of sacred rites there are purifications, and gradual stripping of the clothes they wore before, and going up naked) until, passing in the ascent all that is alien to the God, one sees with one's self alone That alone, simple, single and pure, from which all depends and to which all look and are and live and think: for it is the cause of life and mind and being. If anyone sees it, what passion will he feel, what longing in his desire to be united with it, what a shock of delight! (1.6.7.2–14).

Identification with Intellect occurs through intellectual vision. "For one must come to the sight with a seeing power made akin and like to what is seen," Plotinus explains. "No eye ever saw the sun without becoming sun-like, nor can a soul see Beauty without becoming beautiful. You must become first all deiform (*theoeidēs*) and all beautiful if you intend to see God and Beauty" (1.6.9.29–34).

Postmortem Rule

As in the Pauline form of deification, Plotinus occasionally thinks of godhood as involving cosmic rule. "In heaven with the universal Soul they [individual souls] can share in its government (*sundioikein*)," he says, "like those who live with a universal monarch and share in the government of his empire" (4.8.4.7–8).[28] The philosopher even remarks: "We also will reign as kings" (*basileuomen de kai hēmeis*) (5.3.4.1). Witness the similarity to Paul, who declares: "How much more will those who receive the abundance of grace and the gift of justice reign as kings (*basileusousin*) in life!" (Rom 5:17). Just as in Paul, Plotinus never envisions deified humans as replacing the God who rules the world (in this case the World Soul). Rather, deified souls become agents and ministers in the heavenly court of a higher God.

---

28. Cf. *Enn.* 4.3.12.10–12; 4.8.2.19–31; 5.8.7.32–35; Plato, *Phaedrus* 246c1–2.

Transcendence

Plotinus can conceive of deification as likeness to God, and specifically the likeness of an image to its archetype. "Likeness to the gods," he says, "is likeness to the model (*paradeigma*), a being of a different kind (*allon*) to ourselves" (*Enn.* 1.2.7.30–31). The notion of likeness necessarily acknowledges difference, and Plotinus regularly assumes that God the Intellect is superior to deified humans.

As unified with Intellect, however, one no longer thinks of oneself as a human being (*anthrōpon*). "[B]ut having becoming altogether other (*pantelōs allon genomenon*) and snatching oneself up into the higher world," Plotinus says, one draws up only the better part of one's soul (5.3.4.11–13). For our philosopher, the true human is not the union of body and soul—but soul—and only the better part of it (that linked to intellect).[29] Nevertheless, when the soul comes to Intellect above, "it comes not to something alien (*ouk eis allo*), but to its very self (*eis hautēn*)" (6.9.11.38–40). The human soul is thus capable of receiving God as "another self" (*allon auton*) (5.1.11.10–11). These statements would seem to contradict the notion that the human must become "altogether other." We must keep in mind, however, that in its highest aspect, the human is divine. Deification is the process of purifying and amplifying this divinity. When one is in the body, one is divine in the lowest possible way. When one is wholly purified, one transcends the *type* of divinity possible for one who exists on the human level. The human is already divine, to be sure—but *not* at the level of divinity it truly belongs. One must transcend the divinity of soul to become divine Mind.

Arrogance and Assistance

Although Plotinus paints a bright picture of human nature and destiny, he vigorously opposes deification through pride and self-assertion. In opposition to the Christian Gnostics of his time, he wrote that we must not exalt ourselves over the cosmic or intelligible gods—as if one was superior to the Creator and his cosmic ministers! Plotinus scoffs at the Christian who promotes himself to the highest pinnacle directly beneath God. To concoct a myth in which we are better than the Maker and Governor of the universe, he says, "is like flying in our dreams." Such prideful self-assertion, far from

---

29. Graduating from the body is not the denial of life. Rather, transcending the body is the acceptance of true life, since "the perfect life, the true, real life is in that transcendent intelligible reality; other lives are incomplete, traces of life, not perfect or pure and no more life than its opposite" (*Enn.* 1.4.3.33–37).

leading one toward divinity, will deprive a person of becoming a god (*apos-terounta heauton . . . theōi genesthai*) (2.9.9.50–51).[30]

For Plotinus, deification does not occur by the intervention of a personal God or spirit. He does not need the divine to intervene because the divine is already in him, unseparate from his true self. Nevertheless, deification in Plotinus is not thereby merely *self*-deification. As Pierre Hadot points out, if in Plotinus union with God is not by grace, it is still gratuitous. That is, it comes unexpectedly, as something unplanned, and as a matter of supreme good fortune (6.7.34.8).[31] One does all one can to prepare for it (5.5.7.33–38), but in the end, one's union with God depends on the goodness of Intellect. Although Plotinus' God is impersonal, deified humans still receive something from him as they advance to the realm of Intellect. Plotinus calls it an "outflow" (*aporroēn*), "light" (*phōs*), or "warmth" (*thermasia*) coming from the Good. When this warmth surrounds the soul, it is strengthened, awakened, and becomes truly winged (6.7.22.8–16). The soul mounts to God, the continual dispenser of favors (*charitas*) and love (*erōtas*) (6.7.22.7–8). In Plotinian thought, then, deification is by "grace." Yet the grace he speaks of is the "grace discerned through beauty," the "infinite generosity of a principle which gives itself."[32] God is Beauty. It is this Beauty and this Beauty alone that creates a love so powerful that it can fuel the human voyage past all stars and galaxies into the intelligible world.

In the last (over-quoted) line of the *Enneads*, Plotinus advocates the famous "flight of the alone to the Alone" (*phugē monou pros monon*) (9.9.11.51). It is easy to misconstrue this phrase to mean that Plotinian deification is the lonely quest of a lonely soul for union with a lonely God. In the context of Plotinus' thought, however, we should understand this line in relation to the soul's love of Beauty. "If anyone does not know this experience [of union]," Plotinus writes, "let him think of it in terms of our loves here below, and what it is like to attain what one is most in love with" (6.9.9.38–41). Even on earth, the true lover can so love the beloved that the rest of the world melts away in insignificance. Nothing else matters except being alone with the beloved. This experience is analogous to what occurs in the transcendent realm. "If all the other things around it [the soul] perished," Plotinus says, "it would even be pleased—so that it might be alone (*monon*) with This One" (6.7.34.36–38).[33]

---

30. Cf. Porphyry, *Vit. Plot.*16.

31. Hadot, "Neoplatonist Spirituality," 248.

32. I borrow these phrases from Bergson, quoted in Hadot, *Plotinus*, 49.

33. For the flight of the alone to the Alone, see further Narbonne, *Plotinus in Dialogue*, 97–101.

The Deferral of Divinity

In spite of his bold language about union with God (6.9.10.13–14), Plotinus concurs with the majority of ancient theories of deification that the ultimate destiny of the human soul is not indistinct union with the high God, but identification with a second-tier "Prime Mediate" deity—in this case, Intellect. If souls "are not what the supreme God is," he says, "this is in itself according to the nature of things" (2.9.9.43–44).

Some scholars have argued, however, that Plotinus may have envisioned "the ultimate absorption of the individual soul by the One."[34] Porphyry indicates that Plotinus attained union on several occasions with "the God over All" (*tōi epi pasi theōi*).[35] The "God over all" here is not necessarily the One, however, since the One does not directly control the universe (or "the All"). Nor is union with God in this passage viewed as indistinct. Like many ancient authors, Porphyry seems to equate union (*henōthēnai*) with proximity to God (*pelasai*). The language of union thus does not necessarily mean absorption.

To be sure, in a passage cited above (4.8.1.1–11), we observed Plotinus "waking up" from himself into union with God. As Dominic O'Meara has noted, however, this testimony describes union with Intellect (or Beauty), not with the One.[36] In other passages, Plotinus can speak of touch (*epaphē*) (6.7.36.4) or vision (*horan*) of the One (6.9.9.56). But all the metaphors that Plotinus uses are metaphors of relation, not of indistinct union. The soul always remains "near" (*plēsion*) the One, and is never absorbed (6.7.36.14).[37]

34. Bussanich, "Mystical Elements," 5325.

35. Porphyry, *Vit. Plot.* 23.16–17.

36. O'Meara, *Plotinus*, 104–5. Cf. also Hadot, "La union de l'âme," 14–15. The passage most often cited for union with the One is *Enneads* 6.9.9.9–11: "He [the One] does not give and then cease from it, but he always lavishly bestows until he/it becomes what he/it is (*heōs an ēi hoper esti*)." The unclarity of this text is caused by the unknown antecedents in the last clause. One could read the text to mean that the One lavishly bestows gifts until the soul (the subject of *ēi*) becomes what the One (the subject of *esti*) is. This is not the only possible interpretation. Meijer, for instance, translates *heōs an ēi hoper esti* "as long as it [the One] is what it is." This is probably the simplest reading since in context the human soul is not immediately in view (*Plotinus on the Good or One*, 248–49). This is also the understanding of Armstrong in LCL: "as long as it is what it is." What Plotinus *does* say in this passage is that the soul can see the source of life, intellect, being, and the Good (6.9.9.1–2), that it is not cut off from the One (6.9.9.7), and that the soul can incline toward it (*neusantes pros auto*) (6.9.9.11–12).

37. *Pace* Bussanich who claims that, "in many passages Plotinus talks about the soul . . . 'becoming the One' or of seeing itself as or in the One" ("Mystical Elements," 5325). The passages he cites (6.9.3.10–13; 9.50–52; 10.14–17; 11.14–16; 11.40–45) do not confirm his conclusion. (On these passages, see Bussanich, *The One*, 183–93). At one point, to be sure, Plotinus speaks of the soul "becoming one" (*genomenos hen*)

The soul cannot become one with the One, but only encircle him in a dance (*choreia*) (6.9.9.1; cf. 6.9.8.37–45) of erotic, intellectual love (6.9.9.39; cf. 6.7.22; 6.7.34.3, 14).[38] Lack of union with the One does not impede deification, however, since the One is beyond divinity (6.9.6.12–14). It is those who *revolve* around the One who are gods (*theoi*) (6.9.8.8). "There [in the intelligible realm]," Plotinus says, "one can see both him [the One] and oneself as it is right to see: the self glorified, full of intelligible light—but rather itself pure light—weightless, floating free, having become—but rather, being—a god" (6.9.9.56–59).

Conclusion

Plotinus concludes that in rare moments of deep contemplation, "I have . . . come to identity with the divine (*tōi theiōi eis tauton gegenēmenos*)" (4.8.1.5–6). This passage reminds readers that although Plotinus was one of the greatest thinkers of the ancient world, his theory of union with God grew out of his *experience* of it. The sage not only taught a vision of deification, he *lived* it—if only to taste it briefly. Plotinus was, in other words, not only a philosopher, but one of the world's great mystics and mystagogues. When they entered Christianity, his spiritual teachings shaped the pattern of Christian salvation for over a thousand years.

(6.9.10.16)—but this refers to the soul becoming one *in itself* not one with *the* One (*to Hen*). See further Hadot, "La union de l'âme," 27.

38. Later Christian authors would reserve the language of dance (*perichoresis*) for the relation of the three members of the Trinity.

Chapter 8

"The Flash of One Tremulous Glance"

Augustine and Deification

Manicheism was with him [Augustine] early and late, and was the one truly impassioned religious experience of his life.

—JAMES J. O'DONNELL[1]

Perhaps the most pivotal theologian for the Roman Catholic—and later Protestant—vision of deification is Augustine of Hippo (354–430 C.E.).[2] Although raised a nominal Christian, the young Augustine indicted the Catholicism of his youth for its anti-intellectualism and superstition (it was well-known for the veneration of saints in graveyard ceremonies). During the equivalent of his college days, Augustine's love of intellectual inquiry was kindled by a reading of Cicero's *Hortensius*, an exhortation to philosophy. From this book Augustine absorbed a kind of common-sense anthropology in popular philosophy, namely that the soul was eternal and akin to the divine. Accordingly the soul—if trained in reason and virtue—could ascend to heaven at death.[3] Within a few days of reading the *Hortensius*, Augustine joined a sect of enlightened Christians dedicated to rationality, science, and the pursuit of truth: the Manicheans.[4] Augustine

1. O'Donnell, *Augustine*, 47.

2. Meconi gives the most recent bibliography of deification in Augustine, "Dynamics," 173–74.

3. *Trin.* 14.19.26.

4. *Duab.* 1.

117

was a "Hearer" (a full, but subordinate member) of the Manichean church for about eleven years (from about age nineteen to thirty).[5]

As a Manichean, Augustine conceived of God as "an immense, luminous body." His mind, he thought, was a "fragment" (*frustrum*) of this corporeal Light.[6] Many light particles were separated from their divine source after a violent battle between Light and Darkness. Darkness, according to Manichean teaching, was a substantial reality like Light, bordering it on one side. At a certain point, Darkness invaded the Light and took part of it captive. Augustine describes this event while praying to God in his *Confessions*:

> [S]ome portion of yourself, one of your members, or an offspring from your very substance, was mixed with hostile powers and with the natures of beings not created by you, and was by them so far corrupted and changed for the worse that it was turned from beatitude to misery, and was in need of help by which it could be rescued and purged. This portion is the [human] mind (*animam*).[7]

Consequently, Augustine thought of his mind (or soul) as captured divine light, impure and in a state of misery.

On the face of it, these views contradicted the common Platonic idea that God was incorporeal and immutable (i.e., completely unchanging). Augustine knew by experience that his consciousness was thoroughly alterable—subject to various passions, and able to dance from one opinion to another. He concluded that his mind was not exactly like God. Nonetheless, Augustine was so strong a Manichean that he was better prepared to reject God's immutability than to deny the natural divinity of his mind.[8] Long after he had left Manichaeism, the bishop of Hippo polemically asserted that Manicheans attributed all the aberrations of the mind to the nature of God. God could thus be forgetful, foolish, disturbed, deformed, perverse, and so forth.[9]

Augustine's depiction of the Manichean "perverse" and "deformed" God presents a skewed version of their teaching. Manicheans would prefer to say that divine reality in humans retains its essential goodness even as it is held hostage in a kind of delirium or slumber.[10] The divine soul can be

5. For Augustine the Manichean, see O'Donnell, *Augustine*, 45–53; BeDuhn, *Augustine's Manichaean Dilemma* 1, 21–134.

6. *Conf.* 4.16.31; cf. *Gen. Man.* 2.26.40.

7. *Conf.* 7.2.3. Cf. also *Ver. rel.* 16.

8. *Conf.* 4.15.26.

9. *Nat. bon.* 41. Cf. *Gen. Man.* 2.8.11.

10. *Conf.* 7.2.3.

compelled against its will, like Christ on the cross, to suffer an evil act. In the process, however, the divine element "struggles to maintain its integrity in the face of evil's efforts to divide and conquer it."[11]

At about the age of thirty, Augustine devoured some books of Neoplatonic philosophy.[12] The books, it seems, were Latin translations of some works of Plotinus and Porphyry. The reading of these volumes revolutionized Augustine's theology by convincing him that God was all-powerful and incorporeal. God's omnipotence proved that Light could not succumb to darkness. Similarly, God's bodilessness proved that he could not mix with matter and flesh—the stuff of this physical world. These ideas, Augustine thought, shattered the foundations of the Manichaean corporeal God who was vulnerable to evil.

Nevertheless, Neoplatonism—like Manichean thought—fully maintained the divinity of the soul.[13] Accordingly Augustine, after his conversion to Catholic Christianity in 386 C.E., continued to believe in the natural divinity of the human soul.[14] "As either a Manichaean or a Platonist Christian," Jason BeDuhn observes, "Augustine could express belief that the soul preexisted in a state unsullied by materiality, and would return to that state in the end."[15]

After the spring of 387, however, Augustine replaced the language of the divine soul with more conventional Catholic language of the created soul. The reason is not exactly clear. BeDuhn suggests that Augustine's catechetical training discouraged the language of a divine soul.[16] Another factor is Augustine's reflection on a mystical experience that occurred around this time. In a session of Platonic meditation, Augustine claims to have seen "by whatever kind of eye in my soul that is above the eye of my soul and above my mind—an unalterable Light!"[17] He concluded that the Light

---

11. BeDuhn, *Augustine's Manichaean Dilemma I*, 85. BeDuhn writes that if God is changeable in Manichean thought, it is "not in his essential goodness, but in other features related to his dynamic responsiveness to the coexistence of evil" (ibid., 101).

12. *Conf.* 7.9.13.

13. On the divinity of the soul in Plotinus, see Cary, *Augustine's Invention*, 36–38.

14. *Acad.* 1.1, 3, 11. Cf. BeDuhn, *Augustine's Manichaean Dilemma I*, 160. In *Ord.* 2.46, Augustine does not deny the divinity of the soul, only the Manichean claim that the soul is "not at all" (*nihil . . . omnino*) separate from God. See further O'Connell, *St. Augustine's Early Theory*, 125–27, 130–31. Cary goes so far as to claim that "the initial move in Augustine's philosophical development—the move which leads him to Platonism in the first place—is from Manichaean (and probably Ciceronian) divinity of the soul to neo-Platonist divinity of the soul" ("God in the Soul," 72).

15. BeDuhn, *Augustine's Manichaean Dilemma I*, 258. Cf. *Acad.* 2.9.22.

16. Ibid., 174.

17. *Conf.* 7.10.16.

he beheld was utterly different from created reality. "Nor was it above my mind," Augustine recalled, "like oil above water or the sky above the earth— it was superior because that very Light made me; and I was inferior, because I was made by it."[18] God was Light—so far the Manicheans had been right— but this divine Light did not lose particles of itself to Darkness. Instead, the divine Light *created* the other lights that became human minds.[19]

It is important to understand Augustine's idea of creation. As early as the fourth century B.C.E., Plato had distinguished Being and becoming as two separate planes of reality. Normally Platonists thought of the intellect as existing on the plane of Being, and thus on the side of God. Augustine drew the line differently. He confessed to God: "You are not the mind (*animus*) itself: you are the Lord and God of the mind, and though all these things [the vagaries of consciousness] are entirely changed, you abide unchangeable above them all."[20]

What separated God and the human mind, was not simply the idea that God made the mind, but the Platonic implications Augustine associated with this idea. If God *made* the mind, God was a substance inherently superior to mind. Such a notion did not entirely break with Platonic teaching since Platonists acknowledged that, unlike the human mind, God is also unchangeable and all-powerful. As an immutable and omnipotent substance, God is unlike the human mind, which is currently bottled in a body and subject to sin.

Nonetheless, Augustine radicalized the division between God and the human mind by emphasizing the doctrine of creation from nothing (*creatio ex nihilo*). The mind, he came to believe, was not born of God, but created from that which *does not even exist*. God, on the other hand, remained ultimate Being. Now there can be no greater separation between Being and what derives from nothing. Thus the *essence* of God and of humanity, Augustine concluded, could not and could never be one.[21] After becoming a Catholic Platonist, then, Augustine exchanged a dualism between divine

---

18. Ibid.

19. Augustine later discovered this teaching in the Bible: "The prophet says, 'He [God] who formed the spirit for all people made all things' (Ps 32:15), and in another place he says, 'He who formed the spirit of a person is in him' (Zech 12:1). These testimonies clearly prove," said the bishop, "that the spirit [or mind] of a human being was created" (*Gen. Man.* 2.8.11). I have reversed the order of these passages as they appear in *Gen. Man.* for clarity.

20. *Conf.* 10.25.36. Cf. BeDuhn, *Augustine's Manichaean Dilemma I*, 262.

21. On creation from nothing in Augustine, see Torchia, *Creatio ex nihilo*; Harrison, *Rethinking*, 74–114. Both treatments are conservative. Torchia tends to see *creatio ex nihilo* where it does not exist. Harrison's mission is to see Augustine as orthodox as early as possible. The best overall treatment of the subject is still May, *Creatio ex nihilo*.

Light and demonic Darkness for a dualism between God and the (created) world—a world that included the human mind.

A decade after his conversion, Augustine was bishop of the city of Hippo Regius in North Africa. He had had ten years to reflect on the meaning of his conversion. During this time (397 C.E.), Augustine confessed that by considering his mind to have been divine, he was impious and utterly arrogant.

> What was more proud than for me to have asserted—wondrous madness!—that I was something naturally what you [God] are? For although I am changeable and this was manifest to me by my very desire to be wise—so that from a worse state I could become better—I was nevertheless preferring even to suppose that you were changeable rather than that I was not what you are.[22]

In a tractate Augustine later wrote against the Manicheans, he claimed, "There cannot be a greater sign of pride than that the human soul says that it is what God is, while it still groans under such great burdens of vice and unhappiness."[23]

Pride, which Augustine defined as "love of one's own excellence,"[24] had blocked him from realizing the truth about God's difference from himself. In his own picturesque mode of expression: "By my swelling pride I was separated from you [God], and my bloated face was enveloping my eyes."[25]

Fall

Augustine later came to see his own chronicle of "swelling pride" woven into the story of humanity itself. Humans originally fell from God, Augustine emphasized, through arrogance. "For the beginning of all sin is pride," the bishop was wont to quote, and "the beginning of . . . pride is to turn away from God" (Sir 10:13, 12).[26] The first being to turn away from God was the devil, who attempted to be like God by his own power (Isa 14:12–14). Similarly Satan persuaded Adam and Eve to taste the forbidden fruit by saying: "You shall be as gods [or God]!" (Gen 3:5). Adam's attempt to be "as God" through breaking God's law was, according to Augustine, a surge of pure arrogance. The first man imagined that God was keeping true freedom

22. *Conf.* 4.15.26.

23. *Gen. Man.* 2.8.11.

24. *Gen. litt.* 11.14.18.

25. *Conf.,* 7.7.11. Cf. *Gen. Man.* 2.26.40.

26. *Enarrat. Ps.* 7.4 (*initium autem omnis peccati superbia*). The Septuagint for Sir 10:13 has the reverse "The source of pride is sin" (*archē uperēphanias hamartia*).

and autonomy from him. Based on this suspicion, he refused God's authority, preeminence, and dominion. Adam relied on his own judgment, defied God's law, and on his own strength strove to be equal to God.[27] In consequence, God let him fall into degradation and death. "When against God's command, man desired to be God—not by legitimate imitation, but by illicit pride—he was cast down to the mortality of the beasts."[28]

For Augustine, the only way to reverse Adam's condemnation to mortality was to reverse the cause of death: pride. The prop of this pride was his belief that he was one in essence with God. When he became bishop and defender of the Catholic faith, Augustine vigorously denounced this idea.

The Image of God

In Augustine's mature theology, there remained a link between God and the soul: the image of God. It was traditional Christian teaching that humans were made in or as the image of God (Gen 1:26). Augustine accepted this teaching,[29] but taught that the image had been lost.[30] Later, he revised this hard-line position, asserting that the image was "faded and defaced."[31] The result of both formulations was the same: the natural continuity between humanity and God was removed.

Christian models of salvation were (and are) typically structured in a problem-solution format. Christians—including Manicheans—were generally agreed on the solution: Jesus Christ in his life, death, and resurrection. The problem to fit this solution was variously described. Augustine painted the human problem with dark colors. For the bishop of Hippo, our first parents—although created good and by a good God—mysteriously rebelled against God and chose evil instead. An evil will became something inherent in human nature and was transmitted like a genetic disease from parent to child. The disease in every case was lethal. Due to that first sin, all humans born are condemned to die. But death is only the beginning of human judgment. God will punish human wickedness by subjecting human beings— men, women, and children—to an eternity of conscious torture.

The terror of this story would lead any rational being who accepted it straight into the arms of God's only solution: Jesus Christ and his executor,

27. *Gen. Man.* 2.15.22; cf. *Enarrat. Ps.* 1.4; *Gen. litt.* 11.5.7; *Civ.* 14.13.

28. *Gen. Man.* 2.21.32; cf. *Enarrat. Ps.* 35.17–18.

29. *Conf.*, 7.7.11. For Augustine's teaching that the mind is the image of God, see *Enarrat. Ps.* 4.8; *Gen. Man.* 1.17.28.

30. *Perdita* (Dolbeau *Serm.* 23B.5).

31. *Trin.* 14.8.11. See further on this point Bonner, "Augustine's Doctrine," 504–14.

the Catholic church. Although the image of God was lost or deformed, Christ was the Image of God himself (2 Cor 4:4; Col 1:15). For Catholics who accepted the Nicene Creed, this idea led to the notion that Christ was one in essence (*homoousios*) with God.

The Wondrous Exchange

In the incarnation, Christ performed a striking act of exchange to accomplish human salvation. According to Paul, "for our sake he [Christ] became poor, though he was rich, so that you, by his poverty, might become rich" (2 Cor 8:9). A century and a half later, Irenaeus the bishop of Lyon wrote that Christ "on account of his immense love was made what we are to make us what he himself is."[32] Athanasius, the Alexandrian bishop, said it most forcefully: God "was made human so that we might become God."[33] Augustine devised a similar maxim: "God assumed a human being in order to make human beings gods."[34] In brief, Christ's incarnation effected human deification.

It seemed a plan of perfect symmetry: God shared in humanness, and consequently, human beings shared in deity. "Look what our sharing in him means," said Augustine, "we have been promised a share in his divinity (cf. 2 Pet 1:4). . . . The son of God was made a sharer in our mortal nature so that mortals might become sharers in his Godhead."[35] Deification, for Augustine, was the flipside of the incarnation. Incarnation began the process of salvation, and deification completed it. A Christian cannot accept the first part of the process and reject the second.

Human godhood, for Augustine, must begin with God's act to become flesh, not with the innately divine mind of human beings. In Jesus Christ— and in him alone—God's Being and the human mind became one.[36] The bishop traces this teaching back to Paul:

> The blessed apostle teaches this unity of the person of Christ Jesus, our Lord, including both natures, namely, the divine and the human, so that each of them shares its attributes with the other, the divine with the human, and the human with the divine[;] . . . therefore the divinity took the name of this humanity, . . . the humanity has received the name of that divinity.[37]

32. *Haer.* book 5, *praef.*

33. *Inc.*, 54.3.

34. *Serm.* 344.1; cf. 192.1.1.

35. *Enarrat. Ps.* 52.6.

36. For Augustine's doctrine of the person of Christ, see his *Enchir.* 10.35.

37. *Arian.* 1.8; cf. *Serm.* 265b.3.

Whereas the Manicheans reduced the essential union of God and humanity to the elect, Augustine reduced it to a *single man*. Only one human shared in God essentially: Christ. Thus he became the mediator between God and human beings.

Consequently, the exchange between God and human beings is deliberately asymmetrical. Christ is the limit case: in any other person besides him human and divine natures can never be one in essence. Ordinary humans can never be or become God (or divine). Nevertheless, by participating in Christ's *human* nature, redeemed human beings can share in Christ's divine qualities. Augustine asserted: "Since he [Christ] was the Word of God with God, he both brought down his majesty to human affairs and raised human lowliness to the realm of the divine."[38] For the bishop, deification is God's gracious act to exalt and ennoble *human* nature by allowing it to share—not in God's essence—but in his attributes.

God does not have just one shareable attribute, but many. Consequently Augustine's concept of deification is multidimensional. Below, I will discuss five aspects of it: justification, adoption, incorporation, immortality, and beatitude.[39]

Justification

Justification is God's forgiveness of human sin through the atoning death of Christ. The basis for justification is the incarnation, for the incarnation produced an interchange of human and divine qualities. Augustine summarized his understanding of justification in his work *On the Trinity*:

> By nature we are humans, and through sin we are not righteous human beings. So God, being made a righteous human being, interceded with God for human beings who are sinners. The sinner has nothing in common with the Righteous One [Christ], but humans have humanity in common with humans. Therefore joining to us the likeness of his humanity, he [Christ] took away the unlikeness of our iniquity, and being made a sharer (*particeps*) of our mortality, He made us sharers (*participes*) of his divinity.[40]

38. *Exp. Gal.* 24.8.

39. For a chart (with dates and references) of Augustine's eighteen uses of *deificare*, see Meconi, "Becoming One Christ," 158.

40. *Trin.* 4.2.4.

As Augustine put it elsewhere: "He who justifies is the same as he who deifies" (*qui autem iustificat, ipse deificat*).[41] Only God, the bishop says, is truly just.[42] Indeed, Augustine accepted the Platonic teaching that God is himself Justice. Therefore, only God can justify human beings by sharing what he is—Justice. Christ shared God's justice with humans by sharing in human injustice. He did not share in human injustice by sinning, but by bearing human sin on the cross. Christ's atoning death was the act whereby he shared totally in human injustice, enabling humans to share in divine justice. In the verse of Paul: "He [Christ] who knew no sin became sin for our sake so that we might become the justice of God in him" (2 Cor 5:21).

The logic of participation raises an important question. Christ, as one in nature with God, *is* Justice. If humans—by sharing in Christ's Justice—become just in the same manner as Christ, are human beings also equal to God like Christ? Augustine responded:

> For my part I feel that when there comes to be in us so much justice that nothing more can be added, still the creature will not be equal to the Creator. Yet if some suppose that we will so far be advanced as to be converted into the substance of God and be made directly what he is, let them see how they build up their opinion. I must confess that I am not persuaded.[43]

Augustine is one of the first to formulate the distinction between likeness and identity. Deification means *likeness* to God, and likeness always presupposes difference even in the thick of similarity. Humans are like God by sharing in Christ's justice; they are not just in themselves. "In many just people there seem to be many forms of justice, whereas there is only one justice of God in which they all share."[44] God is absolute justice, as is Christ. Humans take part in justice, but never become it.

Adoption

Justification, according to Augustine, made possible the second aspect of deification—adoption. God could not adopt human beings to be his sons and daughters because of their sins. When Jesus Christ freed people from sin,[45] "he made us sons and daughters of God."[46]

41. *Enarrat. Ps.* 49.1.
42. Ibid.
43. *Nat. grat.* 33.37.
44. *Enarrat. Ps.* 10.11.
45. *Tract. Ev. Jo.* 2.13.
46. *Enarrat. Ps.* 49.2.

For Augustine, then, deification was a form of adoption. "To as many as received him [Christ], to them he gave the power to become the children of God" (John 1:12). The power to become a child of God, according to Augustine, was the power to become a god. He made this connection based on Psalm 82:6, where God was thought to declare to Christians: "I have said 'you are gods, *and sons of the Most High.*'" This text, which affirms the same point in two parallel ways ("you are gods *and sons of God*"), shows that to become a child of God is to become a god as well. "If we have been made children of God," Augustine preached, "we have been made into gods."[47]

Nevertheless—and there is frequently a "nevertheless" with Augustine—the divinity of the adopted sons of God never supplants the divinity of Christ. Humans are God's children by God's mercy. Christ is the natural son, one with the Father's essence.[48] Thus there always remains a division between the status of Christ and human beings. Christ alone was begotten by the Father from all eternity. Human beings, in contrast, are adopted in time.[49] Thus humans, even as scriptural "gods," are not divine as God or Christ is divine.[50]

Incorporation

By sharing in Christ, humans not only share in God's justice and family, they also share in God's "body." This is a third aspect of deification in Augustine: incorporation into Christ. Incorporation means that the Christian enters into Christ's *corpus*, or body. The doctrine was developed in large part from Pauline texts:

> We, who are many, are one body in Christ, and individually we are members of one another. (Rom 12:5)

> Do you not know that your bodies are members of Christ? (1 Cor 6:15)

> Now you are the body of Christ, and individually parts of it. (1 Cor 12:27)

Although modern Christians typically understand these statements as metaphors, Augustine had a deep sense of their reality. For him, Christians were organically related to Christ. As the church suffers, Christ suffers.

47. *En. Ps.* 49.2: *si filii dei facti sumus, et dii facti sumus.* See further Bonner, "Augustine's Conception," 377–78.

48. *Exp. Gal.* 30.6. Cf. *Tract. Ev. Jo.* 2.13; *Serm.* 166.4.4.

49. *Tract. Ev. Jo.* 2.13.

50. *Enarrat. Ps.* 49.2.

When Saul persecuted the church, Christ demanded, "Why are you perse-cuting *me*?" (Acts 9:4). Christ and his church, Augustine emphasized, are one flesh (Eph 5:32).[51] This is the great mystery symbolized in the union of a husband and wife. Christ is one with his church and identifies with it.[52] Augustine underscored this point in the most vivid terms:

> Therefore, let us rejoice and give thanks, not only that we have been made Christians, but that we have been made Christ. Do you understand, brothers and sisters, do you comprehend the grace of God upon us? Be in awe. Rejoice. We have been made Christ. For if he is the Head, we are the members—a whole man, he and we. This is what the Apostle Paul says . . . "until we all attain . . . to a perfect man, to the mature measure of the age to the fullness of Christ" [Eph 4:12–13].[53]

In short, the church becomes divine by forming the body of a divine being.

Lest, however, one think of Manichean sparks of light coalescing into one divine body, Augustine offered some expected qualifications. "Christ never so joined us so as to make no distinction between us and himself."[54] Christians, though they can be called "Christ," are not the essence of Christ. Just as Augustine made a distinction between natural and adopted sons, he also forged a division between the body's *Head* (Christ) and *members* (redeemed human beings). Human beings are truly divine by virtue of being part of Christ's body. Nonetheless, they are not the Head (Christ)—the source of the body's divinity. Without the Head, the body dies and dissolves into dust. Joined to the Head, the body of the church inherits with Christ what he won on earth: resurrection and eternal life.[55]

Immortality

The defining trait of deification in the ancient world was immortality.[56] According to Augustine, humans die by reason of Adam's pride and fall. They have no power to retake the life an obedient Adam would have enjoyed. In response, God in Christ graciously shared his eternal life with

51. *Enarrat. Ps.* 54.3.

52. *Ep.* 140.18.

53. *Tract. Ev. Jo.* 21.8.1.

54. Ibid., 21.3.

55. *Serm.* 22.10.10.

56. Litwa, *We Are Being Transformed*, 44–45.

human beings.[57] Christ as God's essence means that he is Life itself, and thus able to bestow life on dying humanity. The ideas have a Platonic ring, but Augustine appealed to biblical language:

> In him [Christ] was life, and that life was the light of human beings. (John 1:4)

> For as the Father has life in himself, so he has granted the son to have life in himself. (John 5:26)

> I am the Way, the Truth, and the Life; no one comes to the Father except through me. (John 14:6; cf. 11:25)

Again, deification is interchange: in the incarnation, Christ shares human mortality, and thereby gives human beings a share in what makes him divine—eternal life (John 5:21; cf. 6:33, 40; 10:28). Describing this process, Augustine wrote:

> [B]y participating in his [Christ's] divinity we too shall be made immortal in eternal life; and this pledge has been given to us by the son of God [Jesus] . . . that before we should be made partakers of his immortality, he should himself be made a partaker of our mortality. For just as he was mortal, not of his nature but of ours, so we shall be immortal, not of our nature but of his.[58]

As Augustine explained the transfer of immortality to human nature, he was again careful to make a distinction between human beings and Christ. Christians, though they are destined to be immortal, will never be Life itself. Before they share in Christ's life in the resurrection, they will die physically. Their demise accords with Psalm 82:6, where God speaks to the redeemed: "I have said, you are gods . . . *but you will die like human beings.*" For Augustine, eternal life is always deferred to a postmortem state.

Beatitude

Finally, deification in Augustine means the experience of happiness (or beatitude), which for the bishop starts with internal order. The opposite of happiness is loss of self-control. When Adam turned away from God, his desires overpowered his reason, and he began to want earthly things according to base impulses. As children of Adam, humans experience the fickleness of their feelings and desires on a daily basis. Sometimes they are

---

57. *Serm.* 80.5.
58. *Enarrat. Ps.* 146.5.11. Cf. *Serm.* 166.4.4 (*PL* 38.909).

restrained, but often they creep in unawares. Constant indulgence causes deep ruts of expectation. Instead of being satisfied, people become addicted, and demand additional pleasure to satisfy the addiction. Consequently, lusts grow more violent and become uncontrollable passions. Passions like guilt and pride—if they grow strong enough—rend the soul, throwing it into confusion and paralysis. Looking back on his life before his conversion, Augustine confessed his own experience of inward fragmentation. In his own words: "I went to pieces!" (*frustatim discissus sum*).[59] He broke apart because, "I turned away from you, the One [God], and sunk into a multitude of things."[60]

In contrast to human fluctuation, Augustine envisioned God as the singular, unchanging Being, perfectly stable and rational. God's fervent love for justice and vehement hatred of injustice did not flicker and fade with events, but eternally endured. In the book of Exodus, God's voice booms from the burning bush: "*I AM WHO I AM*" (3:14). Augustine took this in a Platonic sense to mean that God was absolute Being. Being, according to Augustine, never was, and never will be, but always *is*. When humans fell from God, they detached themselves from Being. Consequently, they began to shift, dissolve, and veer haphazardly in their emotional life. They became unstable like ocean waves, and so lost their inner calm.

For Augustine, happiness comes when a person molds his or her affections to the stability of the unchangeable God. Such assimilation to God, Augustine learned from the philosopher Porphyry, deified human beings.[61] But whereas Porphyry held that deification came through virtue, Augustine more and more emphasized the singular role of grace.[62]

Unsurprisingly, this grace was made possible by the incarnation. As a man, Christ clung to God, a sign of his full participation in God's nature.[63] His unique share in God's being stabilized his emotional life and made his reason master of his passions. By sharing in Christ's humanness, people can participate in the tranquility of his (human) soul.

The exchange is not automatic: there is a condition to happiness. The only person, Augustine emphasized, who shares in God's stability is the "one who confesses that he is not what God is."[64] One must reject one's *own* godhood to be deified. The logic of this paradoxical deduction is philosophical.

---

59. *Conf.* 2.1.1. Here I adopt the translation of Boulding, *The Confessions*, 33.
60. Ibid.
61. *Civ.* 19.23.
62. Folliet, "Deificari in Otio," 225–36.
63. *Enarrat. Ps.* 118.16, §1.
64. Ibid., 121.8.

Christ alone shares the Being—and thus stability—of God. Humans, on the other hand, came from non-being. "I would not exist," Augustine cried out, "unless you [God] existed in me!"[65] When humans separate from God, they slowly degrade back into the chaos of nothingness.[66] In contrast, Christians are able to advance toward Christ's inward stability. Even at his best moments, however, Augustine admitted that the "temptations of the flesh" still "beat upon me as I groan."[67]

A Distant Vision

Those who would be like God must see God, but that vision is only possible, Augustine believed, in a future life. In the late second century C.E., Irenaeus wrote, "For God is he who is yet to be seen, and the beholding of God is productive of immortality, and 'immortality renders one near unto God' [Wisd 6:19]."[68] The final step in Augustinian deification is the vision of God. Humans, as Scripture teaches, will become like God when they see him as he is (1 John 3:2).[69] Yet the only hope that Augustine offered for seeing God in this world was the "flash of one tremulous glance" (*ictu trepidantis aspectus*). Describing one of his Platonic visions, Augustine laments, "I was not strong enough to fix my gaze there [the intelligible realm]. Beaten back by weakness, I returned to accustomed sights."[70] The weight that dragged Augustine to the earth was his mortal body, as was confirmed by a biblical passage Augustine regularly quoted: "the body which is corrupted weighs down the soul (*animam*), and the earthly habitation presses down the mind thinking many things" (Wis 9:15).[71]

For those whose body died, however, Augustine painted a brighter picture—a heavenly expectation of seeing God face to face.[72] "God promised us eternal salvation," the bishop preached, "a life of happiness with the angels that would never end, an unfading inheritance, everlasting glory,

65. *Conf.* 1.2.2; cf. 1.6.10.
66. *Enarrat. Ps.* 7.19; cf. *Civ.* 14.13.
67. *Conf.* 10.34.51.
68. *Haer.* 4.38.3.
69. Aristotle had written that study or contemplation (*theōria*) is the human activity most akin to the gods' activity, and most productive of happiness (*eudaimonia*) (*Nicomachean Ethics* 1178b1–24).
70. *Conf.* 7.17.23.
71. Cf. *Quant. an.* 33.73; *Ord.* 1.1.3.
72. *Enarrat. Ps.* 35.14.

the delight of seeing his face."[73] When the vision of God becomes a reality, affirmed Augustine, "then the human mind shall be in a way lost [in God]."[74] Seeing God will produce an unspeakable transformation. The fullness and beauty of this metamorphosis Augustine described with the language of deification. The mind, when it is lost in wonder at the sight of God "shall become divine (*et fit divina*)!"[75] In sum, Augustinian deification is not a present possession, but a postmortem goal. As Augustine put it, "So we are in hope, but not yet in reality (*ergo sumus in spe, nondum in re*)."[76]

Grace against Nature

It is conventional to say that Augustinian deification is by grace, and not by nature. Manicheans could claim, however, that their divine mind was just as much a gift of God. God's grace, in this view, was "built-in," since the human mind is created as (or in) the image of God. By contrast, Augustine opposed grace and nature, so that natural grace became something of a contradiction in terms. He insisted that grace come solely from without and made it depend upon an ecclesial rite: baptism. Late in life, Augustine asserted that the image of God in unbaptized infants was subject to the devil by God's judgment.[77] Even infants whose minds were made in God's image—but who died without baptism—would perish in hell. Witness how far Augustine was willing to go in order "to sever the idea of the mind of man as being made in the image of God from any suggestion of natural divinity."[78]

The belief that unbaptized infants go to hell seems today (and to some in Augustine's own time) simply pathological—but it should be recognized as part of Augustine's justified war on human pride. Admittedly, a naturally divine person could conceivably remain humble since natural divinity remains the gift and design of God. (Indeed, if one is truly divine, what room is there for pride?) For Augustine, however, human evil is too radical for natural grace.

Augustine is famous for the theory that original sin—and the corrupt sexual desires that come with it—is passed on naturally through sex and reproduction. Consequently, Augustine saw the selfishness of babies not as

73. *Enarrat. Ps.* 109.1; cf. 37.28.
74. Ibid., 35.14: *perit quodammodo humana mens.*
75. Ibid.
76. *Enarrat. Ps.* 49.2.
77. *C. Jul. op. imp.* 6.20.
78. Bonner, "Augustine's Doctrine," 507.

a drive to survive, but as the proof of perversity.[79] Evil had no explanation—no "whence"—since it become integrated into human nature (the so-called "sin nature"). As a boy of sixteen, Augustine (with a band of other teenagers) stole some pears from a local farmer and threw them before swine. Much later, the bishop struggled to find a motive for this peccadillo, but eventually concluded, "I was gratuitously evil, and my evilness had no other cause than evilness itself."[80] "This statement," comments BeDuhn, "represents a perfect articulation of the dualist account of evil promoted in Manichaeism."[81] Evil, for Augustine, is just as basic to human nature as is (created) goodness. Evil may be a privation (a lack of good), but it still emerges from the abyss of the human will.[82]

Due to their inherent evil, Augustine thought, humans will inevitably claim divinity for themselves alone, and buck their dependence on God. They will want, like the Manicheans, "to be the light—not in the Lord but in themselves! By the very act of supposing that the nature of the mind is what God is, the more densely dark do they become."[83] The natural darkness (or evil) that Augustine imputed to human nature has suggested to some that the saint never fully forsook the Manichean dualism between a primal, unexplained darkness in opposition to divine light.[84]

Conclusion

Augustine's post-conversion relation to Manichaeism will always be debated. We cannot easily uncover the motives for Augustine's theory of deification, but we can present its themes. For Augustine, *divinity is always deferred*. In a sense this emphasis is no different than that of Plotinus, for whom the soul

79. See esp. *Conf.* 1.7.11–12.

80. Ibid., 2.4.9.

81. BeDuhn, *Augustine's Manichaean Dilemma I*, 40.

82. "Our original nature itself sinned" (*ipsa natura nostra prima peccavit*) (*Serm.* 23B.11). Babcock rightly points out that the theory of evil as privation does not account for its origin. Humans are the origin of the evil they do; God is the origin of the evil they suffer (an evil which Augustine calls "punishment") ("Sin and Punishment," 235–36, 241). Augustine's doctrine of an evil will derives, I suspect, just as much from Plotinus' doctrine of a primeval fall of souls as it does from his reading of Paul.

83. *Conf.* 8.10.22.

84. For the influence of Manichaeism on Augustine's later theology, see Coyle, "Saint Augustine's Manichaean Legacy," 18–20. Admittedly, Augustine did not think that evil was a substance eternal like God. Evil was a privation and a result of sin. But, as Lamberigts points out, "the outcome is still the same": evil is basic to human nature ("Was Augustine a Manichaean?" 122).

could never unite in essence with the One. But Augustine is more radical because he removes any natural spark of divinity burning in the human heart. Again and again, he emphasized the division between human beings and God. Humans are not gods by nature (even potentially). They are not even divine (as in Plotinus) by sharing the reality of a mediate God such as Intellect. Rather, humans are divine due to their participation merely in God's *qualities*, a participation that always distinguishes them from "true God."[85] Christ alone is divine by nature. When human beings are called "gods" in Scripture, they are gods in name only (nominally).[86] In eternity, deified humans remain human.[87] In sum, deification in Augustine does not mean that humans unite with God's uncreated essence. Instead, deification becomes a powerful metaphor for the complete salvation and perfection of human nature.

85. Cf. *Enarrat. Ps.* 109.3.

86. "It is therefore clear, because he *called* human beings gods, they are deified by his grace, not born from his essence" (*manifestum est ergo, quia hominess* dixit *deos, ex gratia sua deificatos, non de substantia sua natos*) (*Enarrat. Ps.* 49.2, emphasis mine). Cf. *Serm.* 166.4.4; *Enarrat. Ps.* 146.11. In Dolbeau *Serm.* 23b Augustine remarks that "there is a big difference" (*multum interest*) between the one true, deifying God and those who are made gods by grace and adoption.

87. Augustine comes closest to positing a real transition from humanity to deity in *Serm.* 166.1, where he says, "God commands that we should not be humans" (*hoc iubet deus, ut non simus homines*). Nevertheless, he makes his understanding clear in *Enarrat. Ps.* 94.6 "He is the real God, who makes those into gods. . . . He is the true God because God is in no way made[;] . . . we are not made true gods." Note the emphasis on making. *Creatio ex nihilo*, it appears, makes a strong division between humans and God.

Chapter 9

"I am the Truth"

The Deification of Husayn ibn Mansur al-Hallaj

We are the mirror as well as the face in it.
We are tasting the taste this minute
Of eternity.

—RUMI

I N HIS *BOOK OF Flashes* Abu Nasr as-Sarraj (died 988) writes that Sufis,

> give priority to what God has commanded his servants and avoid
> what God has forbidden. . . . Their way does not include . . . the
> espousal of questionable views, all of which amount to a disregard
> for the religion. . . . On the contrary, their way is to hold fast to
> what is fundamental and most complete in the matter of religion.[1]

This depiction would hardly seem to describe the Sufi Husayn ibn
Mansur al-Hallaj (858–922 C.E.). In the year 912 he was imprisoned for
holding seemingly bizarre beliefs. "The quality of his sayings is stranger
than all others," Ruzbihan Baqli Shirazi (died 1209) observed, adding:

> The path to his spiritual reality became incomprehensible in
> the sight of the imperfect. . . . He entered into that sea with the
> quality of creaturehood, and he departed with the character of
> lordship. . . . None saw, and none heard, for some said he was

---

1. Abu Nasr as-Sarraj, quoted in McGinn, *Knowledge of God*, 72–73.

a magician, and some said he was a conjurer, some said he was mad, and some said he was a heretic.[2]

Hallaj's accusers came to focus on one of Hallaj's declarations:

Ana' l-Haqq: "I am the Truth," or "I am God."

It was for this statement that the reigning vizier in 922 convinced the Baghdad authorities to execute Hallaj. As legend has it, ibn Mansur danced in his chains to the gibbet. His hands and feet were cut off. He was then hung (or possibly crucified). The next day he was taken down, decapitated, burned, and his ashes thrown to the wind. Nevertheless, the echoes of what he proclaimed still hung in the air. Louis Massignon writes that Hallaj, "from the height of the gibbet, uttered the apocalyptic cry that announces the Judge of the Last Judgment: *Ana' l-Haqq*, 'I am the Truth!'"[3]

Ana' l-Haqq. In this statement, Hallaj seemed to deify himself. But appearances can be deceiving. In Hallaj's theology, this confession—and his commitment to die as a result of making it—grew directly out of his studied Sufi understanding of what Carl Ernst calls "the central concept of Islamic theology"—*tawhid*.[4]

Tawhid

What is *tawhid*? Annemarie Schimmel calls it "the central mystery of Islam."[5] For orthodox Muslims it means "affirming the oneness (of God)."[6] Arguably, it is the central teaching of the Qur'an. "Your God is One God. There is no God but he" (sura 2.163). God is not a Trinity (sura 5.76). He has no begotten son (sura 2.116), nor daughters, nor consorts (sura 6.100–101)—no partners or associate deities (sura 6.22–24).[7] The central significance of this doctrine is underscored by the Qur'an's condemnation of *shirk*, which means associating anything with God or allowing anything to usurp God's place. *Shirk* is, as it were, the Islamic "unforgivable sin" (sura 4.48).[8]

Tawhid, in addition to affirming the awesome oneness of God, means for Sufis the "existential [or 'interiorized'] realization" of God's unity; in

---

2. Ernst, *Words of Ecstasy*, 17.

3. Massignon, *Passion*, 1.liv.

4. Ernst, *Words of Ecstasy*, 29.

5. Schimmel, *Mystical Dimensions*, 17.

6. Ernst, *Words of Ecstasy*, 29.

7. Esposito, *Islam*, 22.

8. Ibid.

short, the "making one," or "unification" of the Sufi with God.[9] The classical Sufi formulation of *tawhid* was articulated by Abu'l-Qasim al-Junayd:
"*Tawhid*," he said, "is the isolation of the eternal from the temporal."[10] Ernst
comments that "this is the way of negation. Perfect unity in isolation can be
expressed only by rejecting all concepts tied to the world of multiplicity."[11]
This "way of negation" purging multiplicity is ultimately, for Hallaj, *self-*
negation, the rejection of *aniyah*, or "I-ness."

Hallaj (along with his Sufi predecessor Bayezid Bistami) is perhaps
most famous for repeatedly "losing" his selfhood. As a result of his understanding of *tawhid*, he perceived his "self" as ambiguously and strangely
permeated or "mixed" with the divine Self. As he is quoted in *Sharh-i Sha-
thiyat*: "My spirit mixes with Your spirit, in nearness and in distance, so that
I am You, just as You are I." This statement seems to be a truncated version
of Hallaj's longer statement, in which he confesses to Allah: "Your spirit was
mixed in my spirit, just like wine and clear water, and if something touches
You, it touches me, for You are I in every state."[12] Such statements indicate
that even the strictest monotheism does not prevent deification. In the case
of al-Hallaj, interestingly, monotheism heightens the radicality and reality
of deification for all who are able to follow him.

To be sure, Hallaj believed that an "incommensurable hiatus" divides
God and humankind.[13] He greatly underscored the difference between
qidam, "Allah's absoluteness and Eternity" and *hadath*, "what is created in
time."[14] In his book *Kithab Tawasin*, Hallaj cries:

> Glory be to God, Who is Holy, inaccessible to every device of the
> people of experiment, to every intuition of the people of feeling!
> . . . For his part, God, in his pure divinity, exists, transcending
> all contingencies. Praise be to God, whom no second cause
> affects; his proof is strong; his argument glorious; he, the Lord
> of Splendor, Glory, and Majesty! Indivisibly one, not *one* like
> arithmetical unity! Neither definition, deduction, beginning,
> nor end reaches Him. His existence is a marvel, for he has no

9. Ernst, *Words of Ecstasy*, 28–29; cf. Schimmel, *Mystical Dimensions*, 23.

10. Ernst, *Words of Ecstasy*, 29. Schimmel has a slightly different translation of this
in *Mystical Dimensions*: "*tawhid* is the separation of the eternal from that which has
been originated in time by the covenant," which also means "to go out of the narrow-
ness of temporal signs into the wide fields of eternities" (ibid., 58).

11. Ibid., 29.

12. Ibid., 27.

13. Massignon, *Passion*, 27.

14. Schimmel, *Mystical Dimensions*, 72.

mode of existence! He alone knows himself, the Lord of Splendor and Praise (sura 55.27, 78) . . . ![15]

Even with this extremely exalted view of God, Schimmel argues that "in rare moments of ecstasy [Hallaj believed that] the uncreated spirit may be united with the created human spirit, and the mystic then becomes the living personal witness of God and may declare *Ana' l-Haqq*."[16] In language lisping after infinity, Hallaj declares that God's transcendent

> "He" flows into the pronoun of subjects of persons (living and speaking); (like an arrow). He enters them, surprises them, astounds them; grazes them and dazzles them, while passing through them. That is the whole of created substances and of created qualities; God has nothing to do with chimeras![17]

Annihilation: Orthodox Foundations

Hallaj's radical experiences of self-annihilation (*fana'*) and permanent establishment in God (*baqa'*) are conceptually rooted in the *hadith qudsi*, or the "divine sayings." The *hadith qudsi*, Ernst explains, are "extra-Quranic revelations in which Muhammad reported what God said to Him."[18] They are considered canonical *hadith* by orthodox Muslims. "The most famous of the divine sayings," Ernst asserts, "is the saying on supererogatory worship (*hadith al-nawafil*), which expresses an experience in which the worshiper feels the divine presence so strongly that his volition is taken up by God, and all his actions are performed by God."[19] According to the revelation,

> my servant continues drawing nearer to me through supererog-atory acts until I love him. And when I love him, I become his ear with which he hears, his eyes with which he sees, his hand with which he grasps, and his foot with which he walks . . .[20]

This is the word of God to the Prophet. What it means for our purposes is that Hallaj had a basis in his own scriptural tradition for his experience of being penetrated and assumed by Allah.[21]

15. *Tawasin*, translated in Massignon, *Passion*, 320–21.

16. Schimmel, *Mystical Dimensions*, 72.

17. *Tawasin* in Massignon, *Passion*, 318–19.

18. Ernst, *Words of Ecstasy*, 9.

19. Ibid., 9.

20. Ibid., 9–10.

21. Abu Bakr al-Kharraz (died 899) is credited with originating the theory of *fana'*

The most important commentator on the *hadith qudsi* in the century before Hallaj's birth was the sixth Shii imam, Ja'far al-Sadiq (died 765). It was Ja'far who found the key to the nature of "I-ness" (*aniyah*) in the words by which God identified himself in his encounter with Moses on Mount Sinai (Qur'an 20.12). On this occasion, God said: "I am I, your Lord (*inni ana rabbuka*)." It was after God said this, according to Ja'far, that Moses realized that

> it is not proper for anyone but God to speak of himself by using these words *inna ana*, "I am I." I was seized by a stupor, and annihilation (*fana'*) took place. I said then: "You! You are He who is and who will be eternally, and Moses has no place with you nor the audacity to speak, unless you let him subsist by your subsistence (*baqa'*) and you endow him with your attribute [of existence]." . . . He [God] replied to me: "None but I can bear my speech, none can give me a reply; I am he who speaks and he who is spoken to, and you are a phantom (*shabah*) between the two, in which speech takes place."[22]

The "phantom" nature of creatures is made most clear in Hallaj's development of the Iblis (Satan) tradition. In sura 7 of the Qur'an, Iblis is commanded to prostrate himself before the pre-created image of Adam, endowed with the qualities of the divine Self (*huwa huwa*).[23] In verse 12, Iblis refuses this command by crying out: "*I am better than Adam!*" The assertion of "I-ness," according to al-Hallaj, was the root of Satan's sin. If he had not said "I," he would not have thought himself better than Adam. In reality, Iblis—and all creation—was nothing before the divine Self.

This "nothingness" of all created selves is the flipside of Hallaj's deep understanding of *tawhid*. Only God is a Self; only God can say "I." It is this realization which prevented Hallaj from saying "I" for himself. If he was to express the "I" of anyone, it would have to be the only legitimate "I"—the "I" of God. In this way, his declaration "I am God" can be read as perfectly orthodox. *Ana' l-Haqq* and *la illaha illa Allah* ("God alone is God," the central confession of Islam) have identical meanings. For the "I" in Hallaj's

---

and *baqa'*. He wrote that "only God has the right to say 'I,' for whoever says 'I' will not reach the level of gnosis." Al-Kharraz also said, "The only true subject is . . . God" whose divine "I" is "ontologically connected with the divine name, *al-Haqq*" (Schimmel, *Mystical Dimension*, 55).

22. Ernst, *Words of Ecstasy*, 10.

23. In his *Riwayat*, Hallaj declares, "God made a covenant with the Banu Adam seven thousand years before he created the body of Adam; then there were only spiritualities" (Massignon, *Passion*, 3.331).

"*I* am God" is God's "I." The word of al-Hallaj is in fact God's word.[24] "I wonder at you and me," Hallaj says to God:

> You annihilated me out of myself into you. You made me near
> to yourself, so that I thought that I was you and you were me.[25]
> Is it you or I?
> That would be two gods in me;
> far, far be it from you to assert duality!
> The "He-ness" that is yours is my nothingness forever.
> My "all" added to your "All" would be a double disguise.
> But where is your Essence, from my vantage point when I see you,
> since my essence has become plain in the place where I am not?
> And where is your face? It is the object of my gaze,
> whether in my inmost heart or in the glance of my eye.[26]

Although in innovative—and beautiful—poetic form, this is not a radical new doctrine. Nor is this reading of *tawhid* and its implications for the human self a Hallajian idiosyncrasy. Abu Muhammad al-Ruwaym, a Baghdadi and contemporary of Hallaj (died 915), defined *tawhid* as "the effacement of the characteristics of humanity and the stripping bare of divinity."[27] He refers, according to Sarraj, to "the transformation of the character of the soul, because it pretends to lordship by regarding its own actions, as when the creature says 'I'; but none says 'I' save God, for selfhood (*aniyah*) belongs to God."[28] These comments proceed directly from Junayd's paradigmatic definition of *tawhid*: "*Tawhid* is the isolation of the eternal from the temporal."[29]

Hallaj was familiar with these developments (he was a one-time disciple of Junayd), which we can trace throughout his writings. Once he claimed, "When you become obliterated, you arrive at a place in which nothing is obliterated or confirmed. . . . It is the divine erasings and effacements. . . . It is inexpressible."[30] Here we have a "hook word" reaching back to earlier tradition. Again, to quote al-Ruwaym, *tawhid* is "the *effacement* of the characteristics of humanity and the stripping bare of divinity."[31]

---

24. Ernst, *Words of Ecstasy*, 10–11.
25. Ibid., 27.
26. Ibid., 27–28.
27. Ibid., 29.
28. Ibid.
29. Ibid.
30. Ibid.
31. Ibid., emphasis added.

In Hallaj's understanding of *tawhid*, "transcendent unity existentially merges with divine selfhood."[32] For Hallaj this development is perfectly logical—and entirely orthodox. In fact, for him, those who claimed to be an "I" were the real *kafir* (unbelievers, heretics).

The Original Sin

Allah, Hallaj believed, created Adam from nothing. In this creation, God granted many gifts to Adam, but he did not grant him independent permanent substantiality, that is, "I-ness." To do so would be for God to associate something with himself (an unthinkable instance of *shirk*). But Adam was not left without an "I." He, and all human beings, had "I-ness" in God—but only in God. God is the root of human selfhood and permanence. For Hallaj, "God's nature contains human nature within it."[33]

Any independent "I-ness" that Adam garnered had to be presumptuously produced by Adam himself. It had to be fabricated out of nothing (where human beings came from, and what all human beings truly are). This projection of the sham self, according to Hallaj, is what all human beings typically (indeed, automatically) perform. They are deceived by the first creature to claim an "I"—Iblis. This declaration of independent selfhood was the first and most deeply rooted instance of *shirk*. From this primordial self-assertion flowed all other idolatry.

In one sense, Hallaj seems to say what is commonly preached from contemporary pulpits: "the root of idolatry is egoism." But Hallaj was more radical. For him, the root of idolatry is egoity itself. To claim an ego is to claim only what God can claim. It is a claim to *be*, thus to be what God is (true Being), and thus to be God.

What this means is that Hallaj accused his contemporaries of exactly the sin that they accused him of: claiming to be God. For Hallaj, the case was just the opposite. He was the only Muslim who, by his affirmation *Ana' l-Haqq*, claimed *not* to be God. He claimed to be nothing—for in reality, there was nothing except God.

If this interpretation is correct, it is logical that Hallaj considered himself to be a witness to God, and to God's divine truth.[34] "God," he says, "uttered through me, coming from my heart, my knowledge: with my tongue.

---

32. Ibid.

33. Schimmel, *Mystical Dimensions*, 72. Schimmel also observes that, "human nature was reflected in the creation of Adam and Adam became *huwa huwa*, 'exactly He.'"

34. Ernst writes that "once Hallaj was accused of pretending to prophethood. He said, 'Shame on you! You make so little of my worth!'" (*Words of Ecstasy*, 38).

He brought me near him after I had been far from him. He made me his close friend, and he chose me."[35] Hallaj spoke for God—he could speak *as* God—because he was *in* God. As he says in his final prayer:

> What of you, then, when you have likened yourself in my essence, at the end of my transformations, and you have called my essence, "My Essence." You have shown the realities of my sciences and my miracles, by rising in my ascents to the celestial canopies of my eternities, in the speaking by my creatures . . .[36]

Ernst comments on this prayer:

> the divinized man [Hallaj] experiences the proofs of divinity as divine acts in his soul, acts whose overwhelming Agency completely annihilates the limited role of the separate observer. The transformation is developed with great subtlety. The activities ordinarily considered merely human—"science and explanation, power and proof"—are modes by which the Spirit speaks. Yet when God calls the human essence His, then, as the progression from the human "my" to the divine "My" attempts to show, the human speaks with the authority of God.[37]

Repentance

Ana' l-Haqq. It was a public declaration, and a declaration by which Allah, through the mirage of Hallaj, called his people to repent. As Hallaj once told a disciple, "God Most High is the very one who himself affirms his unity by the tongue of whatever of his creatures he wishes. If he himself affirms his unity by my tongue, it is he and his affair . . ."[38]

By declaring his profound understanding of God's unity, Hallaj called his contemporaries to repent not from any individual or particular sins—nor even from the chief sin (*shirk*)—but rather from the root of all *shirk*: *aniyah*. If he could deliver his people from this sin, they could be true Muslims; they could submit to the unique "I-ness" of Allah.

But few Muslims—particularly the legalists and politicians—understood Hallaj's meaning. Only the Sufis understood. Nevertheless, most Baghdadi Sufis (following Junayd) practiced *isharat*, "subtle allusion to the Truth,"

---

35. *Tawasin*, Massignon, *Passion*, 1.293.

36. Ernst, *Words of Ecstasy*, 41–42.

37. Ibid., 42.

38. Ibid., 45.

as opposed to its direct proclamation.[39] Hallaj spoke from the rooftops—and what he declared sounded like the ravings of a madman: *Ana' l-Haqq.*[40]

This declaration was not meant to confuse. It was meant, I suggest, to jar people out of their egoity. At the very least, it would get people thinking about the boundaries between the human and the divine. What they would discover is that the boundaries of the human self were more permeable and instable than they formerly thought. Human reality, as Hallaj realized, was shot through with God. God was ultimate. God existed everywhere, in everyone—and everyone in God.

There was no disputing the profundity of Allah's oneness as it is taught in the Qur'an and supported in the *hadith qudsi.* Hallaj's interpretation of it, however, was radical: human beings could no longer claim to be an "I." To claim to be an "I" was a lie, and—in the deepest sense—*shirk*, the unforgivable sin. Nevertheless, as Hallaj observed, everyone did it—even those who claimed to submit to the ultimate reality of God (the Muslim community). Even for them, the claim to be an "I" functioned as the universal presupposition of their mental existence, which Hallaj, for all his heroic declarations, could not dislodge. Hallaj could not even dislodge it from himself.

So he conceived an idea. Hallaj knew that he was misunderstood. He knew that he would die misunderstood. But perhaps in that death he could atone for that misunderstanding, and for his own self-willed separation from God. Hallaj once prayed: "Between you and me there is an 'I am' that battles me, so take away, by your grace, this 'I am' from in between."[41] Death would be the answer to his prayer. It would mean that his "I" could never rise again. The final veil between him and God—his selfhood—would be ripped away.

Conclusion: At-one-ment

But there is more to the mystery of Hallaj's death. There is evidence that he conceived of his death as an atonement, not only for him, but for the entire *umma* (or Muslim community) who lived their ordinary existence totally unaware of their idolatry.[42] Hallaj would be aware for them. He would annihilate his "I" for them. He would die for them.

Perhaps some would understand and follow his example. At the very least, they would raise questions. Why would Hallaj not merely recant (or at

39. Schimmel, *Mystical Dimensions*, 59.

40. Schimmel observes that Hallaj sinned by revealing the secrets of his love for God (ibid., 64).

41. Ernst, *Words of Ecstasy*, 27–28.

42. Ibid., 45, 69.

least admit insanity)? Why be imprisoned for eleven years and submit to a death intended only for the worst of unbelievers? What was he saying in his ecstatic utterances? What did he mean by his death? It was, I think, made clear through his final words, spoken from his cross: "It is enough for the ecstatic that the One be single in himself."[43]

On the night of his execution, during the evening prayer, Hallaj was heard whispering *makr, makr* ("a ruse, a ruse") far into the night. Silence followed. Finally Hallaj made the cry *Haqq, haqq* ("Truth, truth!").[44] Hallaj was a witness to the truth of *tawhid*. What follows is his final recorded prayer:

> We are your witnesses (*shawahid*). . . . It is you who manifest as you wish the likeness of your manifestation in your decree, as "the most beautiful form" (i.e., Adam), the form in which is the Spirit speaking by science and explanation, power and proof. You have intimated your essence, of which the quality is "He is," to your witness (*shahid*, i.e., Hallaj), whose quality is "I am."[45]

The motif of Hallaj as witness finds its culmination in perhaps Hallaj's most beautiful poem:

> Between me and the Truth there remains neither
> discursive explanation
> nor evidence
> nor proven signs . . .
> Firm indication of God comes
> from Him and
> through Him
> to one who witnesses the Truth
> as He reveals it in sending down the power of discrimination.
> Firm indication of God from him and through him and toward
> him
> we have found in truth,
> indeed a knowledge clear.
> This is my existence,
> my affirmation,
> my conviction;
> thus God brings into one
> my affirmation of God's transcendent unity
> and my faith.[46]

43. Ibid., 45.
44. Ibid., 41.
45. Ibid., 41–42.
46. Quoted in McGinn, *Knowledge of God*, 102–3.

Chapter 10

"God's Being is My Life"

Meister Eckhart's Birth in God

But *we* are before the foundation of the world, we—because we had to come about in him—were born beforehand in God. We are the rational creations of God's Reason, through whom we exist from the beginning, for "in the beginning was Reason."

—CLEMENT OF ALEXANDRIA, *PROTREP.* 1.6.4

ON MARCH 27, 1329, Pope John XXII condemned the teachings of Meister Eckhart (1259–1327 C.E.) in the papal bull "In the Lord's field." The holy father found the following articles "quite evil sounding and very rash and suspect of heresy, though with many explanations and additions they might take on or possess a Catholic meaning."[1] They are (in their original numbering):

20. . . . the good man is the only-Begotten son of God.

21. The noble man is that only-Begotten son of God whom the Father generates from all eternity.

22. The Father gives birth to me, his son and the same son. Everything that God performs is one; therefore he gives me, his son, birth without any distinction.[2]

---

1. McGinn, *Meister Eckhart*, 80.
2. For a translation of the entire bull, see ibid., 77–81.

These strange sayings cannot merely be passed off as the speculation of a mystic "led astray," in the pope's phrase, "by the Father of Lies."[3] They come from a person, a scholar, an administrator, a spiritual guide, and a beloved preacher who bubbled over with excitement in his profound—if eccentric—experience of God.

Born in 1259 in what is now Germany, Meister Eckhart was named "Johann," or "John." Eckhart's parents were wealthy enough to have him thoroughly educated. Probably around the age of eighteen, he entered the Dominican order, the "Order of Preachers." The Dominicans of Eckhart's time, like Dominicans today, live a life of study, prayer, and preaching to the people.

Academic training in the Dominican order was rigorous. As a bright student, Eckhart pursued his studies for many years. At the age of thirty-four he became lecturer at the University of Paris, where he later twice occupied the chair of Dominican theology—a rare honor. As an instructor in the university, Eckhart was called *Magister*, Latin for "teacher." This was translated into the German "Meister," an honorary title for Eckhart that people used before and after his death.

Despite his sojourns in Paris, Meister Eckhart lived in Germany for most of his adult life, laboring as an administrator in his order. In this capacity, he gradually rose to the highest ranks of his provincial chapter. His administrative role involved him in frequent traveling. As he traveled, he preached to different parishes and religious houses in Germany.

In his late sixties, while teaching in Cologne, he was abruptly put on trial for heresy. Forty-nine "articles" (i.e., short excerpts from Eckhart's sermons and books) were drawn up by his religious and political enemies. These articles were taken as indicative of the elderly man's unorthodoxy. Eckhart had a chance to respond to this set of articles, as well as to another set of fifty-nine articles in the presence of his inquisitors. When they were slow to make a ruling, Eckhart appealed to Pope John XXII. This incident occurred during the period of the so-called "Babylonian Captivity" of the papal court, which was temporarily residing in Avignon, France.

When Eckhart arrived in Avignon, the pope appointed a theological commission to review a revised and abbreviated list of articles pulled from Eckhart's works. Eckhart, though his powers were failing, appeared before this committee to defend his teachings. Later, in consultation with the theological commission and a group of his cardinals, John XXII decided to condemn Eckhart's teachings in the bull described above. A year and a half before the bull was issued, Eckhart had quietly died.

3. Ibid., 77.

Eckhart's works, like his life, are varied and complex. Therefore it is necessary to narrow our scope as we discuss his doctrine and experience of deification. I will focus on only the three articles drawn from the papal bull above. They state, in essence, that the good or noble man is God's only-Begotten son. This man, as we come to intuit, is Eckhart himself. Eckhart, somewhat like al-Hallaj, spoke of his indistinct and eternal union with divinity. He called the realization of this union the "breakthrough" (*durchbrechen*).[4]

Breakthrough

John Tauler, a student of Eckhart, formulated one rule for interpreting the Meister that must always be kept in mind. Tauler wrote, "He [Eckhart] spoke in terms of eternity and you understood in terms of time."[5] Time, Eckhart believed, necessarily involved multiplicity and materiality which drew his hearers away from God.[6] The goal of Eckhart's preaching was to spark his audience's realization of their unity with the incorporeal, simple, and eternal God.

Excluding time from his conception of God produced an original rhetoric for Eckhart, but not an original theology. Christian theologians since the fourth century had thought in these terms. Augustine was among the most profound and eloquent.[7] It was to Augustine whom Eckhart constantly appealed to in order to ground his freedom from time. Twice in the Cologne proceedings, Eckhart quoted Augustine's *Confessions*,[8] where the bishop addresses God:

---

4. Sermon 15 (*DW* 1.251–53 = *Essential Sermons*, 192); Sermon 48 (*DW* 2.417–19 = *Essential Sermons*, 198); Sermon 52 (*DW* 2.503–6 = *Essential Sermons*, 203). See also Sermon 29 (*DW* 2.76–80), translated in McGinn, *Teacher and Preacher*, 288; Sermon 84 (*DW* 3.460–65 = *Teacher and Preacher* 336–37). In Latin, he called the breakthrough the "return" (*reditus*). See Eckhart's *Commentary on John* nn. 546–51 in *LW* 3.477–81.

5. Taken from Tauler's Sermon 15, *Clarifica me, pater charitate*. The saying is commented on in Ruh, *Meister Eckhart*, 11; and Kelley, *Meister Eckhart on Divine Knowledge*, 4.

6. The Meister repeatedly emphasized this point. See, for instance, Sermon 11 (*DW* 1.179–89), Sermon 50 (*DW* 2.454–60); *Commentary on Wisdom* n. 281–82 (*LW*, 2.613–15).

7. *Conf.* 11; *Cons. ev.* 1.35.53; *Enarrat. in Ps.* 2.7. For Augustine on time and eternity, see Cavadini, "Time and Ascent," 171–86; Thompson, "Theological Dimension of Time," 187–94.

8. 1.6.10. See Théry, "Edition critique," 206, 208.

Because your years do not fail, your years are the day of
Today. And now how many of our days and our fathers' days
have passed through your Today.... "Yet you are the very same,"
and all our tomorrows and beyond and all our yesterdays and
before you will make your Today, you have made your Today.[9]

God does not exist in time, but in an eternal present with neither past
nor future. This was standard theology in Eckhart's time. What was original
for Eckhart was his application of God's eternal "Today" to human beings.
"God's day," he preached, "is where the [human] soul exists in the day of
eternity in an essential 'now.' And here [in God's eternal present] God gives
birth to his only-Begotten son."[10] Eckhart concluded that the "heavenly
Father is truly my Father, for I am his son and have everything that I have
from him, and I am the same son and not a different one. Because the
Father performs one work, therefore his work is me, his only-Begotten son
without any difference."[11]

Eckhart's insistence that he is one with the only-Begotten son of
God—a designation Catholic Christians reserved for Jesus Christ—
seemed suspect. The Meister seemed to claim that he was eternal. In this
way, Eckhart's teaching appeared to collide head-on with the orthodox
Christian doctrine of creation from nothing, which strictly separates reality into eternal God and temporal creation. If creation came from nothing,
it could not be eternal.

Eckhart, however, was not considering himself as a created being.
He had tasted eternity, and in eternity there is no multiplicity. In God's
eternal Today, our being is not ours, but God's. Our everyday life on earth
is conditioned by time, matter, and space. These elements of our earthly
existence make possible a story—a sequence of events. But in eternity there
can be no storyline. In the bowels of "forever" all is intensely and joyously
the same. Therefore one cannot "describe" Eckhart's experience of birth in
God—there is no sequence of narration. One can only trace out the path
whereby Eckhart predisposed himself to be struck by the lightning of this
onto-theological deduction: his identity with God's son.

---

9. In his defense, Eckhart also refers to the statements on God's eternity in *Conf.*
11. He also may have been familiar with Augustine's *Serm.* 117, which treats the co-
eternity of the son (McGinn, *Essential Sermons*, 40). Eckhart also quotes this passage in
his *Commentary on John* nn. 580, 638 (*LW* 3.508, 554).

10. Sermon 10 (*DW* 1.166–67 = *Teacher and Preacher*, 263). Cf. also what Eckhart
says about the "fullness of time" in Sermon 24 (*DW* 1.421–23 = *Teacher and Preacher*,
286), and McGinn's comments in *Mystical Thought*, 125–26.

11. Sermon 6, *Essential Sermons*, 188.

Entering the Ground

Eckhart's point of connection between himself and the eternal God is his "intellect," which is neither his brain, nor his faculty for abstract reasoning. It is something much deeper than normal, everyday rationality. "Intellect" as humanity's spiritual core sounds like a throw-back to Hermetic and Plotinian thought, but Eckhart firmly grounds it in biblical teaching. The intellect is part of the image of God. The image of God is not defaced (who or what could remove God's imprint?); nor is the image something merely earthly—constituted by our bodily shape, emotions, or language (all of which are shared on a lower level by animals). When the creator makes his mark on humans, he does not inscribe something created. He stamps on people a part of his true self: his eternity. According to the Bible, God "has put eternity into their hearts" (Eccl 3:11). Eternity is not something created, but proceeds directly from God. This inward bit of eternity Eckhart calls "the ground."

How does one enter "the ground"? Humanly speaking, it is impossible. There are no "ways"—religious or secular—into the ground. "Whoever is seeking God by ways," Eckhart warned, "is finding ways and losing God, who in ways is hidden."[12] Although the breakthrough cannot be manufactured, however, one can predispose oneself to experience it.

Eckhart prepared himself for timeless union with God by trying to understand it. He attempted to think without time. "Take away time," the Meister said, "and evening is the same as morning."[13] Time is the measure of change. Only material reality is subject to change. Therefore in eternity, there is no matter. If there is no matter, there is no space. With no space, there is no distinction between beings. There is, technically, no "thing" in the ground. This great No-thing—whom no one has seen or can see—is God, who is this eternal ground, doing what he does eternally: giving birth to his son, the same reality as himself.

God eternally giving birth to his son (the Word of God) is perhaps a strange image to Christians today. Nevertheless, this was the teaching of the early church. At the councils of Nicea (325 C.E.) and Constantinople (381 C.E.), it was determined that the Father did not create the son of God (Christ), but gave birth to him eternally. Eckhart, speaking from the abyss of eternity, applied this distinction to human beings.

12. Sermon 5b, *Essential Eckhart*, 183.
13. *Commentary on John*, n. 8; *Essential Eckhart*, 124.

Augustinian Background

Speaking in time, Augustine drew a distinction between the son of God by nature (Jesus) and the sons of God by adoption (the elect brothers and sisters of Jesus). God "sent [the son] into this world," Augustine affirmed, "so that he would not be the only one, but have many adopted brothers. For we are not born from God in the manner of that only-Begotten [son], but we are adopted through his grace."[14] God's son, we are told, "never joined us together so as not to make a distinction between us and himself."[15]

In spite of these remarks, Augustine's theology of the Word opposes a distinction between eternal Word and what is eternally "in" the Word. According to the Gospel of John, "In the beginning was the Word, and the Word was with God, and the Word was God" (1:1). The Word is the son of God. What does John mean by calling the son the "Word"? In his Latin commentaries, Eckhart tells us that the word "Word" in Greek is *Logos*, which also means "Idea," "Mind," or "Reason." God's Mind is "in the beginning," eternally begotten as God's child.

God's Reason (whom John says is "with" God and "is" God) contains the essential nature of all things in an ideal state, like thoughts in a thinker's mind. "In him was life" (John 1:4), a life that Eckhart took to refer to the life of all beings. The living beings in God's Mind (or Reason) are not airy and inconsequential. They are forms and models for what corresponds to them in our material world. In God's mind (or son) is the Idea of a flower that is more real than the daisies and tulips and pansies we see around us, since all the flowers that we see are based on the Idea of flower in God's mind. This ideal flower is the very *nature* of flower, the "archetype" of which all other flowers are merely the images. Likewise, the Word or son of God contains the idea or form of Eckhart more real than the Meister himself.

In this line of reasoning Eckhart again adheres close to Augustine. The bishop understood John 1:3 ("all things were made through him" [i.e., the Word]) to mean that all things were eternally pre-contained in God's mind "prior" to their creation. "God is one," says the bishop of Hippo, "he has one Word, he contains all things in one Word."[16] This (Platonic) idea played a central role in Eckhart's works. "In the Father are the images of all created things," he preached. "This piece of wood has a rational image in God. It is not merely rational, but it is pure reason."[17] The wood beam in the Word

14. *In Ioh. Tract.* 2.13.1.

15. *In Ioh. Tract.* 21.3.2. Cf. 21.3.2 and 75.1. See also McGinn, *Essential Eckhart*, 53; Théry, "Edition critique," 198–99; 201, 214–15, 220, 231–32, 243–44, 265, 266.

16. *Tract. Ev. Jo.* 22.

17. Sermon 22 (*DW* 1.376–77 = *Essential Sermons*, 193). Cf. also his *Commentary*

is not material, but ideal. It is also eternal. Since God's Reason is eternal, what is in Reason must be eternal as well. Augustine says: "There [in the Word] . . . there is neither 'was' nor 'will be' but only 'is.'"[18] Moreover, the "knowledge" of the Word is "eternal and from an eternal, and [is] coeternal with him from whom it is [i.e., God]."[19] Eckhart drew the deduction: If human beings are in God's Word (or mind), they are as eternal as God himself.

The realization of humanity's eternal existence in the Word made possible Eckhart's language of indistinct union with God's Mind, or son.

> When we say that all things are in God [this means that] just as he himself is indistinct in his own nature [i.e., totally *one*] and nevertheless the most distinct from everything else [i.e., totally separate from creation], so in himself are all things [in their ideal state] simultaneously most distinct [from what corresponds to them in creation] and indistinct [from God].[20]

Since the Word is *one*, as Augustine said earlier, all things in the Word are one too (even though "down here" on earth they are many).[21] "All things" (cf. John 1:3) includes the adopted sons of God (John 1:12–13). As *in* God's son, they are one *with* God's eternal son. Humans, in other words, insofar as they *are* God's thoughts (i.e., existing as pure intellect) *are* also God's Word.[22] The human intellect in the Word (which Eckhart often calls the "spark" [*vûnklein*], or "little castle" [*bûrgelin*]) is in essence a little word eternally begotten by and in the Word. It is, in Eckhart's terminology, a "son."[23] But this son, as word within Word, is no different in reality from the son (or mind) of God eternally begotten of the Father. Both are intellect, the eternal

---

on Wisdom n. 283 (*LW* 2.616): "The image, however, inasmuch as it is a formal emanation, has the characteristic sense of 'boiling' [i.e., it is identical with the intra-Trinitarian being]."

18. *Trin.* 4.1.3.

19. Ibid.

20. *Sermon* IV, (*LW* 4.27–28; n. 28). For further sources, see, McGinn, *Teacher and Preacher,* 211, n. 12).

21. *Trin.* 4.1.3. The Christian adaptation of the doctrine of the divine ideas was also expressed by Augustine in *De diversis quaestionibus* 83.46.

22. Eckhart points out in his response to the forty-nine articles that the word "insofar as" (*inquantum*) is the key to interpreting his works, particularly his "rare and subtle" passages (McGinn, *Essential Eckhart*, 72). It indicates that one is speaking from a single, limited point of view—the viewpoint of eternity.

23. This "son" is the knowledge of the Word. But the knowledge of the Word, says Augustine, also *is* the Word, for "the knowledge of the son is not one thing and the son himself another" (*Tract. Ev. Jo.* 21.4.4–5.1).

nature of God. In Eckhart's short formulation, "Whatever is in God *is* God; it cannot be removed from him."[24]

The Articles

With this background in place, the language of Eckhart's articles begins to take on if not a Catholic then at least a reasonable meaning! Article 20 ("That the good man is the only-Begotten son of God") is probably a summary of a passage found in part one of Eckhart's book, *Blessed Be* (also called *The Book of Divine Consolation*). Eckhart states that it applies to the good man only "insofar as he is good" (*als verre er guot ist*).[25] That is, only insofar as the person participates in the Form of the Good, and thus is not a particular person but the form of Goodness itself. The "good," Eckhart explains, "names and comprises in itself nothing else . . . than bare and pure Goodness (*güete*)."[26] Goodness and the good, Eckhart wrote in his defense, "are one. For the good, insofar as it is good, signifies Goodness alone; just as white signifies . . . whiteness. These—the good and Goodness—are unequivocally one in the son."[27]

The eternal son of God is the form of Goodness, or absolute Goodness. To the degree that a person participates in Goodness, this person is the son of Goodness. "For I am," Eckhart said, "the son of everything that forms and bears me to be like it and in its likeness."[28] But there is only one Goodness, and only one son. So if someone is to be a child of God, one must be, in varying degrees, God's only-Begotten son (i.e., Goodness itself). For "the son in the divinity according to his proper attribute (*eigenschaft*) gives nothing else than the essence of the son (*sun-wesen*)."[29] The Meister summarized his teaching:

> [A] good man and goodness have a mutual relationship and depend on one another, in this way. Goodness is not created, not

24. Sermon 3 (*DW* 1.56 = *Teacher and Preacher*, 246). The Meister affirmed this teaching also in *Sermon* IV: "a person in God is God" (*homo in deo deus est*) (*LW* 4.27–28; n. 28).

25. *DW* 5.44 = *Essential Sermons,* 229. Eckhart mentions the *inquantum* at least three other times in *Blessed Be*: *DW* 5.8–9; 22–23; and 28–29 (= *Essential Sermons,* 209, 217, 220, respectively).

26. *DW* 5:10 = *Essential Sermons,* 210.

27. "Defense of the Forty-nine Articles" (Théry, "Edition critique," 186).

28. *Blessed Be* (*DW* 5.11 = *Essential Sermons,* 211).

29. *Blessed Be* (*DW* 5.42). The rest of the translation is taken from McGinn, *Essential Sermons,* 227.

made, not born; rather it is what gives birth and bears the good man; and the good man, insofar as he is good, is unmade and uncreated, and yet he is born, the child and the son of Goodness. . . . That which is good and Goodness are nothing else than one single Goodness in everything, apart from the one bearing and the other being born; but that Goodness does bear and that it is born in the good man, this is all one being [one son], one life.[30]

Article 21 ("The noble man is that only-Begotten son of God whom the Father generates from all eternity") comes from a passage in Eckhart's German Sermon 14:

St. John says, "Those who received him he gave the power to become sons of God" (John 1:12–13). Those who are God's son are not of flesh and blood; they are born of God, not outwardly, but inwardly. Our dear Lady [the Virgin Mary] said, "How can that be, that I become the mother of God?" Then the angel said, "the Holy Spirit shall come into you from above." David said, "Today I have given birth to you" [Ps 2:7]. What is "Today"? Eternity. I have born me you and you me eternally. Yet it is not enough for the noble, humble person that he is the only-Begotten son whom the Father has given birth to eternally. He also wishes to be the Father, to enter into the very sameness with the eternal Fatherhood, and to give birth to him from whom I was eternally born.[31]

Eckhart's language flows with a rush of excitement: the eternal son is born in the ground of humanity. In this way, humans recapitulate the experience of the Blessed Virgin, who gave birth to God's son by the Spirit within her. Males too—like king David of old—can give birth in the ground. Soon Eckhart arrives at a paradox: humans give birth to the son in the eternal ground, and in eternity the Father gives birth to them in and as the son (or Word).

As if this paradox did not slake his thirst for truth, Eckhart says more. It is not enough to be the eternal son. He also wants to enter into the sameness of the Father, and thus give birth to the eternal son himself. This idea sounds outrageous until one realizes that it flows from the wells of orthodox Christianity. The Nicene Creed affirms that the son is "one substance" (*homoousios*) with the Father. Although different in person, they are the same in essence. Thus for Eckhart to *be* in essence the son is for him to *be* the Father as well. This deduction only deepens the paradox of thinking

30. *Blessed Be* (DW 5:9 = *Essential Eckhart*, 209–10).

31. DW 1.238–39 = *Teacher and Preacher*, 273–74.

outside of time, for now Eckhart is not only born as the only-Begotten son, he is himself the Father giving birth to the son—and through the son—himself! Eternity is the mirror in which one sees oneself projected eternally backwards. Without the framework of time, the distinctions in the Trinity itself break apart.

Article 22 ("The Father gives birth to me his son and the same son. Everything that God performs is one; therefore he gives me, his son, birth without any distinction") is Eckhart's personal confession excerpted from his German Sermon 6, called "The Just Will Live Forever." The context is as follows:

> The Father gives birth to his son in eternity, equal to himself. "The Word was with God, and God was the Word" (John 1:1); it was the same in the same nature. Yet I say more: He has given birth to him in my soul. Not only is the soul with him, and he equal with it, but he is in it, and the Father gives his son birth in the soul in the same way as he gives him birth in eternity, and not otherwise[;] . . . and I say more: He gives me birth, me, his son and the same son (*den selben sun*). . . . Everything God performs is one; therefore he gives me, his son, birth without any distinction (*âne allen underscheit*).[32]

God gave birth to the son in eternity—but eternity is also *in Eckhart's soul*. So God gave birth to the son within his soul. Eternity outside the soul is the same as eternity within, for eternity is the same wherever one looks (and without time and space, there is no "where").

Eckhart characteristically says more. In eternity past, Eckhart was in the son as word in Word, when there was no difference between Eckhart and the mind of God. There is thus one single son born from all eternity—and Eckhart is part of that son. But to say "part of" already introduces space and time into eternity, which cannot be. Eckhart must be that *same* son born from all eternity. Thus we arrive at the paradox: the son is born in him in eternity and he is born in the son. "Everything that God performs," Eckhart insists, "is one": the out-flowing of the Word (the only-Begotten son) from the Father is the out-flowing of all that is *in* the Word (the adopted children). Eckhart is the Word and the Word is Eckhart. Speaking from the perspective of eternity, Eckhart—and all those who follow his path—is the only begotten son of God.

---

32. Sermon 6 in *DW* 1.109–10 = *Essential Sermons*, 187–88.

Conclusion

Although the teachings of Eckhart can seem tortuous, they are at once the passionate confessions of a man who experienced a deifying breakthrough. Sometimes Eckhart experiences breakthrough, it seems, right in the middle of a sermon. "What is life?" Eckhart once cried out. "God's being is my life! If my life is God's being, then God's existence must be my existence and God's is-ness is my is-ness, neither less nor more."[33] Once again, strict monotheism—even Platonic monotheism—proved no hindrance to deification. In the case of Eckhart, the logic of God's metaphysical singleness radicalized his union with God.

One can ask: What did Eckhart do in eternity? Nothing. But this is the point. There is nothing left to do in eternity. There is no change. All human cares and worries in this world, all pains and sufferings, all sadness and frustration are based on *change*—change within the self, and outside it. But those who are eternal in the Word are beyond change. They have nothing more to become, nothing to wait for, nothing to fret about. They have already reached the goal: indistinct union with God. This is the whole purpose of human existence for Eckhart, and the end to which all human action is (or ought to be) directed. Millions of people through their praying, fasting, confessing, writing, reading, shouting, rolling, weeping, shaking, dancing, meditating, and even self-mutilation have tried to attain union with God. But Eckhart says that this union is already an eternally accomplished fact. One simply has to realize it in the ground of one's being.

Eckhart can lead human beings along the logical path of their union with God, but his reasoning is not itself the breakthrough. It only reveals the possibility for it. The ideal existence of humanity in God's Mind (or Word) is only one (very scholastic!) way of talking about an indescribable reality. It is only one way of making sense of reality in a super-temporal and super-spatial dimension. It is only one way of stumbling into eternity. "Before the mountains were brought forth, or ever you had formed the earth and the world, even from everlasting to everlasting, you are God" (Ps 90:2). But God has buried eternity in the human heart (Eccl 3:11). In the heart, then—in the deepest core of one's being, at the intersection between time and no-time, matter and nothingness, the human and the divine—Eckhart finds the key to overcome the creator-creature divide. This is the breakthrough into the ground, a place—or rather No-place—that Eckhart called the "quiet desert, into which distinction never gazed . . ."[34]

33. Sermon 6, *Essential Sermons*, 187.
34. Sermon 48, *Essential Sermons*, 198.

Chapter 11

"Uncreated by Grace"

Deification in Gregory Palamas

Humans transcend their own nature: being mortal, they become immortal; being perishable, they become imperishable;
being ephemeral, they become everlasting; generally speaking,
being human, they become God.

—GREGORY OF NYSSA[1]

I N THE FOURTEENTH CENTURY within the monasteries of Mount Athos
in northern Greece, certain monks deep in prayer began to glow. Those
who saw the light said that it was the same light that had appeared from the
flesh of Jesus Christ on the Mount of Transfiguration (Luke 9:28–36, par.).
There, on the mountain (identified with Mount Tabor in Galilee) Jesus went
to pray (Luke 9:29). Suddenly he was transfigured, and, as Matthew's Gospel
says, his face shone like the sun (17:2). The monks on Athos who prayed in
imitation of Christ experienced the same luminous result.

The monks prayed in a specific way. Many would crouch down and—
like Elijah on Mount Carmel—put their face between their knees (1 Kgs
18:42). With their chin tucked into their chest, they directed their eyes and
their mind toward their belly. In this posture, monks attempted to free their
minds from earthly images in order to enable the purest form of converse
with God. Some monks helped clear their minds by praying the "prayer of
Jesus"—the slow, mantra-like repetition of: *"Lord Jesus, son of God, have
mercy on me."* Another technique focused on breathing. Hunched over,
monks restrained the inhalation of their breath through their nose. They

---

1. *On the Beatitudes* 7 (PG 44 1280c–d).

imagined their breath entering through their nostrils, coursing down to the lungs until it reached the regions of the heart. In this way the monks would (as they said) help to push their minds into their hearts. The goal of the prayer (in its various forms) was inward stillness—*hēsuchia* in Greek. Accordingly, praying this way was called "hesychasm" and those who prayed it "hesychasts."[2]

When the prominent philosopher and theologian Barlaam of Calabria (1290–1348) heard of hesychastic prayer from some of its leading practitioners in Thessalonica, he was aghast. "But on meeting some of your fellow hesychasts," he wrote in one letter:

> I was initiated by them—it were better I had not been—into some extraordinary and absurd teachings, unworthy of the mind, not to say of the understanding, products of a deluded fancy and unrestrained imagination. What was taught among them was certain strange disjunctions followed by conjunctions of the mind with the soul, and the soul's encounters with demons and various red and white lights, and certain mental entries and departures taking place through the nostrils rhythmically with the breathing, and certain palpitations occurring round the navel, and finally a union within the navel of our ruling element with the soul that takes place with the assurance and certainty of the heart, and such things which, in someone who practices them, seems to me would inevitably lead to sheer insanity or to filling the mind but emptying it of all sense.[3]

Barlaam was to write several letters and treatises against the hesychasts.[4] Behind the smoke and bombast of his rhetoric, we find two important criticisms. First, hesychasm is crudely materialistic. Why must one be in a particular bodily posture to receive divine light? The point of prayer, after all, is to free the mind from the body so that it can make its contemplative ascent toward God. Second—even if the monks saw a light—the light was either (a) an illusion (due to restricted breathing and undernourishment in the monasteries), or (b) an effect of God's grace. But if an effect

2. For the method, meaning and history of hesychasm see Meyendorff, *St. Gregory Palamas*, 30–38, 56–71; Ware, "Origins of the Jesus Prayer," 175–83, 242–55; Mantzaridis, "Spiritual Life in Palamism," 208–22; Corneanu, "The Jesus Prayer and Deification," 6–11; Gunnarsson, *Mystical Realism*, 31–80; 160–70; Krausmüller, "The Rise of Hesychasm," 101–26.

3. Barlaam of Calabria, *Letter* 5.114–27 (ed. Shirò, *Barlaam Calabro*, 323–24). Palamas depicted Barlaam's informants as rather simple monks (*haplousteroi*), but Rigo has shown that this is not the case (*Monaci esicasti*, 44–58, 273–74).

4. Krausmüller, "Rise of Hesychasm," 111.

of grace, the light itself is not divine—let alone God—since God cannot be seen (Exod 33:20).[5]

Gregory Palamas (1296–1359), celebrated by the Greek East as the "light of orthodoxy," was spurred to write against Barlaam in a book called *Defense of the Holy Hesychasts.*[6] This book, now commonly called *The Triads* (since it was published in bundles of three tractates each), became a— and perhaps *the*—definitive account of deification in Eastern Orthodoxy. Palamas—although he never himself claims to have been transfigured in prayer—argued for the full deity and deifying power of the light based upon his direct experience. Although an aristocrat connected with the imperial family, Gregory had entered the religious life around the age of twenty. For decades before replying to Barlaam, he had inculcated the spiritual wisdom of the monastic tradition as a monk and hermit on Mount Athos and in other places. Although Gregory himself did not believe in the development of theology, *The Triads* is a creative treatise expressing the mystery of God and the profound realism of deification in Eastern Christianity.[7]

Essence vs. Energies

"God is light," says the First Epistle of John, "and in him there is no darkness at all" (1:5). In accordance with this scriptural sentiment, Palamas argued that the light shining from the monks during prayer was not a created effect or symbol of God, but *God himself.* God the Father is light, Christ is light, and the "Spirit, too," Palamas adds, "is light, as we read: 'He who has shone in our hearts by the Holy Spirit' [cf. 2 Cor 4:6]."[8] Palamas knew the texts that indicated God's invisibility (Exod 33:20; cf. John 1:18)—but these passages, he believed, only referred to God's *essence*. What Palamas called God's *energies* could be seen by eyes that were themselves deified.

In accord with the traditional Christian emphasis on the transcendence of God, Palamas excoriates "people who teach that we can also share

5. See further on Barlaam, ibid., 110–13; McGuckin, "Barlaam of Calabria," 1.67–69.

6. In the Orthodox liturgy, Palamas is celebrated on two days: November 14 in commemoration of his passage from this life, and the second Sunday of Great Lent. On the latter day, the Orthodox celebrate "the triumph of orthodoxy"—a triumph in which Palamas played a large part.

7. Deification in Palamas has frequently been studied in recent years emphasizing various aspects. See, for instance, Mantzaridis, "La doctrine," 45–160; Flogaus, *Theosis bei Palamas,* 77–284; Savvidis, *Lehre,* 153–94; Lison, "La divinisation," 59–70; Williams, "Light from Byzantium," 483–96; Williams, *Ground of Union,* 102–56; Alfeyev, "Deification," 120–22; Russell, *Doctrine of Deification,* 304–9; Russell, "Theosis," 357–79.

8. Christ as light: *Tr.* 3.1.16; Spirit as light: ibid., 3.1.12.

in God's supra-essential essence."[9] Those who become one spirit with God (1 Cor 6:17) "are not united to God in substance (*kat' ousian*)." Rather, God is "imparticiple (*amethekton*) in substance." Humans united to God, however, do not thereby unite with something *less* than God. Rather, they "are united to God in energy (*kat' energeian*)." The spirit by which they are made one with God "is called and is indeed the uncreated *energy* of the Spirit and not the *essence* of God."[10]

This distinction between the essence and the energies of God has become one of the most (in)famous distinctions in all of Christian theology. Its implications for understanding God are disputed, but its function in Palamas' thought is not: it allows him to express the full reality of deification while simultaneously protecting the mystery of God. To express his theory in brief: there is the *essence* of God which cannot be shared, and the *energies* of God which can.[11] Both essence and energies of God *are* God (since there can be no real division in the Godhead). Thus deified Christians truly participate in the *reality* of God, even if that reality has two different aspects.[12] In Palamas' delicately balanced formulation: "the deifying light is also *essential* (*ousiōdes*), but is not itself the *essence* of God (*ouk auto ousia theou*)."[13] By being illumined, Christians partake of *true* (i.e., "essential") God even though God's reality is not fully comprehended and thus reduced to something less than what it is.

As Palamas stresses, the essence of God is *more than God*. We have already seen this idea in Plotinus, who said that the One is beyond divinity (*Enn.* 6.9.6.12–14).[14] For Palamas, the God beyond God means that the

9. *Hom.* 8.13.

10. *Cap.* 75.

11. Early in *Tr.*, Palamas speaks of the energies of God in the biblical language of God's "glory." "God has given his glory to human nature, but not his essence, even though divine glory and divine nature are inseparable" (2.3.15). Glory is not God's nature even if it is inseparable from that nature (1.3.23). When humans see in themselves the glory of God, they are deified (2.3.17).

12. One can think of God's essence as the transcendent aspect of the divine, and the energies as the immanent aspect. Nevertheless these are not just conceptual distinctions, I would argue, but real distinctions in the Godhead. Note Palamas' formulation in *Cap.* 75: "There are three realities in God: substance, energy, and the Trinity of divine hypostases." On essence and energies, see further Gunnarsson, *Mystical Realism*, 205–52; Ware, "God Immanent yet Transcendent," 157–68; Demetracopoulos, "Palamas Transformed," 263–372. Demetracopoulos points out that Palamas went so far as to distinguish a "superordinate essence of God" (*hyperkeimenē ousia*) and a "subordinate divinity" (*theotēs hypheimenē*) (ibid., 273).

13. *Tr.* 3.1.23, emphasis mine.

14. Cf. also the Gnostic *Secret Book of John*, where the primal God, or "the Invisible Spirit" is unknowable and "superior to deity" (Berlin Gnostic Codex 23.3–6; *NHC* II 2.33–36).

divinity of God is in fact not his essence but his divine energy given as a gift to the saints.[15] In Gregory's language, God is "more-than-God" since God is "the ground and subsistence of divinity."[16] Put another way: God is not only "above all created things, but is even beyond Godhead."[17] God is called "God" not because he can be reduced to being God, but because he can *make* Gods out of human beings.[18] By pushing the essence of God beyond Godhead, Palamas makes a radical attempt to preserve God's transcendence.[19] The result for his theory of deification is clear: to be deified is always to be less than the essence of God. Deification thus never threatens God's transcendence and superiority.

The distinction between the essence and energies of God is a milestone in Christian theology, but it is also an adaptation of an ancient distinction in the Godhead between primal and mediate divinity. In the early days of Christianity, for instance, Justin Martyr was comfortable distinguishing the ultimate primal God from "another God" (*theos . . . heteros*), Jesus Christ.[20] There is one "true" (or "really existing") God (*ho ontōs theos*), and Christians give the "second place" (*deuteron chōran*) to Christ after the unchangeable, ever-existing Father.[21] In this model, one person of the Godhead (the Father) is the primal God, while another person (Christ) is the mediate God.[22]

Palamas adopts this ancient distinction between primal and mediate divinity, but applies it *not* to the *persons* of the Godhead, but to the *nature* of Christian deity itself. By Gregory's time, Christ (or the son) had—along with the Spirit—been identified with the essence (*ousia*) of God in the famous councils of Nicea (325 C.E.) and Constantinople (381 C.E.). Thus Christ and the Spirit could not anymore be identified with a mediate divine being. If there are distinctions in deity—i.e., between primal and mediate divinity—these distinctions must apply to *all three persons* of the Trinity. Accordingly for Gregory, the *whole* Trinity is the essence of divinity, and the *whole* Trinity is the energy of divinity. Thus the essence and energies of God, instead of referring to the Father God and the mediate God Christ, apply to *divinity as such*. For Palamas, then, the *persons* of the Godhead and

---

15. *Tr.* 3.2.10; cf. 1.3.23.

16. *Tr.* 1.3.23.

17. *Tr.* 2.3.8.

18. *Tr.* 3.1.31.

19. *Tr.* 2.3.37.

20. *Dial.* 56.4; cf. *1 Apol.* 63.15.

21. *1 Apol.* 13.3–4. Cf. Origen, *Cels.* 5.39; Eusebius of Caesarea, *Praep. ev.* 7.12, 320c; *Dem. ev.* 5.4.9–14.

22. Cf. also Philo of Alexandria, who distinguishes between the unknowable essence of God and God's "glory," or "powers" that surround him (*Spec.* 1.36–50).

the *degrees* of the Godhead no longer correspond. Yet this asymmetry is the genius of his theology, for it allows him to preserve the ancient distinction between primal and mediate divinity, while maintaining the orthodoxy of three divine persons sharing a single divine essence.

Christ the Model

For Palamas, the great model of deification is Christ transformed on the Mount of Transfiguration. In the account of Luke we read:

> Now about eight days after these sayings Jesus took with him Peter and John and James, and went up on the mountain to pray. And while he was praying, the appearance of his face changed, and his clothes became dazzling white. Suddenly they saw two men, Moses and Elijah, talking to him. They appeared in glory and were speaking of his departure, which he was about to accomplish at Jerusalem. Now Peter and his companions were weighed down with sleep; but since they had stayed awake, they saw his glory. . . . [Suddenly] a cloud came and overshadowed them; and they were terrified as they entered the cloud. Then from the cloud came a voice that said, "This is my Son, my Chosen; listen to him!" When the voice had spoken, Jesus was found alone. (Luke 9:28–36, NRSV)

Despite being a special event in Christ's life, the Transfiguration was not for Jesus alone. In the Transfiguration, says Palamas, Christ "showed how God's splendor would come to the saints and how they would appear. For the righteous shall shine forth as the sun in the kingdom of their Father (Matt 13:43)."[23]

Palamas agrees with his tradition that deification occurs through Christ's incarnation. "Having taken our nature upon him from the Holy Virgin," Palamas preaches, Christ "renewed and restored it. Or rather, he led it up to divine and heavenly heights."[24] In another homily, Gregory says: "If the son of God had not come down from heaven we should have had no hope of going up to heaven. . . . The son of God became man to show to what heights he would lead us. . . . He made men sons of God and partakers of divine immortality. Human nature was shown [by Christ] to have been created in the image of God, unlike the rest of creation, and this kinship with God was such that human nature could be joined to him in one person."[25]

23. *Hom.* 34.11.

24. *Hom.* 14.4.

25. *Hom.* 16.18–19.

When Palamas says that Christ united the human and divine natures in one person, he assumes the formula of the Council of Chalcedon (451 C.E.), which stated that Christ was made up of two natures in one person. This union of the divine and human natures in one person is called the "hypostatic" union since in Greek the word *hypostasis* signifies the reality of a "person": two natures in *one person*. In another context, Gregory clarifies that the hypostatic union is for Christ alone. Other humans are united to God "in energy and Spirit."[26] But since the energies themselves are God, and the Spirit is a person of the Godhead, the union of the divine and human for Christians is not so radically different than the union of the divine and human in Christ. Palamas can preach, for instance, that Christ "ascended to heaven, making our human substance share the same throne as the Father, being equally divine."[27]

The Divine Light

With regard to the Transfiguration, Gregory clarifies that Christ himself is deifying light.[28] Therefore the Taboric light seen by the hesychasts is most surely divine. It is also, Palamas says, the source of divinity. In his formulation: the light "is not only divinity, but deification-in-itself."[29]

> For it is in light that the light is seen, and that which sees operates in a similar light, since this faculty has no other way in which to work. Having separated itself from all other beings, it becomes itself all light and is assimilated to what it sees, or rather, it is united to it without mingling, being light and seeing light through light. If it sees itself, it sees light; if it beholds the object of this vision, that too is light; and if it looks at the means by which it sees, again it is light. For such is the character of the union: *that all is one*, so that he who sees can distinguish neither the means nor the object nor its nature, but simply has the awareness of being light and of seeing a light distinct from every creature.[30]

The Psalmist of old spoke to God: "In your light we shall see light." (Ps 36:9). For Palamas, what Christians see, they become. God is light, and

---

26. *Cap.* 75.

27. *Hom.* 19.1. For the work of the Spirit in Palamas, see Lison, *L'Esprit répandu.*

28. *Tr.* 1.3.5.

29. *Tr.* 1.3.23. Cf. Pseudo Dionysius, *On Divine Names* 11.6; 2.11; 5.8.

30. *Tr.* 2.3.36, emphasis mine.

Christians are deified *by becoming divine light*. As Gregory explains it, they (1) *see* divine light, (2) see *through* divine light, and (3) *become* divine light. Everything in the vision is God's brilliance. In the vision, then, God becomes "all in all" (1 Cor 15:28). Or in Palamas' words: "*all is one*"—God, light, and human being. With this language Palamas comes closest to speaking of an indistinct union of humans and God. He is careful to explain, however, that the deified (or illumined) monk in the moment of vision merely cannot *distinguish* himself from the object of vision (God) and the means of the vision (God the Spirit). Apart from the vision, these realities can be discerned.

It is striking that for Gregory deified Christians "*become* light by grace."[31] In another place, Palamas states that Christians are transformed into "spiritual light."[32] The mind quit of this "impure and grimy world," he says,

> becomes luminous by the power of the Spirit, and mingles with the true and sublime purity; it shines itself in this purity, becoming entirely radiant, transformed into light. . . . And if the true light which "shines in the darkness" comes down to us, we will also be light, as the Lord told his disciples. Thus the deifying gift of the Spirit is a mysterious light and transforms into light those who receive its richness.[33]

To become light is to become God, and "not just God," Palamas adds, "but the God who truly is."[34]

Seeing by the Spirit

Barlaam had accused the monks of claiming to see God with their physical eyes. Palamas argued that seeing God with fleshly eyes was in fact possible since the eyes themselves were deified. Again, to be deified means to become divine light. If only God can see God, then God himself can become the organ of vision for seeing God. For Palamas, the God through whom one sees God is God the Spirit. One sees, Palamas says, "neither by the intellect nor by the body, but by the Spirit, and he knows that he sees supernaturally a light which surpasses light."[35] At the moment of Christ's transfiguration, his disciples passed, "from flesh to spirit by the transformation of their senses . . . and so they saw that ineffable light, when and as much as the Holy Spirit's

31. *Tr.* 2.3.37, emphasis mine.
32. *Tr.* 3.1.34.
33. *Tr.* 3.1.35.
34. *Hom.* 14.1.
35. *Tr.* 1.3.21.

power granted."[36] Since deified Christians become spirit by Spirit (cf. John 3:6), Christians possess deification in a perfect manner.[37] "By nature," Palamas writes, God's Spirit "deifies from all eternity. It is properly called 'Spirit' and 'divinity' by the saints, insomuch as the deifying gift is never separate from the Spirit who gives it."[38] Since the eyes become spirit by Spirit, the difference between physical and spiritual seeing breaks down.

The Deification of the Flesh

The deification of the eyes raises the question of the deification of the whole body. For Plotinus (as for most thinkers formed by Greek philosophy—including Christians!), a necessary step in deification was disengagement from the body. Deification can be consummated only when the body is fully sloughed off at death. For Palamas, by contrast, the freeing of mind from body is "the greatest of the Hellenic errors."[39] Gregory presents a different view of deification because he assumes a different picture of human nature. The true human is not mind alone, but mind plus body. Therefore if the human is to be deified, the body must be deified as well.

The model of fleshly deification is again Christ. When God the son was incarnated, he assumed not only the human soul, but the body as well. Christ "honored this mortal flesh," Gregory says, "so that the proud spirits [angels and demons] should not consider themselves, or be considered, favored above humankind or as deified because of being without bodies and apparently immortal."[40] For Palamas, the deification of the flesh is biblically demonstrated by the glowing face of Moses (Exod 34:29–35) and the angelic face of Stephen (Acts 6:15). It is historically proved by the power of relics—which are typically body parts of saints that communicate divine powers.[41] The supreme confirmation of deified flesh, however, is Christ on Mount Tabor. "The glory that proceeds naturally from his divinity," Palamas declares, "was shown on Tabor to be shared by his [Christ's] body as well because of the unity of his person."[42] Christ's divinity, in other words, shone through his flesh and changed the very nature of

---

36. *Hom.* 34.8. Cf. Maximus Confessor, *Amb.* 10 (*PG* 91.1125d).

37. *Tr.* 2.3.17.

38. *Tr.* 3.1.9.

39. *Tr.* 1.2.4.

40. *Hom.* 16.18–19.

41. *Tr.* 2.2.12.

42. *Hom.* 34.11.

his flesh into divine reality. Palamas adds: "the . . . radiance shared by God and his saints are one and the same."[43]

Thus although deification may involve removal from the *corruptible* body, deification does not require a separation from body *as such*. Rather, the divine light shining upon the hesychasts "transforms the body, and communicates its own splendor." This miraculous participation in divine light consequently "deifies the body."[44] Palamas even identifies the divine light with "the splendor of the deified flesh, flesh which enriches and communicates the glory of the divinity."[45] In this passage he speaks of both the deified flesh of Christ and of Christians in the practice of hesychastic prayer.[46]

The Passions

In accordance with his "corporeal" view of deification, Palamas argues that the Christian must separate only from "evil and earthly passions," *but not from the passions as such.*[47] Again, the body is part of the human self. Since passions are an inherent part of bodily life, completely cutting them off produces—not deification—but a deadening of the self.

> It is thus not the man who has killed the passionate part of his soul who has the preeminence, for such a one would have no momentum or activity to acquire a divine state and right disposition and relationship with God; but rather, the praise goes to him who has put that part of his soul under subjection, so that by its obedience to the mind, which is by nature appointed to rule, it may ever tend towards God, as is right, by the uninterrupted remembrance of him. Thanks to this remembrance, he will come to possess a divine disposition, and cause the soul to progress towards the highest state of all, the love of God.[48]

Controlled passions lead to the love of God. Love in fact *is* a passion: "it is with this [passionate] power of the soul," says Gregory, "that we love."[49] To

---

43. *Hom.* 35.16.

44. *Tr.* 2.3.9.

45. *Tr.* 2.3.20.

46. The deification of the body is not a denial of the deification of the mind. Palamas says that the saints possess God's glory when their minds become super-celestial (*Tr.* 1.3.5.). Nor does the deification of the flesh mean that "divinity and flesh have a common essence" (*Hom.* 35.16).

47. *Tr.* 2.2.12.

48. *Tr.* 2.2.19.

49. *Tr.* 3.3.15.

cut off the passions would be to eliminate the engine of deification: love for God and neighbor. "Those who love the good thus transform this power [i.e., the passionate part], and do not put it to death; they do not enclose it immovable in themselves, but activate it towards love of God and their neighbors."[50]

Love for God is based on the virtues, and virtues are born of love.[51] Palamas, in accord with monastic tradition, supports a form of deification by virtue. The "brilliance [of the divine vision] comes about and shines forth when we draw near to God through the virtues, and our minds are united with him [God]. It is given to all who unceasingly reach up toward God by means of perfect good works and fervent prayer, and is visible to them."[52] Indeed, one can only see the divine light if one is virtuous.[53] In these and similar passages, virtue might only seem to be a preparation for deification—but it is also an inherent part of the deifying process. As Gregory puts it: "the prize of virtue is to become God."[54]

Deification by Grace

When Palamas speaks of deification through love and virtue, he does not deny the classic Christian emphasis on God's grace. As is standard in Christian discourse, deification does not depend solely on the natural resources of human nature.[55] For Gregory, deification demands that one transcend nature. Deification is not, in other words, the natural outcome of a fully perfected human nature. Rather, the *"deifying gift is supernatural."*[56] It lifts humans out of themselves and beyond themselves.[57] It therefore requires more than human faculties.

Gregory's suspicion of the sufficiency of human nature is related especially to his skepticism about human rationality. Palamas accused Christian philosophers of his day of using rational modes of reflection to attain union with God. One mode of rational ascent was the "Way of Negation" (or *via negativa*). The Way of Negation was sketched out most profoundly by Pseudo-Dionysus the Areopagite—a theologian of the sixth

---

50. Ibid.

51. *Cap.* 58.

52. *Hom.* 34.10.

53. *Tr.* 1.3.35.

54. *Tr.* 3.1.34, quoting Basil of Caesarea.

55. *Tr.* 3.1.26.

56. *Tr.* 3.1.30, emphasis mine.

57. For a fuller discussion of deification by grace in Palamas, see Williams, *Ground*, 106–8; 119–22.

century who wrote under the name of a character in the book of Acts (17:34). Pseudo-Dionysus reasoned that God could not be known through normal human ways of knowing. God is in fact higher than any affirmation made about him—even lofty pronouncements like "God is pure goodness," or "glorious" or "immortal" or "divine." To gain a proper sense of God's transcendence, one must negate every affirmation about God. Thus God is *not* good, or glorious, or immortal, or divine—*not* because he is less than these, but because he is *beyond* all goodness, glory, immortality and divinity. This is the way of negation, sometimes called "unknowing." Unknowing, for Pseudo-Dionysus, is a process of intellectual ascent. It begins with a denial of all the names for God. It proceeds to the negation even of these negations. Eventually it leads to, or is concomitant with, the soul's ecstatic union or *henosis* with the ineffable God.

One of the more famous points that Palamas makes in the *Triads* is that God is not only beyond knowing, but beyond *unknowing* too.[58] That is, philosophers who make the *via negativa* a *method* of attaining God are (to paraphrase Meister Eckhart) finding methods and losing God. In contrast, Palamas performs his own way of negation on the way of negation. One attains deification not by methods or means, not by intellect or the process of intellect, not by the way of affirmation or the way of negation—but by the serendipity of grace.[59] "The mind which applies itself to apophatic theology [i.e., the *via negativa*]," Palamas says, "thinks of what is different from God. Thus it proceeds by means of discursive reasoning. But in the other case [i.e., by contemplating divine light], there is union. In the one case, the mind negates itself together with other beings [who are not God], but in the other there is a union of the mind with God."[60] Union with God, says Palamas, occurs *after* the "cessation of all intellectual activity." "It is not the product of a cause or a relationship, for these are dependent upon the activity of the intellect."[61] God is *beyond* mind, and thus if one is to find him, one must transcend rationality itself.[62]

For Gregory, then, grace is typically not opposed to *works*, but to *nature* and the resources of human rationality. As a monk defending monks engaged in the practice of deifying prayer, Gregory assumes that humans will engage in the hard labor of deification. "Contemplation," Gregory

58. *Tr.* 1.3.4.

59. *Tr.* 3.1.27.

60. *Tr.* 2.3.33. In itself, the way of negation does not deify. Although it can liberate the human mind from created beings, "it cannot by itself effect union with transcendent things" (*Tr.* 1.3.20).

61. *Tr.* 1.3.17.

62. See further Krausmüller, "Do We Need," 143–52.

preaches, "is the fruit of a healthy soul; it aims to achieve a certain end and is of a kind that deifies; for it is through contemplation that a person is made divine (*theopoieitai*)."[63] Palamas clarifies that contemplation "is not simply abstraction and negation; it is a union and divinization which occurs mystically and ineffably by the grace of God."[64]

Transcendence

Does the deified person transcend human nature? Palamas answers this question rather directly. The deified person, he declares, becomes as one "better than what is human (*kreitton ē kat' anthropon*), being already God (*genomenos kai theos*) by grace."[65] Later in the *Triads* he says:

> If deification does no more than perfect the rational nature, without elevating those made in the form of God beyond that condition; if it is only a state of the rational nature, since it is only activated by a natural power, [then] the deified saints do not transcend nature, they are not "born of God" [1 John 3:9], are not "spirit because born of the Spirit" [John 3:6] and Christ, by coming into the world, has not "given them power to become children of God" [John 1:12] . . .[66]

Perhaps the classic philosophic definition of the human being is "rational animal." To be the perfect human would thus involve the perfection of rational nature: becoming complete by the full development of the human brain. But Palamas is not satisfied with the perfection of rational nature. He envisions a higher destiny: the *deification* of human nature. For Palamas, deification means transcending the rational state altogether. Transcending rationality, in turn, means that humans "transcend *nature.*" Stepping beyond human capacities and the human constitution is *what it means* to be born of God and God's Spirit and to *become* spirit (all biblical language). To become spirit, a divine entity, is evidently to become something higher than human nature.

63. *Hom.* 53.52.

64. *Tr.* 1.3.17.

65. *Tr.* 2.3.52. The context of the remark comes in a defense of seeing God by a supernatural sight. Becoming God by grace is synonymous to "existing as one with God and seeing God through God." Cf. 1.3.45: "through this [its own energy] it [the mind], by transcending itself (*hyperanabainōn heauton*), is also intimately joined to God"; and 1.3.47: "So our mind comes out of itself (*exo heautou*) and is thus united to God. Rather it comes to be something beyond itself (*hyper heauton*)."

66. *Tr.* 3.1.30.

In another place, Palamas writes that Christians know spiritually—in a manner beyond sense and intelligence—that God is spirit, "for they have become entirely of God (*holoi theou*), and know God in God. . . . We must transcend ourselves altogether (*holous d' heautous holōn heautōn existamenous*), and give ourselves entirely to God, for it is better to belong to God, and not to ourselves. It is thus that divine things are bestowed on those who have come to be with God."[67] His final comment about being "with God" indicates that transcending the self involves not fusion, but communion with the Godhead. Nevertheless, Gregory's bold language suggests that transcending the self does in fact imply transcending one's *human* self. To have the truest fellowship with God, and to truly belong to God, one must become "entirely *of God.*"

Palamas even says that those who attain the deifying gift become "uncreated (*aktistos*), unoriginate (*anarchos*), and indescribable (*aperigraptos*), even if in their own nature they derive from non-existent realities (*ex ouk ontōn*)."[68] A Christian, he says elsewhere, can even attain a "non-being (*mē ōn*) by transcendence, that is by exceeding created things."[69] Christians, like all created beings, come from nothing, a nothingness that is a kind of emptiness and void. As deified beings, however, Christians can paradoxically return to nothingness (or non-being), which is divine fullness. The language of Palamas is admittedly extreme, however, because being "uncreated, unoriginate, and indescribable" are qualities of God that are normally thought to be unshareable.

Perhaps Gregory's most daring declaration is that those who are deified by grace become *homotheoi*. Literally this Greek word signifies that Christians become "joint divinities" or "co-gods" with God.[70] In the singular (*homotheos*), this word means "of the same Godhead, identically God," and is applied to Christ the son of God, the whole Trinity, or to Christ's humanity as wholly one with God.[71] It is analogous to the Nicene term expressing the union of Christ and God—*homoousios*—which means that Christ is "of the same substance" or "consubstantial" with God.[72]

Based on such radical language, it is fair to say that Gregory understood deification (i.e., "becoming God") in a supremely realistic (that is, non-metaphorical) way. To be sure, deified Christians do not become identical

---

67. *Tr.* 2.3.68.
68. *Tr.* 3.1.31. Cf. Maximus Confessor, *Amb.* (PG 91.1144C) cited in *Tr.* 3.2.12.
69. *Tr.* 2.3.37.
70. *On Divine Energies* 36.
71. Lampe, *A Patristic Greek Lexicon*, 953.
72. Cf. Russell, "Theosis and Gregory Palamas," 370.

with God, but they do transcend human nature. "It is only when one or another of these beings [humans or angels] goes out from itself," Gregory declares, "and acquires a superior state that it is deified (*theōthen*)."[73] This deifying union, Gregory says, even angels cannot attain without transcending their nature—how much more human beings?[74]

Present or Future?

Palamite deification is not only radical because it is real, it is radical because it is present. Since his debate about deification arose in the context of a defense of those currently transformed into light, it seems clear that deification for Palamas can be experienced now. Nonetheless Gregory retains Christian emphases: there is a life beyond this life, and thus deification is not yet manifest in its full glory. Not every deified monk will glow, and those who do will not shine with the *fullness* of divine light. "Today this light shines out in part," he says, "a pledge given to those who by dispassion have left behind all that is forbidden, and by pure and immaterial prayer have passed beyond all that is pure." On the Last Day, in contrast, divine light "will deify in manifest fashion 'the sons of the resurrection' (Luke 20:36) who will rejoice in eternity and in glory in communion with the one who has endowed our nature with a glory and splendor that is divine."[75]

Conclusion

How does Palamite deification relate to the models that come before it? Undoubtedly, it has points of contact with Pauline deification. It is based, first of all, on a radical correspondence between Christ and Christians. Christians follow the human God as archetype. By seeing his glory, Christians become "the same image" as Christ (2 Cor 3:18). Or as Gregory puts it: on Tabor Christ "indicated what we once were and what we shall become

---

73. *Tr.* 3.1.33.

74. *Tr.* 2.3.37. If an angel, says Palamas, were to experience deifying union with God, he would explain his experience in the language of Paul: "I know an angel who saw, but I do not know if it was an angel, God knows (cf. 2 Cor 12:2)" (ibid., cf. 2 Cor 12:2). In the words of Williams, for Gregory deification is "the acquisition of a new [divine] identity, as Gregory says of Paul, 'he *was* that to which he was united'" (*Ground*, 125, quoting *Tr.* 2.3.37). For Gregory, Paul ascended to heaven (2 Cor 12:2–4) and became light by grace and non-being by transcendence and exceeded created things. Paul's experience—like Christ's on Mt. Tabor—is not unique. It is another model of deifying transformation for all Christians.

75. *Tr.* 2.3.66.

through him in the future age."[76] Furthermore, the transformation of the body into light is analogous to Paul's transformation into a "pneumatic body," which rises to the stars (1 Cor 15:45–49). In both cases the body has a luminous quality, and—although corporeal—is no longer made of flesh and blood. Third, just as Paul saw the gradual growth of the pneuma within the believer in this life (Rom 8:23; cf. 2 Cor 4:16), Palamas saw the first fruits of corporeal deification in the practice of hesychastic prayer. Those who see God's glory really are being transformed into it from one degree of glory to another (2 Cor 3:18).

Gregory's protests against the human rational faculty seem strongly opposed to Hermes who sees the mind (*nous*) as the access point to divinity and the key to deification. But appearances can be deceiving. For Hermes, *nous* is a kind of creative imagination that far transcends rationality and discursive thought. Although they use different language, then, Hermes and Palamas agree that true contemplation and the vision of God require transcending discursive reasoning. The difference between them is that although Hermes considers rational reflection (in astronomy, for instance) as a stepping stone to contemplation, Palamas seems to bypass it altogether.[77]

One could contrast sharply Gregory's corporeal model of deification with Plotinus' theory of deification through mind. Nevertheless, since for Gregory the body is transformed into divine light—commonly thought of as the substance of mind—perhaps one should not overstress the differences between Plotinian and Palamite deification. It is important to note as well that despite Gregory's inclusion of the body, he ultimately preserves a sense of the mind's superiority. "For it is not the bodily constitution but the very nature of the mind," he says, "which possesses this image [of God] and nothing in our nature is superior to mind."[78] For Palamas, the deification of the mind in fact precedes that of the body. Sounding Hermetic, he cries out: "How much greater is the human mind than the heavens! It is the image of God, knows God, and alone of everything on earth can, if it wishes, become God, exalting man's humble body at the same time."[79]

Perhaps the most interesting aspect of Palamite deification, however, is its realism. The realistic nature of Palamite deification has often been contrasted with Western models of metaphorical deification prominent since Augustine. Indeed, Palamite deification is so radical that it even seems

---

76. *Cap.* 66.

77. See further Krausmüller, "Barlaam," 143–52.

78. *Cap.* 27.

79. *Hom.* 26.2.

to transcend the Creator-creature divide. Palamas says that Christians become *uncreated* by participation in the divine energies.[80]

It is nevertheless true that Palamas preserved Christian orthodox affirmations about the final difference between God and human beings.[81] A Christian can fully participate in God's *energies*—the true reality of God— but is blocked from sharing in the ultimate mystery of God's *essence*. "The person who has been deified by grace," Gregory clarifies in a sermon, "will be in every respect as God is, *except for his very essence*."[82]

In this way of thinking, the Palamite version of deification is both like and unlike the Augustinian model. For Palamas it is the *greatness* of God that is unattainable, *not realistic union with him*. Augustine, by contrast, preserves God's difference precisely by allowing only a participation in God's attributes. Both Augustine and Palamas, to be sure, forestall participation in God's essence. Nevertheless, protecting God's essence from human participation means something different for Palamas than it does for Augustine. For Augustine, *either* one participates in God's essence (which is prohibited) *or* one participates in God's qualities (which, as shared by human beings, are *not God*). Thus Augustinian deification ever retains the savor of unreality, since no human ever ultimately participates in *what God actually IS*. Palamas, although he plunged God's essence in a sea of unknowability, still allowed humans to participate in God's *true reality*—the reality, namely, of God's energies. In neither thinker, however, do we find indistinct union with God (as in Eckhart). In the end, for all Christian theologians who claim the badge of orthodoxy, deification—perhaps the strongest testament of human union with God—is always balanced by equally forceful assertions of God's ultimate and unbridgeable difference.

---

80. *Tr.* 3.1.31.

81. "Every nature is utterly remote and absolutely estranged from the nature of divinity. For if God is nature, other things are not nature, but if each of the other things is nature, he is not nature: just as he is not a being, if others are beings; and if he is a being, the others are not beings" (*Cap.* 78).

82. *Hom.* 8.13 (emphasis mine), quoting Maximus Confessor, *Ad Thalass.* 22 (*PG* 90.320a); cf. *Amb.* (*PG* 91.1308b).

Chapter 12

"By Faith a Human Becomes God"

Martin Luther on Deification

A human becomes so divinized that everything which he is and does, God is and does in him. Such a person is raised so far above any natural mode that he truly becomes by grace what God is essentially by nature. . . . Beloved, to have attained this state is truly to have reached the deepest depth of humility, for in this state we have been brought to nothing.

—JOHN TAULER[1]

THE GERMAN REFORMER MARTIN Luther (1483–1546) is famous for issuing the clarion call of justification by grace alone (*sola gratia*) through Christ alone (*solo Christo*).[2] It goes without saying, then, that for him deification occurs totally by grace, and thoroughly depends on conformity to Christ. "Truly deiform persons (*recht gottformige menschen*)," Luther preaches, are "those who receive everything from God in Christ."[3]

Luther taught Christ-centered deification through the Christian teaching of the "wondrous exchange." In his Christmas sermon of 1514, he preaches: "just as the Word of God was made flesh, so certainly ought the flesh also to become Word. For the Word becomes flesh so that the flesh can become Word. God becomes human so that the human can become God

---

1. Sermon 40 in Shrady, *Johannes Tauler: Sermons*, 143–44.

2. For a realistic account of justification in Luther see Vainio, *Justification and Participation*, 19–53.

3. *WA* 10 I 100.13–20 (Kirchenpostille 1522).

(*deus fit homo, ut homo fiat deus*)."[4] But Luther (at the time an Augustinian monk) introduces Augustinian asymmetry into the exchange. The Word is fully made human, but humans are not fully made Word. To be made Word is only to be "like" (*similes*) him. The young Luther continues:

> we are not made God (*deus*) or truth, but divine (*divini*) and truthful or participants in the divine nature [2 Pet 1:4]. For the Word is not made flesh [John 1:14] by abandoning itself and being changed into flesh, but because it assumes and unites flesh to itself. Through this union it is not only called flesh, but *is* flesh. Likewise, we who are flesh are not made Word in the sense that we are substantially changed into Word, but because we assume [the Word] and through faith unite it to ourselves. Through this union we not only have the Word but can even be called "Word."[5]

Here Luther delicately balances a realistic version of deification (union) with nominalist language (humans are merely "called" Word). One might conclude that for Luther humans are only gods "in name only."

Nevertheless we know from his later writings that Luther was not satisfied with nominal deification. In a sermon of 1530, the Reformer comments on Ps 82:6 where God—according to Christian tradition—calls Christians "gods." What the Most High calls Christians, Luther urges, has a real effect. "God's word sanctifies and deifies everything (*heiliget und vergoettet alle ding*)."[6] Humans are not simply called "gods." God's Word actually transforms them into deities.

In this way, Luther forges a middle path between a substantial and a merely nominal form of deification. For the Reformer, deification is real in the sense that it truly transforms the human and makes the human like (*similes*) the Word. Nevertheless real change is not synonymous with what he calls "substantial" change. After the union between humans and God, humans remain human and Word remains Word. Luther has a succinct way of expressing this nuance in his Christmas sermon: humans become divine (*divini*) but not God (*deus*). In other words, humans participate in a kind of deity that allows them to remain human.[7] Luther's understanding of deifi-

---

4. *WA* 1 28.25–28. Cf. *WA* 57 94.11–13 (Commentary on Galatians): "Thus God is made flesh before flesh is made God. So it ought to be in all things that God first be incarnated before they are divinized (*indivinari*) in God, and thus that Platonic saying will be true: 'like is known by like.'"

5. *WA* 1 28.34–41. Luther then quotes or paraphrases as prooftexts 1 Cor 6:17 ("The one who adheres to the Lord is one spirit [with him]"), John 3:6 (everyone born of Spirit is spirit), and 2 Cor 5:21 (humans are the justice of God in Christ).

6. *WA* 31 I 217.10.

7. On the ontology of deification with reference to this sermon, see Mannermaa,

cation, in short, involves both a strong theory of union as well as the classic genetic separation between humans and God.

In this way, Luther positions himself in a Catholic (broadly Augustinian) tradition of deification—a tradition that seems to have occasioned little surprise in the history of Lutheran theology. Eyebrows began to be raised, however, in the late 1970s when deification in Luther was "rediscovered" by Lutheran scholars working in Finland. Today, one cannot speak of deification in Luther without in the same breath mentioning the Finnish scholar Tuomo Mannermaa and his school. Mannermaa was spurred on to study deification in Luther after being invited by his Archbishop to be part of a preparatory group seeking theological points of contact with the Russian Orthodox Church. In the past thirty years the theology department at the University of Helsinki (where Mannermaa taught) has become a factory of articles, theses, and books on topics focused directly or indirectly on Luther and deification. Even though the theological work has been integrated into the academy, ecumenical unity remains a basic motivating factor in this research.[8]

Although I concur in broad lines with Mannermaa's presentation of Luther's understanding of deification and depend on his and his disciples' research, what follows is not a recapitulation of Mannermaa's theses or theories. Rather, I present a fresh attempt to understand Luther's model of deification in light of the history and categories of deification previously discussed in this book. I make no attempt to adhere to classical "orthodox" Lutheran portrayals of Luther. Nor do I claim to present every side of Luther's theology. The amount that Luther preached and published, the complexity of his character, and the many masks that he wore in life dog every attempt to reconstruct a systematic—let alone comprehensive—picture of his theology. In this chapter I am solely interested in Luther's understanding of deification. In my view, deification is not the core of Luther's theology—but it can *express* that core in a particularly poignant way.

In my chapter on Augustine, I discussed five aspects of deification: justification, adoption, incorporation, immortality, and beatitude. These

---

"Hat Luther eine trinitarische Ontologie?" 16–22; Radler, "Theologische Ontologie," 28–34.

8. For a recent English survey of Finnish scholarship on Luther, see Kärkkäinen, *One with God*, 37–66. A convenient history of research can be found in Saarinen, *Engaging Luther*, 1–26. The essence of Mannermaa's thought is distilled in his book *Christ Present in Faith*. For necessary correctives to Finnish emphases, see Flogaus, *Theosis bei Palamas*; Bielfeldt, "Deification as a Motif," 401–20; Trueman, "Is the Finnish Line a New Beginning?" 231–44; Hailer, "Rechtfertigung als Vergottung?" 239–68.

aspects of deification remain standard for all those who inherited the (broadly) Catholic tradition—including Luther.[9] In what follows I will discuss five ways of talking about deification that are fairly distinctive to Luther. They are: (1) deification and annihilation, (2) the notion of "total deification," (3) participating in God's attributes and essence, (4) the correspondence of believer and Christ, and (5) the hypostatic-like union between believer and Christ.

Deification and Annihilation

One of the better-known slogans of Luther is that a Christian is *simul iustus et peccator* ("at once righteous and a sinner"). We can adapt this saying with reference to his notion of deification. For Luther, the Christian is simultaneously a god and nothing at one and the same time: *simul deus et nihil*.[10] Both poles of this paradox—deity and nothingness—always need to be balanced in order to properly represent Luther's view of deification. To grasp how Luther came to advocate deification under its opposite—nothingness—one must know something of his theological journey.

In his early career, Luther was a self-confessed devotee of John Tauler, a German mystical theologian of the fourteenth century.[11] Luther's first published book in 1516 was a volume of mystical chapters that formed (he believed) a summary of Tauler's teaching. Ten days after editing and printing this treatise, Luther sent a letter to his friend George Spalatin boasting: "I have seen no theological work in Latin or German that is more sound and more in harmony with the gospel than this."[12] After coming across a better manuscript of the work, he published a more complete edition in 1518. Luther called the work *A German Theology* (*Eyn deutsch Theologia*), now commonly referred to by its Latin title *Theologia Germanica*. In his preface to the 1518 edition, Luther confesses that—aside from the Bible and Augustine—he has read no other work in which he has learned more about God, Christ, human beings, and all other things.[13]

---

9. For Luther on adoption see, for instance, *WA* 17 II 324.8–15 with the comments of Saarinen, "Die Teilhabe," 178–81.

10. For simultaneity in Luther, see Nilsson, *Simul*, esp. 209–27.

11. For the relationship of Luther to Tauler, see esp. Otto, *Vor- und frühreformatorische Tauler-Rezeption*, 177–214.

12. *WA* (*Briefwechsel*) 1 79.61.

13. *WA* 1 378.21–23. For a recent, comprehensive introduction to the *Theologia Germanica*, see Zecherle, "Die 'Theologia Deutsch,'" 1–96.

176 176   becoming divine

176 The *Theologia Germanica* is important for our purposes because in it Luther found the description of *ein vergotter mensch*—a deified human being.[14] We know from his own notes that Luther highlighted this phrase, and sought to know what it meant.[15] The unknown author of *Theologia Germanica* associates deification with perfect obedience,[16] divine indwelling,[17] godliness,[18] humility,[19] suffering,[20] love,[21] and self-abnegation.[22] The treatise also speaks of the passive reception of God's transforming grace, and the rejection of human efforts to attain a higher spiritual state or salvation. Deification in *Theologia Germanica* is, in a word, completely passive. Any form of human cooperation involved in the process of deification destroys it. The whole treatise can be summed up in the words, "Cut off your self, cleanly and utterly."[23] Once the self is emptied, God fills it. "When a person surrenders and abandons his own self, God enters with his own, that is his self."[24] The goal in fact is to make oneself nothing so that "there is nothing that is not God or things of God and also so that there is nothing left in the human of which he considers himself to be proprietor."[25]

The *Theologia Germanica* is often categorized as a mystical work. Luther was familiar with another kind of mysticism (often dubbed "Neoplatonic") wherein the soul works out the truth of its own nature in a process of purgation and love. From the beginning of his career, however, Luther emphasizes—with the *Theologia Germanica*—the insufficiency of human nature to attain to the divine. He accepts, in other words, the traditional Christian teaching that the soul is made from nothing. Although the soul can have some appreciation for the invisible things of God (Rom 1:20), there is nothing in the soul that actually links it to God. Although Luther

14. Zecherle calls deification "the central theme (*das zentrale Thema*) of the 'Theologia Deutsch'" (ibid., 47). In the notes that follow, I cite both the chapter of *Theologia Germanica* and the page number in the Hoffman translation (*Classics of Western Spirituality*).

15. WA 59.18.30 (Luther's marginalia to the *Theologia Deutsch*, ca. 1520).

16. *Theologia Germanica*, ch. 14, 80.

17. Ibid., ch. 29, 101.

18. Ibid., ch. 30, 104.

19. Ibid., ch. 33, 107.

20. Ibid., ch. 38, 116.

21. Ibid., ch. 39, 120.

22. Ibid., ch. 55, 147.

23. Ibid., ch. 20, 86.

24. Ibid., ch. 22, 90.

25. Ibid., ch. 55 147. For deification in *Theologia Germanica*, see further Zecherle, "Die 'Theologia Deutsch,'" 47–69.

acknowledges a continuity between God and humans through the human conscience (often called the *synteresis*), he came to emphasize the discontinuity and opposition between unredeemed humans and God.[26] Ironically, it is this natural opposition between humans and God that makes Luther's model of deification possible.[27]

Like Augustine, Luther portrays the human predicament in terms of self-deifying pride. "For he who is prideful strives either to be equal to or superior to God."[28] By their own nature, Luther says in another place, humans strive to be "unhappy and haughty gods." The necessary work of God is to make them "genuine human beings—that is wretches and sinners."[29]

Since humans are made from nothing, they bring nothing to the table. They are by nature weak and have no resources to attain to God. Although made in the image of God, fallen humans are—but for a few remnants—deprived of the image.[30] Scriptural references to the image of God "serve to remind us of what humanity has lost through sin."[31]

To emphasize the starkness of human inability and sin, Luther uses the language of nothingness. In his *Dictata super psalterium* (1514-16), Luther quotes Augustine: "The whole wisdom of a human being is this: to know that one is nothing in oneself (*quod per se nihil est*)."[32] "Nothing is to be preached so much and actually practiced," Luther says (in his own voice), "than the knowledge that we from ourselves are nothing (*quod ex nobis nihil simus*) and have all things only from above."[33]

John Tauler spoke of recognizing one's own natural inability and sin as a form of annihilation.[34] Luther, it would appear, adopts his language. In

---

26. *Pace* Hoffman (*Luther and the Mystics*, 141-42), who emphasizes the continuity—even substantial continuity—between humans and God in Luther. Hoffmann's comments were directed against Ozment, *Homo Spiritualis*, who wrongly depicted Tauler as claiming that one's own soteriological resources were within the deepest part of one's being (the ground). The ground is precisely that aspect of the human self that is not part of the human self, since it is uncreated. The heart of Tauler's message is to reject one's own inner resources and turn to God. See further Otto, *Tauler-Rezeption*, 207-11.

27. For Luther and "mysticism" see in general Hoffman, *Luther and the Mystics*; Neufel, "The Cross and the Living Lord," 131-46.

28. *Quia qui superbit, deo vel equalis vel superior esse nititur* (WA 3 498.6-7 [*Dictata super psalterium* 1513-16]).

29. WA 5 128-29 (*Operationes in Psalmos* 1519-21).

30. WA 42 50.6-12, 16-17. See further Raunio, "The Human Being," 36-38.

31. Wilson-Kastner, "On Partaking of the Divine Nature," 123.

32. WA 3 449:6-8.

33. WA 4 123:5-7.

34. For the necessity of annihilation in Tauler, see Juntunen, *Der Begriff des Nichts*, 116-23.

his Christmas sermon of 1514, the (future) Reformer preaches, "We must, when we assume the Word, forsake and utterly empty our very selves (*nos ipsos deserere et exinanire*). Nothing is to be retained by our mind, but totally rejected (*totum abnegando*)."[35] We must be utterly nothing (*penitus nihil*), empty ourselves of everything (*omnibus evacuemur*), and despoil ourselves (*exinaniamus nosipsos*). But "O how eagerly we are empty," Luther cries out, "so that you [God] may be full in us!"[36]

Annihilation is not a literal destruction of the self, but the recognition of one's utter resourcelessness. In a marginal note on a sermon of Tauler, Luther writes: "Therefore one needs to be naked with respect to the mind, stripped from all our wisdom and righteousness—to lean on God alone and to account oneself nothing (*nihil*)."[37] In the Heidelberg Disputation (1518), the Reformer understands the reduction to nothingness (*ad nihilum redactus*) as the cultivation of humility. It prepares one to take no credit for one's own work, but to see the saving work of God in the ugliness and disgrace of Christ's crucifixion.[38] Annihilation, for Luther, occurs through personal suffering and anguish (*Anfechtung*). "He who has been emptied (*exinanitus*) through suffering no longer does works but knows that God works and does all things in him." Annihilation is part of Luther's theology of the cross, where the glory of God is hidden under its opposite.[39]

Annihilation is not just the preparation for deification. In his *Operationes in psalmos* (1519–21), Luther speaks of nothingness and deification as two sides of the same coin. The Reformer comments on Ps 116:11: ("I said in my ecstasy [*in excessu meo*]: every human is a liar"). Luther clarifies that the ecstasy of the psalmist,

> was his anguish, by which a human is taught that every person who does not hope in God alone is empty and a liar. For a human is a human until he becomes God (*Homo enim homo est, donec fiat deus*), who alone is true. By participation in God, the human is made true, as long as he clings to God in faith and hope, while he is brought back by his ecstasy into nothingness (*redactus . . . in nihilum*). For he who hopes in God where does he advance, if not into his own nothingness (*in sui nihilum*)? Where does the

35. WA 1 29.6–8.

36. WA 56 218.14; 219.7 (Scholia to the Epistle to the Romans).

37. WA 9 103.35–37.

38. "Luther's concept of *theosis*," Mannermaa writes, "is understood correctly only in connection with his *theology of the cross*. The participation that is a real part of his theology is hidden under its opposite, the *passio* through which man is emptied" ("Participation and Love," 304).

39. WA 1 363.27–37.

one who departs to nothingness depart to unless to [the place] where he came? But he came from God and his own nothingness (*ex deo et suo nihilo*). Therefore he who returns to nothingness (*redit in nihilum*) returns to God (*in deum redit*).[40]

In this passage Luther appears to affirm both a doctrine of creation from nothing (*ex nihilo*) and from God (*ex deo*).[41] By becoming nothing—thus returning to one's origin—one becomes God. By returning to one's humble origins, one inevitably discovers one's divine source as well. In itself, humanity is nothing, and thus has no resources to return to God.[42] Yet when one becomes nothing, one comes to—or *into*—God (*in deum*).

Annihilation and deification, therefore, are in fact two simultaneous moments of the Christian life. When one looks at salvation from the perspective of the natural resources of human beings, one sees nothingness. When one observes from the side of God and God's grace, on the other hand, one sees humans made lords and gods.[43] Deification and nothingness are experienced at the same time. They are negative and positive poles of the same reality—poles that can never be fused or reduced wholly to their opposite. It is this paradoxical structure of being at once everything and nothing, high and low, lord and servant, sinner and saint, full and empty that appears again and again in Luther's thought. It is the structure of how Luther thinks of salvation and deification. In short, theosis is kenosis (self-emptying), and—by the grace of God—kenosis entails theosis.

Total Deification

In a sermon on Matthew 3 (Christ's baptism), Luther connects Christ's incarnation as God's "humanization" with humanity's deification: Because of God becoming human, humans can be deified. God "pours out upon us his dear son and [pours] himself into us, and he draws us into himself, so that he becomes totally human and we become totally deified (*gantz*

---

40. *WA* 5 167.38—168.1–7 (*Operationes in Psalmos*), my trans.

41. Juntunen opposes the idea that *ex deo* means from the substance of God (*ex substantia dei*) (*Begriff des Nichts*, 352).

42. *WA* 3 378.27–28.

43. In a recent essay, Alfsvåg implies that there is "an identity between annihilation and deification." ("Deification as *creatio ex nihilo*," 73, n. 80). "This emphasis," he continues, "on humans as nothing corresponds to a similarly strong emphasis on the unfolding of humanity as participation in God, leading to an anthropology which finds deification as the one and only realization of creation" (ibid.)

und gar vergottet)."[44] This emphasis on total deification is consistent with Luther's exposition of Eph 3:19 (". . . that you may be filled up to all the fullness of God"). The Reformer preaches that humans are fully deified (*gantz vergottet*), "not piecemeal or merely having some piece of God, but all the fullness." He continues: "Much has been written about how a human is to be deified. They have taught how one climbs to heaven and many things of this sort. This is all," he says, "beggar's work. Here [in Eph 3:19] the true and nearest way to advance is shown, so that you become full, full of God, so that you not lack anything, but have everything in one fell swoop, and everything you speak, think, do—in short, your whole life may be entirely divine (*Gottisch*)."[45]

Luther presents his notion of full deification in opposition to the "sophists" (i.e., medieval scholastic theologians) who conceived of deification as a process of growth through love. Luther accuses scholastics of making ladders by which to climb to heaven, and of only realizing deification in a partial way.[46]

At first glance, Luther's own understanding of deification seems extreme: humans are full-fledged gods?! Nevertheless Luther quickly adds: "but while we live in the flesh, we are still full of Adam [the old human nature] in manifold fullness."[47] The redeemed remain beggars and sigh in this life, praying to God to remove their weakness.[48] When God gives gifts, he gives them in full. Yet while still in the flesh, Christians struggle in this world. Remaining in God (1 John 2:24b), says Luther, involves deification.[49] But to remain in the Father means struggling against Satan and the world.[50] Such is the paradox of "Lutheran" deification. It is fully realized in faith and hope (*in fide et in spe*), but not actualized in present circumstances (*in re*).[51] The Reformer's ability to look at the Christian life through a double lens

---

44. *WA* 20.229.28–34 (Jan 6, 1526).

45. *WA* 17 I 438.21–28 (A Sermon of 1525). Luther returns to Eph 3:19 in a later sermon: To have the fullness of God and to be deified (*vergottet*) means to be begotten of God and to be unable to sin (*WA* 32.96.13–24 [September 15, 1530]).

46. In another sermon of 1525, Luther says that when humans believe in God, they become a partaker (*particeps*) in all God's goods. They do not receive part (*partem*), but the whole: "eternal justice, wisdom, fortitude—I become Lord and reign over all things!" (*WA* 17 I 93.22–24).

47. *WA* 17 I 438.32–33.

48. *WA* 17 I 438.32–34.

49. *WA* 20 687.2–3 (Lecture on 1 John, 1527).

50. Later in commenting on 1 John 2:29, Luther says that "to be born of God is to acquire the nature of God" (*nasci ex deo est acquirere naturam dei*) (*WA* 20.692.5).

51. Flogaus, *Theosis bei Palamas*, 352; cf. Mannermaa, *Der im Glauben*, 91.

of completed work (on God's part) and continued temptation (in everyday reality) well represents the incongruous texture of Christian life itself.

Attributes and Essence

According to Simo Peura, Luther identifies God's being with his attributes. For instance, in the *Dictata super psalterium*, Luther says that God's deity consists of his truth, wisdom, goodness, light, power, and life.[52] Since God *is* his attributes, when God gives his qualities to human beings, he gives himself. "For just as they are called 'gods' (*dii*) [in Ps 82:6]," Luther remarks, "they are called true, just, holy—attributes of God alone—by whose participation and union humans become such."[53] Based on this language, Mannermaa (Peura's teacher) concludes that justifying faith means "participation in God's essence in Christ."[54]

We have already seen deification as a participation in God's attributes in both Augustine and Meister Eckhart. Justice is an attribute of God and is God. To have justice is to have God; to participate in justice is to be divine. Justification thus implies the deification of justified human beings.

Nevertheless, superficial similarities can mask differences in the Eckhartian and Augustinian theories of participation. Eckhart's understanding of participation in Justice is realistic: to share in God's Justice is to share God's reality without qualification. Augustine's theory of participation, on the other hand, assumes ontological difference: to share in justice is not to be God. For Augustine, the justice one shares is not God, but is some third thing that makes one "like" God. In short: for Eckhart, sharing Justice means *becoming* God, whereas for Augustine sharing justice means becoming god*like*.

With which theologian does Luther agree? The language that the Reformer uses to speak of human participation in God indicates his agreement with Augustine, not Eckhart. Humans who participate in God's attributes do not share God's essence, but in attributes that express God's reality. They become *divine* (i.e., *like* God), but not God.

---

52. Peura, *Mehr als ein Mensch?* 47–49.

53. WA 2 565.15–16 (Commentary on Galatians 1519).

54. Mannermaa, *Christ Present in Faith*, 17. Cf. his article "Hat Luther eine trinitarische Ontologie," 22–23. The text he cites from *Operationes in Psalmos* is as follows: "[T]he justice of God is in a certain manner of speaking (*tropo iam dicto*) the justice by which God is just, so that by the same justice God and we are just, just as by the same Word God makes and we are what he himself is (*et nos sumus quod ipse est*) so that we are in him and his being is our being (*et suum esse nostrum esse sit*)" (AWA 2.259).

Admittedly there is some ambiguity on this question since Luther—and the Christian tradition in general—believe that Christians are "sharers in the divine nature" (2 Pet 1:4). "Nature" in Christian discourse is often equivalent to "essence." Thus to follow the "plain sense" of Scripture Christians would seemingly share the essence of God. In Christian orthodoxy, however, "nature" typically refers to God's attributes, not his essence. This distinction assumes that there is a difference between God's traits and God's selfhood (at least from the human perspective). For Augustinians (Luther included), God's attributes—unlike Palamas' divine energies—are not God when they are shared by human beings.

Moreover, Luther agrees with Augustine that humans do not share in God's qualities directly, but *through Christ*. "Christ himself," Luther underscores, "*is* life, righteousness, and blessing."[55] Christ thus mediates believers' participation in these qualities. Naturally Luther considers Christ to be God, so sharing in such qualities indicates participation in the divine. But the dual (divine-human) nature of Christ allows for a very common theological equivocation often employed by those in the Augustinian tradition: sharing in Christ's qualities means sharing in Christ's perfect *humanity*, and not his divine essence.

Distinctive for Luther is the *mode* of sharing the divine qualities. For the Reformer, faith and faith alone is required for participation. "If I believe in him [God], I become a partaker in all his goods."[56] Commenting on Paul's unbending defense of the gospel, Luther cites 2 Pet 1:4 (Christians as "partakers of the divine nature"), and concludes: "by faith a human becomes God" (*fide enim homo fit deus*).[57] Naturally if faith makes the believer sharer of God's goods (not essence), and if sharing in God's goods is a mode of deification, then by faith a human becomes divine.

The context of Luther's statement, however, heavily qualifies his remark. Luther argues that whereas love tolerates all things, faith cannot bear any deviation in the gospel. Faith thus makes one like God who does not suffer or yield to anything. Deification by faith thus amounts to the saying: "faith is immovable"—a significant point, to be sure, but having little to do with deification in itself.[58]

---

55. *WA* 40 I 440.21–27 (Galatians Commentary, 1531 [1535]).

56. *WA* 17 I 93.22–24 (1525).

57. *WA* 40 I 182.15.

58. *WA* 40 I 182.16–17. In his comments on the faithful Abraham (Gal 3:9), Luther says that one who lives by faith is "clearly a divine human" (*plane est divinus homo*), by which Luther means "a son of God, the inheritor of the universe . . . the victor over the world, sin, death, the devil, etc." (*WA* 40 I 390.22–24).

Correspondence

For Paul, as for Luther, there is a close coordination and conformation of the believer to Christ. According to Mannermaa, Luther portrays Christ and Christians "as having exactly parallel characteristics" with "analogous constitutions."[59] For instance, Luther wrote that "through faith we must be born God's children and gods, lords and kings, just as Christ is born in eternity a true God of the Father."[60] Mannermaa comments: "Christ is begotten by the Father continuously in eternity as true God. In like manner, Christians are born in faith as 'God's children and gods, lords and kings.'" Luther preaches that "we must once again break out through love to help our neighbor with good deeds, just as Christ became human to help us all."[61] Likewise a Christian, writes Mannermaa, "must step into the position of the neighbor and become 'like the poorest of the poor.'"[62] Faith, to put it another way, involves participation in Christ's exaltation: it makes humans lords and gods. Love, on the other hand, entails sharing Christ's incarnation: it makes humans the poorest of the poor.[63] With Christ as model, both exaltation and impoverishment are equally aspects of deification. Mannermaa even states that the believer shares the human and divine nature of Christ, although he understands these terms in a metaphorical way: "The 'divine nature' of the believer is Christ himself" present in faith.[64] Christians take up their "human nature," in turn, by assuming the misery and burden of their neighbors in love.[65]

Deification through love is an important theme in Luther. The idea is as old as Augustine, who proclaimed, "By loving God, we are made gods."[66] For Luther, deification is expressed through love of neighbor. "[T]hrough good works they [Christians] . . . prove to be as if they were gods to others. This is the realization of Ps. 81 [82:6]: 'I say, "You are gods, children of the

---

59. Mannermaa, "Why is Luther So Fascinating?" 14.

60. *WA* 17 II 74.35–37 (*Fastenpostille* on Matthew 8, 1525).

61. *WA* 17 II 74.37—75.2.

62. Mannermaa, "Why Is Luther So Fascinating?" 14.

63. *WA*17 II 74.25–34

64. Mannermaa, "Why is Luther So Fascinating?" 18. For Luther, the Christian no longer lives. Paraphrasing Gal 2:20, Luther says that "Christ remains in me, and that life lives in me, and the life through which I live is Christ" (*WA* 40 I 283.7–9).

65. Mannermaa, "Why is Luther So Fascinating?" 19. See further *Der im Glauben*, 101–5. Mannermaa's phraseology indicates that the "two natures" of believers are not substantial like the humanity and divinity in Christ. He frequently repeats that when we predicate two natures of human beings "nature" is "understood in the theological [not a philosophical] sense" ("Participation and Love," 310).

66. *Serm.* 121.1.

Most High, all of you.'" . . . [W]e are gods through love (*gotte synd wyr durch die liebe*), which makes us do good to our neighbors. For divine nature is nothing else than beneficence plain and simple."[67] By defining divine nature as beneficence, Luther allows all those who do works of beneficence to be called gods.[68]

Quasi Hypostatic Union

Despite Luther's denial of a substantial union with the Word, his language of union with Christ is strikingly vivid and physical. In *The Freedom of the Christian*, Luther writes: "The sort of reality that the Word is, is the sort of reality that the soul becomes from it—just as iron made red-hot glows like fire due to its union" with fire.[69] The Reformer's language is daring because traditionally the image of fire and iron was used to illustrate the union of the human and the divine in Christ.[70] The iron was made to represent the humanness of Jesus totally interpenetrated by the fire of divine nature.[71] Just so, for Luther humans totally assume the divine properties of Christ while remaining human.

This strong union Luther envisions between Christ and Christian is analogous to the hypostatic union, i.e., the union of Christ's two natures (human and divine) in a single person.[72] Christ and believer, though they are two entities, become one person by faith. Faith, Luther writes in his *Lectures on Hebrews*, transfers the human heart into God (*in deum*) such that one spirit (1 Cor 6:17) arises from the human heart and God. The human and God as "one spirit" is analogous (*sicut*) to Christ's human and divine nature

---

67. *WA* 10 I 100.13–20.

68. A similar sentiment is expressed in the second-century C.E. Epistle of Diognetus. "For whoever takes up the burden of his neighbor, whoever wants to use his own abundance to help someone in need, whoever provides for the destitute from the possessions he has received from God—himself becoming a god to those who received them (*theos ginetai tōn lambanontōn*)—this one is an imitator of God (*mimētēs theou*)" (10.6, trans. Bart Ehrman, LCL).

69. *Quale est verbum, talis ab eo fit anima, ceu ferrum ignitum candet sicut ignis propter unionem sui et ignis* (*WA* 7.53.26–28).

70. Basil of Caesarea, *In sanctam Christi generationem* (*PG* 31 1460.36–41); Maximus Confessor, *Quaestiones et dubia* 1.67.10–15; John Damascene, *Expositio fidei* 104–15.

71. For Christ as "deified man" in Luther, see *WA* 4.635.31–32.

72. In the words of Hamm, "It is the classical two-nature doctrine of the true divinity and humanity of Christ in which Luther finds the basic paradigm (*Grundmodell*)—one could even say the primal sacrament (*Ursakrament*)—for the union of Christ with the sinner" ("Wie mystisch?" 249). For further comments, see ibid., 249–52.

united in one person (*una et eadem facta est persona*).[73] Commenting on Gal 2:20 ("I no longer live; Christ lives in me"), Luther adds that Christ and sinner "become like one inseparable person unable to be separated" (*quasi una persona quae non possit segregare*).[74] "You are so cemented (*conglutineris*) to Christ," he continues, "that he and you are as (*quasi*) one person, which cannot be separated but remains attached to him forever and declares 'I am as (*ut*) Christ.' Christ, in turn, says: 'I am that sinner who is attached to me, and I to him. For by faith we are joined together into one flesh and one bone.'"[75] Despite the bold language, however, Luther's qualifiers *quasi* (as if) and *ut* (as) show that the hypostatic union between Christ and believer is simply an analogy, radically expressing the proximity of Christian and Christ.

In another bold analogy, Luther says that believers unite with Christ more closely than a husband and wife.[76] Adapting medieval nuptial mysticism, Luther says that "the soul is joined (*copulat*) with Christ as a bride with her bridegroom. By this mystery, as the Apostle teaches, Christ and the soul become one flesh [Eph 5:31–32]."[77] Christ and soul as "one flesh" is not, for Luther, a statement about fusion, but about participation and exchange. Married to Christ, the soul has all that Christ has—grace, life, salvation, and so on. Likewise Christ takes on all that the soul has—sin, death, and damnation. In a glorious exchange the soul becomes as righteous and alive as Christ himself. "For if he [Christ] gives his body to her [the soul] and his very self, how does he not give her everything he has? [cf. Rom 8:32]"[78] Luther immediately adds, however, that Christ has to assume and appropriate the character of his spouse: sins, death, and hell.[79] Thus Luther adheres to the orthodox understanding of exchange: it is not the communication of identities (the believer *becomes* Christ, and vice versa), but of properties. In itself, the soul has nothing, but in Christ, everything.

---

73. . . . *quia fides ita exaltat cor hominis et transfert de se ipso in Deum, ut unus spiritus fiat ex corde et Deo ac sic ipsa divina iustitia sit cordis iusticia quodammodo, ut illi dicunt, 'informans,' sicut in Christo humanitas per unionem cum divina natura una et eadem facta est persona* (*WA* 57 [Lectures on Hebrews] 187.17—188.3).

74 *WA* 40 I 285.25 (*Galatians Commentary* 1531 [1535]).

75. *WA* 40 I 285.24—286.16.

76. *WA* 40 I 285.24—286.1, 17.

77. *WA* 7 54.31–33 (*The Freedom of the Christian*, 1520).

78. *WA* 7 55.4–5; cf. Rom 8:32.

79. *WA* 7 55.11–14.

Transcending Humanness?

Although Luther presents a bold version of deification, he generally maintains the genetic boundaries between humans and God: Humans remain human and God remains God. There is one text, however, that seems to contradict this conclusion. At Leipzig in 1519, the Reformer tells his audience, "So it is that the human helped by grace is more than human (*mehr ist dann ein Mensch*). Yes, the grace of God makes him deiform (*gotformig*) and deifies him (*vergottet yn*) so that Scripture even calls him 'god' (*got*) and 'God's son' [Ps 82:6]. Thus the human must transcend flesh and blood and become more than human if he wants to be devoted (*frum*)."[80] As we have seen throughout this chapter, Luther was fond of bold rhetorical flourish (the sign of a good preacher). Thus I hesitate to agree that for Luther deified humans transcend humanity. Even though Luther speaks of deification here as transcending human nature, he also associates it simply with being devoted or pious (*frum*). Devotion, although an important Christian virtue, does not involve a transformation to superhuman life.

Even if believers do one day transcend flesh and blood, Luther believes that there will always be a difference between God and humans. First John 3:2 ("we know that when he [Christ] appears, we will be like him [*similes ei*]" [Vulg.]) is a favorite proof-text for denying a present and substantial model of deification. Commenting on this passage, Luther says, "On the last day we will be like (*similes*), not the same as God (*non idem quod deus*), but like (*similes*) to him, who is the life, justice, i.e., everything; we will participate in all which is in God; there will be the experience of what he is; there will be no cover any more; it will be apparent that we are holy [or saints, *sanctos*]."[81] The idea of being holy (*sanctus*) is parallel to being pious (*frum*). In neither case does it involve an actual transfer from humanness into godhood as such. Being "like" God—while affirming proximity—also asserts the difference between God and human beings. Although humans participate in all that God has, they are not what God is. It is implicit in his language that Luther assumes at least two different kinds of deity—what one might call metaphorical deity, and the deity of God. By only acknowledging the former, Luther makes clear that a realistic identification with godhead—even in the postmortem future—is not what he imagines. Even if we grant that deified humans after the resurrection transcend earthly human qualities, they do not thereby become God.[82]

---

80. *WA* 2 247.39—248.4 (Sermon on Matthew 16:13–19, 1519).

81. *WA* 20 698.12–15 (Lecture on 1 John 1527).

82. Cf. Mannermaa, *Der im Glauben*, 192–93.

Conclusion

There is little doubt that deification is an important theme in Luther's voluminous writings. The presence of this theme is immensely significant because Luther is (by most accounts) the first Protestant theologian, a thinker who even more than Augustine emphasizes the passivity of human beings and the need for salvation by God's intervention alone. Luther remained positive toward the idea of deification throughout his career, and carefully interwove it into the structure of his own thought.

Today deification in Luther seems astounding since in later Lutheran teaching, the notion and vocabulary of deification swiftly dropped out of theological discourse.[83] Recovering the Reformer's doctrine of deification is thus important since it shows that Protestants have in fact lost an important part of their own tradition by interpreting salvation (more narrowly: justification) in a purely forensic way (i.e., God declares the sinner just, thus creating a sort of legal fiction). In this light, Luther scholarship owes the Mannermaa school a debt of gratitude for reviving the importance of real salvific transformation (i.e., deification) in Luther's thought.

Nevertheless it must be admitted that deification is not absolutely central to the thought of the Reformer. The verb "to deify" and its derivatives is found only about twenty times in the standard edition of Luther's works (the Weimarer Ausgabe)—which consists of well over a hundred stout volumes. Moreover, to my knowledge Luther never brings up deification as a topic for independent discussion, never offers it sustained treatment, or expounds on it in detail. When he does employ the language of deification (many times in sermons), he uses it to describe (or redescribe) the traditional benefits of salvation. Deification means Christians are God's children (Ps 82:6), priests and kings (Rev 1:6; 5:10; 20:6),[84] saints (1 Cor 1:2, etc.),[85] and participants in the nature and qualities of God (2 Pet 1:4).[86] Throughout, Luther uses the vocabulary of deification to emphasize the reality and effectiveness of salvation in a colorful and rhetorically effective way.

---

83. For the German Protestant reception of deification after Luther, see Kretschmar, "Rezeption," 61–84. See further Mosser, "The Greatest Possible Blessing," 36–57; Kärkkäinen, *One With God*, 67–115.

84. *WA* 20 687.2–3 (Lecture on 1 John, 1527).

85. *WA* 20 698.12–15 (Lecture on 1 John 1527).

86. Luther nicely draws these images together in *WA* 17 II 74.25–75.11 (Fastenpostille, 1525). It is true that Luther's repeated use of biblical language to refer to deification indicates that he was eager to employ his principle of *sola Scriptura* to expound a traditionally Catholic doctrine. (For Protestants since Luther's day, if deification is to exist it must be biblical.) Nevertheless, the use of biblical proof-texts for deification (esp. Ps 82:6) accords with patristic tradition.

Where does Luther stand in the history of deification? In my view, Luther finds himself securely in the Augustinian tradition, with some important nuances. As we have seen, what Augustine gives with the one hand in reference to deification, he tends to take away with the other. That is, Augustine proclaims that Christians are sons of God—but not the true Son. He announces that they are justified—but not Justice. He even declares that Christians are gods—but not God. The style of Augustine is thus "affirmation plus limitation"—limitation that ever threatens to undermine the reality of the affirmation.

Luther's style of thought—and thus his presentation of deification—is both similar and different. It is similar in that Luther often qualifies what he means after using the bold language of deification. What differentiates him from Augustine, however, is his tendency to simultaneously affirm two opposite realities (e.g., humans are nothing in themselves and yet fully divine) without letting one side of the paradox undermine the other. For Luther, in other words, seemingly contradictory assertions (e.g., nothingness and godhood) do not cancel each other out, but intensify the paradox of Christian life.

Is Luther's understanding of deification "real-ontic" (a point often emphasized by the Finns)? To a certain extent, both Luther and Augustine can be described as "realist" in their account of deification, for both accept the Platonist theology that participating in God's qualities means participating in divinity (even if one never becomes what God is). Nevertheless there remains something profoundly non-realist about both Augustinian and "Lutheran" deification. Augustine was a true metaphysician. He formulated a trend in medieval theology that upheld a strict metaphysical barrier between humans and God (in short, the "creator/creature divide"). In previous chapters we saw how both Eckhart (and to a certain extent Palamas) overcame this restriction at once philosophically and experientially. In my reading, Luther—even if he did at one point speak of creation *ex deo*[87]— never overcomes the genetic separation between humans beings and God.[88] Although the Reformer shows no penchant for substance metaphysics, his emphasis on humanity's utter resourcelessness and God's awesome omnicompetence assumes a thick theological and existential boundary between

---

87. *WA* 5 168.3 (*Operationes in Psalmos* 1519–21).

88. "The believer is in faith one with what is believed. Luther understands this union not metaphysically, i.e., in the sense of a (platonic) participation in being, even if in his Christmas sermon of 1514 he describes becoming Word with the help of a realistic epistemology. Individual positive statements with reference to Aristotelian and Platonic ontology, as can be demonstrated above all during the first years of Luther's activity in the university at Wittenberg, should not be overestimated" (Flogaus, *Theosis bei Palamas*, 412).

God and human beings.[89] This boundary generates a paradox in Luther's thought—a paradox that expresses the inner structure of his theory of deification. Although in Christ humans can become gods and lords of all, from ourselves we are nothing at all.[90]

89. Wilson-Kastner suggests two reasons for Luther's general avoidance of strictly metaphysical language and concepts: his nominalist theological training, and his primarily pastoral theology. According to her, "Luther did not really care about the ontological foundations of participation in God either by nature or by grace. In certainty that he was preaching God's unmerited grace to a world to be judged on the last day, Luther correspondingly shaped the content of his preaching and his commentaries. If the language of participation in the divine life and transformation in God could be used within the context of *sola gratia* [grace alone theology], Luther would employ that part of the theological tradition." ("On Partaking of the Divine Nature," 123).

90. *WA* 4 123:5–7.

Chapter 13

"Then Shall They be Gods . . ."

The Mormon Restoration of Deification

The fluidity and materiality of the Mormon view of God enables
it to capture the essential sameness of Jesus Christ with us in a
most striking manner. Mormons go so far as to insist that God
was once a man just like us, which can sound confusing, but it
is, in a way, the flipside to the belief that we will become, in the
afterlife, just like him.

—STEPHEN H. WEBB[1]

IN A "BLESSING MEETING" of 1836, Joseph Smith Sr. (the prophet Joseph
Smith's father) told Lorenzo Snow, a potential convert, "You will become
as great as you can possibly wish—EVEN AS GREAT AS GOD—and you
cannot wish to be greater."[2] Snow was shocked, calling the declaration a
"dark parable." Four years later, however, he (now a converted Mormon)
received an "extraordinary manifestation" in which the mystery of the dark
parable was revealed.

> At the time, I was at the house of Elder H. G. Sherwood; he was
> endeavoring to explain the parable of our Savior, when speaking
> of the husbandman who hired servants and sent them forth at
> different hours of the day to labor in his vineyard [Matt 20:1–16].
> While attentively listening to his explanation, the Spirit of the
> Lord rested mightily upon me—the eyes of my understanding

1. Webb, *Jesus Christ, Eternal God*, 247.
2. Eliza R. Snow Smith, *Biography*, 10.

were opened, and I saw as clear as the sun at noonday, with wonder and astonishment, the pathway of God and man. I formed
the following couplet which expresses the revelation, as it was
shown me, and explains Father Smith's dark saying to me. . . . As
man now is, God once was: As God now is, man may be.[3]

Snow felt that the couplet was "a sacred communication," which he
revealed only to a few. When he returned from England in January 1843,
Snow related the couplet to the prophet Joseph Smith in Nauvoo, Illinois.
The founder of the Mormon movement replied: "Brother Snow, that is true
gospel doctrine, it is a revelation from God to you."[4]

The King Follett Discourse

A year later on April 7, 1844, Joseph Smith preached to a crowd of followers
estimated at 20,000 people. To them the prophet daringly proclaimed: "You
have got to learn how to make yourselves gods in order to save yourselves
and be kings and priests to God, the same as all Gods have done!"

Today this sermon is known as the "King Follett discourse."[5] The
discourse had a humble occasion. King Follett, an Elder in the Mormon
church, was "crushed to death in a well, by the falling of a tub of rock on
him." Joseph agreed to offer his final condolences after a major church conference in the morning. That afternoon, crowds gathered in a grove along
the banks of the Mississippi. The prophet, soon to be martyred in an Illinois
jail, stood up. His goal was to console his people by edifying them "with
the simple truths of heaven." Yet these "simple truths" turned out to be the
deepest mysteries and highest revelations Joseph Smith ever made known.

Smith began at creation, and with the nature of God. The nature of
God is important, since according to John 17:3, eternal life consists in
knowing God, along with Jesus Christ. Smith understood this knowledge of
God to mean the knowledge of God's nature. Knowing God's nature is not
just a game of theological speculation. One must know the nature of God
to have eternal life. Smith determined to preach the knowledge of God. He
began by telling his people about "the designs of God for the human race."

3. Ibid., 46. Cf. Snow's account given later in life (1901) in Williams, *The Teachings
of Lorenzo Snow*, 1–2. For more history on the couplet, its ideas and its influence in the
Mormon church, see Huggins, "Lorenzo Snow's Couplet," 549–68.

4. LeRoi C. Snow, "Devotion to Divine Inspiration," 656.

5. I use the reconstructed text of Larson, "King Follett Discourse," 193–208. The
original notes are printed in parallel columns in Cannon and Dahl, *The Prophet Joseph
Smith's King Follett Discourse*. For historical background, see Cannon, "The King Follett
Discourse," 179–92; and Widmer, *Mormonism and the Nature of God*, 108–26.

First, God Himself who sits enthroned in yonder heavens is a Man like unto one of yourselves—that is the great secret! If the veil were rent today and the great God that holds this world in its sphere and the planets in their orbit and who upholds all things by His power—if you were to see Him today, you would see Him in all the person, image, fashion, and very form of a man, *like yourselves*.[6] For Adam was a man formed in His likeness and created in the very fashion and image of God. Adam received instruction, walked, talked, and conversed with Him as one man talks and communicates with another.

Smith knew from the book of Genesis that God had appeared in human form—walking (apparently with legs) in the garden of Eden. Throughout Christian history, the anthropomorphic appearances of God in the Bible were played down. Every sophisticated (that is, Platonist) thinker knows that God is an invisible, incorporeal spirit. This Platonic concept of God was absorbed into Christianity and made staple by the fourth century C.E. (witness Augustine). Smith tosses out this long Platonic heritage without blinking. He spoke from experience. At the age of fifteen, Smith himself had seen a vision of the Father and the Son, and they were both in the shape of a man.[7] In the King Follett discourse, he makes clear that this anthropomorphic shape is not simply a form that God takes on and off in an effort to condescend to human needs. God does not lie in his words or in his appearance. The human form is his true form, the form he has always had. This is the form, or image, in which he created the first human (Gen 1:26)—and through him the whole human race.

Smith then proceeded to unfold God's history. "I am going to tell you how God came to be and what sort of a being He is." God was not, contrary to common opinion, divine from eternity. Rather, the Father "once was *a man* like one of us" and "*once* dwelled on an earth the same as Jesus Christ himself did in the flesh *and like us*." From this statement, we might think that the history of the Father is like the history of the son: incarnation leads to the assumption of divine power and status. But Smith indicates that the Father never needed to *become* incarnate. Instead, it is of his very nature to be human. As he evolved, the Father presumably took on higher and higher forms of body until he became the refined body (or spirit) he is now.

This story of God's own evolution is distinctive in Christian history. Previous Christian theologians had held up Christ as a forerunner and

6. Words in italics reflect the independent testimony of Wilford Woodruff, who wrote down the sermon in his journal from notes soon after it was given (Larson, "King Follett Discourse," 194, 198).

7. For the vision, see Joseph Smith, *History of the Church*, 1.5–6. Cf. DC 130:22.

model of human deification. Now the Father himself, in the long view of history, appears to be an even earlier forerunner and model of human destiny. Lorenzo Snow—who later became the fifth president of the Mormon church, taught that "Through a continual course of progression, our Heavenly Father has received exaltation and glory, and He points us out the same path; and inasmuch as He is clothed with power, authority, and glory, He says, 'Walk ye up and come in possession of the same glory and happiness that I possess.'"[8]

By the late nineteenth century, this idea was "common property" among Latter-day Saints.[9] In 1844, however, Joseph Smith realized the audacity of his theory, and clung to a biblical anchor. "I will show it from the Bible!" he says in the King Follett discourse. The prophet then paraphrases a verse from the Gospel of John: "As the Father has power in Himself, even so has the son power *in himself.*" The verse most closely resembles John 5:26, where Jesus says, "For as the Father has life in himself, so he has granted the son to have life in himself." At first glance, Smith seems to have misquoted the passage, exchanging "life" for "power." In the context of John, however, Jesus is indeed speaking about the power of raising people from the dead— and thus giving them life. Just as the Father has life-giving power, so he has given this power to the son (John 5:24–30).

Smith added that the son has power to do "what the Father did." Here the prophet had in mind Jesus' remark that comes a little before John 5:26, namely v. 19: "the Son can do nothing on his own, but only what he sees the Father doing; for whatever the Father does, the Son does likewise." This is a theology of recapitulation: the son repeats the action of the Father in the world. But if the son repeats the action of the Father, the Father must have once done what the son now does. The son sojourns on earth, but ascends to receive all power in heaven and on earth. This was once the path of the Father, then it became the work of the son. Thus Father and son follow the same course to deification. Humans themselves, Smith taught, are also destined to follow this track. They follow the son who followed the Father. Their destiny is his. History has a single arc, and all who become gods traverse it. The prophet cried out:

> You have got to learn how to make yourselves gods in order to save yourselves and be kings and priests to God, the same as all gods have done—by going from a small capacity to a great capacity, from a small degree to another, from grace to grace, until the resurrection *of the dead,* from exaltation to exaltation—till

8. Williams, *Teachings of Lorenzo Snow,* 3–4.
9. Ibid., 2.

you are able to sit in everlasting burnings and everlasting power
and glory as those who have gone before sit enthroned.

Deification is a process of cosmic evolution. By small steps and degrees, humans advance into yet higher and higher forms of life. "When you climb a ladder," Smith notes, "you must begin at the bottom rung." The higher and higher "rungs" of existence are likened to states of kingship and priest-hood on earth. They are positions of power. Eventually these earthly posts of authority lead to cosmic promotion. Humans evolve into cosmic kings and queens. These cosmic states are also corporeal states. The redeemed will *sit* enthroned, says Smith—which should not be taken metaphorically. Deified humans will need bodies to sit on their heavenly thrones. Nevertheless, the cosmic bodies of exalted humans must be able to endure what Smith calls the "everlasting burnings." These fires seem to refer to the celestial bodies above, or possibly to the fiery presence of God himself.

This evolution into higher—indeed, divine—forms of life is what it means, for Smith, to be "heirs of God and joint-heirs with Jesus Christ" (Rom 8:17). It means, in short, to "inherit *and enjoy* the same glory, powers, and exaltation until you ascend a throne of eternal power *and arrive at the station of a God*, the same as those who have gone before." This is the path of Jesus Christ. Christ himself was following his Father's lead. This Father was following his God and Father, and so on, for all eternity.

What does the Father do? He builds a kingdom. But this is no earthly kingdom; it is the world, the solar-system, the whole universe itself. The Father was there "when worlds came rolling into existence." Christ, accord-ingly, builds his kingdom as well—this universe. He will hand over this world to God, according to 1 Cor 15:28. By doing this, Jesus "treads in the tracks" of the Father and "inherits what God did before." As Plato knew, there is no jealousy in the divine choir. "God is glorified," Smith declares, "in the salvation and exaltation of His creatures." They will follow in the same path of deification and world-building as Christ.

Deification is part of God's eternal plan. "The Head One of the Gods," Smith continued, "called together the Gods and the grand councilors sat in grand council *at the head* in yonder heavens to bring forth the world and contemplated the creation of the worlds that were created at that time." The depiction of God standing in the midst of the Gods is reminiscent of Ps 82:1: "God has taken his place in the divine council; in the midst of the gods he holds judgment." The minutes of the most ancient divine council, accord-ing to Smith, reveal the creation and deification of human beings. Human beings, by divine ordination, were created to become gods.

In the discourse, Smith immediately proceeded to attack the doctrine of *creatio ex nihilo*, or creation from nothing. The word for "create" in Genesis 1:1 (*bārā'*), Smith claimed, means to organize, "the same as a man would organize and use things to build a ship." Smith infers that "God Himself had materials to organize the world out of chaos—chaotic matter—which is element [*sic*] and in which dwells all the glory." Matter, contrary to the Platonic understanding, is not opposed to God. Instead, it is a receptacle to house his splendor. The purest elements of matter, says Smith, "may be organized and reorganized, but not destroyed. Nothing can be destroyed. They never can have a beginning or an ending; they exist eternally."

Undercutting *creatio ex nihilo* was important for Smith, since it protects the eternity—and eternal dignity—of human beings. Smith shuddered at the thought of human annihilation. He feared that if something is made from nothing—including the human spirit—to nothing it might return. This horrifying prospect contradicted everything Smith knew about the sanctity and ultimate value of the human spirit, as well as God's own history. If God was once a man, he was not made from nothing. Likewise, humans who have the destiny to be gods cannot emerge from pure nothingness. This, then, is the mystery that Smith revealed: the human spirit must be eternal, as eternal as God himself.

What, then, did God do when he created the first human being? "God made *the tabernacle* [i.e., the body] *of* man out of the earth," said Smith, "and put into him Adam's spirit (which was created before), and then it became a living body *or human soul.*" God made Adam's body, the prophet claimed, but not his spirit. He could not have made Adam's spirit, for it is as eternal as God himself. "*Man existed in spirit*; the mind of man—the intelligent part—is as immortal as, and is coequal with, God Himself." Here, interestingly, Smith's teaching veers close to Platonism. The second-century Christian Platonist Clement of Alexandria once wrote: "But *we* [humans] are before the foundation of the world, we—because we had to come about in him—are born beforehand in God. We are the rational creations of God's Reason, through whom we exist from the beginning, for 'in the beginning was Reason (*Logos*)' (John 1:1)" (*Protrepticus* 1.6.4). For Smith, however, human preexistence is not only ideal (in the mind of God), but real. Humans were independent spirits in eternity past. There was never a point, then, when humans were not God's children and heirs.

The eternality of the human spirit as an independent "intelligence" does not mean that this intelligence is incorporeal like a platonic Form. "Intelligence *is eternal*," preached Smith, "*and* exists upon a self-existent principle. It is a spirit from age to age and there is no creation about it. The first principles of man are self-existent with God." By nature, then, humans have a certain equality with God. Philippians 2:6 says that Christ, who existed in the form of God, was equal with God. For Smith, the privilege of divine likeness is part of humankind's eternal constitution.

God, like a great artificer, sends his spirit children into the world with a capacity to grow in intelligence and knowledge. This is the way they are enlarged and improved. It is also the way they are deified.

The Father gives his children the chance to grow just as he did of old. In eternity past, "God Himself found Himself in the midst of spirits and glory. Because He was greater He saw proper to institute laws whereby the rest, who were less in intelligence, could have a privilege to advance like himself *and be exalted with Him*, so that they might have one glory upon another in all that knowledge, power, and glory." For Smith, deification is by grace, even if that grace is built into the cosmos and planted into the human spirit. God, like a good Father, helps his fellow spirits by graciously bringing them up to his level.

Smith concluded the King Follett discourse with a note of consolation. "Your expectation and hope is far above what man can conceive." This hope has a firm ground. The sermon is no mere idle foray into the ivory castle of Smith's imagination. The prophet declared that the knowledge he reported had "the authority of the Holy Ghost." What he preached, he preached "by the testimony of the Holy Ghost that is within me." In this way, the prophet authoritatively encouraged his people with the hope of re-joining deified loved ones in the upper world. "Some shall rise to the everlasting burning of God, for God dwells in everlasting burnings."[10]

Impact

The King Follett discourse is as electrifying today as it was 170 years ago. Due to its shock value, perhaps, it has never been pronounced official Latter-day Saints (LDS) doctrine. Soon after the sermon, faithful followers of Smith called him a fallen prophet since he taught a plurality of gods. In modern times, even committed LDS members—in light of similar criticism—are hesitant about these teachings. Such hesitation, however, does not shake the historical fact that Smith meant the King Follett discourse to serve as inspired teaching. Two months after the speech (June 16, 1844), Smith attacked his enemies in a sermon, strongly reasserting his divine inspiration and divinely inspired power to interpret the Bible.[11] To many

10. For the initial Mormon response to the King Follett Discourse, see Hale, "The Doctrinal Impact," 209–25.

11. The sermon can be found in Joseph Fielding Smith, *Teachings*, 369–76.

Mormons then and now, the King Follett discourse is the culmination of his preaching, the fullness of revelation the prophet bestowed on his people before his martyrdom.

To fully understand Mormon deification, however, we must turn to revelations of Joseph Smith that have attained canonical status. Historically speaking, Mormonism begins with the revelations given to Smith from 1820 until his death in 1844. Deification (which Mormons often call "exaltation") is not a prominent feature of Smith's early revelations, in particular, the *Book of Mormon*. The truth of deification is a higher mystery, progressively revealed to the prophet as time went on. It appears that Smith began receiving revelations about humanity's divine destiny in the early 1830s. Some of these revelations are printed in the Mormon canonical book called *The Doctrine and Covenants* (*DC*).

The Three Kingdoms

Section 76 of the *Doctrine and Covenants*—called the "Vision of the Glories"—is a revelation revealed to Joseph Smith and his associate Sidney Rigdon on February 16, 1832 (twelve years before the King Follett discourse). This revelation flows directly from a reading of Scripture. In fact, the revelation came immediately after Smith and Rigdon read and translated John 5:29: "and they will come out, those who have done good to the resurrection of life, and those who have done evil to the resurrection of condemnation."

The dualism of this passage is stark: there will be life for the good, and judgment for evildoers. For the Mormon prophet, the "fullness of the gospel" (*DC* 76:14) is more complex than this simple binary. His revelation announces that punishment is eternal only for those who have denied God's word and thus have (in effect) spat in the face of God. For most, however, hell becomes purgatory: punishment is temporary, souls are given a second chance, and heavenly blessing becomes available after the final judgment. In accordance with the variety of deeds, there are different levels of blessing. There are very few pure evildoers and still fewer sinless saints. A fair and just God does not simply divvy up humanity into sheep and goats, sending one party to everlasting agony, and the other to a monochrome experience of halcyon bliss. Smith's comment about his revelation appeals to logic and common sense: "It appeared self-evident from what truths were left [in Christian Scripture], that if God rewarded everyone according to the deeds done in the body [cf. 2 Cor 5:10], the term 'Heaven,' as intended for the Saints' eternal home, must include more kingdoms than one."[12]

In the "Vision of the Glories," the kingdoms receive names: celestial, terrestrial, and telestial (cf. DC 88:17–31). All three realms of heaven have majesty and felicity, but they ascend in grades of glory. The glory of the lower, telestial realm is like that of the stars (DC 76:81). Those who inherit this kingdom did not receive Christ's gospel. Nevertheless, they did not deny the Holy Spirit (vv. 82–83). This complex state of affairs results in an equally nuanced destiny. The spirits of these people abide in hell until their promotion in the final resurrection. At the resurrection, these souls come to participate in the glory and powers of the Holy Spirit (v. 86).

Above the inhabitants of the telestial realm are the occupants of the terrestrial kingdom. They too have a complex history. Many "terrestrials" died before Christ. Later, they had the opportunity to hear and receive the gospel when Christ preached to them after his resurrection (DC 76:71–74; cf. 45:54). Few, it seems, reject the message. Accordingly, they go on to receive a share of God's glory, "but not of his fullness" (v. 76). Their bodies become "terrestrial," shining like the brilliance of the moon (v. 78). They receive the presence of God's son, the Mormon second God (v. 77).

Those who receive the highest destiny enter the celestial realm. Even though the inhabitants of the telestial and terrestrial realms live a life higher than (normal) human life, only the peoples of the celestial world are formally deified. They are called "gods, even the sons of God" (DC 76:58, cf. Ps 82:1). "All things are theirs," said Smith—adapting 1 Cor 3:21—"whether life or death, or things present, or things to come, all are theirs and they are Christ's, and Christ is God's" (DC 76:59). Celestials overcome all things (DC 76:60), just as the faithful in the book of Revelation (2:26; 3:5; 21:7). For them, deification means dwelling in the presence of God and Christ (DC 76:62), and taking part in Christ's resurrection and rule (vv. 63–67). To fit in the celestial world, these saints receive "celestial" bodies, like in nature to the brilliance of the sun, and "even the glory of God, the highest of all" (v. 70; cf. 1 Cor 15:39–49). In this way, they receive "the fullness of the Father" (v. 71; cf. John 1:16; Eph 3:19; 4:13).

Biblical Grounds

The relation of these revelations to the Bible is an important issue for traditional Christians. It is impossible to determine precisely how much of Joseph Smith's ideas derive from his searching study of Christian Scripture and how much

12. Joseph Smith, *History of the Church*, 1.245.

from new revelation. Nonetheless, the constant biblical echoes and phraseology reveal his heavy debts to previous revelation. Although the prophet might not have put it this way, his revelation in *Doctrine and Covenants* §76 can be viewed as an illuminating interpretation of Christian Scripture. It seeks, in short, to make revelation clearer—to tune it to reason and make it more faithful to a progressively enlightened concept of God.

To give an example of Smith's Spirit-empowered (re-)interpretation of Christian Scripture, I point out the three levels of heaven themselves. Although technically not in ancient Scripture, Paul does distinguish three types of glory in 1 Cor 15:41–42: "There is one glory of the sun, and another glory of the moon, and another glory of the stars; indeed, star differs from star in glory. So it is with the resurrection of the dead." In the context of 1 Corinthians itself, Paul's analogy is rather vague. The term "glory" is never explained, and how he relates resurrected individuals to sun, moon, and stars is left open. Smith's periphrastic revelation clears up some of the difficulties:

> And the glory of the celestial is one, even as the glory of the sun is one. And the glory of the terrestrial is one, even as the glory of the moon is one. And the glory of the telestial is one, even as the glory of the stars is one; for as one star differs from another star in glory, even so differs one from another in glory in the telestial world. (*DC* 76:96–98)

The revelation explains that the different glories correspond to different levels of heaven. Paul also spoke of three heavens (2 Cor 12:2–4)—so this teaching was ready to hand. According to their level of heaven, Smith said, saints shine with different brilliance. He appears to envision different intensities of brilliance within individual levels of heaven. On the lower, telestial level at least, saints shine brighter or dimmer—like the lights of the stars.

When Smith defines deification itself, he continues to speak in Pauline terms:

> Then shall they be gods, because they have no end; therefore shall they be from everlasting to everlasting, because they continue; then shall they be above all, because all things are subject unto them. Then shall they be gods, because they have all power, and the angels are subject unto them. (*DC* 132:20)

In short, godhood means immortality (everlasting continuance) and the possession of power. The power is specifically the power to rule. As in Paul's teaching, the saints are said to rule angels (1 Cor 6:2–3).

Also agreeing with Pauline thought, the "Vision of the Glories" declares that the saints do not become gods apart from participating in the godhood of Christ. When the son reigns, they reign (*DC* 76:108). Those in the lower realms of heaven are subordinate to Christ. In Phil 2:10–11, it is said that three levels of being bow to Christ: those on earth, those under it, and those above it. Smith's revelation makes clear that those who bow the knee to Christ are members of the telestial world (*DC* 76:109). They become servants of the Most High God, and always subordinate to the divine Christ (v. 112).

Christ the Exemplar

For Latter-day Saints, Christ sets the pattern of deification. Christ was called "son of God" because at first he did not possess the fullness of the Father (*DC* 93:14). When he received the fullness, the spirit of Christ became God's firstborn son. All those begotten through Christ partake of Christ's glory and become the "church of the firstborn" (*DC* 93:22, a phrase borrowed from Heb 12:23). Christ's mission is to deify human beings so "that where I am ye shall be also" (John 14:3, quoted *DC* 132:23). As Paul envisioned believers being transformed into the "same image" as Christ (2 Cor 3:18), fully redeemed saints will be "made equal" with their Lord, the Lamb of God (*DC* 88:107).

Celestial Marriage

Nevertheless, Mormon deification diverges from Christ's story at one point: marriage. Although Christ (at least according to traditional Christian teaching) was not married, marriage is essential to receive deification in the celestial kingdom.[13] *Doctrine and Covenants* speak of three degrees of celestial glory (131:1–4). In order to attain the highest—and divine—level, one must be married "by the new and everlasting covenant," sealed "by the Holy Spirit of promise" by an anointed priest. This is the language of *Doctrine and Covenants* section 132 (from a revelation recorded on July 12, 1843). Once a couple is "sealed" in marriage, they remain together for eternity. Thus they have the power to continually produce offspring (called the "continuation of the seeds forever and ever," or "fullness," *DC* 132:19). In their afterlives, couples "shall inherit thrones, kingdoms, principalities, and powers, dominions, all heights and depths . . . and they shall pass by the angels, and the gods which are set there, to their exaltation and glory in all things" (*DC* 132:19).

13. Shortly before writing this, Karen King of Harvard revealed a Coptic fragment from an ancient gospel referring to Jesus' wife. The papyrus fragment reveals an unknown gospel currently dubbed *The Gospel of Jesus' Wife*. See further http://www.hds. harvard.edu/faculty-research/research-projects/the-gospel-of-jesuss-wife.

People who remain single, in contrast, do not have the ability to produce seed or ascend in the spirit world. Those married but not sealed become separate (i.e., divorce) at death, and thus cap their spiritual productivity. They are saved to be sure, but they only become ministering angels, serving those sealed in higher matrimony (132:29).[14]

About a month after Smith received the revelation recorded in *Doctrine and Covenants* 132, he preached a sermon in which he declared "No man can attain to the Joint heirship with Jesus Christ without being administered to by one having the same power & Authority of Melchisedec."[15] The only one with that power was himself ordained a "King and Priest" of Jesus Christ—the prophet himself. Thus in addition to celestial marriage, deification required initiation into the highest level of Mormon blessing—the Melchizedek priesthood. This gift is sometimes referred to as the "endowment" or "second anointing." Joseph Smith first administered this special priesthood in September 1843. From that time it has been administered to thousands of Mormons in secret temple rituals.[16]

Deification and Grace

In Mormon thought, the deified cannot take credit for their destiny. It is God who subdues all enemies for them, just as he did for Christ (*DC* 76:61, cf. 1 Cor 15:24–28). Nonetheless, in Mormon thinking, grace is not opposed to nature. That humans are naturally fitted by God for deification does not undermine God's grace, but underscores it. In the canonical Book of Moses 1:39 (part of the *Pearl of Great Price*), God reveals his work: to immortalize human beings. This is God's eternal plan.

The Book of Abraham (also in the *Pearl of Great Price*) allows us to glimpse the "back-story" of grace. In eternity past, God found himself among other spirits, less intelligent and less glorious than he. Not satisfied with this inequality, the Father endeavored to bring these spirits up to his fullness. Employing the service of some "noble and great" souls (3:22), God created the earth as a space for the dwelling of spirits (3:24). The earth then becomes their testing ground (3:25). There the spirits are "tabernacled" or clothed in bodies (cf. John 1:14) and given freedom to exercise their will. Those who follow God and his revelation in this life (or "estate") and the next evolve into gods (3:26).

14. Compare Joseph Fielding Smith, *Teachings*, 300–301.

15. Quoted by Buerger, *Mysteries of Godliness*, 61.

16. For a history of the endowment ritual in the time of Joseph Smith, see esp. ibid., 35–68.

The eternity of the human spirit is basic to Mormon thought. In the Gospel of John we learn that "God is spirit" (4:24). According to a revelation of Joseph Smith, "man is spirit" as well (*DC* 93:33). Human spirits are eternal. They were in the beginning with the Father, existing as intelligences (93:23, 29). Every human spirit was innocent at first (93:38), but some go astray while in the body. Most spirits, however, graduate to higher levels after their sojourn in the body. The increased glory and intelligence of human spirits advances the glory of God, because the glory of God is intelligence, light, and truth (93:36).

In sum, humans are of the same race as God (cf. Acts 17:28), made in God's image, eternal, and endowed with unlimited potential.[17] One of the first theologians of the Latter-day Saints movement, Parley Pratt, expressed this point as follows:

> Gods, angels and man are all of the same species, they comprise a great family which is distributed over the whole solar system in the form of colonies, kingdoms, nations, etc. The great decisive difference between one part of this race and the other consists in the differing degrees of intelligence and purity and also in the difference of the spheres, which each of them inhabit, in a series of progressive Being.[18]

In the words of Ernst Benz, "Man is of the same family as God and the Gods, but like God himself he must first unfold his being in an act of self-creation through eternal progression."[19] According to former LDS president John Taylor (served 1880–87), each human being is a "God in embryo" who possesses "in an embryonic state all the faculties and powers of a God. And when he shall be perfected, and have progressed to maturity, he will be like his Father—a God. . . . As the horse, the ox, the sheep, and every living creature, including man, propagates its own species and perpetuates its own kind, so does God perpetuate his."[20]

Conclusion

To some, the claim that God and humans are of the same species suggests a radically different view of God than that proposed in classical Christian theology. Mormons point out, however, that classical Christian theology

17. Ibid., 345–46.
18. Pratt, *Key to the Science of Theology*, 39.
19. Benz, "Imago Dei," 212.
20. Taylor, *Teachings of the Presidents*, 2–3.

itself represents the gradual merging of the Platonic and biblical views of God. This merger only prevailed in the early Middle Ages and never deeply affected the masses of ordinary Christian believers. Augustine, who was raised Christian in the late fourth century, grew up assuming a Stoic view of God as a kind of gas permeating the entire universe.[21] Around age thirty, he converted to the Platonic notion of an incorporeal God in part because it was the theology with the most claim to philosophical respect. Today, however, Platonic theology—which views God as Being itself and beyond earthly sorts of being—hardly carries the same philosophical prestige, and to many seems abstruse and even unintelligible.

Historically speaking, the Platonic view of God has no claim to being the original Christian view. Paul, who saw the divine Christ as Christians' elder brother (Rom 8:29) and who promised believers a body like Christ's own body of light (Phil 3:21) was no Platonist. The theological claim of Mormons is that they have restored a pre-Platonic and indeed "original" view of God. Till the present day, this claim continues to be challenged and defended.

Since his death in 1844, Mormon theologians have developed Smith's understanding of deification in new and creative ways.[22] What is truly distinctive about Mormon deification is the doctrine of spiritual increase: the capacity to enlarge, to be productive, and to create eternally. Paul's older contemporary Philo of Alexandria likened parents to gods because of their power to create.[23] Mormon teaching ratchets up this insight to a new level. Human gods in the celestial kingdom go on producing more spirit beings, "tabernacling" (i.e., incarnating) them in new worlds, thus playing the role of God the Father. In this way, cosmic evolution advances.

To outsiders, these teachings can admittedly seem like science fiction. Leaving the bizarre aside, however, one must admit that the Mormon doctrine of deification presents something heartwarming. Deification among the Latter-day Saints is not a matter of the lonely individual buried in contemplation. To become a god, one must become a god *in the midst of family*—as a husband, wife, daughter, son, father, or mother progressing with the family into higher and higher levels of godhood. Mormonism does not so much teach the deification of the individual as the deification of the family and the larger family of the church. Godhood is eternal communion, and the increase of this communion with God and with each other. It is not just

21. Augustine, *Conf.* 7.1.2.

22. For deification in contemporary Mormon thought, consult the articles on "exaltation" and "deification" in *The Encyclopedia of Mormonism*. See also Roberts, *Mormon Doctrine of Deity*, 32–43, 135–37; Peterson, "Ye Are Gods," 471–594; Ostler, *Of God and Gods*, 359–90.

23. Philo, *Dec.*, 51, 107, 120; *Spec.* 2.2, 224–25.

the rule and domination of other planets; it is the progression and infinite multiplication of love.

In short, Mormon deification connects the saints to their spiritual family. The path to godhood was tread long ago by ancient patriarchs, prophets, and saints. It was tread by Jesus Christ, and even God the Father himself. This connection to cosmic history and a high view of human destiny is delightfully expressed in a poem of Lorenzo Snow which he composed early in 1892:

> This royal path has long been trod
> By righteous men, each now a God:
> As Abra'm, Isaac, Jacob, too
> First babes, then men—to gods they grew
> As man now is, our God once was;
> As now God is, so man may be,—
> Which doth unfold man's destiny.[24]

24. Williams, *Teachings of Lorenzo Snow*, 8–9.

Chapter 14

"Rather be a God Oneself!"

Nietzsche and the Joy of Earthly Godhood

The shepherd . . . bit as my cry counseled him; he bit with a good bite. Far away he spewed the head of the snake—and he jumped up. No longer shepherd, no longer human—one changed, radiant, *laughing*! Never yet on earth has a human being laughed as he laughed! O my brothers, I heard a laughter that was no human laughter . . .

—NIETZSCHE, *THUS SPOKE ZARATHUSTRA* 3.2 §2

JOSEPH SMITH DIED THE year Friedrich Nietzsche was born (1844). Although Nietzsche came to reject Christianity, he did not reject a version of deification. From 1883 to 1884, he composed his most famous work—*Thus Spoke Zarathustra*. He wrote it in a frenzy of inspiration.[1] "Wrapped in his overcoat and a woolen scarf (for the wretched stove smokes only and does not give warmth), his fingers freezing, his double glasses pressed close to the paper, his hurried hand writes for hours—words the dim eyes can hardly decipher. For hours he sits like this and writes until his eyes burn."[2] This is the testimony of Nietzsche's contemporary Stephan Zweig, an eyewitness of the philosopher's writing habits. Nietzsche wrote the first three books of *Zarathustra* in the space of a mere ten days each. The book is a flamboyantly personal testament of Nietzsche's own struggle, a struggle that to some extent has become that of the post-Christian West.

---

1. For *Thus Spoke Zarathustra* as an inspired work, see *Ecce Homo* "Thus Spoke Zarathustra" §3.

2. Quoted in Kaufmann, *Portable Nietzsche*, 104.

Nietzsche could not stress enough the importance of this work for understanding his philosophy. In his autobiography he boasts,

> Among my writings my *Zarathustra* stands to my mind by itself. With that I have given humankind the greatest present that has ever been made to it so far. This book, with a voice bridging centuries, is not only the highest book there is, the book that is truly characterized by the air of the heights—the whole fact of man lies *beneath* it at a tremendous distance—it is also the *deepest*, born out of the innermost wealth of truth, an inexhaustible well to which no pail descends without coming up again filled with gold and goodness.[3]

Zarathustra is no prophet, Nietzsche says, and no bearer of tradition. He is a creator, a *"world-governing* spirit, a destiny," even "the *supreme type of all beings*."[4]

Admittedly, Zarathustra is an odd choice for godhood, given his self-proclaimed godlessness. "Yes, I *am* Zarathustra the godless," he declares. "Who is more godless than I?"[5] But though Zarathustra likes to prankishly shout his irreverence in the ears of his enemies, his reputation of being godless does not exhaust the depth of his character.[6] Truth be told, Zarathustra is not godless. He is an extremely pious individual: "the most pious of all those who do not believe in God."[7] Even if Zarathustra does not "fold his hands like a child," peeping, "Dear God";[8] and even if his piety leads him to reject all former concepts of divinity, Zarathustra still believes in the divine. "Precisely this is godliness: that there are gods but no God!" (III 12.11). "All things," he proclaims, "shall be divine to me!"[9] Zarathustra is so spiritual that he even perceives himself to be possessed by a deity: "Now I am light, now I fly, now I see myself beneath myself, now a god dances through me!"[10] But Zarathustra's identification with deity penetrates deeper than possession by a god. By the end of Part I of *Thus Spoke Zarathustra*, Zarathustra

---

3. *Ecce Homo*, Preface §4.

4. Ibid., "Thus Spoke Zarathustra" §6.

5. *Thus Spoke Zarathustra*, "On the Virtue that Makes Small," III.5, §3. For *Thus Spoke Zarathustra* (hereafter *Zarathustra*), I use the Kaufmann edition in *Portable Nietzsche*, 103–439.

6. Lampert, *Nietzsche's Teaching*, 229.

7. *Zarathustra*, "Retired," IV.6.

8. Ibid., "The Ass Festival," IV.18, §2.

9. Ibid., "The Tomb Song," II.11.

10. Ibid., "On Reading and Writing," I.7. At least one other person also thinks that Zarathustra is divinely possessed. The old pope says to Zarathustra in Part IV: "Some god in you must have converted you to your godlessness" ("Retired," IV).

is a creator, a sun-like giver of abundant grace. By the end of Part III, his soul has become master of time and circumambulates the universe. In short: Zarathustra the godless has become a god.

Throughout his exhilarating quest, Zarathustra presents and embodies two distinct understandings of deification. At first (from Part I.1 to Part II.8), Zarathustra thinks that he can deify himself by willing the "overman" (*Übermensch*). Later (from Part II.9 to the end of Part III), when he realizes that the hope of the overman keeps his will in bondage, he wills something more ultimate: the identification of his will with Fate.[11]

The Way of the Creator

The most (in)famous catch-phrase of part I is Zarathustra's remark (first muttered only to himself) that "*God is dead!*"[12] Walter Kaufmann emphasizes that this statement is not a "metaphysical speculation about ultimate reality" but an "attempt at a diagnosis of contemporary civilization."[13] In other words, "God is dead!" is not a remark about a being that exists beyond nature, but an assertion that people in modern society do not believe in the supernatural anymore. Nietzsche, who rarely spoke as a theologian, preferred to speak as a psychologist.[14] Thus he was more concerned with the psychological *worth* of believing in God's existence than he was with speculating about whether any kind of divine reality exists. "What differentiates *us*," Nietzsche clarifies in *The Antichrist*, "is not that we find no god—neither in history, nor in nature, nor behind nature. Rather, we are separated by the fact that we view the thing worshipped as God as pathetic, absurd, and harmful, not as 'divine.'"[15]

If "God is dead!" is taken as a theological statement, it refers to the non-existence of the Judeo-Christian God. He is that "old grimbeard of a god," the jealous one, who pronounced, "There is one god. Thou shalt have no other gods before me!" For Nietzsche, the Judeo-Christian God is the great Lawgiver and Platonic universal who justifies all moral universals ("thou shalts"). Zarathustra once believed in a God like this,[16] but he later claimed

11. Part IV, not originally planned by Nietzsche to be part of *Thus Spoke Zarathustra*, does not present any new theory of deification, but helps to interpret the material in Parts I–III.

12. *Zarathustra*, Prologue, §2. Nietzsche used this statement earlier in his parable of "The Madman." See *The Gay Science* §125.

13. Kaufmann, *Nietzsche*, 100.

14. *Ecce Homo*, "Beyond Good and Evil," §1.

15. *Antichrist* §47. See further Hatab, "Apollo and Dionysus," 45–46.

16. In "On the Afterworldly," (I.3), Zarathustra confesses that he once believed in the doctrine of God's creation of the world, but he could only conceive of the world as

that this God was the self-denigrating projection of a dying civilization, and thus no God at all.

Zarathustra clears away the gods to make room for his own godhead. At one point he asks, "[W]hat could one create if gods—were there?"[17] As for all the rest of the gods, Zarathustra advances an ingenious proof for their non-existence. "If there were gods," he says, "how could I endure not to be a god? *Hence*, there are no gods."[18] The inference is bizarre, and humorous, not only because Zarathustra characteristically avoids syllogisms of this kind, but because the apodosis (or "then clause") discloses so much about Zarathustra's desires. If gods existed, Zarathustra says, then he would be so consumed with envy that he would, it seems, implode (cf. Yahweh the jealous God). In this light, Zarathustra's extravagant repudiation of all gods—far from establishing that he is an atheist in the strict sense—leads us to be curious about his own divine pretensions.[19]

Zarathustra does not simply deny the reality of all previous deities. He knows that the death of other gods opens a horrific emotional and moral black hole in the human spirit. The sudden meaninglessness and profanity produced in society by the negation of the Judeo-Christian God is one of Zarathustra's chief problems. The God-shaped vacuum produces the nihilism justifying what he calls "the last man": a mediocre, pusillanimous believer in the equality of all. To halt the arrival of the last man, Zarathustra intends to re-sacralize reality—starting with himself. He states this project in bold terms in two places of *Zarathustra* Part IV:

> Now this [Judeo-Christian] god has died. . . . Only now the great noon comes; only now the higher man becomes—lord.[20]

> Rather no god, rather make destiny on one's own, rather be a fool, rather be a god oneself![21]

---

the creation of a "suffering and tortured god." Zarathustra, agreeing with the philosopher Arthur Schopenhauer, says that nature is too passionate, rapacious, and disordered for a perfect, tranquil divine Mind to have created it. If God did create it, it could only be a product of his fitful, drunken attempt to turn away from himself.

17. *Zarathustra*, "On the Blissful Islands," II.2.

18. Ibid.

19 Admittedly, Nietzsche later calls Zarathustra "an old atheist" (Colli and Montinari, *Kritische Gesamtausgabe*, VIII 17.4, §5, May–June 1888). The context of Nietzsche's remark is his lament that almost two thousand years have passed without the advent of any new god. Nietzsche jubilantly says immediately before this statement: "And how many new gods are still possible!"

20. *Zarathustra*, "On the Higher Man" IV.13.

21. Ibid., "Retired," IV.6.

For Zarathustra it is not good enough for humans to be images and imitators of God (Gen 1:26; Eph 5:1). One must *will* oneself to be god.[22] This is the essence of his project of deification in *Zarathustra* I.1—II.8.

After he has denied God, Zarathustra no longer considers himself to be "dust and ashes" (Gen 18:27). Instead, he carries his own ashes "to the mountains."[23] Like Lucifer, Zarathustra dares to announce, "I will sit on the mount of the assembly, in the far reaches of the north; I will ascend above the heights of the clouds; I will make myself like the Most High!" (Isa 14.13–14). But though brimming with hubris, Zarathustra is not violently thrown down from the heavenly heights. Rather, he becomes a "brighter flame"—a god himself.

How did he do it? Zarathustra tells us expressly in the section "On the Afterworldly":[24] Zarathustra became a god by overcoming himself. He did this, evidently, during his ten years of solitude in the mountains before he began his ministry. During this time, he first conceived of and created for himself his new ideal for secular humanity after the death of God: the overman (*Übermensch*). His first gospel preached to the people when he descends from his mountain peak is: "*I teach you the overman!*"[25]

When the townspeople reject his teaching, Zarathustra vows to reject them and pass on the teaching of overman to a select number of disciples. They too, Zarathustra urges, must overcome themselves. Their self-overcoming does not involve a slavish imitation of Zarathustra. Instead, each disciple must overcome himself in his own way.

In "On the Way of the Creator" (I.17), Zarathustra discusses three common elements in the ethics of self-overcoming, which are at the same time the ethics of deification. First, Zarathustra teaches the necessity of self-legislation. The self-deifier must escape uncreative obedience to laws (heteronomy) and become a law unto himself. "Let your spirit and your virtue serve the sense of the earth, my brothers; and let the value of all things be posited newly by you."[26]

Zarathustra ensures that the rewriting of new values makes one a "creator" in the place of the old Judeo-Christian creator God. In the Judeo-Christian myth of creation, God created the garden of Eden, the first law—and the first threat: "But of the tree of the knowledge of good and evil thou shalt not eat, for in the day that thou eatest thereof, thou shall surely die"

---

22. Ibid., "On the Way of the Creator," I.17.
23. Ibid., "On the Afterworldly," I.3.
24. Ibid.
25. Ibid., Prologue, §3, emphasis original.
26. Ibid., "On the Gift-Giving Virtue," I.22, §2.

(Gen 2:17 KJV). Zarathustra rewrites the story of the origin of good and evil. In his version, there is no tree of the knowledge of good and evil existing separate from the valuation of human beings. "Verily, men gave themselves all their good and evil. Verily, they did not take it, they did not find it, nor did it come to them as a voice from heaven. Only man placed values in things to preserve himself—he alone created a meaning for things, a human meaning."[27] The knowledge of good and evil for Zarathustra is partly that good and evil do not exist as eternal divine "things." They only exist as temporal human valuations. This is the truth that opens the eyes. But does it make one "as God" (Gen 3:5)? Yes. The only god who can exist now is the "I" who esteems. For Zarathustra, "to esteem is to create."[28] The power to esteem or valuate is based on the will. So Zarathustra refines his statement in "On Old and New Tablets": "to will is to create."[29] "Creativity," says Herman Cohen, "is the basic attribute of God, identical with his uniqueness."[30] Zarathustra, through his creation of new laws, wills himself into godhood.

Though self-legislation is the only real way to have personal freedom, says Zarathustra, it demands the greatest courage. The common people (or herd), jealous of the freedom and horrified by the pride of the self-legislators, will reject and attack them.[31] In response, Zarathustra counsels creators to reject society, which leads to the second element of Zarathustran deification—self-isolation. One must reject involvement in politics (I.11), instruction under other teachers (I.2), the people of the marketplace (I.12), the love of neighbor (as it is commonly conceived, I.16), friendship (I.14)—and when one relates with females (Zarathustra was unfortunately a chauvinist), one must not forget the "whip" (I.18). In Zarathustra's view, the way of self-creation is also "the way to yourself"—and to no one else.[32]

The third element in the ethics of deification in *Zarathustra* I.1—II.8 is self-love. The irony of the self-love that Zarathustra calls for, however, is that it is simultaneously self-contempt. The creators who truly love themselves will also hate themselves, because they see what they ought to become. They have an ideal—overman—which Zarathustra gives his disciples. At the same time, however, he gives them no real hope of attaining it in this life. Their only hope, as Zarathustra relates in Part II, is to make themselves the

27. Ibid., "On the Thousand and One Goals," I.15.

28. Ibid.

29. Ibid., III.12, §16.

30. Cited in Manser, *Westminster Collection*, 127; cf. Bauckham, *God Crucified*, 9–13.

31. *Zarathustra*, "On the Way of the Creator," (I.17). Cf. "On Old and New Tablets," III.12, §26.

32. Ibid., "On the Thousand and One Goals," I.15.

fathers and forefathers of the overman, attempting to create him through their progeny. They themselves remain mere "apes" in comparison to the overman.[33] Zarathustra's disciples must accept this fact. They will—indeed, they *must*—perish or "go under" before overman comes. They must hate what they are, but love what they hope for.

The ideal of overman is an important concept in the first major section of *Zarathustra* (I.1—II.8). This ideal determines the character of all three elements of Zarathustran deification. Thus it is necessary to discuss the *Übermensch* in more depth.

Overman

Overman, Zarathustra stipulates, is the meaning of the earth, the new goal of human flourishing. He supplies the motive for human growth. He is the expression of human destiny. Without overman, modern secular people will perish in their self-sufficiency because they (so Zarathustra) have reached the pinnacle of self-satisfaction. Their scientific gadgets have conquered the forces of nature, provided abundant food, and made life comfortable. Now humanity's greatest temptation is to sit back and be entertained. This attitude, urges Zarathustra, is the way of death. All life requires struggle and self-overcoming to continue. The way to motivate this struggle is a new ideal: overman. All of Zarathustra's ethics of deification in Part I.1—II.8 are designed to produce him.

Overman must be willed. "Let your will say: let overman be the meaning of the earth." Overman himself is the will to life, expressing Zarathustra's hope for the redemption of himself and the other elite men of society (the "creators"). Overman is what is most difficult and rare for the elite, because his advent requires them to discipline themselves, subjugating their own humanity to the humanity that overman represents. He requires the creators to see their life as only having meaning and purpose to realize a future end, as instruments for a higher cause. He demands warriors ready to sacrifice themselves for a greater purpose. He commands them to die. "I love him," says Zarathustra, "who wants to create over and beyond himself and thus perishes."[34]

This is a hard teaching, reminiscent of the saying of Christ that "Whoever wants to follow me must deny himself, and pick up his cross" (Mark 8:34). Zarathustra will begin to have deep doubts about his ethics of self-sacrifice for the overman beginning in II.9. These doubts, and the

33. Ibid., Prologue, §3.
34. Ibid., "On the Thousand and One Goals," I.15.

bold means Zarathustra uses to overcome them, transform and expand his view of deification.

Fall and Redemption

"Night Song" (II.9) is Zarathustra's most searching and melancholy song of self-doubt, eerily and abruptly sounding out of nowhere. Zarathustra had not shown any signs of sadness or self-doubt since the herd rejected his preaching. He had been chewed up by flies in the marketplace (1.12), bitten by a poisonous adder (1.19), and visited by awful nightmares (II.1) all seemingly undaunted and beaming with happiness. By the time that Zarathustra croons Night Song, however, he is empty of knowledge—both of himself and his mission. He whines pathetically to his lonely heart, "A craving for love is within me."

What has happened to Zarathustra? What has happened to his self-confidence and poise? Suddenly his heart is restless. He no longer wants to be the gift-giving sun he boasted of becoming in Part I. He wants to be night and darkness. The waves of joy and knowledge that flowed out from him at the opening of Part II are now the flames that he drinks back into himself. He is filled with malice, envy, and the desire to hurt other people. His happiness is dead. Dead also is his confidence in his disciples. Dead is his feeling of being understood by anyone. He is alone—though he knew the way was lonely! He is over-sensitive—though he claimed that fly bites did not hurt him! He is full of revenge—though he laughed at the adder's vengeful poison! Zarathustra has become the devil that stared back at him through the mirror in II.1—though he thought he could transform his devil into a god! Zarathustra's first attempt at deification has failed to give him the deep joy that he desired. He has not become a god, but a frightened, sentimental worm. Why?

Zarathustra has troubling doubts about whether or not he truly loves life. But this is a secret that he does not wish anyone to know about—even his closest disciples (II.20–21). He railed against the preachers of future worlds, branding them "preachers of death," unfaithful to the earth, and proponents of life-denying fabrications (I.3–4, 9). Yet he admitted in Part II that the blood of priests and world-haters was his own blood (II.4). By Night Song, it shows. From here on, Zarathustra has the smoldering sense that he too has denied life by his poetic creation—overman. The overman makes humanity a bridge, life a means, and all past human action unredeemable. With the hope of overman as the true goal of human beings, current human life, including his own, is only justified by what comes after it. This hope is similar to the expectation of the second coming of Christ—which Zarathustra understands as a pie-in-the-sky panacea and justification for all suffering. Just as the Christians who died waiting for Christ, so will Zarathustra die in expectation of the overman. Zarathustra is tired of a redemption that always requires one more generation to be achieved. He is tired of the theology that justifies waiting, that always repeats *"next year* in Jerusalem!" He yearns for redemption now, in this time, and equally for all times of his life.

Zarathustra cannot escape the conclusion that his philosophy of overman is ultimately a philosophy of pessimism. Though it proposes a distant hope, this very hope denigrates all of life and lulls Zarathustra into accepting death for a supposed higher cause. The ethics of overman are ultimately the ethics of martyrdom and self-hatred that Zarathustra tried to overcome in I.16.

The philosophy of overman is Zarathustra's "wild wisdom" (II.1). The problem with this wisdom is that it does not show Zarathustra how his life is worth living now, in and for itself. So Zarathustra finds himself unable, like the believers in the old Judeo-Christian God, to praise life as life. He has not yet learned to subordinate his wisdom to his lust for life. Though he supports mortal, earthly life as an ultimate principle, he has not yet learned how to *love* life. These inner tensions in Zarathustra's former theory of deification provide the growth factor for the development of a new, yet bolder theory.

The Will

Zarathustra's hope of salvation is still his will. With his will he can fully love life. Formerly his will created the vision of the overman. Now with his will he will transform this vision out of a new love of life. His will, Zarathustra still insists, can redeem and resurrect him.

But his will, Zarathustra admits, is chained. He can will overman for the future, to redeem the future—but he cannot will something in the past to redeem the past. It is necessary to redeem the past also, for overman throws a gigantic question mark against the status of all human beings who come before him. Like the Messiah of old, overman makes all people simply preparation for his coming. *All* reality, including Zarathustra, is past for the overman. Zarathustra, though he wills overman in the present, is quickly becoming his own past, which cannot be redeemed. Even Zarathustra's present life does not justify *itself* if overman is yet to come. The entirety of Zarathustra's life is quickly entering the dustbin of history, with his will powerless to do anything. For who could teach the will, Zarathustra asks with a tinge of despair, "to will backwards?"[35]

When we look deeper, Zarathustra's problem with his will is a problem about time. He finds linear time to be oppressive. What happened in the past will never happen again. So it is impossible to will something to happen in the past—it is already gone and will never return. Thus the will has this extraordinary limitation: it wants to redeem all of life, to *will* all of life, but it cannot will what happened before (in preparation for overman). But Zarathustra demands that his will be able to will and redeem the past, not just the future. What Zarathustra demands is impossible, unless the past somehow comes back—unless Zarathustra the poet can envision the past as eternally coming back, unless there is an eternal recurrence of all events.

Eternal Recurrence

The one who sparks the idea of eternal recurrence in Zarathustra is one called "the Soothsayer" (II.19). "All is the same," he preaches, and "all has been." Based on these premises, the Soothsayer draws a dismal conclusion (similar to the Preacher in the biblical book of Ecclesiastes 1:2): "all is empty." Time is cyclical, says the Soothsayer, which makes life meaningless.

Zarathustra was open to the first proposition ("all has been") because of his need to redeem and love all of life. But along with it, Zarathustra blindly accepted the Soothsayer's cynical interpretation of cyclical time ("all is empty"). As a result, Zarathustra drops into despair. He does not eat or drink for three days and slips into a week-long comatose state.

On the seventh day, Zarathustra is startled awake by a bizarre nightmare. He finds himself as the guardian of dead people who lay before him in glass coffins. Suddenly there are three thunderous knocks at the outer gate. Zarathustra tries to open the gate with his keys, but the keys stick in the lock. All at once a violent wind bursts open the gate, throwing up a black coffin before Zarathustra. The coffin, representing death, bursts open and unleashes the cruelest laughter. The laughter is so violent and hideous that Zarathustra is thrown to the ground and weeps convulsively. The sound of his own weeping wakes him.

Zarathustra, with his voice sounding as if it came from a great distance, asks for an interpretation of the dream. After his "beloved disciple's" abortive attempt, Zarathustra grasps its significance in a flash. Yet he tells no one. Immediately, he calls for the Soothsayer to be invited to a meal, and boasts that he is the sea in which the Soothsayer will drown.

---

35. Ibid., "On Redemption," II.20.

We immediately come to the section "On Redemption" (II.20) within which Zarathustra begins to reveal what has been tormenting him since "Night Song." His torment is the crippled nature of humanity. Though he strives not to pity humankind, Zarathustra bewails human beings who are unable to cross over the bridge to overman. Unable to attain the ultimate purpose for their existence, humans break into "fragments of the future." Their present life is not worth living in and for itself. It is not whole. Wholeness is overman, but he cannot be born now. Thus all past and present is broken on the stone of overman, and life cannot be affirmed in and for itself. The best way to affirm the past is to will it to happen again. But recurrence, given linear time, cannot come about. Thus the will, Zarathustra says, is chained.

The "people" teach that crippled humanity should not desire to be healed. For them, the chained will is part of life in linear time. But this view is not good enough for Zarathustra, since it requires all the "hunchbacks" and "lame-foots" to wait for some future era of redemption, and die waiting. Although Zarathustra cannot heal cripples now, he demands that their life be viewed as intrinsically valuable. Life should be enough to justify life. Recognizing this point is already the first step toward healing the lameness of humanity. Nevertheless a full healing—which pulls overman from the future and puts him in the ever-repeating present—will require a whole new view of time—eternally repeating time. Zarathustra finally accepts this truth in Part III.

In the second section of Part III ("On the Vision and the Riddle"), we are more fully introduced to Zarathustra's secret "abysmal" thought. Yet even at this point the thought is still embryonic. Zarathustra wields this thought to counteract the melancholy persuasion of the "spirit of gravity" (represented here by a dwarf-like monster). "Behold this moment!" Zarathustra cries out:

> From this gateway, Moment, a long, eternal lane leads *backward*: behind us lies an eternity. Must not whatever *can* walk have walked on this lane before? Must not whatever *can* happen have happened, have been done, have passed by before? And if everything has been there before—what do you think, dwarf, of this moment? Must not this gateway too have been here before? And are not all things knotted together so firmly that this moment draws after it *all* that is to come? Therefore—itself too? For whatever *can* walk—in this long lane out *there* too, it *must* walk once more.

Peter Berkowitz points out that Zarathustra received intimations of this idea from the dwarf—just as he did from the Soothsayer in II.19.[36] Accordingly, Berkowitz interprets cyclical time itself to be the dwarf's "leaden thought," which he whispered to Zarathustra, a thought full of revenge and the denial of this mortal life. Admittedly, cyclical time could be viewed as a "leaden thought" *if* one, like the Soothsayer, interprets it pessimistically to signify the meaningless of all life. Nevertheless, eternal return is not a doctrine of melancholy and revenge. The leaden thoughts the dwarf drops into Zarathustra's mind do not penetrate to the depth of his abysmal thought. His abysmal thought is not the thought of eternal return itself, but his *interpretation* of it. Instead of concluding with the Soothsayer that infinite repetition of time makes life vain, Zarathustra proposes that it makes life worthwhile and intrinsically valuable. By this new valuation (which he forms haltingly in Part III), Zarathustra overcomes the spirit of gravity. In this way, he makes the doctrines of his devil into the doctrines of a god.[37]

Zarathustra shows courage by interpreting eternal recurrence as a doctrine of redemption and joy—for it implies a bitter truth. It implies that all the small people with their small-making virtues can return with Zarathustra—exactly the same as they are now. This nauseating idea is represented by the snake that Zarathustra sees crawl down a shepherd's throat. Zarathustra commands the shepherd to bite hard (III.2). This shepherd, Zarathustra says later (III.13, §2) represents himself. In this section, Zarathustra admits his

> great disgust with man—this choked me and had crawled into my throat; and what the Soothsayer said: "All is the same, nothing is worthwhile, knowledge chokes." . . . "Eternally recurs the man of whom you are weary, the small man"—thus yawned my sadness and dragged its feet and could not go to sleep. . . . My sighing sat on all human tombs and could no longer get up; my sighing and questioning croaked and gagged and gnawed and wailed by day and night: "Alas, man recurs eternally! The small man recurs eternally!"

Zarathustra's only way to avoid suffocating from this truth is to accept it—life is intrinsically valuable *even with the small man*. Zarathustra's acceptance of this truth is represented by his biting off the head of the snake and spewing it far from him. When he bit, Zarathustra became what he

---

36. Berkowitz, *Nietzsche*, 195–201.

37. In *Gay Science* §341, where the doctrine of eternal return is stated by a demon, the person who rightly accepts this doctrine proclaims the demon to be a god.

always longed to become—one who overcomes himself. In Zarathustra's vision, after the Shepherd bites off the head of the snake, he rises and laughs triumphantly, a true lover of life.

Eternal return is the final test to discern whether or not Zarathustra can accept life as it is. There is no progress in the cycle. Nor is there any purpose to fulfill outside of life. Life must be enjoyed for itself. By affirming eternal return—even the eternal return of his enemies—Zarathustra says "yes" to life even though it has no ultimate end. Zarathustra learns to express his love of life in his laughing remark, "Was that life? Well, once more!"

This is the laugh of the redeemed shepherd. But his laughter, Zarathustra testifies, is "no human laughter." By his laugh, the shepherd—Zarathustra himself—shows that he is "no longer shepherd, no longer human," but one who is changed, radiant. Zarathustra has become a god, even the joy-giver Dionysus.

Yet Zarathustra's deification is not yet complete. Eternal recurrence is his highest peak and deepest abyss not only because it helps him to love life in itself, but also because it is the expression of Zarathustra's fate. To love life is to love the kind of life that Fate brings: infinitely repeated mortal life (eternal return). To love life is to love Fate (*amor fati*).[38]

Amor Fati

Fate—the will of the universe—is not the word for a new metaphysical system but a natural fact. Fate could be oppressive to Zarathustra if he viewed it as something external to him, compelling his will, and crushing it. Instead, he accepts Fate, loves Fate, and so redeems himself and all of time. Zarathustra's love of Fate is expressed in his formula, "Become who you are,"[39] later revised in his book *Ecce Homo* to read, "Become what you are." To understand Zarathustra's full experience of deification in II.9—III.16, it is necessary to explain this formula.

"Become what you are!" What is "are"? It might seem as if we need a Platonic metaphysics to explain this word, for "are" seems to imply permanent, static being. Meister Eckhart conceived of our "are" as our ideal, eternal existence in God. For him to say, "Become what you are" is to say, "Become what you fundamentally are in God—God himself." But this is

---

38. Love of fate (*amor fati*) Nietzsche says, is "my formula for human greatness: that you do not want anything to be different, not forwards, not backwards, not for all eternity. Not just to tolerate necessity, still less to conceal it . . . but to *love* it" (*Ecce Homo*, "Why I Am So Clever," §10).

39. *Zarathustra*, "The Honey Sacrifice" IV.1, 351.

not what Nietzsche meant by "Become what you are!" A point crucial to his philosophy is "a radical rejection of the very concept of 'being.'"[40] So would not Nietzsche more properly state his formula: "Become what you become"? No, because there is a genuine sense in Nietzsche that human beings *are*—not because of their ideal existence in God's mind, but because of their fate. According to Zarathustra, there is really only one way in which we can become. Our "are-ness" is determined by our inward spirit of creativity. Zarathustra's "Become what you are" means "Become what you must be!"

This counsel would be frightening and burdensome were it not for Zarathustra's doctrine of the will. For Zarathustra, "to will is to create."[41] In Part I of *Zarathustra*, the wild sage wants to create the overman. In Part III, he is still trying to create the overman—now not in some distant future—but in himself. To himself, Zarathustra says, "Become!" The place of this word in his formula ("*Become* what you are") reveals that the whole statement is an imperative, an imperative directed at Zarathustra's own will. In Zarathustra's thought, a person does not possess "free will." Free will, Nietzsche says in *Ecce Homo*, is a fabrication of the ascetic mind, which requires it to subjugate and rule the passions. Zarathustra's doctrine of the will focuses on "the will to power." Will to power became, for Zarathustra, the fundamental force of nature, which he comes to employ as the central explanatory principle for all events, including human action.[42] The will of an individual, Zarathustra seems to say, is a particular instantiation of cosmic will to power, or Fate. By commanding himself to "Become what you are," Zarathustra is asking himself to identify his will with Fate.[43] Fate is what must be at all times. To will Fate is to will what is. To will Fate transforms all "it was" into "thus I willed it."[44] It is not just a matter of willing that the past eternally recur. It means willing all events at all times. This truth becomes clear at the end of "On Redemption," where Zarathustra views himself as willing from all points of time: "thus I willed it" (spoken from the future), "thus I will it" (spoken in the present), and "thus I shall will it" (spoken in the past). As Julian Young points out, "since most of the 'it was' happened

---

40. *Ecce Homo*, "The Birth of Tragedy," §3.

41. *Zarathustra*, "On Old and New Tablets," III.12, §16.

42. Ibid., "On Self-Overcoming," II.12.

43. Zarathustra had premonitions of his identification with Fate in ibid., "On the Blissful Islands," II.2.

44. Ibid., "On Redemption," II.20.

before its birth, the 'I' that 'willed it' cannot be the individual ego but must be the ecstatic, individual-transcending, divine 'I.'"[45]

"Become *what* you are" is a nod to Fate. Fate is the "are"—the state of affairs. It is reality working in nature. Nature is not a person, nor an organism, nor a machine.[46] It can only be described as an impersonal phenomenon—a "*what.*" Therefore, to become *what* you are is to become Fate.

I take this word "become" in a literal sense. It does not merely command Zarathustra to will Fate, but commands him to become what Fate is. It is Zarathustra's identification with Fate. Zarathustra, who is commanding himself, is the "you" in "Become what *you* are." The formula assumes that you *are* Fate. Fate is what you "are." So to "become what you are" is to become what you have always been—one with the force of Necessity that determines all cosmic events.

What then is Zarathustra saying by "Become what you are"? He is commanding his spirit to identify itself with the creative force in the cosmos. It always was a part of nature, and always will be, but it has not been conscious of it. Zarathustra demands that his spirit now recognize its own identity with Fate.

Although the Stoics identified Nature and God, for Zarathustra identity with Fate is admittedly different from identity with God. The *results*, however, of both identifications, are strangely alike. After his union with Fate, Zarathustra has the expansive sense of being timeless, omnipresent, uncreated, free, necessary, and unlimited—in essence, a god. In "On the Great Longing" (III.14), Zarathustra speaks to his soul:

> O my soul, I taught you to say "today" and "one day" and "formerly" and to dance away over all Here and There and Yonder
> . . .
>
> O my soul, I gave you back the freedom over the created and the uncreated . . .
>
> O my soul . . . I called you "destiny" and "circumference of circumferences" and umbilical cord of time, and "azure bell." . . .
> O my soul, now there is not a soul anywhere that would be more loving and comprehending and comprehensive.

These cosmic claims only make sense if Zarathustra identifies his will (representing the most fundamental element of his being) with Nature. For him to love Fate leads to a true union with it. Identity with Necessity—the

---

45. Young, *Nietzsche's Philosophy of Religion*, 199.

46. *Gay Science* §109.

greatest, most irresistible force in the cosmos—means that Zarathustra loves life in an infinite sense. He has become infinite. He has become God.

Does not Zarathustra's identification with Fate imply the destruction of his will—his last hope for redemption? On the contrary, Zarathustra's identification with Fate is his ultimate act of deifying freedom. In the Hermetic tradition, "God wills all that is good, and he has all that he wills."[47] Likewise, Zarathustra's will is fully liberated and empowered because now, what he wills *must* be. Nothing can ever frustrate his will anymore. If his will wills Fate, it can never go wrong, never fail, never lack power, and never be chained.

In *Zarathustra* I.1—II.8, the best Zarathustra could do was to will what he wanted—the rise of overman. But Zarathustra's will could still at that point be compromised. Indeed, his will *was* compromised because it stood in conflict with his past and present reality. In II.9—III.16, however, Zarathustra's will attains love of life—past, present, and future—and supreme power when it wills as one with Necessity.

Thus instead of being the end of Zarathustra's original project to create himself, his union with Fate is the culmination of this project. To identify with Fate is not to become Fate's pawn, but to help create it. In Christian theology God's will is functionally equivalent with Necessity—what *must* be. God's will, moreover, is the means by which God creates. "Let there be light!" (Gen 1:3) is an expression of God's creative will (cf. Rev 4:11)—which has the power to instantly generate light. The Qur'an has a masterful way of expressing this extraordinary divine power: "God says Be! And it is." Zarathustra asks himself to say and do no less. He claims the power to transform all "it was" into "thus I willed it!" (II.20). This act of will is more than his simply accepting reality, or "letting being be." It means something more powerful and surprising. It means that, through his identity with Fate, he can proclaim "Be!" and it is, was, and will be. His "Be!" is the "Be!" of the universe.

Zarathustra and Fate speak the same creative word. Fate is from the Latin *fatum*, which literally means "what is said." What is said, in this view, is what is and must be. Fate is a creator. Fate created Zarathustra, but Zarathustra wills and creates Fate. By this organic relationship Zarathustra not only creates himself, but the entire universe.

Conclusion

By "The Other Dancing Song" (III.15), Zarathustra has become a cosmic personality, and thus a worthy dance partner with a cosmic goddess, Life. This Shiva-like dance expresses his joy because of his union with Fate. Like

47. *Ascl.* 26.

Fate, the dance of Shiva has no purpose. It is random, but harmonious and vibrant. Human dancers, when they are fully absorbed in the dance, cannot predict their next move. They catch the spirit of the dance—or the spirit catches them. They move faster and faster than expected, and perform feats that surprise themselves. The dance partners feel themselves to be one as the joy of the dance wells up in their inner being.

Zarathustra's dance with Life is his vision of cosmic joy, which seeps from the margins of Nietzsche's book. His overflowing freshness and cheerfulness in the final section of the book expresses the pure joy of his divinity.

> If my virtue is a dancer's virtue and I have often jumped with both feet into golden-emerald delight; if my sarcasm is a laughing sarcasm, at home under rose slopes and hedges of lilies—for in laughter all that is evil comes together, but is pronounced holy and absolved by its own bliss; and if this is my alpha and omega, that all that is heavy and grave should become light; all that is body, dancer; all that is spirit, bird—and verily, that is my alpha and omega . . .[48]

Zarathustra has finally overcome his fear and pity. He has crushed the spirit of gravity underneath his feet, and his spirit has become a singing, fluttering, flipping, twirling bird.[49] Though he preserves traces of the old humanity—and is thus susceptible to bouts of pity and melancholy—his fundamental nature is now the "laughing lion." He laughs and overflows with joy. In Part IV of *Zarathustra*, laughing and joy-giving become Zarathustra's sacred "work."[50] It is truly the work of a god—and specifically Dionysus—whom Nietzsche viewed as the symbol of the supreme affirmation of life, the greatest love of fate, and the apotheosis of joy.

48. *Zarathustra*, "The Seven Seals," III.16 §6.
49. Cf. *Ecce Homo*, "The Birth of Tragedy," §3.
50. *Zarathustra*, "The Sign," IV.20.

Chapter 15

The Posthuman God

I sing the body electric,
The armies of those I love engirth me and I engirth them,
They will not let me off till I go with them, respond to them,
And discorrupt them, and charge them full with the charge of
the soul.
Was it doubted that those who corrupt their own bodies conceal
themselves?
And if those who defile the living are as bad as they who defiled
the dead?
And if the body does not do fully as much as the soul?
And if the body were not the soul, what is the soul?

—WALT WHITMAN, "I SING THE BODY ELECTRIC"

NIETZSCHE REPRESENTS SOMETHING OF a turning point in the spirit of Western thought. He presents not so much a polemic against the divine as against a Platonist understanding of it. That is, he argues against locking divinity with its unshareable essence in an inaccessible transcendent realm. Instead, he roots divinity in the soil of the earth, so that it can also course through the veins of earth's children lately born—human beings.

This relocating of divinity makes possible a new view of the destiny of human beings. In former times, people whose happiness was inevitably frustrated in this life by dearth, death, and disease longed for a good afterlife.[1] They longed to transcend the earth and this earthly life. This other-

---

1. Sorgner, "Nietzsche," 39–40. According to Sorgner, Nietzsche is a forerunner of the transhumanist movement. Few transhumanists, however, would agree that Nietzsche's

222

worldly spirit was predominant in Western consciousness roughly from Plato to the Enlightenment. With the birth of scientific thinking, however, dreams of another realm had to compete with this-worldly hopes.

In a popular school of modern sociology, humans are basically reasonable creatures who search for happiness and strategize to maximize their goods.[2] In the past, people naturally sought for powerful exchange partners to obtain what was for them the ultimate good: eternal life. Over time, people traded ideas and information about where such a reward could be obtained. Philosophy built upon imagination to suggest that there existed a supernatural realm where superhuman exchange partners dwelled—partners who might be willing to help humans fulfill their most desperate need. At the same time, some people used this situation to attain status in their society as religious specialists, priests, and hierophants whose role it was to mediate the will and power of supernatural beings. Over the centuries, magic and religion arose as sisters in human culture to provide ultimate goods. Gradually, local nature-religions arose, woven of innumerable promises with symbols of powerful plants and animals who provided gateways to the transcendent. The rise of agricultural civilization and the invention of writing allowed many primitive legends and laws to be preserved and codified—a valuable legacy for an emerging professional priesthood. Religious reformers began to appear like Moses, Jesus, and Mohammed. Soon after their deaths they were transformed into messengers of God or even gods, whose stories served as magnets for a plethora of religious symbols. They became models of attaining the highest goods, including immortality. In the fourth century C.E., Christianity as a state religion developed a large religious bureaucracy. Priests and bishops began to suppress magical and mystical movements, since they threatened the monopoly on supernatural gifts mediated by an established sacral authority.

In the present time as well, conservative religious providers claim to have the only key unlocking the transcendent. Therefore they resist a new enemy—not magic—but science. Science and its wild daughter, technology, are movements that promise to provide earthly solutions to human problems of powerlessness and disease. Already technological advances have effectively eliminated food shortages in industrialized nations, produced cures formerly considered to be miraculous and—in the last century alone—doubled the average span of human life.

---

ideas fundamentally resemble transhumanism. For one, Nietzsche denied personal immortality, saying that the very desire for it was destructive. See further Hauskeller, "Reply to Stephan Sorgner," 5–8, and Sorgner's response in "Beyond Humanism," 1–19.

2. In this section I adapt the language of Bainbridge, "The Transhuman Heresy," 92.

Today, some people claim that within the near future the advance of technology will in fact provide what was formerly considered to be solely a supernatural good—a healthy, vibrant life *with no end*. Among these "techno-optimists" are the transhumanists.

Transhumanism is a broad movement that has developed over the past quarter century. According to Max More, "Transhumanism is a class of philosophies of life that seek the continuation and acceleration of the evolution of intelligent life beyond its currently human form and human limitations by means of science and technology, guided by life-promoting principles and values."[3] Speaking from the perspective of evolutionary biology and biotechnology, transhumanists believe that "the human species in its current form does not represent the end of our development but rather a comparatively early phase."[4] Biological evolution has taken humans far, but it can only bring us part of the way. Guided by the hand of natural selection, people need only live long enough to generate progeny that are healthy and adapted to their environment. Currently there is no evolutionary mechanism favoring a longer, more healthy life after the peak of our reproductive years. Now, however, humans have the capacity to take evolution into their own hands.

Technology, according to the transhumanists, is the great mechanism for the next step of human evolution. At our current stage of development, humans have already employed technologies to overcome the limitations of flesh and blood bodies. We have injected into our bloodstream vaccines, hormones, mood-controlling drugs, insulin, pain-killers, vitamins, and other perceived enhancements. Currently technology has modified the very architecture of our bodies. Many of us have knee and hip replacements, pacemakers, cochlear implants, retina replacements, donated organs, prosthetic limbs, and so on. All these enhancements help extend our lives and radically improve their quality.

If present technologies already slow bodily breakdown, transhumanists believe that future technologies can be used to stop bodily degradation altogether. Extended health, expanded cognition, and even immortality can be obtained by technological means. The end goal is nothing short of transcending the human (biological) condition as we know it. The result is what transhumanists call the "posthuman."[5]

3. More, quoted in "Philosophy," n. p. (cited 12 Oct 2012). Online: http://humanityplus.org/philosophy/philosophy-2/.

4. Bostrom, "Transhumanist FAQ," n.p. (accessed 22 May 2012). Online: http://humanityplus.org/philosophy/transhumanist-faq/.

5. Ibid., "What is the Posthuman?"

The Posthuman

The posthuman is variously defined, but he or she is in essence a being that so radically exceeds the capacities of present people "as to be no longer unambiguously human by our current standards."[6] Part flesh and part machine, the posthuman will be a type of cybernetic organism, or in techno-speech, a "cyborg."[7] Whatever the exact shape of the posthuman, such a being will have advanced far beyond present human beings. As far as we exceed apes, we are told, so far will the posthuman mind outpace current humanity. No longer restricted by the limitations of flesh, the posthuman will be "resistant to disease and impervious to aging" bursting with "unlimited youth and vigor," and in full control over moods and mental states. Unsurprisingly, such a grand vision of human destiny has led some writers to envision the posthuman as a kind of god.[8]

Of old a god was understood to be an immortal being with superhuman power. In the theology of the ancient Greeks, such gods did not exist in an inaccessible supernatural realm—but in the upper reaches of this cosmos, or even on the high mountain of Olympus in Thessaly. For transhumanists, science and technology promise to give human beings the power and immortality enjoyed by these gods of old. Today we only see premonitions of that increase in power. Formerly, couples prayed to the gods to overcome barrenness. Today, sperm and egg can unite in a petri dish. In biblical history, Yahweh threw down fire and sulfur on the cities of Sodom and Gomorrah. Presently, whole cities can be wiped out by the firing of a nuclear missile. Generations ago, devout people viewed the stars as rulers of fate and foretellers of the future. In the modern world, stars seen by powerful telescopes can tell us about our distant past—as far as 14 billion years ago. Now science promises to give human beings the ultimate good: fruit from the tree of life.

For transhumanists, imagining ourselves as one with God now or living godlike lives in some postmortem fairyland ("heaven") is not enough: "Radical technological modifications to our brains and bodies are needed."[9] Flesh and silicon must cooperate and act as one. Cognition, booted up with

6. Ibid.

7. Thweatt-Bates distinguishes between a "Cyborg" version of posthumanity and what she calls a transhumanist "upload" (*Cyborg Selves*, 1–65). The first version is based on the reflections of Haraway in her essay "A Cyborg Manifesto." The second version, more closely identified with the transhumanist movement, will be the focus of my discussion.

8. For transhumanism and deification, see Zimmerman, "The Singularity," 347–70.

9. Ibid.

advanced technology, must run at a faster speed. Hunger, sickness, and even death must be eliminated from the human condition.

If this is a version of "self-deification," one should realize that the "self" in this case represents a broad community of scientists and professionals advancing current technology and deeply respecting individual rights. Advancement, transhumanists agree, cannot be imposed by the state, but only willed by the individual. Freedom is an ultimate good which transhumanists intend not to remove, but to maximize.

Singularity

What is the transhumanist vision of the end? Ray Kurzweil calls it "the Singularity": "the nearly vertical phase of exponential growth that occurs when the rate of development is so extreme that technology appears to be expanding at infinite speed."[10] When the Singularity comes, the present human mind will no longer be sufficient to keep up with the explosion of knowledge. This explosion thus assumes the advent of a "rapidly self-enhancing greater-than-human intelligence"—the posthuman.

The posthuman is not a machine that is different than ourselves, infinitely smarter than the human race, and bent on destroying it. The god(s) we create will be *ourselves* enhanced by technologies that become part of our bodies. It is even possible, according to Kurzweil, that with the advance of scanning technology our brains could be xeroxed down to the last neuron and our consciousness uploaded onto a vast network that connects all our brains to an overarching cyber intelligence.[11] In this state, humans would have the opportunity to infinitely expand their cognitive capabilities in a vast kingdom of knowledge. Swimming in the paradise of virtual reality, humans would achieve cybernetic immortality.[12]

Although some have accused transhumanists of (implicit) hatred of the body, supporters of the movement declare that they want the full range of embodied experiences: "an increased capacity for pleasure, love, artistic appreciation, and serenity."[13] Uploading human consciousness onto a supercomputer does not assume a hatred of the biological "wet platform" (i.e., our present, fleshly condition). It is an attempt to attain a body less vulnerable to decay. Presumably, transhumanists would inhabit any sort of

---

10. Kurzweil, *Singularity*, 24.

11. Ibid., 198–99.

12. On uploading see Broderick, *The Spike*, 192–235.

13. Bostrom, "What is the Posthuman?" n.p.

body—biological, mechanized, or a hybrid of the two—that allowed them a maximum scope of sensory experience, mobility, pleasure, and love.

Admittedly, transhumanists can be portrayed as rebelling against "nature." They point out, however, that what is "natural" is not always desirable. Racism, sexism, and class inequality were once viewed as "natural." It is not rebellion to envision—and create—a better world. Technology can increase inequality, but it can also help eliminate basic inequalities: making the paralyzed mobile, the hungry full, the purblind see, the genetically impaired person healthy and vibrant. Transhumanists are committed to reducing the prohibitive costs of medical procedures that allow miracle cures, and (in the future) to giving all people freedom to accept or deny enhancements.

Transhumanism and Religion

As a form of utopianism, transhumanism resonates (as transhumanists admit) with religious visions. It is part of the Christian narrative, for instance, to believe that this world is "fallen" or incomplete. Death is not God's design; nature groans for redemption. The final vision is of a "new heaven and a new earth" where justice reigns. Jesus told his followers that those who live in heaven will be like or equal to the angels (Luke 20:36). Paul promised his converts a future transfiguration in which human bodies would become "pneumatic" and ascend to the stars (1 Cor 15:44–49).[14] The kingdom of God is in fact a renewed earth where death, crying, and pain will be no more.[15] In sum, it is part of the West's religious heritage to envision a transformation of our nature and our world into a state transcending its current condition. Transcendence is built into Western religious thought. The question is *how we attain it*. Do we take the ultimate gamble and sacrifice our lives for a supernatural dream, or use every opportunity to extend what is already intrinsically and infinitely valuable—*life on earth*?

Contemporary Christians often assert that the "new creation" of humanity and the cosmos must be brought about after death or by God at the end of time. There is no reason to think, however, that God demands that humans die before their bodies are "redeemed" (to use the Pauline phrase, Rom 8:23). "[W]hat kind of creator," Simon Young asks, "would

14. Incidentally, Paul who envisioned Christians as inhabiting a pneumatic "super body" is not accused of hating the flesh. To the contrary, he has become the standard bearer of the notion of bodily resurrection. For a brief history of celestial corporeality in later Christian thought, see Smith, *The Wisdom of Ancient Cosmology*, 83–106.

15. For transhumanism and Christianity, see Steinhart, "Teilhard de Chardin," 1–22.

wish his creation to remain in suffering and torment, plagued by the agonies of death and disease?"[16] God, if he is truly good, is already working in us and through our technology to make us more like him. The total depravity of the human heart and the ultimate destruction of human civilization in a divinely determined future apocalyptic catastrophe are not consonant with the loving nature of the Christian—or any—benevolent deity.

Although it may be selfish to will one's own eternity, the vision of the posthuman is not necessarily individualistic. Posthumans will not simply be sitting on lotus petals meditating—like Aristotle's supreme God—on their own consciousness. They will together make up a renewed society. A new creation within implies the kingdom of God without. As I noted, humans hooked up to the same cybernetic interface will in fact be supremely *together*—perhaps even cognitively one.

The major conservative religious objection to transhumanism (influenced by Augustinian theology) is hubris: it is prideful to make oneself posthuman. Yet this objection too often assumes a jealous god resentful of humans attaining his status (even though we were made in his image!), and that humans are born to rebel against their all-powerful suzerain. Such a picture of deity and humanity, although popular among modern Fundamentalists, is not the picture of mainstream Christianity. In fact, Christian theology from Paul to Palamas, from Luther to the Latter-day Saints, has presented a God open to sharing divinity. Human deification in these thinkers at least, is not God's dismay, but his design.

The Place of Divinity

Admittedly, since most transhumanists are secular, they would resist calling post-humanity "divine humanity."[17] But as Nietzsche shows us, one does not have to be "religious" to believe in the divine. Whatever its precise meaning in the various religions, from a humanistic perspective the divine is something that humans construct as an ideal for themselves. According to transhumanists, some religious communities have constructed a deity so high as to be ineffable, inimitable and imparticipable. He is a pure limit concept, restricting what human nature can be—an idol traditionalists use to keep humans under a glass ceiling. Transhumanists question every attempt to define "human nature" as a fixed, immutable essence and thus make it fit an orthodox box.

16. Young, *Designer Evolution*, 49.

17. On transhumanism and religion, see Hopkins, "Transcending the Animal," 13–28; LaTorra, "Trans-Spirit," 41–55; Jordan, "Apologia," 55–72; Manoj, "Spiritual Transcendence," 1–10; Thweatt-Bates, *Cyborg Selves*, 59–61.

"[T]ranshumanists do not *believe* in the human condition," Young writes, "rather in its *transcendence*, through technology."[18]

The faith of transhumanists is fundamentally positive: humans can transcend their present condition! Transhumanists do not see this reality now. "It is," to use the biblical phrase, "not yet revealed what we will be" (1 John 3:2).[19] Nevertheless transhumanists, like religious people, have faith in their ideal. Distinguishing themselves from some religious communities, however, transhumanists have confidence that their ideal can and will be attained on earth. Consequently, the posthuman ideal invites people to develop their full potential, and never discourages present advancement.

Given the long view of human history, transhumanists claim, people have every reason to "think big" about their future. If humans evolved from single-celled organisms like amoebas, it is not unlikely that present-day humans could at some future time inhabit god-like bodies lifted from the earth—more like photons than flesh—coursing through the stars. Is this pure science-fiction? History proves the rule: today's fiction is tomorrow's science.

Now and in the future human nature will have to be constantly re-negotiated and re-defined. But self-definition is part of human creativity. One of the greatest gifts humans have is the ability to construct themselves and their own identities. We might say that the very fact that humans have the freedom to construct and choose their identity is in fact part of their existence as God's image.

The divine is not far from any one of us. Admittedly, a transhumanist could choose to see the origin of human beings as a chance product of atoms engineered in stars, joining and coming alive in primeval ponds, complexifying in the contest of survival, forming ganglions upon ganglions until the birth of consciousness in a 1400cc cranium. Alternatively, transhumanists could choose to see humans "as the intentional product of a 13-billion-year process, in which the naturalistic processes through which we have reached our current stage of complexity are nothing less than the creative actions of God."[20] This "God," naturally, can be variously interpreted as anything from an incorporeal Platonic "Other" to a panentheistic prescient power to Nature with a capital "N."[21]

18. Young, *Designer Evolution*, 52.

19. See further Thweatt-Bates, *Cyborg* Selves, 1–3.

20. Knight, "*Homo Religiosus*, 38. Gregory Jordan believes that "It is possible to see evolution as forming a kind of sacred history—an understanding of the past, and how the present came to be, which informs religious attitudes, beliefs, and behaviors" ("Transhumanism and Religion," 64).

21. For scientific theology, see Sharpe, *Sleuthing the Divine*.

If in fact there is a personal God out there guiding the process of human evolution, it is not inconceivable that he is like a parent rearing his children. As in every family, there will come a time when our divine parent will joyfully let his children go to shape their own destiny. If we truly are the children of God, and "of his race (*genos*)" (Acts 17:28), then it may be God's will that someday we be adults of the same species.

In the transhumanist vision, however, it is more likely that God (as Kurzweil believes) does not yet exist—or is at least not yet conscious.[22] Transhumanists like Kurzweil recognize that the wondrous ideal of divinity we project onto the cosmos has the possibility of becoming real—of being incarnated—not in some Great Beyond, but *in ourselves*. The classical Christian tradition conceived of God as a vast Mind—the Logos—with individual human minds as participants in that Logos. Might it be that the minds we currently have are mere fragments of God, and that when our intellects cybernetically unite, all the candles of the Logos will suddenly converge into one flame, and God will be born in us?

22. Kurzweil, *Singularity*, 375, 389.

Conclusion

This book is an introduction to the variety of deification as it manifests itself in various discourses across a history spanning over thirty centuries and a multitude of lands. Such discourses have clearly been influential for Western intellectual traditions. The road following these discourses has been one of many windings with surprising turns up lofty heights offering broad vistas.

The road, with all its meanderings and way stations, has not been well traveled. One can safely guess why. There is neither one storyline connecting the competing discourses of deification, nor a single line of tradition, nor a shared pool of symbols and myths kept sacred by a particular religion.

In the theological traditions of (especially Eastern) Christianity, the exploration of deification is old. Today, however, we stand at the beginning of systematic, academic research into deification. No one discipline has claimed—or can claim—to oversee its study. It has been treated by specialists in ancient Egyptian religion, Greek and Roman ruler cult, mystery religions, magic, ancient philosophy, biblical studies, comparative mythology, patristics, medieval mysticism, Mormon thought, Western esotericism, and modern philosophy of science. A comprehensive history of the subject has yet to be written. In-depth comparisons of deification traditions are non-existent.

The present brief conclusion does not furnish another chapter summary (already supplied in the introduction). Instead I offer reflections that sum up the major themes of this book. This study's main "thesis," if you will, is that deification comes in many types. Such types can be described in terms of content (deification of the body? the soul?), chronology (postmortem? pre-mortem? gradual? instant?), mode (through ritual? moral practice?), motivating power (divine benefaction? human action?), result (union with a greater deity? independent godhood?), and so on. It is not my purpose here to provide a comprehensive typology, which would in any case reduce the complexity of the figures I have discussed. Instead, I draw attention to two central questions continually posed by this study. First, what do the manifold types of deification assume about the divine nature? Second, what, if any, is the natural connection of the divine and the human that makes deification possible? These are questions that properly situate deification as part of the larger history religious thought.

The Nature of God

It seems that in most forms of deification there is assumed to be both a transcendent and an immanent pole of God. In my own terminology, the transcendent pole represents "primal deity," and the immanent pole "mediate deity." The basic pattern is that the deified person participates in or identifies with mediate deity (whether it be thought of as personal or impersonal), leaving primal deity integral and protected. For instance, in pharaonic theology, there is no strict identification of the individual king with Amun-Re in his transcendent majesty. Instead, deification occurs through a mediate divine entity: the royal *ka* that inhabits each individual pharaoh when he comes to office. Similarly, Dionysus functions as a mediate divinity with whom the Orphic initiate can claim kinship. It is because Dionysus serves as a mediator that the initiate can become a demigod, and share table with more powerful Gods. In the "Mithras Liturgy," Helios is a mediate deity controlling access to his Father Helios Mithras. It is by participating in Helios—through the scarab ointment and by sucking in solar breath—that one experiences ascent and deification.

The distinction between primal and mediate deity is especially prominent in Platonism, where there is typically a mediate God called "Mind" or "Intellect" (*Logos* or *Nous*) and a primal deity called "the Good" or "the One" or "Father." In Platonism, humans are already endowed with the central characteristic of the mediate God (mind, *logos*, *nous*), but they never reach so far as the Unknown God who is pushed beyond being and divinity.

Likewise, in Christian thought there is a primal God called "Father" and a mediate God called "Christ." Christ is called "Logos" and the "Image" of God in the New Testament (John 1:1; Col 1:15). Christians can identify with and take on the attributes of Christ (being "conformed to his image" in Pauline language) while simultaneously remaining "other" than and separate from the Father. In this way, the Father's supreme deity is preserved in its undiminished mystery.

Gregory Palamas, as we have seen, shifts the concepts of primal and mediate deity away from the persons of Christ and the Father to the aspects of the entire Godhead. Primal deity is not the Father alone, but the essence of the entire Godhead. Likewise, mediate deity is not Christ (or the Holy Spirit) alone, but the energies of the entire deity. By this means, Gregory is able to maintain the dialectic between an immanent and a transcendent God after Christ was promoted to be one in essence with the Father. Despite the novelty of the essence/energies distinction, then, Gregory remains consistent with his tradition in that deification occurs only through the mediate aspect of God: humans are deified by God's energies, but do not become God's essence.

Thinkers who do away with the distinction between primal and mediate deity (for instance, Meister Eckhart) or who do not even countenance such a distinction (al-Hallaj) are sometimes categorized as "mystical" thinkers. They fuse categories that most conventional votaries of Western religions tend to keep separate—especially God and human beings.

Modern secular thinkers (Nietzsche, transhumanists) tend to reject the transcendent pole of deity altogether. By doing so, they do not automatically rid the world of deity, but (in the case of Zarathustra) see deity shining in and through this world. Although in theory the loss of transcendent deity might threaten to collapse the distinction between humanity and deity (since the earth embodies divinity already), in practice most modern secular people see humans as what they are: fallible and sometimes violent animals. Nevertheless, transhumanists see a vast potential in people, given certain technological interventions. In this way, even if there is no transcendence, there is still an open recognition of what humans are and what they have the potential to become. Transhumanists push this potential into the future, making it a definable and attainable goal. Nietzsche, by contrast, focuses that potential within. We can become what we are because we *are* always more than we are. We know not our own greatness—and such ignorance (regardless of what we think of Zarathustra) should make us humble.

The distinction between primal and mediate deity indicates that, for most advocates of deification, God is not mathematically one. Rather, the divine is a "fullness" containing different aspects, and inviting others to participate in them. Trinitarian monotheism is one way to express both the primal and mediate aspects of God, as is Egyptian henotheism and Greek philosophical monotheism. In these systems, divinity—though often professed to be one or focused on one being—actually represents a manifold reality or a larger family of beings (spirits, angels, saints, etc.). The "family model" of Godhead is most clearly expressed in Mormon deification: we are already part of God's larger divine family. Mormons might be accused of lessening God's transcendence, but they still work with obvious limits. Humans, although of the same species as God, never attain the status of

God the Father. Even in eternity, they always remain subordinate deities, not the supreme God, whose true greatness is inexpressible.

In Christian systems influenced by Augustine, the transcendence of God is so emphasized that deification becomes only a metaphor. Following the Nicene Creed (325 C.E.), he considers the mediate God, Christ, to be one substance with the Father. Humans are still conformed to Christ, but can never become divine like Christ is divine. Humans called "gods" in Scripture are just immortal beings—angelic or saint-like figures. There is actually only one God, whose deity is, strictly speaking, exclusive. Given such a view of God, deification still involves a superhuman transcendence—humans become immortal, invulnerable, and powerful beings. But they do not cease to be human. Deification thus becomes a metaphor for human perfection—what "God created humans to be"—however that it is understood. Understandably, upholders of Augustinian forms of deification thus look askance at *unio mystica*, and those versions of deification in which humans truly do attain the status of gods (e.g., Mormon, Platonic, and magical forms).

One of the chief doctrinal supports of the Augustinian understanding of God is the doctrine of *creatio ex nihilo*, or creation from nothing. Creation from nothing means that God did not create the world out of a preexistent stuff or from God's own self. Instead, God miraculously created the world from nothing at all. There is nothing so different from God as nothingness itself. Therefore God creates the world as something entirely different and other than himself. The master metaphor in this model is God the builder. But unlike the human builder, the divine builder does not use preexistent material, but by fiat brings the finished product out of the abyss of non-being.

One might think that such a view of creation would automatically exclude deification, but Luther's understanding of deification disproves this. For this Reformer, the deified individual realizes his nothingness. It is this recognition of one's utter resourcelessness and non-being before God that is the key to achieving godhood. In the biblical phrase: the one who humbles himself will be exalted. If God chose (and the decision, for Luther, is his), God could make what is nothing become everything he is.

The prophet Joseph Smith rejected *creatio ex nihilo* and presented an immanent God rather different from Augustine's transcendent Trinity. An important question in Christian theology is whose view of God more closely approximates that of the first Christian theologian, Paul? The question is not easy to answer, but it would seem that Augustine's incorporeal, super-mental Light is not necessarily closer to Paul's theology than the humanized and embodied God of Joseph Smith. Although we cannot attribute the saying to Paul, what the author of Acts places in Paul's mouth is highly significant: humans are the class (*genos*) of God (Acts 17:28–29). The verse (actually a quotation from Aratus of Soloi) is translated by the NRSV "for we too are his [God's] offspring." More literally, it means that humans are the same "class," "type," or "family" of God (all fair translations of *genos*)—an idea very similar to the Mormon view. If in his genuine letters Paul does not indicate that God and Christians are members of the same species, he does portray the latter as siblings (*adelphoi*) of Christ—a divine being (Rom 8:29). That humans are conformed to the image of God's (older) son—who is the image of God (2 Cor 4:4)—may suggest that they come to share a similar body, just as Seth, Adam's son and image, shared a similar body with his father (Gen 5:3). Children do, at any rate, share the same genes (a word deriving from *genos*) as their parents. To share genes is a modern way of talking about sharing a particular nature. The idea that humans as God's children are "adopted" and thus not "true" children seems to be derived from an unfortunate misunderstanding of Paul's term *huiothesia* (usually translated "adoption"; Gal 4:5; Rom 8:15, 23). *Huiothesia* is not a secondary sonship; it means "establishment as a [true] son." In Roman law, the one *made* son has the same rights, privileges, and status as the one *born* son. For Paul, similarly, humans are "co-heirs" (*sugklēronomoi*) with their divine brother (Rom 8:17). This is an extraordinary relationship with a mediate deity. Needless to say, however, there is little in Paul to suggest that humans will share the same status as the Father, or that God the Father himself was once human.

A Natural Connection?

When viewed from the side of humanity, there are two basic models of deification: deification "from within" and deification "from without." Deification from without involves the reception of a divine quality (e.g., power or immortality) not previously possessed. Deification from within involves the realization that those same divine qualities are already built into the human self but require realization or development. As is to be expected, most forms of deification manifest elements of both models.

Deification from without is often expressed by the Christian slogan "deification by grace." The phrase is something of a misnomer because deification from within involves grace as well—what we might call "built-in" or "natural" grace. Inward, unrealized divinity is often spoken of metaphorically as a "seed," "spark," "ground," "image," or "inward light." But the one who planted the seed, lit the spark, and created the image is often a divine agent who graciously bestows an inner potential in those destined to be deified. Deification assumes that "there is no jealousy in the divine choir" (Plato, *Phaedrus* 247a). God, in other words, does not resent our natural likeness to the divine and our ability to become more like God, and to become gods ourselves.

Our natural likeness to God is often thought of as a kind of kinship. There is no more natural kinship with God than that displayed by Amenhotep III. He is the natural son of Amun-Re born from the God's body. But the divine pharaoh is made a god both from within and without. The pharaoh's status as "son of the Sun" expresses a natural potential that must be realized in his military ventures and in the various rituals of renewal. Were he to lose his kingship, he could also lose his kinship with the God.

The deification of Antony seems to be entirely his own production. It is achieved by his deeds, his propaganda, his acts of self-invention amidst all the hullabaloo of ancient political theater. Still, Antony playing the role of a god was part of a system of expectations for a divine ruler external to his own program. Fulfilling this template of expectations eventually had a profoundly transformative effect on his person, not to mention the views of his subjects who honored him as *Neos Dionysos*.

It seems that the kinship between humans and Christ in Paul is very much like the kinship between Dionysus and initiates in the Orphic mysteries. Such kinship with a mediate god can turn into identification with that god. In both versions of deification, kinship with the god is fictive, not natural. It must be established through rituals (baptism and a ceremonial meal in Paul's churches; various purifications and sacrifices in Orphic communities). It provides a way for the individual to become part of the larger family of holy and divine beings.

The magician in the "Mithras Liturgy," it seems, has no natural connection with the Sun God. That connection must be forged through the use of amulets, spells, ointments, and magical words. As in Paul, divine pneuma has to be received from without, but it is soon integrated into the human self. For the magician, pneumatic substance briefly becomes the sole carrier of the self. In Paul, this wondrous form of existence is only experienced after death or at Christ's return.

In popular (Hermetic) and elite (Plotinian) Platonism, the human mind is already a fragment of divinity. Yet that spark of inner godhood will not grow into a fire until one acts morally and engages in a system of strictly disciplining the body and its passions. The god within is matched by a God without who draws the human soul above itself to the full realization of its true divine nature.

For al-Hallaj, deification might be the result of an inner realization, but it is wholly dependent on an external, immutable reality. Humanity is absorbed in God—a wondrous necessity of God's own greatness. Eckhart's sense of the eternality of human beings consubstantial with God's Mind tends in the same direction.

Such "fusion" models of deification are not to the taste of moderns, schooled since youth to value individuality and the ultimate importance of the single, conscious self (classic Enlightenment values). What is important in our day is to remain human even as we improve ourselves. This emphasis on the ultimate value of humanness has been embraced by Christian theologians.[1] In their view, God created us human and that is what we will always be. For these interpreters, deification translates as "becoming fully human." According to one recent interpreter, "This authentication and self-realization of human nature is the *raison d'être* of deification."[2] Deification does not mean becoming God or gods, but becoming *like* God (and such likeness assumes a final difference).[3] Accordingly, Christian theologians have come to prefer the term "theosis" over deification.[4] Theosis is often distinguished

---

1. Hans Küng asks: "But does a reasonable man *today* want to become God? . . . Our problem today is not the deification but *the humanization of man*" (*On Being a Christian*, 442).

2. Daniel M. Rogich, *Becoming Uncreated*, 90. In *The Orthodox Study Bible* (1993), we are informed about "*What Deification Is Not*: When the Church calls us to pursue godliness, to be more like God, this does not mean that human beings then become divine. We do not become like God in his nature. That would not only be heresy, it would be impossible. For we are human, always have been human, and always will be human. We cannot take on the nature of God" (ibid., 561). In the 2008 *Orthodox Study Bible*, we are assured that partaking of the divine nature "does not mean we become divine by nature. If we participated in God's essence, the distinction between God and man would be abolished. What this *does* mean is that we participate in God's energy, described by a number of terms in scripture, such as glory, life, love, virtue, and power. We are to become like God by His grace, and truly His adopted children, but never become God by nature" (ibid., 1691). In the rhyming phrase of Kallistos Ware: "In the Age to come God is 'all in all,' (1 Cor. 15:28); yet Peter is Peter and Paul is Paul" (*The Orthodox Way*, 125).

3. Gorman, *Inhabiting*, 4–5; Finlin and Kharlamov, *Theōsis*, 1.

4. Etymologically the term *theosis* comes from the Greek *theos* ("god") and the Greek suffix *-sis*, which designates action or process. Theosis could thus be translated "godding" or "god-making." Ironically, most users of the term believe that it refers to the perfection of the human being, not the transformation of a human into a god. Frederick Norris says this about theosis: "It was not first a Christian word nor always employed by only Christians after they made it central. From within his deep contemplative life and from previous Church Tradition the Theologian [Gregory of Nazianzus] picked it up, cleaned it up [!] and filled it with Christian sense. He and his fellow theologians took it captive and used it to speak about Christian realities" ("Deification," 415).

from "apotheosis"—which implies actually becoming a god—an idea on which most Christian theologians cast aspersion.[5]

The theology of Gregory Palamas presents a beautiful balance between deification from within and deification from without. For Gregory, deification occurs through God's incarnation (in fact, deification is something like the incarnation in reverse), but cannot be completed without the practice of contemplation and the hard work of transforming the passions.

Luther's understanding of deification by grace alone seems to be an extreme form of deification from without. One must carefully take into account, however, Luther's insistence that deification is expressed through concrete deeds of love for neighbor. But even here, as most Protestants would affirm, love of neighbor is the result of deification, not its cause.

It is important to add here that being the image (or "in" the image) of God is no longer thought of as indicative of kinship in Christian circles (even though Seth was the image of Adam in Gen 5:3). Nevertheless the image of God, however marred, still leaves open the possibility of a natural connection to God. Despite the classic Protestant emphasis on human sin, in practice most Christians would assert that being in the divine image at least makes one able to assume divine qualities (most importantly, a capacity to love). Humans in the image are in some sense *capax Dei*: capable of receiving God and his goodness. All the same, the classically negative view of "fallen" humanity in Christian circles certainly discourages—though it does not ultimately exclude—a realistic understanding of deification. The point of Christianity is to make humans "unfallen." If they are unfallen, they can become something more.

For Mormons, humans are gods in embryo. They have all the potential of their heavenly Father, just as a human child has the DNA of its father. But anyone who has raised a child knows how long a process it is, how much nourishment, education, and discipline the child needs to reach its potential. There is a synergy or cooperation between God and his children. But humans could not grow to be gods if they were not in some sense what God is already.

For Nietzsche's Zarathustra, the notion of external divinity "up there" or attached to a future *Übermensch* figure is already a kind of self-inflicted alienation from one's true (divine) nature. Deification occurs almost entirely from within, in the course of our self-realization. During this process

5. In the words of the theologian Paul Gavrilyuk: "To their credit, most present-day critics of deification recognize that pagan *apotheosis* and Christian *theosis* are not quite the same thing" ("The Retrieval of Deification," 649). "With apotheosis, then, the crowning symbol of imperial paganism," writes Benjamin Drewery, "the church clearly could not compromise" ("Deification," 48).

we learn to affirm life as it is. Although in most cases one undergoes this journey in some kind of community (even Zarathustra had disciples), Nietzsche insists that each individual must find his or her own way.

In transhumanism, deification is again both within and without. One requires the implantation of technology to advance to one's full potential, but the technology is created by us and eventually identified as part of our own make-up. In this form of deification, the individual engages in a process of technological self-creation. Yet it is a process realized in community. When we interface with each other through technology we become more than we are; and only together—in shared knowledge—can we become divine.

A common feature of deification is that the process comes to its culmination after death (e.g., in Egyptian, Orphic, Platonist, and Christian forms of deification). This feature is a nod to our present fallible condition and the eternal value of human beings (alive or dead). Indeed, deification is perhaps the boldest attempt to transform the darkest feature of human life—its end. In many systems, the final stage of deification is not only realized *after* death, but *through the process* of death. Conversely, forms of deification that occur presently must somehow explain the tension between spiritual truth and biological necessity (sickness and death). Sometimes the tension is explained by the fact that present deification is temporary (the Mithras Liturgy), or requires ritual renewal (Amenhotep III), or that it actually occurs outside of time (Meister Eckhart). Whatever it is, deification cannot simply be written off as a radical form of compensation, for no human suffering matches so bright a glory.

———————— ◅◦▻ ————————

It is time to close this study. I have tried to show that deification, though often marginalized and feared, is an important part of the intellectual and spiritual heritage of the West. Even if one cannot believe in it, the very exploration of deification is exhilarating. It is true that deification is (and will remain) "other" to us in modern Western culture. But the "other" is within. Deification is part of our history and our religious heritage regardless of the particular religion that has served as carrier of its traditions. Deification has long been part of the human aspiration to be better, and better than it is humanly possible to be. It is, if I can use the expression, optimism incarnate—optimism, that is, about our potential to definitively (and perhaps infinitely) improve our station by internal or external means before and after death. In ancient times, this aspiration was expressed in the language of metaphysics, mystery, and magic. In modern times, the aspiration is expressed in the (relatively) new language of evolution and technological advance. But whether deification be viewed as supernatural or merely "super" and natural, we are forced to humbly confess: "it has not yet been revealed what we will be" (1 John 3:2).

Bibliography

Primary Sources

Adler, Ada, editor. *Suidae Lexicon*. 5 vols. Stuttgart: Teubner, 1989–94.

Apostolic Fathers. Translated by Bart D. Ehrman. 2 vols. Loeb Classical Library. Cambridge: Harvard University Press, 2003.

Apuleius, Metamorphoses. Translated by J. Arthur Hanson. 2 vols. Loeb Classical Library. Cambridge: Harvard University Press, 1989.

Aristotle. *Fragmenta*. Edited by Valentinus Rose. Leipzig: Teubner, 1886.

———. *Fragmenta*. Translated by H. Rackham, et al. 23 vols. Loeb Classical Library. Cambridge: Harvard University Press, 1926–2011.

Artemidorus, *Oneirocritica*. Edited by R. A. Pack. Leipzig: Teubner, 1963.

Athanassakis, Apostolos N., editor. *The Orphic Hymns: Text, Translation and Notes*. Missoula, MT: Scholars, 1977.

Athenaeus. Translated by Douglas S. Olson. Loeb Classical Library. Cambridge: Harvard University Press, 2007–11.

Attridge, Harold, editor. *The Harper Collins Study Bible Fully Revised and Updated: New Revised Standard Version*. New York: Harper Collins, 2006.

Augustine. *The Confessions*. Translated by Mary Boulding. Works of Saint Augustine I/1. Hyde Park, NY: New City, 1997.

———. *Confessionum Libri XIII*. Edited by Lucan Verheijen. CCSL 27. Turnholt: Brepols, 1981.

———. *De Genesi contra Manichaeos*. Edited by Dorothea Weber. CSEL 91. Wien: Österreichischen Akademie der Wissenschaften, 1998.

———. *De natura et gratia liber unus*. Edited by Carolus F. Urba and Joseph Zycha. CSEL 60. Lipsiae: G. Freytag, 1913.

———. *De Trinitate Libri XV*. Edited by W. J. Mountain. CCSL 50. Turnholt: Brepols, 1968.

———. *Enarrationes in Psalmos*. 3 vols. CCSL 38–40. Turnholt: Brepols, 1956.

———. *Epistulae Pars III*. Edited by Al. Goldbacher. CSEL 44. Lipsiae: Freytag, 1904.

———. *In Iohannis Evangelium Tractatus CXXIV*. CCSL 36. Turnholt: Brepols, 1954.

———. *Sermones de vetere testamento I–L*. Edited by Cyrillus Lambot. CCSL 41. Turnholt: Brepols, 1961.

Bernabé, Alberto, editor. *Poetae Epici Graeci*. 3 vols. Teubner: Leipzig, 2003–7.

Betz, Hans Dieter. *The Greek Magical Papyri in Translation Including the Demotic Spells.* 2nd ed. Chicago: University of Chicago Press, 1992.

Burleigh, John H. S., editor. *Augustine: Earlier Writings.* The Library of Christian Classics 6. Philadelphia: Westminster, 1953.

Cannon, Donald Q., and Larry E. Dahl, editors. *The Prophet Joseph Smith's King Follett Discourse: A Six Column Comparison of Original Notes and Amalgamations.* Provo, UT: BYU Printing Service, 1983.

Church of Jesus Christ of Latter-day Saints. *The Book of Mormon, The Doctrine and Covenants of the Church of Jesus Christ of Latter-Day Saints and The Pearl of Great Price.* Salt Lake City: Church of Jesus Christ of Latter-days Saints, 1981.

Clement of Alexandria. *Le Protreptique.* Translated by Claude Mondésert. 2d ed. Sources chrétiennes 2. Paris: Éditions du Cerf, 1961.

Colli, Giorgio, and Mazzino Montinari, editors. *Nietzsche: Kritische Gesamtausgabe.* 15 vols. Berlin: de Gruyter, 1967.

Cooper, John M., editor. *Plato: Complete Works.* Indianapolis: Hackett, 1997.

Copenhaver, Brian, editor. *Hermetica: The Greek Corpus Hermeticum and the Latin Asclepius in a New English Translation with Notes and Introduction.* Cambridge: Cambridge University Press, 1992.

Der Manuelian, Peter, editor. *The Ancient Egyptian Pyramid Texts.* Translated by James P. Allen. Writings from the Ancient World. Leiden: Brill, 2005.

Diels, Hermann, and Walther Kranz, editors. *Die Fragmente der Vorsokratiker.* 7th ed. Vol. 1. Berlin: Weidmannsche, 1954.

Dio Cassius. Translated by Earnest Cary and Herbert Baldwin Foster. 9 vols. Loeb Classical Library. London: Heinemann, 1914–27.

Dio Chrysostom. Translated by J. W. Cohoon et al. 5 vols. Loeb Classical Library. Cambridge: Harvard University Press, 1932–51.

Diodorus of Sicily. Translated by Charles Henry Oldfather. 12 vols. Loeb Classical Library. London: Heinemann, 1933–67.

Diogenes Laertius. Translated by R. D. Hicks. 2 vols. Loeb Classical Library. Cambridge: Harvard University Press, 1925.

Dittenberger, Wilhelm, editor. *Orientis Graeci Inscriptiones Selectae.* 2 vols. Lipsiae: Hirzel, 1903–5.

Dolbeau, Françoise, editor. *Vingt–six sermons au peuple d'Afrique.* Paris: Institut d'Études Augustiniennes, 1996.

Furley, William D., and Jan Maarten Bremer, editors. *Greek Hymns: Selected Cult Songs from the Archaic to the Hellenistic Period.* Studien und Texte zu Antike und Christentum 9. 2 vols. Tübingen: Mohr Siebeck, 2001.

Graf, Fritz, and Sarah Iles Johnston. *Ritual Texts for the Afterlife: Orpheus and the Bacchic Gold Tablets.* 2nd ed. London: Routledge, 2012.

Hammer, Gerhard, and Manfred Biersack, editors. *AWA.* Köln: Böhlau, 1981.

Herodotus. Translated by A. D. Godley. 4 vols. Loeb Classical Library. Cambridge: Harvard University Press, 1920–25.

Hoffman, Bengt, editor. *The Theologia Germanica.* The Classics of Western Spirituality. New York: Paulist: 1980.

Homer. Translated by A. T. Murray. 4 vols. Loeb Classical Library. Cambridge: Harvard University Press, 1919–25.

Hornung, Erik, and Theodor Abt, editors. *The Egyptian Amduat: The Book of the Hidden Chamber.* Translated by David Warburton. Zurich: Living Human Heritage, 2007.

Inwood, Brad, editor. *The Poem of Empedocles: A Text and Translation with an Introduction*. Toronto: University of Toronto Press, 1992.

Irenaeus. *Contre les hérésies*. Edited and translated by Adelin Rousseau et Louis Doutreleau. 5 vols. Sources chrétiennes 100, 150, 152–53, 210–11. Paris: Éditions du Cerf, 1965–82.

Jacoby, Felix. *FGH*. Leiden: Brill, 1923–58.

Janus, C. *Musici Scriptores Graeci*. Leipzig: Teubner, 1895.

Kaufmann,Walter, editor. *The Portable Nietzsche*. New York: Penguin, 1982.

Kirchner, Iohannes, editor. *IG: Inscriptiones Atticae Euclidis anno posteriores*. 2nd ed. Minor Pars Prima. Preussische Akademie der Wissenschaften. Berlin: Reimer, 1916.

Kouremenos, Theokritos, et al., editors. *The Derveni Papyrus: Edited with Introduction and Commentary*. Firenze: Olschki, 2006.

Lactantius. *Divine Institutes*. Translated by Anthony Bowen and Peter Garnsey. Liverpool: Liverpool University Press, 2003.

Largier, Niklaus, editor. *Meister Eckhart: Werke*. 2 vols. Frankfurt: Deutsche Klassiker, 1993.

Larson, Stan. "The King Follett Discourse: A Newly Amalgamated Text." *BYU Studies* 18 (1978) 193–208.

Lucian. Translated by A. M. Harmon. 8 vols. Loeb Classical Library. Cambridge: Harvard University Press, 1913–67.

Luther, Martin. *Werke: kritische Gesamtausgabe (Weimarer Ausgabe)*. 60 vols. Weimar: Böhlaus Nachfolger, 1883–1980.

Maehler, Herwig, editor. *Pindarus: Fragmenta*. Leipzig: Teubner, 1971–89.

Majercik, Ruth. *The Chaldean Oracles: Text, Translation, and Commentary*. Leiden: Brill, 1989.

McGinn, Bernard, editor. *Meister Eckhart: The Essential Sermons, Commentaries, Treatises, and Defense*. Translated by Edmund Colledge and Bernard McGinn. The Classics of Western Spirituality. Mahwah, NJ: Paulist, 1981.

————. *Meister Eckhart: Teacher and Preacher*. Translated by Frank Tobin. The Classics of Western Spirituality. Mahwah, NJ: Paulist, 1986.

Merkelbach, Reinhold, and Martin West, editors. *Fragmenta Hesiodea*. Oxford: Clarendon, 1967.

Meyendorff, John. *Gregory Palamas: The Triads*. Translated by Nicholas Gendle. Classics of Western Spirituality. Mahwah, NJ: Paulist, 1983.

Migne, J.-P., editor. *Patrologiae cursus completus: Series Graeca*. 161 vols. Paris: Garnier Fratres, 1857–94.

————. *Patrologiae cursus completus: Series Latina*. 221 vols. Paris: Garnier Fratres, 1884–1904.

Minns, Denis, and Paul Parvis, editors. *Justin, Philosopher and Martyr, Apologies*. Oxford: Oxford University Press, 2009.

Nietzsche, Friedrich. *The Anti-Christ, Ecce Homo, Twilight of the Idols, and Other Writings*. Edited by Aaron Ridley. Translated by Judith Norman. Cambridge: Cambridge University Press, 2005.

————. *The Birth of Tragedy and Other Writings*. Translated by Ronald Speirs. Cambridge: Cambridge University Press, 1999.

————. *Ecce Homo*. Translated by Walter Kaufmann. New York: Vintage, 1967.

————. *The Gay Science*. Translated by Walter Kaufmann. New York: Vintage, 1974.

Oriental Institute Epigraphic Survey. *The Tomb of Kheruef: Theban Tomb 192*. University of Chicago Oriental Institute Publications 102. Chicago: Oriental Institute, 1980.

———. *The Festival Procession of Opet in the Colonnade Hall: With Translations of Texts, Commentary, and Glossary*. University of Chicago Oriental Institute Publications 112, Reliefs and Inscriptions at Luxor Temple. Chicago: Oriental Institute, 1994.

Origen. *Contra Celsum*. Translated by Henry Chadwick. Cambridge: Cambridge University Press, 1953.

———. *On First Principles, Being Koetschau's Text of the De principiis*. Translated by G. W. Butterworth. Gloucester, MA: Smith, 1973.

Parrott, Douglas M., editor. *Nag Hammadi Codices V,2–5 and VI with Papyrus Berolinensis 8502, 1 and 4*. Nag Hammadi Studies XI. Leiden: Brill, 1979.

Pelling, C. B. R., editor. *Plutarch: Life of Antony*. Cambridge: Cambridge University Press, 1988.

Perrella, Ettore, editor. *Gregorio Palamo: Atto e luce divina: Scritti filosofici e teologici*. Bompiani Il Pensiero Occidentale, 2003.

Pliny. Translated by H. Rackham et al. 11 vols. Loeb Classical Library. Cambridge: Harvard University Press, 1914–63.

Plotinus. Translated by A. H. Armstrong. 7 vols. Loeb Classical Library. Cambridge: Harvard University Press, 1966–88.

Plutarch. Translated by Frank Cole Babbit et al. 28 vols. Loeb Classical Library. Cambridge: Harvard University Press, 1914–2004.

Preisendanz, Karl, and Albert Henrichs. *Papyri Graecae magicae. Die griechischen Zauberpapyri*. 2nd ed. 2 vols. Stuttgart: Teubner, 1973.

Pritchard, James B., editor. *ANET*. 3rd ed. Princeton: Princeton University Press, 1969.

Quint, Josef, and Georg Steer, editors. *Meister Eckhart: Die deutschen Werke*. 5 vols. Stuttgart/Berlin: Kohlhammer, 1958–.

Rice, E. E. *The Grand Procession of Ptolemy Philadelphus*. London: Oxford University Press, 1983.

Salaman, Clement. *Asclepius: The Perfect Discourse of Hermes Trismegistus*. London: Duckworth, 2007.

Seneca the Elder. Translated by Michael Winterbottom. 2 vols. Loeb Classical Library. Cambridge: Harvard University Press, 1974.

Seneca the Younger. Translated by John W. Basore, et al. 13 vols. Loeb Classical Library. Cambridge: Harvard University Press, 1913–2004.

Shirò Giuseppe, editor. *Barlaam Calabro, Epistole greche*. Palermo, Italy: Istituto Siciliano di Studi Bizantini e Neogreci, 1954.

Sinkewicz, Robert E., editor. *Gregory Palamas: The One Hundred and Fifty Chapters: A Critical Edition, Translation, and Study*. Toronto: Pontifical Institute of Mediaeval Studies, 1988.

Smith, Joseph. *History of the Church of Jesus Christ of Latter-day Saints Period 1: History of Joseph Smith, the Prophet*. 2nd ed. 5 vols. Salt Lake City: Deseret, 1964.

Steer, Georg, and Lors Sturlese. *LECTURA ECKHARDI: Predigten Meister Eckharts Von Fachgelehrten Gelesen Und Gedeutet*. Stuttgart: Kohlhammer, 1998.

Strabo. Translated by Horace Jones. 8 vols. Loeb Classical Library. Cambridge: Harvard University Press, 1917–32.

Strutwolf, Holger, et al, editors. *Nestle-Aland Novum Testamentum Graece*. 28th ed. Stuttgart: Deutsche Bibelgesellschaft, 2012.

Suetonius. Translated by J. C. Rolfe. 2 vols. Loeb Classical Library. Cambridge: Harvard University Press, 1914.

Taylor, John. *Teachings of the Presidents of the Church: John Taylor.* Salt Lake City: Church of Jesus Christ of Latter-day Saints, 2001.

Theophilus of Antioch. *Ad Autolycum.* Translated by Robert M. Grant. Oxford: Clarendon, 1970.

Théry, Gabriel. "Edition critique des pieces relatives au process d'Eckhart continues dans le manuscript 33b de la bibliothèque de Soest." *Archives d'histoire doctrinale et littéraire du moyen âge* 1 (1926–27) 129–268.

Velleius Paterculus, Compendium of Roman History (Res gestae divi Augusti). Translated by Frederick W. Shipley. Loeb Classical Library. Cambridge: Harvard University Press, 1992.

Veniamin, Christopher, editor and translator. *Gregory Palamas: The Homilies.* Waymart, PA: Mount Tabor, 2009.

Weiss, Konrad, et al., editors. *Meister Eckhart: Die lateinischen Werke.* Stuttgart: Kohlhammer, 1936–.

West, M. L. *Greek Epic Fragments From the Seventh to the Fifth Centuries BC.* Loeb Classical Library. Cambridge: Harvard University Press, 2003.

Wright, M. R., editor. *Empedocles: The Extant Fragments.* New Haven: Yale University Press, 1981.

Secondary Sources

Alexander, Philip. "From Son of Adam to Second God: Transformations of the Biblical Enoch." In *Biblical Figures outside the Bible*, edited by M. E. Stone and T. A. Bergren, 87–122. Harrisburg, PA: Trinity, 1998.

Alfeyev, Hilarion. "The Deification of Man in Eastern Patristic Tradition (with Special Reference to Gregory Nazianzen, Symeon the New Theologian and Gregory Palamas." *Colloquium* 36 (2004) 109–22.

Alfsvåg, Knut. "Deification as *creatio ex nihilo.* On Luther's Appreciation of Dionysian Spirituality in *Operationes in Psalmos.*" In *Hermeneutica Sacra: Studien zur Auslegung der Heiligen Schrift im 16. und 17. Jahrhundert*, edited by Torbjörn Johansson et al., 59–84. Berlin: de Gruyter, 2010.

Ancelet-Hustache, Jeanne. *Meister Eckhart and the Rhineland Mystics.* Translated by Hilda Graef. New York: Harper Torchbooks, 1957.

Assmann, Jan. "Chepre." In *LÄ* 1:934–40.

———. "Magic and Theology in Ancient Egypt." In *Envisioning Magic: A Princeton Seminar and Symposium*, edited by Peter Schäfer and Hans G. Kippenberg, 1–18. Leiden: Brill, 1997.

Aune, David E. "Magic in Early Christianity." In *ANRW* II.23.2:1507–57

Babcock, William S. "Sin and Punishment: The Early Augustine on Evil." In *Augustine: Presbyter Factus Sum*, edited by Joseph T. Lienhard et al., 235–48. Collectanea Augustiniana. New York: Lang, 1993.

Bainbridge, William Sims. "The Transhuman Heresy." *JET* 14 (2005) 91–100.

Bauckham, Richard. *Jesus and the God of Israel: God Crucified and Other Studies on the New Testament's Christology of Divine Identity.* Grand Rapids: Eerdmans, 2008.

Beck, R. "Interpreting the Ponza Zodiac, II." *Journal of Mithraic Studies* 2 (1977–78) 87–147.

———. "In the Place of the Lion: Mithras in the Tauroctony." In *Studies in Mithraism*, edited by J. R. Hinnells, 29–50. Rome: Bretschneider, 1994.

———. "Mithraism since Franz Cumont." *ANRW* II.17.4:2051.

BeDuhn, Jason. *Augustine's Manichaean Dilemma 1: Conversion and Apostasy, 373–88 c.e.* Philadelphia: University of Pennsylvania Press, 2010.

Bell, John M. *An Introduction to Greek Mythology: Story, Symbols, and Culture.* Edited by Padraig O'Cleirigh and Rex Barrell. Lewiston, NY: Mellen, 2000.

Bell, Lanny. "The New Kingdom 'Divine' Temple." In *Temples of Ancient Egypt*, edited by Byron E. Shafer, 127–84. Ithaca, NY: Cornell University Press, 1997.

Bengtson, Hermann. *Marcus Antonius: Triumvir und Herrscher des Orients.* Munich: Beck, 1977.

Benz, Ernst. "Imago Dei: Man in the Image of God." In *Reflections on Mormonism*, 201–22. Provo, UT: Religious Studies Center, 1978.

Berkowitz, Peter. *Nietzsche: The Ethics of an Immoralist.* Cambridge: Harvard University Press, 1995.

Berman, Lawrence M. "Overview of Amenhotep III and His Reign." In *Amenhotep III: Perspectives on His Reign*, edited by David O'Connor and Eric H. Cline, 2–3. Ann Arbor, MI: University of Michigan Press, 1998.

Bernabé, Alberto. "Autour le myth orphique sur Dionysos et les Titans." In *Des Géants a Dionysos. Melanges offerts a F. Vian*, edited by D. A. P. Chuvin, 25–39. Alexandria: Edizioni dell'Orso, 2003.

———. "Imago Inferorum Orphica." In *Mystic Cults in Magna Graecia*, edited by Giovanni Casadio and Patricia A. Johnston, 95–130. Austin: University of Texas Press, 2009.

Bernabé, Alberto, and Ana Isabel Jiménez San Cristóbal. "Are the 'Orphic' Gold Leaves Orphic?" In *The "Orphic" Gold Tablets and Greek Religion: Further along the Path*, edited by Radcliffe Edmonds III, 68–101. Cambridge: Cambridge University Press, 2011.

———. *Instructions for the Netherworld: The Orphic Gold Tablets.* Leiden: Brill, 2008.

Betz, Hans Dieter. *Antike und Christentum: Gesammelte Aufsätze IV.* Tübingen: Mohr Siebeck, 1998.

———. *Hellenismus und Urchristentum: Gesammelte Aufsätze I.* Tübingen: Mohr Siebeck, 1990.

———. *The "Mithras Liturgy": Text, Translation, and Commentary.* Studien und Texte zu Antike und Christentum 18. Tübingen: Mohr Siebeck, 2003.

Bianchi, Robert S. *Cleopatra's Egypt: Age of the Ptolemies.* Brooklyn, NY: Brooklyn Museum, 1988.

Bielfeldt, Dennis. "Deification as a Motif in Luther's *Dictata Super Psalterium*." *The Sixteenth Century Journal* 28 (1997) 401–20.

Blackwell, Ben. *Pauline Soteriology in Light of Deification in Irenaeus and Cyril of Alexandria.* WUNT 2/314. Tübingen: Mohr Siebeck, 2011.

Blumenthal, Henry. "On Soul and Intellect." In *Cambridge Companion to Plotinus*, edited by Lloyd P. Gerson, 82–104. Cambridge: Cambridge University Press, 1996.

Bohak, Gideon. *Ancient Jewish Magic.* Cambridge: Cambridge University Press, 2008.

Bonner, Gerald. "Augustine and Mysticism." *Augustine: Mystic and Mystagogue*, edited by Frederick Van Fleteren et al., 113–58. Collectanea Augustiniana. New York: Lang, 1994.

———. "Augustine's Conception of Deification." *Journal of Theological Studies* 37 (1986) 369–86.

———. "Augustine's Doctrine of Man: Image of God and Sinner." *Augustinianum* 24 (1984) 495–514.

Bostrom, Nick. "Transhumanist FAQ: What is the Posthuman?" No pages. Online: http://humanityplus.org/philosophy/transhumanist-faq/.

Bousset, Wilhelm. "Die Himmelsreise der Seele." *Archiv für Religionswissenschaft* 4 (1901) 136–69, 229–73

Brashear, William M. "The Greek Magical Papyri." In *ANRW* II.18.5:3380–3684.

Bremmer, Jan. "Death and Immortality in Some Greek Poems." In *Hidden Futures: Death and Immortality in Ancient Egypt, Anatolia, the Classical, Biblical and Arabic-Islamic World*, edited by Jan Bremmer, 109–24. Amsterdam: Amsterdam University Press, 1994.

———. "Greek Fallen Angels: Kronos and the Titans." In *Greek Religion and Culture, the Bible and the Ancient Near East*, edited by Jan Bremmer, 73–99. Leiden: Brill, 2008.

Brisson, Luc. "Le corps 'dionysiaque': L'anthropogonie décrite dans le *Commentaire sur le Phédon de Platon* [1, par. 3–6] attribute à Olympiodore est-elle orphique?" In *Orphée et l'Orphisme dans l'Antiquité gréco-romaine*, 481–99. Aldershot, UK: Variorum, 1995.

Broderick, Damien. *The Spike: How Our Lives Are Being Transformed by Rapidly Advancing Technologies*. New York: Tomb Doherty, 2001.

Brunner, Hellmut. *Die Geburt des Gottkönig: Studien zur Überlieferung eines altägyptischen Mythos*. Wiesbaden: Harrassowitz, 1986.

Budde, Dagmar. "Harpare-pa-chered: ein ägyptisches Götterkind im Theben der Spätzeit und griechisch-römischen Epoche." In *Kindgötter im Ägypten der griechisch-römischen Zeit: Zeugnisse aus Stadt und Tempel als Spiegel des interkulturellen Kontakts*, edited by Dagmar Budde et al., 15–110. Leuven: Peeters, 2003.

Bussanich, John. "Mystical Elements in the Thought of Plotinus." In *ANRW* II.36.7:5300–30.

———. *The One and Its Relation to Intellect in Plotinus*. Leiden: Brill, 1988.

———. "Plotinus' Metaphysics of the One." In *The Cambridge Companion to Plotinus*, edited by Lloyd P. Gerson, 38–65. Cambridge: Cambridge University Press, 1996.

Buxton, Richard. "Metamorphoses of Gods into Animals and Humans." In *The Gods of Ancient Greece: Identities and Transformations*, edited by Jan N. Bremmer and Andrew Erskine, 81–91. Edinburgh: Edinburgh University Press, 2010.

Cary, Phillip. *Augustine's Invention of the Inner Self: The Legacy of a Christian Platonist*. Oxford: Oxford University Press, 2000.

———. "God in the Soul: Or, the Residue of Augustine's Manichaean Optimism." *University of Dayton Review* 22 (1994) 69–82.

Cavadini, John C., "Time and Ascent in *Confessions XI*." In *Presbyter Factus Sum*, edited by Joseph T. Lienhard et al., 171–86. Collactanea Augustiniana. New York: Lang, 1993.

Chamoux, Françoise. *Marc Antoine: dernier prince de l'Orient grec*. Paris: Arthaud, 1986.

Clauss, Manfred. *The Roman Cult of Mithras: The God and his Mysteries.* Translated by Richard Gordon. New York: Routledge, 2000.

Clay, Jenny Strauss. *The Wrath of Athena: Gods and Men in the Odyssey.* Lanham, MD: Rowman & Littlefield, 1997.

Cole, Susan Guettel. "Voices from beyond the Grave: Dionysus and the Dead." In *Masks of Dionysus*, edited by Thomas H. Carpenter and Christopher A. Faraone, 276–96. Ithaca, NY: Cornell University Press, 1993.

Corneanu, Nicolae. "The Jesus Prayer and Deification." *St. Vladimir's Theological Quarterly* 39 (1995) 3–24.

Corrigan, Kevin. *Reading Plotinus: A Practical Introduction to Neoplatonism.* West Lafayette, IN: Purdue University Press, 2005.

Coyle, J. Kevin. "Saint Augustine's Manichaean Legacy." *Augustinian Studies* 34 (2003) 1–22.

Cranfield, C. E. B. *A Critical and Exegetical Commentary on the Epistle to the Romans.* 6th ed. Edinburgh: T. & T. Clark, 1975.

Demetracopoulos, John A. "Palamas Transformed: Palamite Interpretations of the Distinction between God's 'Essence' and 'Energies' in Late Byzantium." In *Greeks, Latins, and Intellectual History 1204–1500*, edited by Martin Hinterberger and Chris Schabel, 263–372. Leuven: Peeters, 2011.

Detienne, Marcel. "Le chemins de la déviance: orphisme, dionysisme et pythagorisme." In *Orfismo in Magna Grecia: Atti del quarttordicesimo convegno di studi sulla Magna Grecia*, 49–80. Napoli: Arte Tipografica, 1975.

———. *Dionysos Slain.* Translated by Mireille and Leonard Muellner. Baltimore: Johns Hopkins University Press, 1979.

Dickie, Matthew W. *Magic and Magicians in the Greco-Roman World.* London: Routledge, 2001.

Dieterich, Albrecht. *Eine Mithrasliturgie.* 3rd ed. Leipzig: Teubner, 1923.

Dillon, John. "An Ethic for the Late Antique Sage." In *Cambridge Companion to Plotinus*, edited by Lloyd P. Gerson, 315–35. Cambridge: Cambridge University Press, 1996.

———. "Plotinus, Philo, and Origen on the Grades of Virtue." In *The Golden Chain*, 92–105. London: Variorum, 1990.

Dodds, E. R. *The Greeks and the Irrational.* Boston: Beacon, 1957.

Drewery, Benjamin. "Deification." In *Christian Spirituality: Essays in Honour of Gordon Rupp*, edited by Peter Brooks, 33–62. London: SCM, 1975.

Dunand, Françoise. "Les associations dionysiaques au service du Pouvoir Lagide (III s. av. J.-C.)." In *L'Association dionysiaque dans les sociétés anciennes: Actes de la Table Rond organisée par l'École Française de Rome*, 85–104. Palais Farnèse: L'École française de Rome, 1986.

Dunn, James D. G. *Romans 1–8.* Word Biblical Commentary Vol. 38. Nashville: Thomas Nelson, 1988.

Edmonds, Radcliffe III. "At the Seizure of the Moon: The Absence of the Moon in the Mithras Liturgy." In *Prayer, Magic, and the Stars in the Ancient and Late Antique World*, edited by Scott Noegel et al., 223–40. University Park, PA: Pennsylvania State University Press, 2003.

———. "A Curious Concoction: Tradition and Innovation in Olympiodorus' 'Orphic' Creation of Mankind." *American Journal of Philology* 130 (2009) 511–32.

————. "Did the Mithraists Inhale? A Technique for Theurgic Ascent in the Mithras Liturgy, the Chaldaean Oracles, and Some Mithraic Frescoes." *Ancient World* 32 (2000) 10–24.

————. "The Faces of the Moon: Cosmology, Genesis, and the *Mithras Liturgy*." In *Heavenly Realms and Earthly Realities in Late Antique Religions*, edited by Ra'anan S. Boustan and Annette Yoshiko Reed, 275–95. Cambridge: Cambridge University Press, 2004.

————. *Myths of the Underworld Journey in Plato, Aristophanes, and the 'Orphic' Gold Tablets*. Cambridge: Cambridge University Press, 2004.

————. "Tearing Apart the Zagreus Myth: A Few Disparaging Remarks on Orphism and Original Sin." *Classical Antiquity* 18 (1999) 35–73.

Engberg-Pedersen, Troels. *Cosmology and Self in the Apostle Paul: The Material Spirit*. Oxford: Oxford University Press, 2010.

Ernst, Carl. *Words of Ecstasy in Sufism*. Albany, NY: State University of New York Press, 1985.

Esposito, John L. *Islam: The Straight Path*. 3rd ed. New York: Oxford University Press, 1998.

Faraone, Christopher A. "Rushing into Milk: New Perspectives on the Gold Tablets." In *The "Orphic" Gold Tablets and Greek Religion: Further along the Path*, edited by Radcliffe G. Edmonds III, 310–30. Cambridge: Cambridge University Press, 2011.

Fauth, Wolfgang. *Helios Megistos: Zur synkretistischen Theologie der Spätantike*. RGRW 125. Leiden: Brill, 1995.

Festugière, Jean-André. *La Révélation d'Hermès Trismégiste*. 4 vols. Paris: Lecoffre, 1944.

Feuerbach, Ludwig. *The Essence of Christianity*. Translated by George Eliot. New York: Harper & Row, 1957.

Finlan, Stephen, and Vladmir Kharlamov. *Theōsis: Deification in Christian Theology*. Eugene, OR: Pickwick, 2006.

Fishwick, Duncan. *The Imperial Cult in the Latin West: Studies in the Ruler Cult of the Western Provinces of the Roman Empire*. Leiden: Brill, 1987.

Fletcher, Joann. *Chronicle of a Pharaoh: The Intimate Life of Amenhotep III*. Oxford: Oxford University Press, 2000.

Flogaus, Reinhard. *Theosis bei Palamas und Luther: Ein Beitrag zum ökumenischen Gespräch*. Göttingen: Vandenhoeck & Ruprecht, 1994.

Folliet. "Deificari in Otio: Augustin, Epistula 10.2." *Recherches Augustiniennes* 2 (1962) 225–36.

Forman, Werner, and Stephen Quirke, editors. *Hieroglyphs and the Afterlife in Ancient Egypt*. Norman, OK: University of Oklahoma Press, 1996.

Fowden, Garth. *The Egyptian Hermes: A Historical Approach to the Late Pagan Mind*. Cambridge: Cambridge University Press, 1996.

Frandsen, Paul John. "Aspects of Kingship in Ancient Egypt." In *Religion and Power: Divine Kingship in the Ancient World and Beyond*, edited by Nicole Brisch, 47–73. Chicago: Oriental Institute, 2008.

Fraser, P. M. *Ptolemaic Alexandria*. 2 vols. Oxford: Clarendon, 1972.

Frede, Dorothea. "Die Orphik—Mysterienreligion oder Philosophie?" In *Der Orpheus-Mythos von der Antike bis zur Gegenwart*, edited by Claudia Maurer Zenck, 229–46. Frankfurt am Main: Lang, 2004.

Gerson, Lloyd P. *Plotinus*. London: Routledge, 1994.

Gertz, Sebastian Ramon Philipp. *Death and Immortality in Late Neoplatonism: Studies on the Ancient Commentaries on Plato's* Phaedo. Leiden: Brill, 2011.

Giversen, S. "Hermetic Communities?" In *Rethinking Religion: Studies in the Hellenistic Process*, edited by J. P. Sorensen, 49–54. Copenhagen: Museum Tusculanum, 1989.

Gorman, Michael. *Inhabiting the Cruciform God: Kenosis, Justification, and Theosis in Paul's Narrative Soteriology.* Grand Rapids: Eerdmans, 2009.

Graf, Fritz. "Dionysian and Orphic Eschatology: New Texts and Old Questions." In *Masks of Dionysus*, edited by Thomas H. Carpenter and Christopher A. Faraone, 239–58. Ithaca, NY: Cornell University Press, 1993.

———. "Magic and Divination." In *The World of Ancient Magic: Papers from the first International Samson Eitrem Seminar at the Norwegian Institute at Athens, 4–8 May 1997*, edited by David R. Jordan et al., 283–98. Bergen: Norwegian Institute at Athens, 1999.

———. "The Magician's Initiation." *Helios* 21 (1994) 161–78.

———. *Magic in the Ancient World.* Translated by Franklin Philip. Cambridge: Harvard University Press, 1997.

———. "Orpheus: A Poet among Men." In *Interpretations of Greek Mythology*, edited by Jan Bremmer, 80–106. Totowa, NJ: Barnes & Noble, 1986.

Griffin, Jasper. "Propertius and Antony." *JRS* 67 (1977) 17–26.

Gunnarsson, Håken. *Mystical Realism in the Early Theology of Gregory Palamas: Context and Analysis.* Göteborg: Göteborgs Universitet, 2002.

Guthrie, W. K. C. *The Greeks and Their Gods.* London: Methuen, 1950.

———. *Orpheus and Greek Religion: A Study of the Orphic Movement.* New York: Norton, 1966.

Haase, Wolfgang et al., editors. *ANRW.* Berlin: de Gruyter, 1972–.

Hadot, Pierre. "Neoplatonist Spirituality: Plotinus and Porphyry." In *Classical Mediterranean Spirituality: Egyptian, Greek, Roman*, edited by A. H. Armstrong, 230–49. New York: Crossroad, 1986.

———. *Plotinus, or The Simplicity of Vision.* Translated by Michael Chase. Chicago: University of Chicago Press, 1993.

———. "La union de l'âme avec l'intellect divin dans l'expérience mystique plotinienne." In *Proclus et son influence*, edited by G. Boss and G. Seel, 3–28. Zürich: Grand Midi, 1987.

Hadzisteliou-Price, Theodora "To the Groves of Persephoneia. . . . A Group of 'Medma' figurines." *Antike Kunst* 12 (1969) 51–55.

Hailer, Martin. "Rechtfertigung als Vergottung? Eine Auseinandersetzung mit der finnischen Luther-Deutung und ihrer systematisch-theologischen Adaptation." *Lutherjahrbuch* 77 (2010) 239–68.

Hale, Van. "The Doctrinal Impact of the King Follett Discourse." *BYU Studies* 18 (1978) 209–25.

Hamm, Berndt. "Wie mystisch war der Glaube Luthers?" In *Gottes Nähe unmittelbar erfahren: Mystik im Mittelalter und bei Martin Luther*, edited by Berndt Hamm and Volker Leppin, 237–88. Tübingen: Mohr Siebeck, 2007.

Harrison, Carol. *Augustine: Christian Truth and Fractured Humanity.* Oxford: Oxford University Press, 2000.

———. *Rethinking Augustine's Early Theology: An Argument for Continuity.* New York: Oxford University Press, 2006.

Hatab, Lawrence J. "Apollo and Dionysus: Nietzschean Expressions of the Sacred." In *Nietzsche and the Gods*, edited by Weaver Santaniello, 45–56. Albany, NY: SUNY Press, 2001.

Hauskeller, Michael. "Nietzsche, the Overhuman and the Posthuman: A Reply to Stephan Sorgner." *JET* 21 (2010) 5–8.

Hay, David H. *Glory at the Right Hand: Psalm 110 in Early Christianity*. Nashville: Abingdon, 1973.

Heintz, Florent. *Simon "Le Magicien": Actes 8,5–25 et l'accusation de magie contre les prophètes thaumaturges dans l'antiquité*. Cahiers de la Revue Biblique. Paris: Gabalda, 1997.

Helck, Wolfgang, and Eberhard Otto, editors. *LÄ*. 7 vols. Wiesbaden: Otto Harrassowitz, 1975.

Helleman-Elgersma, Wypkje. *Soul-Sisters: A Commentary on* Enneads *IV 3 (27), 1–8 of Plotinus*. Amsterdam: Rodopi, 1980.

Hennig, Beate. *Kleines Mittelhochdeutsches Wörterbuch*. Tübingen: Niemeyer, 1995.

Henrichs, Albert. "Changing Dionysiac Identities." In *Jewish and Christian Self-Definition: Self-Definition in the Greco-Roman World*, 3 vols., edited by E. P. Sanders, 3:137–60; 3:213–36. Philadelphia: Fortress, 1982.

Herrero de Jáuregui, Miguel. "Dialogues of Immortality from the *Iliad* to the Gold Leaves." In *The "Orphic" Gold Tablets and Greek Religion: Further along the Path*, edited by Radcliffe G. Edmonds III, 271–90. Cambridge: Cambridge University Press, 2011.

———. "Orphic Ideas of Immortality: Traditional Greek Images and a New Eschatological Thought." In *Lebendige Hoffnung—ewiger Tod?! Jenseitsvorstellungen im Hellenismus, Judentum und Christentum*, edited by Michael Labahn and Manfred Lang, 289–314. Arbeiten zur Bible und ihrer Geschichte 24. Leipzig: Evangelische Verlagsanstalt, 2007.

Hoffman, Bengt. *Luther and the Mystics*. Minneapolis: Fortress, 1976.

Hoffman, C. A. "Fiat Magia." In *Magic and Ritual in the Ancient World*, edited by Paul Mirecki and Marvin Meyer, 179–96. Leiden: Brill, 2002.

Hölbl, Günther. *A History of the Ptolemaic Empire*. Translated by Tina Saavedra. London: Routledge, 2001.

Hopkins, Patrick D. "Transcending the Animal: How Religion and Transhumanism Are and Are Not Alike." *JET* 14 (2005) 13–28.

Hornung, Erik. *Akhenaten and the Religion of Light*. Translated by David Lorton. Ithaca, NY: Cornell University Press, 1999.

———. *Conceptions of God in Ancient Egypt: The One and the Many*. Translated by John Baines. London: Routledge, 1982.

———. *Knowledge for the Afterlife: The Egyptian Amduat—A Quest for Immortality*. Zurich: Living Human Heritage, 2003.

Hoskins, Paul M. "The Use of Biblical and Extrabiblical Parallels in the Interpretation of First Corinthians 6:2–3." *Catholic Biblical Quarterly* 63 (2001) 287–97.

Huggins, Ronald V. "Lorenzo Snow's Couplet: 'As Man Now Is, God Once Was; As God Now Is, Man May Be': 'No Functioning Place in Present-day Mormon Doctrine?' A Response to Richard Mouw." *Journal of the Evangelical Theological Society* 49 (2006) 549–68.

Huzar, Eleanor Goltz. "The Literary Efforts of Mark Antony." In *ANRW* II.30.1:639–57.

———. *Mark Antony: A Biography*. Minneapolis: University of Minnesota, 1978.

Idel, Moshe, and Bernard McGinn, editors. *Mystical Union and Monotheistic Faith*. New York: Macmillan, 1989.

Jacq, Christian. *Egyptian Magic*. Translated by Janet M. Davis. Chicago: Bolchazy-Carducci, 1985.

Janda, Michael. *Elysion: Enstehung und Entwicklung der griechischen Religion*. Innsbruck: Institut für Sprachen und Literaturen der Universität Innsbruck, 2005.

Janowitz, Naomi. *Magic in the Roman World: Pagans, Jews and Christians*. London: Routledge, 2001.

Johnson, Luke Timothy. *Among the Gentiles: Greco-Roman Religion and Christianity*. New Haven: Yale University Press, 2009.

Johnson, W. Raymond. "Images of Amenhotep III in Thebes: Styles and Intentions." In *The Art of Amenhotep III: Art Historical Analysis: Papers Presented at the International Symposium Held at the Cleveland Museum of Art, Cleveland, Ohio, 20–21 November 1987*, edited by Lawrence Michael Berman, 26–46. Cleveland, OH: Cleveland Museum of Art, 1990.

———. "Monuments and Monumental Art under Amenhotep III: Evolution and Meaning." In *Amenhotep III: Perspectives on his Reign*, edited by David O'Connor and Eric H. Cline, 63–95. Ann Arbor, MI: University of Michigan, 1998.

Johnston, Sarah Iles. *Ancient Greek Divination*. Chichester, UK: Wiley Blackwell, 2008.

———. "Rising to the Occasion: Theurgic Ascent in its Cultural Milieu." In *Envisioning Magic: A Princeton Seminar and Symposium*, edited by Peter Schäfer and Hans G. Kippenberg, 165–94. Leiden: Brill, 1997.

Johnston, Sarah Iles, and Peter T. Struck. *Mantikê: Studies in Ancient Divination*. RGRW 155. Leiden: Brill, 2005.

Jordan, Gregory E. "Apologia for Transhumanist Religion." *JET* 15 (2006) 55–72.

Juntunen, Sammeli. *Der Begriff des Nichts bei Luther in den Jahren von 1510 bis 1523*. Helsinki: Luther-Agricola-Gesellschaft, 1996.

Kärkkäinen, Veli-Matti. *One with God: Salvation as Deification and Justification*. Collegeville, MN: Liturgical, 2004.

Kaufmann, Walter. *Nietzsche: Philosopher, Psychologist, Antichrist*. Princeton: Princeton University Press, 1974.

Kelley, C. F. *Meister Eckhart on Divine Knowledge*. New Haven: Yale University Press, 1977.

Kertz, Karl. "Meister Eckhart's Teaching on the Birth of the Divine Word in the Soul." *Traditio* 15 (1959) 339–63.

Kingsley, Peter. *Ancient Philosophy, Mystery, and Magic: Empedocles and Pythagorean Tradition*. Oxford: Clarendon, 1995.

———. "An Introduction to the Hermetica: Approaching Ancient Esoteric Tradition." In *From Poimandres to Jacob Böhme: Gnosis: Hermetism and the Christian Tradition*, edited by Roelof van den Broek and Cis van Heertum, 17–40. Amersterdam: In de Pelikaan, 2000.

Klodt, Claudia. "Der Orpheus-Mythos in der Antike." In *Der Orpheus-Mythos von der Antike bis zur Gegenwart*, edited by Claudia Maurer Zenck, 37–98. Frankfurt am Main: Lang, 2004.

Knight, Christopher C. "*Homo Religiosus*: A Theological Proposal for a Scientific and Pluralistic Age." In *Human Identity at the Intersection of Science, Technology and Religion*, edited by Nancey Murphy and Christopher Knight, 25–38. Farnham, UK: Ashgate, 2010.

Kozloff, Arielle, and Betsy M. Bryan, editors. *Egypt's Dazzling Sun: Amenhotep III and His World*. Cleveland, OH: Cleveland Museum of Art, 1992.

Kozloff, Arielle. *Amenhotep III: Egypt's Radiant Pharaoh*. Cambridge: Cambridge University Press, 2012.

Krausmüller, Dirk. "Do We Need to be Stupid in Order to be Saved? Barlaam of Calabria and Gregory Palamas on Knowledge and Ignorance." In *Salvation according to the Fathers of the Church: The Proceedings of the Sixth International Patristic Conference, Maynooth/Belfast, 2005*, edited by D. Vincent Twomey and Dirk Krausmüller, 143–52. Dublin: Forecourts, 2010.

———. "The Rise of Hesychasm." In *The Cambridge History of Christianity: Volume 5, Eastern Christianity*, edited by Michael Angold, 101–26. Cambridge: Cambridge University Press, 2006.

Kretschmar, Georg. "Die Rezeption der orthodoxen Vergöttlichungslehre in der protestantischen Theologie." In *Luther und Theosis: Veröffentlichungen der Luther-Akademie e. V. Ratzeburg*, edited by Joachim Heubach, 61–84. Erlangen, Germany: Martin Luther, 1990.

Küng, Hans. *On Being a Christian*. Garden City, NY: Doubleday, 1976.

Kurzweil, Ray. *The Singularity Is Near: When Humans Transcend Biology*. New York: Viking, 2005.

Lamberigts, Mathijs. "Was Augustine a Manichaean? The Assessment of Julian of Aeclanum." In *Augustine and Manichaeism in the Latin West*, edited by Johannes van Oort et al., 113–36. Leiden: Brill, 2001.

Lampe, G. W. H. *A Patristic Greek Lexicon*. Oxford: Clarendon, 1961.

Lampert, Lawrence. *Nietzsche's Teaching*. New Haven: Yale University Press, 1986.

LaTorra, Michael. "Trans-Spirit: Religion, Spirituality, and Transhumanism." *JET* 14 (2005) 41–55.

Layton, Bentley. *Gnostic Scriptures*. New York: Doubleday, 1987.

Lerner, Robert. *The Heresy of the Free Spirit in the Later Middle Ages*. Berkeley: University of California, 1972.

Lewy, Hans. *Chaldean Oracles and Theurgy: Mysticism Magic and Platonism in the Later Roman Empire*. Paris: Études Augustiniennes, 1978.

Lison, Jacques. "La divinisation selon Grégoire Palamas." *Irénikon* 67 (1994) 59–70.

———. *L'Esprit répandu: la pneumatologie de Grégoire Palamas*. Paris: Cerf, 1994.

Litwa, M. David. *We are Being Transformed: Deification in Paul's Soteriology*. Beihefte zum Zeitschrift für neutestamentliche Wissenschaft 187. Berlin: de Gruyter, 2012.

Lüdemann, Gerd. *Untersuchungen zur simonianischen Gnosis*. Göttingen: Vandenhoeck & Ruprecht, 1975.

Ludlow, Daniel, editor. *The Encyclopedia of Mormonism*. New York: Macmillan, 1992.

Mahé, Jean-Pierre. *Hermès en Haute-Égypte*. 2 vols. Québec: L'université Laval, 1982.

———. "A Reading of the *Discourse on the Ogdoad and the Ennead* (Nag Hammadi Codex VI.6)." In *Gnosis and Hermeticism from Antiquity to Modern Times*, edited by Roelof van den Broek and Wouter J. Hanegraaff, 79–86. Western Esoteric Traditions. Albany, NY: SUNY Press, 1998.

———. "La voie d'immortalité à la lumière des Hermetica de Nag Hammadi et de découvertes plus récentes." *VC* 45 (1991) 347–75.

Mannermaa, Tuomo. *Christ Present in Faith: Luther's View of Justification*. Minneapolis: Fortress, 2005.

———. *Der im Glauben gegenwärtige Christus.* Hannover: Lutherisches Verlagshaus, 1989.

———. "Hat Luther eine trinitarische Ontologie?" In *Luther und Ontologie: Das Sein Christi im Glauben als strukturierendes Prinzip der Theologie Luthers,* edited by Anja Ghiselli et al., 9–27. Helsinki: Luther-Agricola-Gesellschaft, 1993.

———. "Participation and Love in the Theology of Martin Luther." In *Philosophical Studies in Religion, Metaphysics, and Ethics: Essays in Honour of Heikki Kirjavainen,* edited by Timo Koistinen and Tommi Lehtonen, 303–31. Helsinki: Luther-Agricola-Society, 1997.

———. "Why Is Luther So Fascinating?" In *Union with Christ: The New Finnish Interpretation of Luther,* edited by Carl E. Braaten and Robert Jenson, 1–20. Grand Rapids: Eerdmans, 1998.

Mannsperger, Dietrich. "Apollo gegen Dionysos: Numismatische Beiträge zu Octavians Rolle als Vindex Libertatis." *Gymnasium* 80 (1973) 381–404.

Manoj, V. R. "Spiritual Transcendence in Transhumanism." *JET* 17 (2008) 1–10.

Manser, Martin. *The Westminster Collection of Christian Quotations.* Louisville: Westminster John Knox, 2001.

Mantzaridis, George. "La doctrine de Saint Grégoire Palamas sur la deification de l'être humain." In *Saint Grégoire Palamas de la Déification de l'être humain,* translated by M.-J. Monsaingeon, 45–160. Lausanne: L'Age d'Homme, 1990.

———. "Spiritual Life in Palamism." In *Christian Spirituality: High Middle Ages and Reformation,* edited by Jill Raitt, 208–22. New York: Crossroad, 1987.

Marasco, Gabriele. "Marco Antonio 'Nuovo Dioniso' e il *De sua ebrietate.*" *Latomus* 51 (1992) 539–48.

Massignon, Louis. *The Passion of al-Hallaj, Mystic and Martyr of Islam.* Translated by Herbert Mason. 4 vols. Princeton: Princeton University Press, 1982.

May, Gerhard. *Creatio ex nihilo: The Doctrine of "Creation Out of Nothing" in Early Christian Thought.* London: T. & T. Clark, 2004.

McGinn, Bernard. "Eckhart's Condemnation Reconsidered." *The Thomist* 44 (1980) 390–414.

———. *The Foundations of Mysticism.* Vol. 1 of *The Presence of God.* New York: Crossroad, 1991.

———. *Knowledge of God in Classical Sufism: Foundations of Islamic Mystical Theology.* Translated by John Renard. The Classics of Western Spirituality. New York: Paulist, 2004.

———. *The Mystical Thought of Meister Eckhart: The Man from Whom God Hid Nothing.* New York: Crossroad, 2001.

McGuckin, John A. "Barlaam of Calabria (ca. 1290–1348)." In *The Encyclopedia of Eastern Orthodox Christianity,* 2 vols., edited by McGuckin, 1:67–69. Chichester, UK: Wiley-Blackwell, 2011.

Meconi, David Vincent. "The Dynamics of Augustinian Deification." In *Tolle Lege: Essays on Augustine & on Medieval Philosophy in Honor of Roland J. Teske, SJ,* edited by Richard C. Taylor et al., 155–74. Milwaukee: Marquette University Press, 2011.

Meeks, Dimitri. "Harpokrates." In *LÄ* 2:1003–11.

Meijer, P. A. *Plotinus on the Good or the One (Enneads VI,9): An Analytical Commentary.* Amsterdam: Gieben, 1992.

Merkelbach, Reinhold. *Abrasax: ausgewählte Papyri religiösen und magischen Inhalts.* 5 vols. Opladen: Westdeutscher, 1990–2001.

Meyendorff, John. *St. Gregory Palamas and Orthodox Spirituality.* Translated by Adele Fiske. Crestwood, NY: St. Vladimir's Seminary Press, 1974.

Miller, Patrick Lee. *Becoming Divine: Pure Reason in Early Greek Philosophy.* London: Continuum, 2011.

Morand, Anne-France. *Études sur les* Hymnes Orphiques. RGRW 143. Leiden: Brill, 2001.

Mosser, Carl. "The Greatest Possible Blessing: Calvin on Deification." *SJT* 55 (2002) 36–57.

Mysliwiec, Karol. "Atum." In *The Ancient Gods Speak: Guide to Egyptian Religion*, edited by Donald B. Redford, 25. Oxford: Oxford University Press, 2002.

Narbonne, Jean-Mark. *Plotinus in Dialogue with the Gnostics.* Leiden: Brill, 2011.

Neufel, Franceen. "The Cross and the Living Lord: The Theology of the Cross and Mysticism." *SJT* 49 (1996) 131–46.

Nilsson, Kjell Ove. *Simul: Das Miteinander von göttlichem und menschlichem in Luthers Theologie.* Göttingen: Vandenhoeck & Ruprecht, 1966.

Nock, A. D. "Notes on Ruler Cult IV." In *Essays on Religion and the Ancient World*, 2 vols., edited by Zeph Stewart, 1:134–59. Oxford: Clarendon, 1972.

Norris, Frederick W. "Deification: Consensual and Cogent." *Scottish Journal of Theology*, 49 (1996) 411–28.

O'Connell, Robert J. *St. Augustine's Early Theory of Man, A.D. 386–91.* Cambridge: Harvard University Press, 1968.

O'Donnell, James J. *Augustine: A New Biography.* New York: Harper Collins, 2005.

O'Meara, Dominic. *Plotinus: An Introduction to the Enneads.* Oxford: Clarendon, 1993.

Orthodox Study Bible. Edited by Peter E. Gillquist et al. Nashville: Thomas Nelson, 1993.

———. Edited by Jack Norman Sparks et al. Nashville: Thomas Nelson, 2008.

Ostler, Blake. *Of God and Gods.* Vol. 3 of *Exploring Mormon Thought.* Salt Lake City: Kofford, 2008.

Otto, Henrik. *Vor- und frühreformatorische Tauler–Rezeption.* Heidelberg: Gütersloher, 2003.

Ozment, Stevan. *Homo Spiritualis: A Comparative Study of the Anthropology of Johannes Tauler, Jean Gerson and Martin Luther.* Leiden: Brill, 1969.

Parker, Robert. "Early Orphism." In *The Greek World*, edited by Anton Powell, 483–510. London: Routledge, 1995.

Pelster, Franz. "Eine Gutachten Aus Dem Eckehart–Prozess in Avignon." In *Aus Der Geisteswelt Des Mittelalters: Festgabe Martin Grabmann*, 1099–1124. Münster: Aschendorff, 1935.

Peterson, Daniel C. "'Ye Are Gods': Psalm 82 and John 10 as Witnesses to the Divine Nature of Humankind." In *The Disciple as Scholar: Essays on Scripture and the Ancient World in Honor of Richard Lloyd Anderson*, edited by Stephen D. Ricks et al., 471–594. Provo, UT: Foundation for Ancient Research and Mormon Studies, 2000.

Peura, Simo. *Mehr als ein Mensch? Die Vergöttlichung als Thema der Theologie Martin Luthers von 1513 bis 1519.* Mainz: von Zabern, 1994.

Pratt, Parley. *Key to the Science of Theology.* 7th ed. Salt Lake City: Deseret, 1915.

Radler, Aleksander. "Theologische Ontologie und reale Partizipation an Gott in der frühem Theologie Luthers." In *Luther und Ontologie: Das Sein Christi im Glauben als strukturierendes Prinzip der Theologie Luthers*, edited by Anja Ghiselli et al., 28–34. Helsinki: Luther-Agricola-Gesellschaft, 1993.

Raunio, Antti. "The Human Being." In *Engaging Luther: A (New) Theological Assessment*, edited by Olli-Pekka Vainio, 27–58. Eugene, OR: Cascade, 2010.

Reitzenstein, Richard. *Die hellenistischen Mysterienreligionen nach ihren Grundgedanken und Wirkungen*. 3rd ed. Stuttgart: Teubner, 1973.

Riedweg, Christoph. "Initiation-death-underworld: Narrative and Ritual in the Gold Leaves." In *The "Orphic" Gold Tablets and Greek Religion: Further along the Path*, edited by Radcliffe G. Edmonds III, 219–56. Cambridge: Cambridge University Press, 2011.

Rigo, A. *Monaci esicasti e monaci bogomili. Le accuse di messalianismo e bogomilismo rivolte agli esicasti ed il problema dei rapporti tra esicasmo e bogomilismo*. Florence: Olschki, 1989.

Roberts, B. H. *The Mormon Doctrine of Deity*. Bountiful, UT: Horizon, 1903.

Robertson, Archibald, and Alfred Plummer. *A Critical and Exegetical Commentary on the First Epistle of St. Paul to the Corinthians*. 2nd ed. International Critical Commentary 33. Edinburgh: T. & T. Clark, 1914.

Rogich, Daniel M. *Becoming Uncreated: The Journey to Human Authenticity*. Minneapolis: Light and Life, 1997.

Rohde, Erwin. *Psyche: The Cult of Souls and Belief in Immortality among the Greeks*. Translated by W. B. Hillis. New York: Harcourt, Brace & Company, 1925.

Ruh, Kurt. *Meister Eckhart: Theologe, Prediger, Mystiker*. München: Beck, 1985.

Russell, Norman. *The Doctrine of Deification in the Greek Patristic Tradition*. Oxford: Oxford University Press, 2004.

———. "Theosis and Gregory Palamas: Continuity or Doctrinal Change?" *St. Vladimir's Theological Quarterly* 50 (2006) 357–79

Saarinen, Risto. "Die Teilhabe an Gott bei Luther und in der finnischen Lutherforschung." In *Luther und Ontologie: Das Sein Christi im Glauben als strukturierendes Prinzip der Theologie Luthers*, edited by Anja Ghiselli et al., 167–82. Helsinki: Luther-Agricola-Gesellschaft, 1993.

Salaman, Clement. *The Way of Hermes*. London: Duckworth, 1999.

Savvidis, Kyriakos. *Die Lehre von der Vergöttlichung des Menschen bei Maximos dem Bekenner und ihre Rezeption durch Gregor Palamas*. St. Ottilien: Eos, 1997.

Schimmel, Annemarie. *Mystical Dimensions of Islam*. Chapel Hill, NC: University of North Carolina, 1975.

Scott, Kenneth. "Octavian's Propaganda and Antony's 'De Sua Ebrietate.'" *Classical Philology* 24 (1929) 133–41.

Seaford, Richard. *Dionysos*. London: Routledge, 2006.

Segal, Alan F. "Heavenly Ascent in Hellenistic Judaism, Early Christianity and their Environment." *ANRW* II.23.2:1333–94.

———. "Hellenistic Magic: Some Questions of Definition." In *Studies in Gnosticism and Hellenistic Religions*, edited by R. van den Broek and M. J. Vermaseren, 349–75. Leiden: Brill, 1981.

———. "Paul and the Beginning of Jewish Mysticism." In *Death, Ecstasy, and Other Worldly Journeys*, edited by John J. Collins and Michael Fishbane, 93–120. Albany, NY: SUNY Press, 1995.

Segal, Charles. *Orpheus: The Myth of the Poet*. Baltimore: Johns Hopkins University Press, 1989.

Sharpe, Kevin. *Sleuthing the Divine: The Nexus of Science and the Spirit*. Minneapolis: Fortress, 2000.

Silverman, David P. "The Nature of Egyptian Kingship." In *Ancient Egyptian Kingship*, edited by David O'Connor and David Silverman, 49–94. Leiden: Brill, 1995.

Smith, Eliza R. Snow. *Biography and Family Record of Lorenzo Snow*. Salt Lake City: Deseret, 1884.

Smith, Jonathan Z. "Trading Places." In *Ancient Magic and Ritual Power*, edited by Marvin Meyer and Paul Mirecki, 13–28. RGRW 129. Leiden: Brill, 1995.

Smith, Joseph Fielding. *Teachings of the Prophet Joseph Smith*. 12th printing. Salt Lake City: Deseret, 1961.

Smith, Morton. *Clement of Alexandria and a Secret Gospel of Mark*. Cambridge: Harvard University Press, 1973.

———. "Transformation by Burial (1 Cor 15:35–49; Rom 6:3–5 and 8:9–11)." *Eranos Jahrbuch* 52 (1983) 87–112

Smith, Wolfgang. *The Wisdom of Ancient Cosmology: Contemporary Science in Light of Tradition*. Oakton, VA: Foundation for Traditional Studies, 2003.

Snow, LeRoi C. "Devotion to Divine Inspiration." *Improvement Era* 22 (1919) 653–63.

Sorgner, Stefan Lorenz. "Beyond Humanism: Reflections on Trans- and Posthumanism." *JET* 21 (2010) 1–19.

———. "Nietzsche, the Overhuman, and Transhumanism." *JET* 20 (2009) 29–42.

Sourvinou-Inwood, Christiane. *Reading' Greek Death: To the End of the Classical Period*. Oxford: Clarendon, 1995.

Southern, Pat. *Mark Antony*. Stroud, UK: Tempus, 1998.

Sprinkle, Preston. "The Afterlife in Romans: Understanding Paul's Glory Motif in Light of the Apocalypse of Moses and 2 Baruch." In *Lebendige Hoffnung—ewiger Tod?! Jenseitsvorstellungen im Hellenismus, Judentum und Christentum*, edited by Michael Labahn and Manfred Lang, 201–34. Leipzig: Evangelische Verlagsanstalt, 2007.

Steinhart, Eric. "Teilhard de Chardin and Transhumanism." *JET* 20 (2008) 1–22.

Tabor, James. "Paul's Notion of Many 'Sons of God' and its Hellenistic Contexts." *Helios* 13 (1986) 87–97.

———. *Things Unutterable: Paul's Ascent to Paradise in Its Greco-Roman, Judaic, and Early Christian Contexts*. Lanham, MD: University Press of America, 1986.

Taylor, Rabun. *The Moral Mirror of Roman Art*. Cambridge: Cambridge University Press, 2008.

Theissen, Gerd. "Simon Magus—die Entwicklung seines Bildes vom Charismatiker zum gnostischen Erlöser. Ein Beitrag zur Frühgeschichte der Gnosis." In *Religionsgeschichte des neuen Testaments: Festschrift für Klaus Berger*, edited by Axel von Dobbeler et al., 407–32. Tübingen: Francke, 2000.

Thompson, Christopher J. "The Theological Dimension of Time in *Confessions* XI." In *Presbyter Factus Sum*, edited by Joseph T. Lienhard et al., 187–94. New York: Lang, 1993.

Thweatt-Bates, Jeanine. *Cyborg Selves: A Theological Anthropology of the Posthuman*. Farnham, UK: Ashgate, 2012.

Tobin, Vincent Arieh. "Amun-Re." In *The Ancient Gods Speak: A Guide to Egyptian Religion*, edited by Donald B. Redford, 18–21. Oxford: Oxford University Press, 2002.

Tondriau, J. "La dynastie ptolemaique et la religion dionysiaque." *Chronique d'Égypte* 49–50 (1950) 283–316.

———. "Rois Lagides comparés ou identifiés à des divinités." *Chronique d'Egypte* 45–46 (1948) 137–38.

Torchia, Joseph. *Creatio ex nihilo and the Theology of St. Augustine.* New York: Lang, 1999.

Traina, Giusto. *Marco Antonio.* Roma: Laterza & Figli, 2003.

Trueman, Carl R. "Is the Finnish Line a New Beginning? A Critical Assessment of the Reading of Luther Offered by the Helsinki Circle." *Westminster Theological Journal* 65 (2003) 231–44.

Tzifopoulos, Yannis. *Paradise Earned: The Bacchic-Orphic Gold Lamellae of Crete.* Washington, DC: Center for Hellenic Studies, 2010.

Ulansey, David. "Mithras and the Hypercosmic Sun." *Studies in Mithraism,* edited by John R. Hinnels, 257–64. Rome: Bretschneider, 1994.

———. *The Origins of the Mithraic Mysteries: Cosmology and Salvation in the Ancient World.* Oxford: Oxford University Press, 1989.

Vainio, Olli-Pekka, editor. *Engaging Luther: A (New) Theological Assessment.* Eugene, OR: Cascade, 2010.

———. *Justification and Participation in Christ: The Development of the Lutheran Doctrine of Justification from Luther to the Formula of Concord (1580).* Studies in Medieval and Reformation Traditions 130. Leiden: Brill, 2008.

Van De Mieroop, Marc. *A History of Ancient Egypt.* Blackwell History of the Ancient World. Chichester: Wiley Blackwell, 2011.

Van den Broek, Roelof. "Religious Practices in the Hermetic 'Lodge': New Light from Nag Hammadi." In *From Poimandres to Jacob Böhme: Gnosis: Hermetism and the Christian Tradition,* edited by Roelof van den Broek and Cis van Heertum, 77–96. Amsterdam: In de Pelikaan, 2000.

Van den Broek, Roelof, and Wouter J. Hanegraaf, editors. *Gnosis and Hermeticism from Antiquity to Modern Times.* Albany, NY: SUNY Press, 1998.

Van den Kerchove, Anna. *Le voie d'Hermès: Pratiques rituelles et traits hermétiques.* Leiden: Brill, 2012.

Walbank, F. W. "Monarchies and Monarchic Ideas." In *Cambridge Ancient History,* 7:1:62–100. 2nd ed. 14 vols. Cambridge: Cambridge University Press, 1984.

Wald, George. *Self-Intellection and Identity in the Philosophy of Plotinus.* Frankfurt am Main: Lang, 1990.

Warden, John editor. *Orpheus: The Metamorphosis of a Myth.* Toronto: University of Toronto Press, 1985.

Ware, Kallistos. "God Immanent Yet Transcendent: The Divine Energies according to Saint Gregory Palamas." In *In Whom We Live and Move and Have Our Being: Panentheistic Reflections on God's Presence in a Scientific World,* edited by Philip Clayton and Arthur Peacocke, 157–68. Grand Rapids: Eerdmans, 2004.

———. "The Hesychasts: Gregory of Sinai, Gregory Palamas, Nicolas Cabasilas." In *The Study of Spirituality,* edited by Cheslyn Jones et al., 242–55. Oxford: Oxford University Press, 1986.

———. "The Origins of the Jesus Prayer: Diadochus, Gaza, Sinai." In *The Study of Spirituality,* edited by Cheslyn Jones et al., 175–83. Oxford: Oxford University Press, 1986.

―――. *The Orthodox Way*. Reprint. Crestwood, NY: St. Vladimir's Seminary Press, 1999.

Watterson, Barbara. *Gods of Ancient Egypt*. Stroud, UK: Sutton, 1996.

Webb, Stephen. *Jesus Christ, Eternal God: Heavenly Flesh and the Metaphysics of Matter.* New York: Oxford, 2012.

Weeks, Andrew. *German Mysticism from Hildegard of Bingen to Ludwig Wittgenstein: A Literary and Intellectual History*. Albany, NY: SUNY Press, 1993.

Weiss, Johannes. *Der erste Korintherbrief.* 2nd ed. Göttingen: Vandenhoeck & Ruprecht, 1977.

West, M. L. *The Orphic Poems*. Oxford: Clarendon, 1983.

Wickkiser, Bronwen. "Augustus, Apollo, and an Ailing Rome." In *Studies in Latin Literature and Roman History XII*, edited by Carl Deroux, 267–89. Bruxelles: Éditions Latomus, 2005.

Widmer, Kurt. *Mormonism and the Nature of God: A Theological Evolution: 1830–1915.* Jefferson, NC: McFarland, 2000.

Wilkinson, Richard H. *The Complete Gods and Goddesses of Ancient Egypt*. New York: Thames & Hudson, 2003.

Williams, A. N. *The Ground of Union: Deification in Aquinas and Palamas*. Oxford: Oxford University Press, 1999.

―――. "Light from Byzantium: The Significance of Palamas' Doctrine of Theosis." *Pro Ecclesia* 3 (1994) 483–96.

Williams, Clyde J. *The Teachings of Lorenzo Snow.* Salt Lake City: Bookcraft, 1984.

Wilson-Kastner, Patricia. "On Partaking of the Divine Nature: Luther's Dependence on Augustine." *Andrews University Seminary Studies* 22 (1984) 113–24.

Young, Julian. *Nietzsche's Philosophy of Religion*. Cambridge: Cambridge University Press, 2006.

Young, Simon. *Designer Evolution: A Transhumanist Manifesto.* Amherst, MA: Prometheus, 2006.

Zangenberg, Jürgen. "Δύναμις τοῦ θεοῦ: Das religionsgeschichtliche Profil des Simon Magus aus Sebaste." In *Religionsgeschichte des neuen Testaments: Festschrift für Klaus Berger*, edited by Axel von Dobbeler et al., 519–40. Tübingen: Francke, 2000.

Zecherle, Andreas. "Die 'Theologia Deutsch'. Ein spätmittelalterlicher mystischer Traktat." In *Gottes Nähe unmittelbar erfahren: Mystik im Mittelalter und bei Martin Luther*, edited by Berndt Hamm and Volker Leppin, 1–96. Tübingen: Mohr Siebeck, 2007.

Zhmud, Leonid. "Orphism and Graffiti from Olbia." *Hermes* 120 (1992) 159–68.

Zimmerman, Michael E. "The Singularity: A Crucial Phase in Divine Self-Actualization?" *Cosmos and History: The Journal of Natural and Social Philosophy* 4 (2008) 347–70.

Zuntz, Günther. *Persephone: Three Essays on Religion and Thought in Magna Graecia.* Oxford: Clarendon, 1971.

Subject Index

adoption, 124, 125–26, 133n.86, 149, 175n.9, 235
Alexander the Great, 3, 22, 27–28
Amduat, 22–23
Amor fati, 217–20
Amun–Re, 3, 9–25, 232, 236
Ana' l-Haqq, 6, 135, 137–38, 140–42
aniyah, 136, 138–39, 141
Antony, Marc, 4, 30–41, 68, 236
apotheosis, 2, 53, 238
Athanasius of Alexandria, 123

Barlaam of Calabria, 156–57, 162
beatitude, 118, 124, 128–30
"Become what you are." See *Amor fati*
bodily transformation, 61–63, 163–64, 170, 226, 227n.14
breakthrough, 146–48, 154

Celsus, 73
Cleopatra, 4, 33–37
contemplation, 5, 94, 105, 116, 130n.69, 166–67, 170, 203, 238
coronation titulary, 11–12
creatio ex nihilo, 120, 133n.87, 195, 234

daimon, 52–54, 91, 95, 101, 103, 104n.10, 106–8
Dayboat and Nightboat, 15, 19
deification
    as annihilation, 7, 137–40, 175–79
    as becoming fully human, 237–38

as metaphor, 6, 133, 168, 170–71, 183, 234
defined, 1–2
ethics of, 55–56, 84, 209–11, 213
postmortem, 22–24, 40, 54–55, 57, 68, 109, 128, 131, 236, 239
nominal, 133, 173
temporary, 81, 239
total, 175, 179–81
Dieterich, Albrecht, 49n.46, 71, 84
Dionysus, 3–4, 7, 26–41, 43–45, 46n.27, 47–51, 56, 58, 217, 221, 232, 236,
divination, 80–81
Dominican, 145

Empedocles, 52–54, 74n.35, 76, 106
essence/energies distinction, 157–60, 171, 182, 232–33
eternal return, 7, 216–17
evolution, 7, 24, 192, 194, 201, 229

fate, 7, 51, 56, 82, 207, 217–21

glorification, 58, 62–63, 66, 116,
gnosis, 92, 98, 100–101, 138n.21
Gnostic, 89, 105n.13, 113, 158n.14
God
    as a human being, 91–92, 192–93, 195
    as Being, 203
    as Intellect, 5, 91–93, 95–100, 103–6, 108–15, 133, 232
    as light, 156–58, 161–66, 169–70

as primal/mediate, 159–60,
    232–35
as Soul, 103–6, 112
as the One, 5, 103, 105–6, 115–16,
    129, 133, 158, 232
beyond divinity, 103, 116, 158–59
death of, 207–8
different than humanity, 82
essence vs. attributes, 97, 123–24,
    138, 151, 171, 175, 181–82,
    232
Hermetic, 89–91
identification with, 5, 12, 19,
    39–40, 48, 68, 73n.29, 112,
    115, 186, 206–7, 219–20,
    232, 236
in embryo, 202, 238
Mormon conception of, 202–3
secular concept of, 229–30
vision of, 100, 130–31, 162–63,
    170
gold tablets, 4, 42–44
grace (inherent and applied), 56,
    83, 100–101, 112, 114, 127,
    129, 131–32, 133n.86, 142,
    149, 156–57, 162, 165–67, 168,
    169n.74, 171, 172, 176, 179,
    185–86, 189n.89, 193, 196,
    201–2, 207, 235–36, 237n.3,
    238
ground, 6, 148, 152, 154, 177n.26,
    235

Helios, 73, 76n.50, 77–78, 81, 84,
    232
Helios Mithras, 5, 71, 78–80, 83, 232
Hermetic community, 87–858
heroization, 51–52
hesychasm, 156–57
Holy Spirit, 157–59, 161–63, 167,
    173n.5, 190, 198–200, 233
homoousios, 123, 152, 168,
humility, 7, 101, 131, 152, 178–79,
    234
hypostatic union, 161, 184–85

image of God, 5, 59, 66, 106, 122–23,
    131, 148, 160, 170, 177, 192,
    232, 235, 238
imagination. See *noēsis*
immortality, 1, 4, 8, 57, 59–63, 68,
    70, 81n.75, 92, 124, 127–28,
    130, 160, 166, 174, 199, 223–26,
    235
Immortalization, rite of, 4, 71–80
incarnation, 3, 11, 39–40, 51–53,
    74n.34, 123–24, 128–29, 160,
    179, 183, 192, 238,
incorporation, 124, 126–27

Jesus
    as model of deification, 58–59,
        160–61, 169, 175, 183–85,
        200
    transfiguration of, 155, 160–62
justification, 18, 124–25, 172, 181,
    187

ka, 11, 16–18, 21, 232
King Follett Discourse, 191–97
kingdoms, three, 197–200
kinship with the divine, 4, 43, 46–48,
    51–52, 59, 160, 232, 236, 238
Kurzweil, Ray, 226, 230

lightning, 50–51
love of neighbor, 183, 210, 238

magic, 72–74, 81n.69, 85, 88n.12,
    223, 231, 239
Mannermaa, Tuomo, 174, 178n.38,
    181, 183, 187
Manicheism, 5, 117–32
marriage, celestial, 200–201
memory, 43, 46, 56
monotheism, 136, 154, 233
mysticism, 116, 119, 137, 145, 167,
    175–76, 177n.27, 185, 223, 231,
    233

Neoplatonism, 102–16, 119
Neos Dionysos, 29, 236
New Kingdom, 3, 10, 14

Nietzsche, 205–7, 208n.19, 217n.38, 218, 221, 222, 228, 233, 238–39
noēsis, 96–99

Opet Festival, 3, 15–19
original sin, 45n.22, 93, 131–32, 140–41
Osiris, 3, 11, 15, 21–26, 27n.4, 35, 40

Papyri Graecae Magicae, 71–72
passions, 5, 31, 91n.36, 94, 99, 105, 108–9, 118, 129, 164–65, 218, 236, 238
Pearl of Great Price, 201
Peura, Simo, 181
Platonism, 5, 30, 37, 45, 47, 54n.85, 60, 73, 89, 103, 105, 118–20, 125, 128–30, 149, 154, 173n.4, 188, 192, 195, 203, 207, 217, 222, 229, 232, 234, 236, 239
pneuma (see also "Holy Spirit") , 4–5, 59–63, 74, 77, 83–84, 170, 236
pneumatic body, 60–62, 83, 170
Poimandres, 90–91, 93–94, 98–99, 101
posthuman, 8, 224–29
prayer, 6, 49, 74–79, 87, 98, 141–43, 145, 155–57, 164–66, 169–70
Pseudo-Dionysus, 2n.3, 165–66
Ptolemy II, IV, XII 4, 28–30
purification, 5, 17, 43, 50, 53–54, 57n.107, 108–13, 236

rebirth 3–5, 15, 18, 20, 22–4, 40, 43, 48–50, 55, 70, 78–80, 83
repentance, 141–42
reverence, 101

Yahweh, 76–77, 208, 225

Zagreus myth, 44–45

rule (of the world), 4, 10, 13–14, 64–66, 68, 112, 198–99, 204

scarab ointment, 70, 84, 232
Sed Festival, 3, 19–22
Seth, son of Adam, 235, 238
shirk, 135, 140–42
silence, 74–77, 101
Simon of Samaria, 73
Singularity, 226–27
Snow's Couplet, 190–91, 204
Soleb, 21–22
stars, 4, 47, 50–51, 60, 63n.11, 75–76, 109
Stoics, 60, 219
Sufism, 134–36
synteresis, 177

tawhid, 6, 135–43
Theologia Germanica, 175–76
theosis, 2, 179, 237–38
titans, 44–47, 51
transcending human nature, 87, 97, 113, 155, 165–69, 171, 186, 222, 229

Übermensch, 7, 207, 209, 211–12, 238
unio mystica, 5, 115, 146, 150, 154, 162, 171, 234
uploading of human consciousness, 8, 226

via negativa, 165–66
Vision of the Glories, 197–99

wondrous exchange, 123–24, 128, 172

Ancient Document Index

HEBREW BIBLE

Genesis

1:3	76, 220
1:26–27	59, 122, 192, 209
2:7	92
2:17	210
3	59
3:5	121, 210
5:1–3	59
5:3	235, 238
18:27	209
24:3	77n.58

Deuteronomy

32:36	66n.17

Judges

4:4	66n.17
3:10	66n.17
3:30	66n.17
10:2–3	66n.17
12:7–9	66n.17
12:11	66n.17
12:13–14	66n.17
15:20	66n.17
16:31	66n.17

Ruth

1:1	66n.17

1 Samuel

4:18	66n.17

1 Kings

18:42	155

2 Chronicles

26:21	66n.17

Psalms

2:7	152
2:10	66n.17
9:9	66n.17
32:15	120,n.19
36:9	161
49:1 (LXX)	77n.58
66:5	66n.17
71:2, 4	66n.17
82:1	194, 198
82:6	173, 181, 183, 186–87
90:2	154
95:10, 13	66n.17
96:13	67
97:9	66n.17
110:1	66
116:11	178
134:14	66n.17

Proverbs

29:14	66n.17

Ecclesiastes

3:11	148, 154

Isaiah

14:12–14	121, 209
19:20	66n.17
51:22	66n.17

Jeremiah

31:34	92

Dan

2:47	77n.58

Hosea

13:9–10	66n.17

Micah

4:3	66n.17

Zechariah

12:1	120n.19

Tobit

3:2	66n.17
7:17	77n.58
10:14	77n.58

Wisdom of Solomon

1:1	66n.17
3:8	66n.17

6:19	130
12:13–14	66n.17
12:18	66n.17

Sirach

4:15	66n.17
10:12–13	121
45:26	66n.17

1 Maccabees

9:73	66n.17

3 Maccabees

2:29	29n.12

Psalms of Solomon

17:29	66n.17

Odes of Solomon

3:10	66n.17

NEW TESTAMENT

Matthew

7:7–8	81n.72
11:25	77n.58
13:43	75n.45, 160
20:1–16	190
21:22	81n.72

Mark

8:34	211

Luke

9:28–36	155, 160
10:21	77n.58
20:36	169, 227
22:30	66n.17

John

1:1	149, 153, 195, 232
1:3	149–50
1:4	128, 149
1:12–13	126, 150, 152, 167
1:14	173, 201
1:16	198
1:18	157
3:6	163, 167, 173n.5
4:24	202
5:22–23	66
5:19	193
5:24–30	193

5:26	128, 193
5:29	197
6:33	128
6:40	128
10:28	128
10:30	78,n.60
11:25	128
14:3	200
14:6	79, 128
17:3	191

Acts

8:9–11	73
6:15	163
9:4	127
17:24	77n.58
17:28–29	202, 230, 235
17:34	166

Romans

1:4	59, 68
1:20	94, 176
3:6	67
5:17	64–65, 112
6:4	58–59
6:5	58
6:6	58
6:8	58
8:14	59

8:15	235
8:17	58, 64, 67, 194, 235
8:18	64
8:23	170, 227, 235
8:26	77
8:29–30	59, 62, 65, 203, 235
8:32	65, 185
8:38	64
11:36	65n.16
12:5	126

1 Corinthians

1:2	187
1:24	73
3:6	58
3:21	64, 198
3:22	64
4:8	65n.15
4:9	65
6:2–3	58, 64, 199
6:15	126
6:17	58, 158, 173n.5, 184
8:6	65
9:25	64
12:1	58
12:27	126
13:1	77n.53
15:24–28	201
15:24	66
15:25–27	64
15:26	66
15:27	65–6
15:28	162, 194, 237n.2
15:35–53	59–61
15:39–49	62, 198
15:39	61
15:40	61
15:41–42	199
15:42–43	61
15:44	60
15:44–49	227
15:45–9	170
15:45	59, 61, 83
15:47	62
15:48–9	63
15:49	62
15:50–52	63
15:50	66
15:53–56	68

2 Corinthians

1:5	58
3:17	59
3:18	59, 63, 66, 169–70, 200
4:4	66, 106, 123, 235
4:6	157
4:10	58
4:16	170
4:17	61
5:10	64, 67, 198
5:21	125, 173n.5
8:9	123
12:1–4	63, 169n.74, 199

Galatians

2:19–20	4, 58, 183n.64, 185
3:9	182n.58
3:26	59, 67
4:5	235
4:6	59

Ephesians

2:5	59n.1
2:6	59n.1
3:6	58
3:19	180, 198
4:12–13	127, 198
5:1	209
5:31–32	127, 185

Philippians

2:10–11	64, 66, 200
2:14–15	62
3:10	58
3:20	63
3:21	59–61, 63, 65, 203

Colossians

1:15	59, 106, 123, 232
1:24	58
2:12	58, 59n.1
2:13	59n.1
2:20	58
3:1	59n.1

1 Thessalonians

2:19	64
4:17	63

2 Thessalonians

2:14	58

2 Timothy

2:11	58
2:12	59n.1, 64–65
4:8	64

Hebrews

12:23	200

2 Peter

1:4	123, 173, 182, 187

1 John

2:24b	180
2:29	180n.50

3:2	130, 186, 229, 240
3:9	167

Revelation

1	79
1:6	187
1:14	79n.62
1:16	79n.62
1:17	79
4:1	77n.55
4:11	200
5:10	187
20:6	187

GRECO-ROMAN WRITINGS

Achilles Tatius

Leucippe and Clitophon

2.37.4	50n. 60

Apuleius

Met.

11.23	47n.36
11.23–24	18n.36

Aristophanes

Ran.

144–6	43n.9
1032–33	55

Aristotle

An.

411a7	38

Fragments

15 (Rose)	56

Nicomachean Ethics

1178b1–24	130n.69

Arrian

Anab.

6.28.1	28n.6
6.28.2	27n.5

Artemidorus

Oneirocritica

2.9.76–77	50n.58

Chaldean Oracles (editor,

Majercik)

Fragments

123	83n.84

Corpus Hermeticum (CH)

Ascl. 1	86, 89
Ascl. 6	93
Ascl. 10	89
Ascl. 13	95
Ascl. 16	90n.34
Ascl. 19	91
Ascl. 20	89, 99n.81
Ascl. 22–24	91
Ascl. 22	92n.39
Ascl. 27	89
Ascl. 29	90
Ascl. 30	89, 94n.56
Ascl. 31	89
Ascl. 37–38	91
CH 1.4	94
CH 1.9–11	94
CH 1.10–11	91
CH 1.12	91
CH 1.18	93
CH 1.21	93
CH 1.24–25	94
CH 1.26	98–99
CH 2.4	100
CH 2.14	90, 99–100
CH 2.16	90, 100
CH 2.17	90
CH 3.1	89

CH 3.2–3	91
CH 4.1	91n.35
CH 4.4	93
CH 4.6	93
CH 4.8–9	96
CH 4.10	90
CH 5.1	89, 99n.81
CH 5.2	96
CH 5.3	95
CH 5.4	94
CH 5.5	95
CH 5.10	90, 99n.81
CH 7.2	96
CH 8.2	100
CH 9.1	100
CH 10.1	100
CH 10.5	96
CH 10.25	94n.51
CH 11.19	97
CH 11.20	96
CH 11.22	94
CH 12.1	92, 99
CH 12.8	96
CH 12.19	92
CH 12.21	95
CH 13.3	98, 100
CH 13.6	89, 90

Diodorus of Sicily
Bibl. hist.

1.2.5.1	70n.8
1.94.2	70n.8
3.64.5	27
3.64.7	33
3.65.8	27n.5
4.7.4.18	70n.8
4.25.4	51n.63
4.38.4–5	50
4.39.2	50
5.52.2	51n.63

Euripides
Alc.

1–4	51n.63

Andromache

1260–62	51n.65

Bacchae

4	39n.56

53–54	39n.56

Hesiod
Fragments

1.5–7	54
25.25–28	50
109	50
125	51n.63

Op.

108	46n.26
170–71	52

Theogony

106	46

Homer
Il.

4.61	52n.70
5.342	61
9.214	2
14.113	51n.64
20.241	51n.64
21.187	51n.64

Od.

4.563	52
11.36–50	44
11.602–4	50n.54
24.1–18	44

Horace
Ars poetica

464–66	53n.82

Isocrates
Busiris

7–8	44

Julian
Or.

5.17	80n.64
12.14–32	80n.64

Lucian
Cal.

16	30

Dial. mort.

13	50

Manilius

Astron.

1.275–93   79n.61

Nonnus

Dionysiaca

8.409   50n.60
9.206   50n.60

Orphic Hymns (editor,
Athanassakis)

4   47n.32
26   47n.32
37.1–2   46
52.11   49
64.9–11   56

Orphicorum Fragmenta
(editor, Bernabé)

33   55
34   55n.95
83   46
280–83   44
293–300   44
301–17   45
318–31   45
470, col. XX   55
474–84a   46
474.1   56
474.10   46
474.15–16   54
475.2   52
476.7   47
476.11   52
476.12   56
477.9   47, 75n.43
484.4   47
485.2   56
485.3–5   48
485.6   54
485.7   47n.37
486.3–4   48
487.3   48
487.4   48
487.5   48n.38
487.6   87
488–90   50n.55
488   50n.55
488.1   55
488.5   53

488.7–10   49
488.8   42
488.9–10   48n.39
489.1   55
489.3   47n.33
489.4   54
489.7   54
490.1   55
490.3   47n.33
490.4   54
490.7   54
491.1   55
491.3–4   56
491.4   42
492   43
492.8   52
493.2   54n.84
501   43
502   43
578   49

Ovid

Metamorphoses

10.1–77   44n.12

Papyri Graecae Magicae
(PGM)

I.178–80   74
I.190–91   74, 81n.75
IV.170–79   73
IV.179–208   73
IV.215–16   74
IV.219–20   74
IV.475–820   71
IV.475–78   70
IV.476   72
IV.478–82   72n.17
IV.482   71
IV.501–2   83
IV.503–4   82
IV.506   74n.35
IV.516–17   70
IV.517–21   82
IV.520–21   77n.51
IV.522   84
IV.525–26   82
IV.529–32   82
IV.534–35   82
IV.537–38   74
IV.541–45   75

IV.548	71
IV.559–60	75
IV.566–68	75
IV.573–75	75
IV.586–87	83
IV.588–602	76
IV.588–94	76
IV.605–6	82
IV.610–16	77
IV.617–20	77
IV.625	77
IV.639–41	77
IV.645–49	82
IV.647–48	70
IV.696–97	79
IV.699–700	79
IV.700	79
IV.703	79
IV.718	80
IV.727–32	80
IV.725–26	80
IV.739–43	84
IV.741	70
IV.747	70
IV.747–48	81
IV.750–71	70n.2
IV.771	70
IV.772–92	70n.2
IV.777–78	81n.72
IV.792	70n.2
IV.797	81
XIII.339–40	81

Pausanias

Descr.

2.31.2	51n.63
2.37.5	51n.63
8.2.4–5	52n.69

Philo

Aet.

46	75n.38
112	75n.38

Dec.

51	203n.23
107	203n.23
120	203n.23

Opif.

27	75n.38

QE

2.40	74n.34

QG

1.42	75n.38
4.157	75n.38

Spec.

1.19	75n.38
1.36–50	159n.22
2.2	203n.23
2.224–25	203n.23

Philostratus

Imagines

1.14	50n.60

Vit. Apoll.

8.5.1	73n.26
8.7.1	73n.26

Pindar

Fragments

33	52n.73
129.1–2	47n.36

Nem.

6.1–3	46n.26

Ol.

2.27	50n.60
2.79–80	51n.66

Plato

Crat.

400c	54

Epistles

II.312e	103

Gorg.

493	54n.85
493b–c	43n.9

Leges

701b–c	47n.30

Meno

81b–c	52n.73, 55

Phaedo

62b	54n.85
69b–d	43
81e–82b	107n.18

Phaedrus

247a	194, 236

Resp.

363c–d	54–55
364b–c	55
364e	43, 57n.107
588c7	105n.12
590a9	105n.12

Symp.

179d–180b	51n.66
179d	44n.11
211b–212a	112

Theaetetus

176b	94

Tim.

40d	75n.38
41d	105
90a	107

Plotinus

Enneads

1.1.5.1	105
1.1.5.9	105
1.1.5.17	105
1.1.7.18–19	105
1.1.10.7–8	105
1.2.1.17–21	109
1.2.6.2	102
1.2.6.4	108
1.2.6.24–28	109
1.2.7.27–28	109
1.2.7.30–31	113
1.4.9.29	110
1.6.5.54–59	108
1.6.6.14–15	108
1.6.6.31	105
1.6.7.2–14	112
1.6.9.9–12	108
1.6.9.29–34	112
2.3.9.25–26	109
2.9.1.12–16	103n.6
2.9.2.7–19	105
2.9.9.38–40	104
2.9.9.43–44	115
2.9.9.50–51	114
3.2.8.5	104
3.2.8.9–12	106
3.4.3.18–21	107
3.4.3.21–23	106
3.4.6.3–4	107
3.4.6.31–32	107
3.8.8.1–9	110
3.8.8.6–8	110
3.8.11.33	110
4.2.1.5–7	110
4.3.2.1–3	105
4.3.6.13–14	105
4.3.12.1–25	104
4.4.2.26–33	110
4.7.10.20–21	106
4.7.10.40	106
4.7.10.46–47	109
4.7.11.2	104
4.8.1.1–11	111, 115
4.8.4.7–8	112
4.8.5.25–27	106
4.8.7.6–8	106
4.8.8.1–6	105
5.1.2.41–47	105
5.1.3.8	106
5.1.10.1–4	103
5.1.11.10–11	113
5.3.4.1	112
5.3.4.10–11	111
5.3.4.11–13	113
5.3.4.29–32	111
5.3.8.47–49	106
5.5.7.33–38	114
5.10.10.11–13	105
5.3.14.19–20	103
5.8.3	103
6.7.6.28–32	107
6.7.12.23	103
6.7.22.7–8	114
6.7.22.8–16	114
6.7.34.8	114
6.7.34.36–38	114
6.7.36.4	115
6.7.36.14	115
6.9.6.12–14	103, 116
6.9.8.8	116
6.9.9.1	116
6.9.9.38–41	114
6.9.9.56–59	116
6.9.9.56	115

6.9.10.13–14		115
6.9.11.38–40		113
6.9.11.45		106
9.9.11.51		114

Plutarch

Adul. am.

12		35, 37

Alex.

67.1–6		28

Ant.

5.9		31
9.5–9		30–31
14.1		31
17.5–6		35
24.1–4		33
26.1–5		34
29.2–3		31
29.4		35
75.4–6		37

Cleom.

33.2		29
34.2		29

Esu carn.

996b–c		47n.30

Quaest rom.

36		48n.43

Sera

27		51n.63

Porphyry

Antr. nymph.

23		80n.64

De abstinentia

3.25		46n.26

Vit. Plot.

1		102
2.26–27		102
10.15–25		107
16		114,n.30
23.16–17		115

Ps.-Apollodorus

Bibl.

2.7.7		50n.59
3.4.3		48
3.5.3		51n.63

Strabo

Geog.

7.3.5		70n.8

Suetonius

Div. Aug.

70.2		35

Virgil

Aen.

6.641		47n.36

Georg.

4.467–505		44n.12

EARLY CHRISTIAN WRITINGS

Ambrose

De Virginibus

3.176.7		51n.63

Athanasius

Inc. 54.3		123

Augustine

Arian.

1.8		123

Civ.

19.23		129

C. Jul. op. imp.

6.20		131

Conf.

1.2.1		130
1.7.11–12		132n.79
2.1.1		129
2.4.9		132
4.15.26		118, 121
4.16.31		118
7.1.2		203
7.2.3		118
7.7.11		121–22

Conf. (cont.)

7.9.13	119
7.10.16	119
7.17.23	130
8.10.22	132
10.25.36	120
10.34.51	130

Duab.

1	117

Enarrat. Ps.

7.4	121
7.19	130
10.11	125
35.14	130–31
49.1	125
49.2	125–26, 131, 133n.86
52.6	123
54.3	127
94.6	133n.87
109.1	131
109.3	133n.85
118.16, §1	129
121.8	129
146.5.11	128

Enchir.

10.35	123n.36

Ep.

140.18	127

Exp. Gal.

24.8	124
30.6	126

Gen. Man.

2.8.11	118, 120n.19, 121
2.15.22	122
2.21.32	122

Nat bon.

41	118

Nat grat.

33.37	125

Ord.

1.1.3	130

Quant. an.

33.73	130

Serm.

22.10.10	127
23B	133n.86
23B.5	122
23B.11	132n.82
80.5	128
166.1	133n.87
344.1	123

Tract. Ev. Jo.

2.13	125–26
21.3	127
21.8.1	127

Trin.

4.2.4	124
14.8.11	122
14.19.26	117

Irenaeus of Lyon

Haer.

4.38.3	130
5, *praef.*	123

Justin Martyr

1 Apol.

13.3–4	159
21.3	71n.8
21.6	71n.8
26	73
30.1	29n.11

Lactantius

Div. Inst.

5.9.17	73n.23

Minucius Felix

Octavian

23.7	50n.61

Origen

Cels. 5.39	159n.21

Comm. Jo.

2.21.138	65n.14

Princ.

1.1.2	60n.3

Made in the USA
Lexington, KY
14 October 2016